Educating Toward
a Culture of Peace

Educating Toward a Culture of Peace

Edited by

Yaacov Iram

Associate Editors

Hillel Wahrman
Zehavit Gross

INFORMATION AGE
PUBLISHING

Greenwich, Connecticut • www.infoagepub.com

Library of Congress Cataloging-in-Publication Data

Educating toward a culture of peace / edited by Yaacov Iram, Hillel Wahrman.
   p. cm.
 Includes bibliographical references and index.
 ISBN 1-59311-483-4 (pbk.) – ISBN 1-59311-484-2 (hardcover)
 1. Education–Political aspects. 2. Education–Social aspects. 3.
Education, Humanistic. 4. Peace. I. Iram, Yaacov. II. Wahrman, Hillel.
 LC71.E287 2006
 370.116–dc22

                                                        2006005239

ISBN-13:

  978-1-59311-483-1 (pbk.)
  978-1-59311-484-8 (hardcover)

Printed in the United States of America

CONTENTS

PART III
Culture of Peace Perceptions

PART IV
Religiosity and Culture of Peace

PART V
Peace Education Initiatives

INTRODUCTION

Yaacov Iram

This volume, *Education Toward a Culture of Peace*, is a timely undertaking, since the United Nations has proclaimed the years 2001–2010 as the "International Decade for a Culture of Peace and Non-Violence for the Children of the World." A culture of peace as defined by the UN is "a set of values, attitudes, modes of behaviour and ways of life that reject violence and prevent conflicts by tackling their root causes to solve problems through dialogue and negotiation among individuals, groups and nations" (UN Resolutions A/RES/52/13 1998: Culture of Peace and A/RES/53/243, 1999: Declaration and Programme of Action on a Culture of Peace).

Achieving a culture of peace within a society and between societies is a complex task. It implies more than a passive and quiescent state due to an absence of war or violence, or a formal agreement between rivals. To attain a culture of peace, a society must actively strive toward positive values, which enable different cultures and nations to coexist harmoniously. Understanding the shared and unique values of different people and cultures also paves the way to establishing a pluralistic society. These goals are hard to achieve in countries, which suffer the outcomes of an existing conflict, where tensions and past patterns of aggression remain obstacles to reconciliation and change.

Of the three possible strategies to achieve peace, "peacekeeping," "peacemaking," and "peace building" (Harris, 1988), education is concerned with the latter, namely conveying a commitment to nonviolence

Educating Toward a Culture of Peace, pages ix–xviii
Copyright © 2006 by Information Age Publishing

and enhancing the capacity for peace. This volume is based on the work of prominent scholars and educationalists from various countries in the field of peace education.

Contemporary peace education research and practice, focusing on the theoretical exploration and practical implications of educating toward a culture of peace, are presented, reviewed analytically, and analyzed in the five sections of this volume, as follows: Peace Education Paradigms; Globalization and Peace; Culture of Peace Perceptions; Religiosity and Culture of Peace; and Peace Education Initiatives.

PART I. PEACE EDUCATION PARADIGMS

The first section of this book discusses four paradigms of peace education.

In Chapter 1, "Culture of Peace: Definition, Scope, and Application," Iram presents UNESCO's definitions of the term and deliniates the scope as well as the promise and problems involved in the practice of its application.

In Chapter 2, Steinberg presents a model code of conduct for peace studies programs and peace education in which academic values upheld. He claims that peace education, like many other issues in the social sciences, are susceptible to being caught in the tension between advocacy of particular policies and values, on the one hand, and the academic requirement for value-free analysis, on the other. Peace studies programs and faculty, particularly at the advanced level and in higher education, often fail to acknowledge this inherent tension. As a result, in many cases, such programs cross the line between neutral analysis and advocacy, not only of specific programs and ideologies but, in some instances, of particular parties and positions in dispute. Hobbesian and "realist" perspectives on the nature of violence and the use of force to manage conflicts are frequently ignored, while the strong "idealist" models are often presented uncritically. As a result, one-sided and highly distorted analysis of conflicts is often presented, thereby providing support for one of the parties, at the expense of the other.

In the third chapter, Nalapat confronts education of peace with education of terror. Elaborating on the Indian concept of *Vasudhaiva Kutumbakam*, "the world is one family," Nalapat refers to the reality that all humanity shares certain common values and characteristics that dwarf the differences. Unfortunately, the differences receive much more attention than the commonalities.

However, much of today's education conveys the wrong concept that one's own culture and history are superior to others, that by being born within a particular society, one is automatically part of the elite. By teaching the young that the world is vertically divided into "superior" and "inferior" cultures and higher and lower civilizations, attitudes are created that generate aggressive responses toward those belonging to different belief systems. This is indeed an "education of terror." Rather, what is needed is the teaching of social science to follow a *horizontal* model in which each society studied is regarded as at the same level of all others, only different. Educating the young about the incredible diversity in humankind is the education for peace. This chapter confronts the "vertical" and "horizontal" models and presents normative guidelines for peace education.

Dajani (Chapter 4) asserts that the Oslo Peace Process in 1993 initiated a radical change in the identity of the protagonists. The identity of the two conflicting parties to the Middle East conflict are transformed from being national in character (Arab-Israeli) to being more sociopolitical in character (pro-peace/anti-peace). As the peace process progressed, this identification has crystallized more into cultural/psychological character, which assembled in one camp those who are for the "big dream" in mortal combat with those in the other camp of "small hope." Advocates of the "big dream" are those, at present in the majority, who struggle for the eventual triumph of their perception of good over evil, as resembled by the other, and as a result seek to establish their state on the historic land of Palestine/Israel fully exclusive of the other. In their effort to achieve its goal, the "big dream" camp implements a highly nationalistic curriculum in its educational system that delegitimizes and demonizes the other. It promotes conflict education, which teaches the new generation the war philosophy of the old generation. It appeals to the emotional bondage of the people to the land and focuses on history. It denies the narrative of the other and ignores their history. Whereas advocates of the "small hope" are those, at present in the minority, who believe in peace as a coexistence between the two peoples and who call for the establishment of a two-state solution living next to each other in peace and security with Jerusalem as a shared capital for both.

PART II. GLOBALIZATION AND PEACE

Globalization is construed as a multidimensional process mostly in economic and political terms. This section deals with the possible impact of globalization on peace education.

Waterkamp, in Chapter 5, employs two concepts for the analysis of peace education. He claims that two fundamental conceptions construe the field of comparative education today: globalization and mankind. The first is more widely used: globalization points at the phenomenon that every group of human beings is being affected by the same worldwide currents and developments in terms of economy, technology, and mass media production. Comparative education investigates the effects of these unifying forces on education of individual countries. Mankind, as an alternative conceptual framework, is an idealistic concept, pointing at the humane destination of humanity. It stresses what human beings do and should share. These two concepts are indeed separate paradigms for comparison. Waterkamp analyzes the two paradigms and their implications for peace education.

In Chapter 6, Epstein claims that in communities at the cultural periphery—myths taught by schools about mainstream society—come to displace in children's consciousness myths about their indigenous past taught in traditional, less formal ways by parents and elders. Myth displacement is an important part of resocialization that allows globalization to take place. This process of transformed consciousness creates the conditions of susceptibility to world forces. The school often becomes the leading authority in the village, interpreting a new social reality and filtering out unflattering images of the dominant culture and the exogenous world. Children learn to be citizens of a nation—to participate with others in the polity, obey laws, function in the marketplace, and render allegiance to the state. Yet, abetted by the school, globalization cuts the pillars of normative thought and behavior from the traditional village and expands into the periphery.

This process of myth displacement is central to building or impeding a culture of peace in peripheral communities. It is a process that must be understood by all who are concerned about why marginalized people engage in conflict or peaceful means in relationships with their neighbors and the mainstream community. This chapter discusses alternative theories and empirical research that shed light on the role education plays in myth displacement and marginalization.

In Chapter 7, Werdmölder discusses the growing confrontations and conflicts between Moroccan and Dutch youth. Moroccan adolescents who have grown up in the Netherlands and traditional Dutch youth are locked in cultural and economic conflicts. The Moroccan community in the Netherlands came up with a number of initiatives in order to improve the understanding between the Dutch and the Dutch-Moroccan. These formal and informal peace education initiatives are discussed in light of the forces changing Dutch society today.

Al-Rfouh (Chapter 8) claims that globalization as a multidimensional and complex process is mostly construed in theory of economic liberalization and political reform. He claims that in the context of the Middle East, the economic dimensions of globalization are accentuated, while political and cultural aspects continue to be a serious subject of debate owing to the historical, religious, and cultural background of the region. The particularities of the Middle East globalization issues are discussed, and their implications for peace are explored.

PART III. CULTURE OF PEACE PERCEPTIONS

The chapters in this section present analytically varied perceptions of peace in the context of the Israeli–Palestinian conflicts.

Yuchtman-Ya'ar, in Chapter 9, discusses the Peace Index project of the Steinmetz Center for Peace Research in Israel. As a culture of peace indicator, its purpose is to monitor how the Israeli public—Jews and Arabs—perceive the relations with the Arab states and the Palestinians and its political, social, and economic implications. The main focus of the chapter is a paradox that seems to emerge in the opinion polls regarding the Oslo Agreement between Israel and the Palestinians in 1993. On the one hand, the Oslo Agreement has never been widely accepted by the Israeli-Jewish public. However, despite the substantial shrinkage of the pro-Oslo camp and the corresponding shift of the Israeli-Jewish electorate to the political right, it appears that when asked about specific issues concerning the conditions for a peace agreement between Israel and the Palestinian Authority, this public has adopted some of the major elements of the Oslo principles. In particular, a majority of the Israeli-Jewish public supports the establishment of a viable independent Palestinian state, and accepts the pre-1967 border, with minor modifications, as the territorial basis of the two states. Furthermore, a clear majority supports the evacuation of all the Jewish settlements in the Gaza Strip as well as the settlements, which are located in the midst of the Palestinian population in the West Bank. In other words, the Israeli Jewish public rejects Oslo yet accepts much of its spirit. This apparent paradox is explained and the contribution of a Peace Index to peace education is discussed.

Sagy (Chapter 10) discusses and measures "hope" as a "culture of peace" component, examining levels and contents of hope among young people in the conflicted region of the Middle East. "Hope" is defined in this study as the interaction between wishes and positive future expectations (Staats & Stassen, 1985). The differentiation between personal and collective hopes among Israeli and Palestinian students looking for stability and/or changes of levels of hope in the context of a changing reality and in times of greater threat are examined. Data were collected at two points in time: The first stage took place in the first semester of the 1999–2000 academic year, during the period of the Oslo Accords talks; the second stage was carried out during the events of Al-Aksa Intifada in January–March 2002. Adolescents' hopes, wishes, and expectations of the future are compared and discussed from individual, social, and cultural perspectives. Conclusions are reached on the usefulness of measuring levels of hope in society in the larger attempt to educate and promote a culture of peace.

Cohen (Chapter 11) presents an analytical summary of a pilot study among visiting students in Israel, their perception of peace and its potential implication for peace education. Cohen seeks to develop a common understandings of the connotations and denotations of the concept of peace. Multitude understanding of this concept reveal fundamentally different social and cultural paradigms. This problem is particularly crucial in the Middle East, which currently is in the midst of a devastating period marked by unprecedented violence between Israelis and Palestinians. There is a need to develop a common understanding of basic terms in order to advance a culture of peace.

In Chapter 12, Witenberg and Gali Cinamon claim that understanding of the various dimensions of a culture of peace requires research of values and attitudes of different age groups and the development of research tools and terminology. This study investigated context- and age-related differences in racial tolerance judgments using a developmental approach and methodology. The participants were 129 students from three different age groups (9–11, 14–16, and 18–24 years). Results indicate that the majority of students supported tolerance; judgements were influenced by both within- and between-subject variations. As anticipated, both situational context (content of the stories) and behavioral context (belief, speech, and act) were found to influence tolerance judgments. Between subjects, differences were also evident with level of tolerance decreasing with age but mediated by context. Gender differences that emerged with females found to be more tolerant than males. Implication for theory and practice of peace education are discussed.

As the cognitive aspects of the conflict are directly addressed and seem deeply imbedded in the structure of the peace programs, the emotional aspects are often overlooked as consequences of the conflict. They are neither seen as the core of peace education programs nor directly affecting the success or failure of the peace programs. However, many studies do stress the relationship between emotions and behavior, and that negative emotional reactions have implications on behavior.

In the present study Yablon (Chapter 13) used structural equation modeling in order to analyze the role that emotions may play on improving interrupted relations by enhancing positive perceptions and motivation to meet and have further contact with members of another group. The results of this study show that although in many other studies the enhancement of positive emotions toward members of conflict groups is considered to be one of the intervention outcomes, it is the positive emotions that enhance cognitive change. It is suggested that emotions should be considered as a facilitator of positive contact between conflict groups. Peace education programs should therefore give more emphasis on the emotional rather than cognitive aspects, and studies should move beyond the assessment of cognitive modification to the examination of affective modification.

PART IV. RELIGIOSITY AND CULTURE OF PEACE

The authors in this section explore the potential advantages and impediments of religion and religiosity in peace education.

Perko's chapter (14) compares and contrasts the role played by religion in both the creation of social conflict and in its amelioration in Northern Ireland and Israel/Palestine. Religion plays a key role in the self-definition of communities living in both places and, as a result, in the ensuing social and political conflicts. In the case of Northern Ireland, whether one is Catholic or Protestant defines, to a significant degree, both one's politics and place in civil society. The overwhelming majority of Palestinians are Muslims, and increasingly, this society is taking on an identity in which Islam is a significant factor. Likewise, Israel, in defining itself as the "Jewish state," makes religion an important focus of identity for its population. Specifically, this chapter focuses on the ways in which the respective communities either have tried, via education, to contribute to the process of establishing peace and reconciliation, or have instead used religion to enhance the conflict.

In Chapter 15, Mollov and Lavie explore the potential of the interreligious dialogue to serve as a basis for peace building between Arabs and Jews within the State of Israel. It presents and evaluates the paradigm of Israeli–Palestinian interreligious dialogues held between Jewish and Arab citizens of the State of Israel, with a particular focus on women. Conclusions based on these dialogues suggest that the interreligious encounter can be effective. In other words, religiosity can be a positive factor in the success of the dialogue. However, there is no conclusive evidence that women's contribution to dialogue and peace building is greater than that of men. Religiosity as a potential factor to peace education is discussed in this chapter.

Gross's chapter (16) analyzes a case study (following Yin, 2003, and Stake, 2000) concerning the attitude of graduates of State Religious schools in Israel to the peace process. The State Religious Education System in Israel is identified mainly with the Religious Zionist movement. The majority of this social and ideological movement rejects the Israeli–Palestinian peace process. The settlements in the West Bank are inhabited mainly by graduates of this educational system, and therefore the understanding of the theological and pedagogical background and premises of their socialization might contribute to the understanding of the issue of peace education within religious settings in general and in Israel in particular.

PART V. PEACE EDUCATION INITIATIVES

The last and concluding section of this volume evaluates theories put into practice. Although the case studies in this section vary in many respects, they represent the complexities and challenges faced by peace educators.

Feuerverger's study (Chapter 17), is based on a 9-year study that the author carried out as an educational ethnographer in the cooperative Jewish-Arab village of Neve Shalom/Wahat Al-Salam in Israel. Neve Shalom/Wahat Al-Salam (the Hebrew and Arabic words for "Oasis of Peace") is a village that began as an intercultural experiment. There, Israeli Jews and Arabs founded a community aimed at demonstrating the possibilities for living in peace—while maintaining their respective cultural heritages and languages. Feuerverger shares narrative portraits of some remarkable educators who are working together in an everyday journey toward reconciliation and peaceful coexistence. She offers insights into the extraordinary landscape of this cooperative village with its cultural encounters, educational innovations, moral dilemmas, traumas, and reconciliations that form the basis for creating the spirit of this community against all odds. Thus, it is about hope in the midst of a deadly conflict.

In Chapter 18, Fritzsche presents the project "Tolerance Matters" (1998–2003), which identifies fundamental issues in the field of education for democracy, human rights, and tolerance. The case studies of this project examine educational responses in a wide range of cultural, social, and economic contexts. Set against an analytical framework that allows for comparison, the case studies explore the complexities, challenges, and opportunities inherent in attempting to use education as a mechanism for fostering understanding and tolerance. With contributions from Brazil, Chile, Germany, Israel, the Netherlands, Northern Ireland, the Philippines, Poland, South Africa, and the United States, this unique collection of case studies offers a cross- and intercultural approach to the issue of education for democracy, tolerance, and coexistence.

Minimal peace building during a violent conflict is a strategy for future post-conflict peace processes, as suggested by Bar-On and Adwan in Chapter 19. They describe a process of six workshops in which Palestinian and Jewish-Israeli teachers developed a joint school textbook of two narratives (an Israeli and a Palestinian) in regard to six dates in their mutual conflict: the Balfour Declaration (1917), the 1920's, the 1930's, the 1948 and 1967 wars, and the 1987 Intifada. The teachers developed these two narratives to be taught in their classrooms in Hebrew and Arabic. All these activities took place under severe conditions of occupation (of the Palestinians) and suicide bombers (against Israelis) throughout the project. The two-state solution requires, in the authors' view, textbooks of two narratives, so students learn to respect the narrative of the "Other" in addition to their own narrative. This unique attempt at developing an innovative textbook is exposed and discussed in this chapter.

In Chapter 20, Bhowon claims that good governance is considered vital for the development of human capital, for transparent and participatory decision making, and for the effective and efficient use of resources. Some examples of peace initiatives and conflict management are drawn from Mauritius and other developing countries. In particular, the role of Gandhi as a peace lover and spiritual leader, that unleashed the power of man to fight the crusade toward freedom, is also considered side by side with the justification of military means as self-defense. This presentation draws also from personal experience in the Republic of Mauritius with respect to openness—inclusive, dialogic, and interactive—in order to reduce military means and to foster a culture of peace and create a prosperous foundation for learning to live together.

It is believed that education can play a prominent role in imparting the values of tolerance, human rights multiculturalism, and peace to the next generation. It is our hope that this volume will contribute to a better understanding of the educational factors working to facilitate peace.

The experience and findings presented in this volume may benefit societies throughout the world in coping with animosity resulting from diversity. The presentation of theoretical and analytical framework and the analysis of the Israeli–Palestinian case and the international context might benefit societies striving to solve conflicts by integrating a nonviolent conflict resolution approach to achieve peaceful coexistence.

ACKNOWLEDGMENTS

Most of the chapters in this book are based on lectures that were presented at the international conference, "Education Toward a Culture of Peace." This conference was convened in December 2003 by the the Josef Burg Chair in Education for Human Values, Tolerance, and Peace—UNESCO Chair on Human Rights, Democracy, Peace and Tolerance School of Education at Bar Ilan University, Israel. This international gathering was attended by prominent scholars of *Human Rights and Peace* from *Canada, Chile, Croatia, Germany, Mauritius, The Netherlands, the United States, the Palestinian Authority,* and *Israel. Australian, Indian, Jordanian,* and *Moroccan* colleagues also submitted papers.

This conference was held under the auspices of the Israel National Commission for UNESCO and supported also by the Ministry of Foreign Affairs, Jerusalem, the Office of Public Affairs of the U.S. Embassy in Tel Aviv, and the Fulbright–United States–Israel Educational Foundation.

The editor wishes to express gratitude to the authors for revising, extending, and updating their original papers for this volume, and for presenting them in a scholarly format following a rigorous referral procedure.

Thanks are also due to Hillel Wahrman and Zehavit Gross for their skillful contribution in editing this volume.

Special thanks are also owed to the secretary of the Chair, Tzila Pollak.

REFERENCES

Harris, I. M. 1988. *Peace education.* Jefferson, NC: McFarland.

Staats, S. R., & Stassen, M. A. (1985). Hope: An affective cognition. *Social Indicators Research, 17,* 235–242.

Stake, R. B. (2000). Case studies. In N. K. Denzin & Y. S. Lincoln (Eds.), *Handbook of qualitative research* (2nd ed., pp. 435–454). Thousand Oaks, CA: Sage.

United Nations General Assembly. (1998). Culture of Peace *Document* A/RES/52/13 adopted by the General Assembly, 52nd session, Agenda item 156.

United Nations General Assembly. (1999). Declaration and Programme of Action on a Culture of Peace *Document* A/RES/53/243, adopted by the General Assembly, 53rd session, Agenda item 31.

Yin, R. K. (2003). *Case study research design and method.* New York: Sage.

Part I

PEACE EDUCATION PARADIGMS

CHAPTER 1

CULTURE OF PEACE

Definition, Scope, and Application

Yaacov Iram

This chapter discusses issues related to "Education Toward a Culture of Peace" in light of UNESCO's proclamation of the year 2000 as the year for the Culture of Peace and Non-Violence, and the United Nations General Assembly's declaration of the years 2001–2010 as the "International Decade for a Culture of Peace and Non-Violence for the Children of the World" (UN Resolutions A/RES/52/13: Culture of Peace and A/RES/53/243: Declaration and Programme of Action on a Culture of Peace).

Before moving on, we need to define the following three terms: tolerance, pluralism and peace, all of which are prerequisites for peace education (Vogt, 1997).

Tolerance implies willingness to tolerate a position, idea, or behavior that is expressed by a person but considered wrong by another. Nevertheless, the other acknowledges its existence, respecting the right and freedom of the other person to express them and to conduct his life according to those ideas and beliefs. The tolerant may react in a "negative," passive way, namely ignore or overlook views that he or she objects to. He or she might also react in a "positive," active manner by supporting and defending the right of another person to express ideas, which he or she may consider wrong politically, morally, or in the social sphere (Vogt, 1997, p. 17).

Educating Toward a Culture of Peace, pages 3–12
Copyright © 2006 by Information Age Publishing
All rights of reproduction in any form reserved.

Tolerance as a concept affecting attitudes and behaviors of individuals as well as governmental policies (toleration) developed initially in religious societies where majority–minority patterns of interaction existed and tolerance was manifested by respecting the rights of minority groups or of individuals, different in beliefs, views, and behavior from those of the majority. Tolerance, which leads to the establishment of a pluralistic society, requires an understanding of both the shared and unique aspects of different peoples and cultures.

Pluralism developed in liberal–secular societies. Pluralism implies more than toleration of attitudes and views ideologies and modes of behavior that deviate from those of the majority. These are viewed not only as tolerated, but valuable, though different and therefore both the ideas and their supporters have to be respected.

The pluralistic attitude might also appear in a "passive way," namely, a factual recognition of diversity in a society, or could be expressed in an "active–normative" form of assigning equal value to the other's views, attitudes, and modes of behavior. The *pluralist*, as opposed to the *tolerant*, is determined to get into a dialogue with those whose beliefs and values are different from his.

Most societies and states are diversified nationally, religiously, linguistically, culturally, and ethnically. In order to achieve a state of peaceful coexistence instead of constant struggle, there is a need for a meaningful and continuous dialogue leading to mutual acceptance and viewing cultural pluralism as a valuable asset to societies. The pluralistic attitude is a prerequisite for peaceful coexistence.

Following Galtung (1973, 1996), *peace* might be defined as absence of war and other forms of violence ("negative" peace). In a wider connotation, peace means a state of social justice and cooperation among and between groups and individuals ("positive" peace). The latter refers also to the absence of "structural violence," namely negation of built-in individual and societal inequalities and injustice. These distinctions lead us to still a wider concept of peace.

CULTURE OF PEACE DEFINITION

As defined by the United Nations, a culture of peace is "a set of values, attitudes, modes of behavior and ways of life that reject violence and prevent conflicts by tackling their root causes to solve problems through dialogue and negotiation among individuals, groups and nations" (UN Resolutions A/RES/52/13: Culture of Peace and A/RES/53/243: Declaration and Programme of Action on a Culture of Peace).

Achieving a culture of peace within a society and between societies is a noble goal and also a complex task. A culture of peace implies more than a passive and quiescent state due to an absence of war or violence, or a formal agreement between rivals. To attain a culture of peace, a society must actively strive toward positive values, which enable different cultures and nations to coexist harmoniously. Understanding the shared and unique values of different people and cultures paves the way to establishing a pluralistic society. These goals are hard to achieve in countries that suffer the outcomes of ongoing intractable conflicts (Bar Tal, 1998, 2000, 2002) and present tensions and past patterns of aggression remain obstacles to reconciliation and change.

Of the three possible strategies to achieve peace—"peacekeeping" (peace through strength), "peacemaking" (i.e., peace through communication), and "peace building" (Harris, 2002, p. 18)—education is concerned mainly with the latter, namely conveying a commitment to nonviolence, enhancing the capacity for peace, and fostering positive attitudes (Brock-Utne, 1985; Harris, 1998; Reardon, 1988).

The following section presents, discusses, and analyzes different documents and programs of a culture of peace and the role that education can play imparting the values of tolerance, multiculturalism, and peace. It is expected that dialogue between groups in conflict and national adversaries will result in a better understanding of the educational factors working to facilitate peace, and provide educators with a peace-building "tool chest" (Alger, 2003, pp. 45–53).

Bellow are pertinent quotes from culture of peace documents, which might provide the ideological foundations of this "tool chest."

Manifesto 2000 for a Culture of Peace and Non-Violence

- The year 2000 must be a new beginning, an opportunity to transform—all together—the culture of war and violence into a culture of peace and non-violence.
- This transformation demands the participation of each and every one of us, and must offer young people and future generations the values that can inspire them to shape a world based on justice, solidarity, liberty, dignity, harmony, and prosperity for all.
- The culture of peace can underpin sustainable development, environmental protection, and the well-being of each person.
- [Every individual has a] share of responsibility for the future of humanity, in particular to the children of today and tomorrow.

Therefore, every individual should pledge to:

- Respect the life and dignity of each human being without discrimination or prejudice;
- Practice active non-violence, rejecting violence in all its forms: physical, sexual, psychological, economical, and social, in particular toward the most deprived and vulnerable such as children and adolescents;
- Share my time and material resources in a spirit of generosity to put an end to exclusion, injustice, and political and economic oppression;
- Defend freedom of expression and cultural diversity, giving preference always to dialogue and listening without engaging in fanaticism, defamation, and the rejection of others;
- Promote consumer behavior that is responsible and development practices that respect all forms of life and preserve the balance of nature on the planet;
- Contribute to the development of my community, with the full participation of women, and respect for democratic principles in order to create together new forms of solidarity (Manifesto 2000— UNESCO.org).

The above six key points of the Manifesto present an opportunity to turn, all together, the culture of war and violence into a culture of peace and non-violence. This transformation implies: respect all life; reject violence; share with others; listen to understand; preserve the planet; rediscover solidarity (http: www3.unesco.org/manifesto2000/2000/uk/uk_6 points.htm).

In another document, "Mainstreaming the Culture of Peace" (UN Resolutions A/RES/52/13: Culture of Peace and A/RES/53/243: Declaration and Programme of Action on a Culture of Peace), those key points were formulated in action terms: "For peace and non-violence to prevail, we need to:

> Foster a culture of peace through education by revising the educational curricula to promote qualitative values, attitudes and behaviors of a culture of peace, including peaceful conflict-resolution, dialogue, consensus-building and active non-violence. Such an educational approach should be geared also to: Promote sustainable economic and social development by reducing economic and social inequalities, by eradicating poverty and by assuring sustainable food security, social justice, durable solutions to debt problems, empowerment of women, special measures for groups with special needs, environmental sustainability.... Promote respect for all human rights and a culture of peace are complementary: whenever war and violence dominate, there is no possibility to ensure human rights; at the same time, without human rights, in all their dimensions, there can be no culture of peace.... Ensure equality between women and men through full participation of

women in economic, social and political decision-making, elimination of all forms of discrimination and violence against women, support and assistance to women in need.... Foster democratic participation indispensable foundations for the achievement and maintenance of peace and security are democratic principles, practices and participation in all sectors of society, a transparent and accountable governance and administration, the combat against terrorism, organized crime, corruption, illicit drugs and money laundering.... Advance understanding, tolerance and solidarity to abolish war and violent conflicts we need to transcend and overcome enemy images with understanding, tolerance and solidarity among all peoples and cultures. Learning from our differences, through dialogue and the exchange of information, is an enriching process.... Support participatory communication and the free flow of information and knowledge freedom of information and communication and the sharing of information and knowledge are indispensable for a culture of peace. However, measures need to be taken to address the issue of violence in the media, including new information and communication technologies.... Promote international peace and security the gains in human security and disarmament in recent years, including nuclear weapons treaties and the treaty banning land mines, should encourage us to increase our efforts in negotiation of peaceful settlements, elimination of production and traffic of arms and weapons, humanitarian solutions in conflict situations, post-conflict initiatives..." (http:www3.unesco.org/iycp/uk/uk_cp.htm)

CULTURE OF PEACE SCOPE AND APPLICATION

The following presentation and discussion on the scope and application of peace education is based on a teacher education program constructed by "Education for Europe as Peace Education" (EURED). This project aimed to provide in-service teacher training on peace education. The author of this chapter was part of the International EURED Advisory Board that constructed a curriculum of a European Peace Education Course (EURED, 2002).

When defined in a narrow sense, peace education is usually focused on specific issues such as uncovering the roots of aggression and war or on specific conflict-resolution strategies such as premeditation to cope with violence in classrooms.

In its broad sense "peace education" is a field of theory and practice of education related to the idea of promoting knowledge, values, attitudes, and skills conducive to peace and non-violence, and to an active commitment to the building of a cooperative and caring democratic society. It is targeted toward the empowerment of an individual and the promotion of social well-being through the protection of human dignity of all. It aims at promoting social justice, equality, civil responsibility, and solidarity, and the accepting of a dynamic global perspective by utilizing the concepts and practices of peaceful conflict resolution and non-violence (EURED, 2002, pp. 10, 20).

Peace education appears in a great number of terms such as peace pedagogy, education for: peace and disarmament, conflict resolution, tolerance, conflict/violence prevention, constructive conflict resolution, reconciliation, promoting friendly relations in the classroom, mutual understanding, and so on.

The multifaceted and integrated concept of peace education is illustrated in Figure 1.1.

The UNESCO International Commission on Education for the 21st century, chaired by Jaques Delores (1996), proposed four educational pillars for learning: (1) Learning to know—acquisition of concepts or knowledge about peace and non-violent means of conflict resolution, as well as about

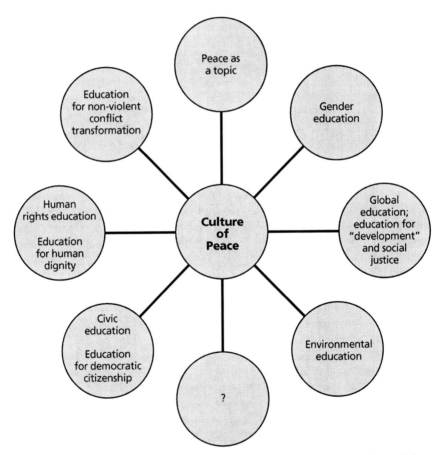

Figure 1.1.   The question mark indicates that other areas and approaches might be added in different contexts (EURED, 2002, Figure 5, p. 21).

its counterparts, violence and war; (2) learning to do—the preparation of students for peace and non-violence. It relies on certain types of knowledge but primarily encompasses a number of procedural and constructive skills as necessary tools for the non-violent resolution and transformation of tensions that emerge in interpersonal or intergroup encounters, mostly on small group or local community levels; (3) learning to be (individually)—the dimension of peace education that refers to an educational climate that enables students to learn from experience by living in a peaceful and non-violent learning environment; it is the climate best defined in terms of the share of power, reinforcing and responsive relations and dynamic horizontal diversity; (4) learning to live together—an environment of inclusion, mutual assistance, and solidarity where tasks are shared and fulfilled with responsibility and care, and where conflicts are understood in positive terms as an opportunity to learn for change. This fourfold learning scheme can be adapted to the four dimensions of competence that peace education should impart, as indicated above.

The state of the world today clearly indicates that educators, educationists, and other professionals involved and in charge of education have failed in their goals to make the world a place that improves the material well-being of peoples and promotes a peaceful state of existence for all. Indeed, they have not defined a proper "tool chest" for peace builders (Alger, 1996, 1999). As a result, what we have now is a world in which social exclusion, alienation, intolerance, violence, and war are widespread. Poverty abounds and the division between north and south is growing (Galtung, 2005). Race, ethnicity, gender, and religion are the basis for social exclusion, alienation, intolerance, and war. There are of course some enclaves of success here and there, and promising projects (i.e., Vriens, 1996, 2003; Feuerverger, Chapter 17, in this volume) but in general, politicians, policy initiators, decision makers, educationists, and educators have failed in improving the human condition.

Not only arms or weapons, but also poverty, poses a threat to social stability and peaceful coexistence within nations and between nations. Thus, for example, India's President Narayan in a speech on India's 50th Anniversary (reported in the *Herald Tribune,* January 26, 2000) warned, The "rich–poor gap endangers India's existence." Well-known studies in the United States, England, and Germany show that youth of lower socioeconomic strata are less tolerant and more often engaged in racist incidents and hate crimes. The same is true for marginalized groups who turn to alienation, violence, and xenophobia (UNESCO, 2004). Indeed, social injustice endangers not only peaceful coexistence within societies but also international peace as well (Galtung, 2005).

CONCLUSIONS

I would like to conclude this chapter with a Rabbinic quote from the Mishna more than 1,800 years old (codified in < 200 C.E.): "The world rests on three pillars: on justice, on truth and on peace which are one and the same: for if there is justice, there is truth and if there is truth, there is peace." We live in an age saturated with advances in information technology and telecommunications. In this turbulent era of change, people rediscover the need for regional identity as well as the need for values. Stable values provide security in a continually changing world. The dignity of the individual represents a basic value that serves as a stepping-stone to other values: freedom of speech, freedom from suffering, and tolerance, which is a prerequisite to attaining an enduring peace. This corresponds with the "Four Freedoms" declared by President Franklin Delano Roosevelt back in 1941: "freedom of speech and expression; freedom of every person to worship God in his own way; freedom from want; freedom from fear" (1941, Vol. 87, Pt. 1).

Education plays a paramount role in imparting the values of tolerance, multiculturalism, and peace to the next generation. Through tolerance, one can strive to transcend religious and political boundaries and bridge cultural and ethnic differences. Tolerance and pluralism require both knowledge of what people share in common, as well as an understanding of their differences. Without this awareness, there can be no multi cultural education, and no peace education. (Reardon, 1988; Rohrs, 1995; Vogt, 1997).

The overarching aim of peace education is to help a new generation build a tolerant society by respecting the rights of individuals and groups, and thus contributing to the greater good of all. The future of all democratic societies will be determined by the ability of the next generation to internalize an informed understanding of the meaning of human values, tolerance, and peace, as well as intercultural and geopolitical peaceful coexistence. The experience and findings generated by ongoing projects aimed at education toward a culture of peace may benefit both the Israeli and Palestinian societies, as well as other societies, in coping with animosity resulting from diversity.

Education toward pluralism, tolerance, and peace in diverse multicultural and multiethnic societies requires two conditions:

Knowledge of the *common* and understanding of the *differences*. Without the knowledge of the *common* there is not and cannot be pluralism. Without understanding of the *differences*, there will not be pluralism. We share common values even though they come from different religious-cultural sources.

Should the present grave situation of destitution, illiteracy, intolerance, and war lead us to despair or hopelessness? Not at all. To the contrary—peace educators should increase their efforts.

I dare to think that if the mythical Sisyphus was alive in these days, Zeus would condemn him to heave the rock of peace up the steep hill. But is it a curse or rather a blessing? Following Albert Camus's *Le Mythe de Sisyphus*, I would suggest to accept his interpretation that it is a blessing, representing humans' relentless drive to improve the human condition, and in our case through peace education.

REFERENCES

Alger, C. (1996), The emerging tool chest for peace builders. *International Journal of Peace Studies, 1*(2), 21–45.

Alger, C. F. (1999). The expanding tool chest for peacebuilders. In H.-W. Jeong (Ed.), *The new agenda for peace research* (pp. 13–44). Aldershot, UK: Ashgate.

Alger, C. F. (2003). What should be the foundations of peace education? In Y. Iram (Ed.), *Education of minorities and peace education in pluralistic societies.* Westport, CT: Praeger.

Bar-Tal, D. (1998). Societal beliefs functional in times of intractable conflict: The Israeli case. *International Journal of Conflict Management, 9,* 23–50.

Bar-Tal, D. (2000). From intractable conflict through conflict resolution: Psychological analysis. *Political Psychology, 21*(2).

Bar-Tal, D. (2002). The elusive nature of peace education. In G. Salomon & B. Nevo (Eds.), *Peace education: The concepts, principles and practices around the world* (pp. 27–36). Mahwah, NJ: Erlbaum.

Brock-Utne, B. (1985). *Educating for peace: A feminist perspective.* New York: Pergamon Press.

Camus, A. (1991). *The myth of Sisyphus: And other essays.* New York: Vintage.

Delores, J. (1996). *Learning: The treasure within.* Report to UNESCO of the International Commission on Education for the Twenty-First Century UNESCO.

EURED (European Network for Peace Education). (2002). *The EURED Teacher Training Programme: Curriculum of a European peace education course.* Klagenfurt, Austria.

Galtung, J. (1973). *Peace: Research, education, action.* Copenhagen, Denmark: Christian Ejlers.

Galtung, J. (1996), *Peace by peaceful means: Peace and conflict, development and civilization.* Thousand Oaks, CA: Sage.

Galtung, J. (2005, March). *Peace studies: A ten point primer.* Paper presented at the Peace Studies Conference, Nanjing University, China.

Harris, I. M. (1998). *Peace education.* Jefferson, NC: McFarland.

Harris, I. M. (2002). Conceptual underpinnings of peace education. In G. Salomon & B. Nevo (Eds.), *Peace education: The concept, principles, and practices around the world* (pp. 15–25). Mahwah, NJ: Erlbaum.

Reardon, B. (1988). *Comprehensive peace education.* New York: Teachers College, Columbia University.

Röhrs, H. (1995) The pedagogy of peace: A fundamental science of practical relevance for the humanization of life. In Y. Iram (Ed.), *The humanities in education.* Israel: Bar Ilan University and the World Association for Education Research.

Roosevelt. F. D. (1941). (U.S. Congressional Record, 1941, Vol. 87, Pt.1)

United Nations General Assembly, 1998: Culture of Peace *Document* A/RES/52/13 adopted by the General Assembly, 52nd session, Agenda item 156.

United Nations General Assembly (1999). Declaration and Programme of Action on a Culture of Peace *Document* A/RES/53/243, adopted by the General Assembly, 53rd session, Agenda item 31.

United Nations *Mainstreaming the Culture of Peace* UN Resolutions A/RES/52/13: Culture of Peace and A/RES/53/243, Declaration and Programme of Action on a Culture of Peace.

UNESCO.org. Manifesto 2000. Available at http://www3.unesco.org/manifesto2000 /uk/uk_6points .htm

UNESCO, Division of Human Rights and Struggle against Discrimination. (2004). *Studies on Human Rights 2004.* Paris: UNESCO.

UNESCO (1945) Constitution. Available at http://www3.unesco.org/iycp/uk/ uk_cp.htm.

Vogt, W. P. (1997). *Tolerance and education—Learning to live with diversity and difference* London: Sage.

Vriens, L. (1996). Postmodernism, peace culture and peace education. In R.J. Burns & R. Aspeslagh (Eds.), *Three decades of peace education around the world: An anthology.* New York: Garland.

Vriens, L. (2003). Education for peace: Concepts, contexts and challenges In Y. Iram (Ed.), *Education of minorities and peace education in pluralistic societies.* Westport, CT: Praeger.

CHAPTER 2

THE THIN LINE BETWEEN PEACE EDUCATION AND POLITICAL ADVOCACY

Toward a Code of Conduct

Gerald M. Steinberg

EVOLUTION OF PEACE STUDIES

The origins of "peace studies" (including conflict resolution, conflict studies, etc.) as an academic discipline can be traced to the late 1940s, and the field has been developing steadily since then.[1] By 2000, the number of academic peace studies and conflict-resolution programs numbered in the hundreds, located all over the world, and organized in professional frameworks such as the Peace Studies section of the International Studies Association and the Political Studies Association (UK).[2]

The peace studies approach to international relations and conflict was founded by a group of scholars with backgrounds in economics and the social sciences, including Kenneth Boulding, Howard Raiffa, and Anatol Rapaport. The backdrop of the Cold War and the political reaction against the threat of nuclear war provided a major impetus for the growth of peace

Educating Toward a Culture of Peace, pages 13–22
Copyright © 2006 by Information Age Publishing

studies, which many people saw as an antidote to programs in war studies, strategic studies, and so on, that also developed on many campuses during this period.

In the early 1960s, during the Kennedy Administration the U.S. Arms Control and Disarmament Agency (ACDA) was created in order to "balance" the influence and power of the Defense Department and Pentagon. The emphasis on arms control negotiations, and the transformative game theory approach developed by influential academics (many of whom served as government advisors on these issues) such as Thomas Schelling and Roger Fischer, strengthened the link between government and academia in the area of peace studies. The 1962 Cuban Missile Crisis, and the concern that the policies of strategic deterrence had brought the world to the brink of nuclear annihilation, accelerated the growth of peace and conflict-resolution studies in academic frameworks.

In parallel, the concept of peace and disarmament studies began to develop in Scandinavia, including the establishment of the Stockholm International Peace Research Institute (SIPRI), the Peace Research Institute, Oslo (PRIO), and related programs at a number of universities. Alva Myrdal, a prominent Swedish diplomat who wrote *The Game of Disarmament* (1976), played a central role in the founding of SIPRI and the promotion of this area of research and analysis.

In addition, the controversies and political upheaval over the Vietnam War, including large-scale protests centered on university campuses, contributed to the growing interest in peace studies. The late 1960s and early 1970s saw a major increase in research projects and courses related to "problems of war and peace," and these often evolved into full-fledged degree-granting peace studies programs. One of the first, at Colgate University, explicitly noted the link between the founding of a peace studies program on campus and "the continuing nuclear arms race and the protracted war in Indochina."[3] In other instances, the role of religious institutions in the development of academic programs was central. The Department of Peace Studies at Bradford University in England was established in the early 1970s, under the influence of the Quaker denomination (Society of Friends).

Funds from philanthropic organizations such as the Institute for World Order and the Ford and McArthur foundations were allocated to the development of courses and research programs on conflict resolution on many campuses, particularly in the United States. This process reinforced the links between policy, politics, and academic activities in the realm of peace studies.

The trend continued during the era of negotiations between East and West during the 1970s, including the SALT agreements, as well as the Helsinki process, with its emphasis on confidence-building measures (CBMs) and links between the three baskets—security, economic interdependence, and civil society (democracy, human rights, freedom of the press, etc.). In these processes, academic involvement in the negotiations, as well as track two meetings and publication of analyses, was very significant. Quasi-academic groups such as Pugwash provided informal and unofficial frameworks for discussions that were designed to influence public policy. At the same time, the academic community published analyses, developed theories, and held conferences based on these activities.

Major universities in different countries opened such programs, some based on the discipline of international relations or international law, others in the framework of political studies or psychology, and yet others as interdisciplinary programs. Over the years, these programs became independent, offering advanced degrees and hiring specialized tenured faculty. In addition, a number of journals in this field have been established, such as the *Journal of Conflict Resolution,* the *Journal of Peace Studies,* and *International Negotiation.* The creation of the government-funded U.S. Institute of Peace (USIP) in the 1980s marked a further stage in this process.

The journals helped to promote the development of a number of theories and models including approaches based on game theory, "reconciliation," prenegotiation, and "ripeness." A wide research literature has developed focusing on these frameworks and their applications. Many of these publications seek to apply the models and analytical frameworks to real cases such as Israeli–Palestinian conflict resolution, India and Pakistan, Cyprus, Northern Ireland, etc. However, as the continuing conflicts in most of these areas illustrate, the field of peace studies has not been able to make much of a difference, in terms of providing empirically useful description or realistic prescription. Furthermore, peace and conflict studies are subject to increasing criticism, reflecting the impact of ideological and subjective political positions that go far beyond the boundaries of careful and value-free academic discourse.

THE IDEOLOGY AND LIMITED CURRICULUM
OF PEACE STUDIES

The failure of peace studies to provide empirically useful analysis and prescriptions for resolving or managing protracted ethnonational conflicts is, in part, a reflection of the complexity of the subject. However, there are additional factors, including a tendency to emphasize a single approach, as well as a dominant ideology of peace studies that strongly rejects, on normative grounds, the legitimacy of the use of force for reducing conflict and self-defense.

In the curricula and syllabi of many peace studies and conflict-resolution programs, the dominance of the Kantian and idealist ideological framework stands out. Many of these programs focus on theories and approaches that are based on sociopsychological concepts and models such as reconciliation, dialogue, forgiveness, historic justice, empathy for victims, etc. The normative models, publications, and simulation exercises of Kelman, Montville, Kriesberg, Lederach, Rothman, etc., are featured centrally in the reading lists and case studies. International law, norms, and frameworks, as well as resolutions and reports of the United Nations and its ancillary groups, such as the UN Commission on Human Rights, supported by the powerful NGO community,[4] are also emphasized in this idealist school (i.e., Falk & Mendlovitz, 1982). Many peace studies programs emphasize the goal of defining and furthering "ways of working toward a just and harmonious world community" (Forcey, 1989, p. 7).

In contrast, approaches that are anchored in the Hobbesian approach to international conflict and conflict resolution, and that include realist theories and models based on deterrence, the security dilemma, and the use of force to prevent or resolve conflict, are all but ignored, or, in some cases, explicitly rejected on ideological grounds. As a result, students in peace studies programs rarely encounter the analyses of Hobbes, Morgenthau, E. H. Carr, and other realists. Similarly, peacekeeping and war prevention strategies based on the use of force for self-defense, preemption, prevention, etc., are also quite rare in standard peace studies curricula. Although some idealist-based reading lists include discussions on just war (in particular, Michael Walzer's 1977 volume on *Just and Unjust Wars*), this is also far from the norm.

The rapid adoption of postmodernism among many academics, including the ideology of critical theory in which subjective concepts are concretized, has amplified this process. Exploiting the terminology of universal human rights and other norms and values, adherents to this ideology, such as Noam Chomsky and Edward Said, have supported "empowerment," meaning political action and even including support for terrorism and violence, in the name of social justice. In peace studies, the adoption of this approach insists that objective criteria exist by which to distinguish between aggressor and oppressor, or victim and perpetrator. See, for example, Mitchell and Schoeffel (2002), Chomsky (1994), and Said (2002). These are a few examples of dozens of such publications that repeat the same theme, in which ideology becomes the basis for political analysis.

Furthermore, the idealistic approach to peace studies—including dimensions such as reconciliation, apology, rebalancing of power relationships, and historic justice—are based on inherently subjective and often highly political judgments. In considering power relationships, the orthodox (idealist) approach to peace studies and conflict resolution inherently assumes that weaker parties and instances of historic injustice can be readily identified.

The danger of distortion from subjective judgments was enhanced with the spread of critical theory, and the enthusiasm with which it was embraced and propagated. Critical theory, in its various forms, easily descends into aggressive political correctness, which claims to distinguish between justice and injustice. Adherents of the critical theory approach seek to empower the disenfranchised and oppressed, or at least to rebalance an asymmetric power relationship. But justice and power relationships are subjective, and when transferred from the philosophical to the political realm, are readily manipulated.

This problem is particularly acute in consideration of the Arab–Israeli conflict in the context of peace studies programs. In general, this dispute is truncated into its Israeli–Palestinian component, and in this very limited and artificial context, Israel is automatically portrayed as the more powerful or dominant party, while the Palestinians are depicted as powerless victims of historic injustice. This assessment is highly subjective, based on a narrow and self-reinforcing criteria, which generally ignores the objective impact of Palestinian terror and the explicit and continuing threats to Israelis security from the region and the wider Islamic and Arab world. Similarly, the standard claims of historic injustice focus on Palestinian refuge claims, Israeli settlements, etc. But these are based entirely on the Palestinian narrative, which ignores responsibility for central historical events, such as the long-standing Arab rejectionism beginning with the 1947 UN Partition resolution and the violence that resulted, or the context of the 1967 war, which led to the Israeli occupation.

Similarly, in this and in many other cases, historic injustice is a matter of perception and interpretation, often depending on the determination of a particular starting point, and therefore outside the realm of useful academic analysis. (The South African case and the clear distinctions between the apartheid regime and the Black majority is exceptional.) Efforts to learn and apply lessons from the South African experience to other conflict situations generally create distortions and reflect political and ideological biases. In this context, the use of the term "apartheid" in different contexts is politically and ideologically judgmental, rather than academic, and the demonization of Israel becomes part of the conflict, rather than contributing to its management or resolution.

These deficiencies resulting from a narrow idealist approach to conflict and peace studies and from uncritical adoption of postmodernist critical theory are reinforced by the relative lack of systematic investigation and empirical evaluation of the relevant theories and models. While descriptive case studies and normative articles have been published dealing with conflict-resolution efforts, particularly with respect to protracted ethnonational conflicts (the Middle East, Cyprus, Northern Ireland, and others), critical evaluations of failed peace processes are generally lacking. Evaluative and comparative methodologies, such as the single analytical framework approach developed by Alexander George, and based on empirically observable variables that are derived from the theories and models in the peace studies literature, are necessary to remedy this weakness in the field. (For a notable and insufficiently cited exception, see Hamson, 1996.)

This overall absence of useful empirical analysis that can ascertain the applicability of the various theories and approaches to peace studies is illustrated in the case of the treatment of the Oslo process in the literature. Following the initial agreement in 1993 (the Declaration of Principles), many scholars "explained" this apparent success and failed to predict the subsequent failure (Kelman, 1998; Kriesberg, 2001; Pruitt, 1997). Most theories and models appear to be tautological in nature, without independent and externally measurable variables with which to determine the link between cause and effect or to measure success or failure. This constitutes a major weakness in the academic approach to peace studies.

ADVOCACY: TALKING PEACE WHILE PROMOTING WAR

As a result of these factors, in recent years, academic peace and conflict studies programs have also drawn increasing scrutiny and criticism, both from within and from external analysts (Cox & Scruton, 1984; Mercer, 1986; Scruton, 1985). George Lopez, Senior Fellow and Director of Policy Studies, Kroc Institute for International Peace Studies, University of Notre Dame, has acknowledged the ideological nature of peace studies (Lopez, 1989, p. 9). This ideology enhances the tendency inherent in peace studies to move from academic inquiry and research to advocacy, and without careful navigation, it is all to easy for peace studies programs to be drawn into the conflicts that students and faculty claim to be studying.

Furthermore, in an idealist framework in which all use of military force by state actors is essentially anathema, and is strongly influenced by external nonacademic and often ideological factors, the framework of peace studies has often been exploited for attacks against specific countries, specifically the United States and Israel. The policies of both countries are routinely subject to condemnation (such political judgments are in themselves outside the realm of academic inquiry) and the context in which force is used in self-defense is often ignored. In a major departure from academic norms of conduct, and in a manner that undermines the credibility of peace studies, faculty members encourage their students to participate in political rallies, boycotts, and similar activities (Sayre, 2003).

While a detailed analysis of this negative phenomenon is beyond the scope of this chapter, a few examples of such abuse to pursue an anti-Israel and pro-Palestinian ideology provide indications of the overall trend. As noted above, the Palestinian side is consistently labeled as the weaker party and a victim of Israeli power and aggression. In a particularly blatant example of the political abuse, Stuart Rees, the head of the Centre for Peace and Conflict Studies (CPACS) at the University of Sydney, has long championed a pro-Palestinian position and ideology, disguised within the postmodern jargon of support for the "disempowered." In November 2003, Rees and the Sydney Peace Foundation (which he also heads and which is closely linked to CPACS) awarded its annual peace prize to Dr. Hanan Ashrawi, a member of the PLO hierarchy and a former minister in the Palestinian cabinet. Ashrawi has been a major figure in the political campaign against Israel (e.g., in the Durban conference in 2001), and in the strident Palestinian organization known as MIFTAH.[5] This award and ceremony, which took place in a university facility, was highly controversial and stood in sharp contrast to the Sydney Peace Foundation's explicit criteria for awarding the prize, which include the pledge to "use the prize to further the cause of peace with justice." The process also undermined Rees's claims to be advancing the cause of peace.

Similarly, the peace studies program at Bradford University in the United Kingdom has also become the setting for anti-Israeli propaganda. In a recent example, the UK Peace Studies association, which is hosted by Bradford University, advertised demonstrations against the Israeli separation fence. ("On the anniversary of the fall of the Berlin Wall, members of Leeds Coalition Against the War will demonstrate in graphic form, with the aid of cardboard boxes, what they believe needs to happen to the wall that the Israeli government is erecting between Israel and the Occupied Territories. Palestinians are being cut off from their livelihoods and families, and Israelis are being separated from neighbors with whom they have lived in peace. This symbolic action is taking place to draw the attention of the Leeds public to the conflict in Israel-Palestine, in order to mobilize the voices of peace.") In this call for action, the facts are greatly distorted and the context of Palestinian terrorism is entirely absent. Under the umbrellas of peace studies, this program, as in the example of Sydney University, is, in fact, promoting conflict.

A third example is found in the December 2001 Newsletter of the Peace Studies Section of the International Studies Association, in an article entitled "Another Voice against the War," written by Mohammed Abu-Nimer from the Program on International Peace and Conflict Resolution at American University, Washington, DC. On its masthead, this publication notes that "The aim of the PSS/ISA is to seek a better understanding of the causes of war and violence and of the conditions of peace in the international system. To this end, the Peace Studies Section links scholars of various disciplines and methodologies, develops, encourages, and disseminates research, and facilitates research-based teaching in peace and conflict studies."

Abu-Nimer's essay begins by focusing on the terrorist attacks of September 11, 2001, agreeing that this "was a horrible act and everyone should agree that there is no religious or political motivation that justifies such a crime." However, he then goes on to address the question of possible causes for Islamic anger and violence, including U.S. policy in the Middle East, and turns the essay into an anti-Israel polemic that is entirely inconsistent with the mission statement of PSS/ISA, as noted above. Abu-Nimer refers to the Israeli–Palestinian conflict as "the main thorn in the Middle East and in the relationship between western countries and Islamic countries." In particular, in this analysis, the conflict is based on the denial of self-determination to the Palestinians. Furthermore, "Every Muslim believes that the U.S. and European governments, if they want, are capable of placing enough pressure on Israel to withdraw from the occupied territories and allow Palestinians to live in freedom. This might not be a totally accurate belief, however it is derived from the fact that such governments act as suppliers of weapons and protectors of Israeli interests and policies in every international setting; the recent decision to pull out of the conference on anti-Racism in South Africa is a prime example of such policy" (Abu-Nimer, 2001).

TOWARD A CODE OF CONDUCT

As in other forms of deviance, the first step in efforts to end the politicization of peace and conflict studies is to acknowledge that the problem exists. Following this stage, specific policies must be formulated and implemented to combat the tendency of academic programs to become players in the conflicts themselves.

A code of conduct for peace studies faculty and students could provide an important step toward implementing this necessary goal. Such a code should include the following dimensions:

1. The academic discipline of peace studies should seek to encourage reading lists, lectures, and related activities that fully present the different ideologically based depictions and paradigms regarding the sources of conflict. In particular, the literature presenting the realist perspective on conflict, beginning with Hobbes, should be included in addition to the Lockian and Kantian (idealist) approaches, allow-

ing students to consider the different perspectives in the free marketplace of ideas.

2. In presenting the details of any conflict, it is important that academic standards of objectivity and nonintervention are scrupulously heeded.

3. Academic programs in general, and peace studies in particular, avoid advocacy or any other actions that would constitute participation in a conflict, taking sides, or promoting the claims of any of the parties.

The purpose of this approach is not to impose, in any sense, uniformity of ideas or to prevent free and open discussion, but rather to break the existing "politically correct" straightjacket that often characterizes peace and conflict studies in the university. Given the deviation from academic norms of open debate and the tradition that encourages questioning of accepted doctrine and orthodoxy in some peace studies programs, a wide discussion of the ideas expressed in this draft code of conduct would be beneficial, in and of itself.

NOTES

1. Claims for earlier origins are far-fetched and demonstrate the absence of continuity with the more modern versions. The first post–World War II Peace Studies program was established in 1948 at Manchester College (Indiana) by the pacifist Brethren, but this was also an isolated example. (Annals of the American Academy of Political and Social Science, v. 504: "Peace Studies: Past and Future"; Harris, Fisk, & Rank, 1998 (http://www.gmu.edu/academic/ijps/vol3_1/Harris.htm).

2. http://www.earlham.edu/~psa/history.html

3. Colgate University Peace Studies Program, http://departments.colgate.edu/peacestudies/default.htm

4. See the analysis posted on www.ngo-monitor.org

5. http://www.ngo-monitor.org/editions/v1n02/v1n02-1.htm

REFERENCES

Abu-Nimer, M. (2001, December). *Another voice against the war* [Newsletter]. Peace Studies Section of the International Studies Association.

Chomsky, N. (1994). *World orders old and new.* New York: Columbia University Press.

Cox, C., & Scruton, R. (1990). *Peace studies: A critical survey.* New York: Hyperion Books.

Forcey, L.(1989). Introduction to peace studies. In L. Forcey (Ed.), *Peace: Meanings, politics, strategies.* New York: Praeger.

Hamson, F. O. (1996). *Nurturing peace: Why peace settlements succeed or fail.* Washington, DC: United States Institute of Peace Press.

Harris, I. M., Fisk, L. J., & Rank, C. (1998). A portrait of university peace studies, in North America and Western Europe at the end of the millennium. *International Journal of Peace Studies, 3*(1), http://www.gmu.edu/academic/ijps/vol3_1/Harris.htm

Lopez, G. (1989). Peace studies: Past and future. *Annals of the American Academy of Political and Social Science, 504.*

Kelman, H. C. (1998). Social-psychological contributions to peacemaking and peacebuilding in the Middle East. *Applied Psychology, 47*(1), 5–29.

Kriesberg, L. (2001). Mediation and the Transformation of the Israeli–Palestinian Conflict. *Journal of Peace Research, 38*(3), 373–392.

Mercer, P (1986). *Peace of the dead.* Policy Research.

Mitchell P. R., & Schoeffel, J (2002). *Understanding power: The indispensable Chomsky.* New York: New Press.

Pruitt, D. G. (1997). Ripeness theory and the Oslo talks. *International Negotiation, 2,* 91–104.

Said, E. (2002, September 30). Low point of powerlessness. *Al Ahram.*

Sayre, B (2003, April 30). Peace studies' war against America. *FrontPageMagazine.com.* http://www.frontpagemag.com/Articles/ReadArticle.asp?ID=7583

Scruton, R. (1990). *World studies: Education or indoctrination.* New York: Hyperion Books.

Walzer, M (1977). *Just and unjust wars.* New York: Basic Books.

CHAPTER 3

TOWARD A HORIZONTAL
VIEW OF SOCIETY

Madhav D Nalapat

A theory widely accepted as reasonable states that around 100,000 years ago, a catastrophe wiped out all but a few thousand members of the human race. Subsequently, it was from this small pool in Africa that the 6 billion of us now inhabiting this planet came from (for an account of this theory, see, e.g., the prehistoric life section in the Science & Nature website of the BBC at news.bbc.co.uk/1/hi/world/science/cavemen/chronology/contentpage6 .shtml).

Geographical location created differences in skin color. Those who migrated to sun-starved climes saw Mother Nature remove much of the pigment from their skin to maximize absorption of sunlight, while others in sunnier climes experienced an abundance of pigment as protection against ultraviolet rays. Similarly, local conditions also crafted differences in culture. Still, at the "foundation" level, the genetic differences between individual humans remained tiny, as shown by the fact that DNA variations between an Australian Aboriginal and a descendant of the Vikings, for example, fall within a definable but infinitesimal range (Holmes, 2005).

Educating Toward a Culture of Peace, pages 23–37
Copyright © 2006 by Information Age Publishing
All rights of reproduction in any form reserved.

Sadly, the formal education systems that have evolved in almost all the countries on the planet have ignored this fundamental kinship between human beings. Instead of educating us that we are all first cousins—if not siblings—the systems and curricula have created the perception that there are huge, and occasionally insurmountable, differences between individual peoples and cultures.

Of course there are substantial differences in mindset, but these are not inherent in our chemical composition. A Mohawk brought up in a Tahiti would behave in the same way as the others on that tropical island—as would someone born of Polynesian parents but brought up on a reserve in Canada. This is very clear with the increasing numbers of interracial adoptions. Thousands of Chinese girls have been adopted in Canada since the late 1980s. These girls came from wholly different backgrounds from their adoptive families yet, within a few years, they had integrated into the cultures and societies into which they had been transplanted (Karin, 2000).

It is not just children that can adapt. Interracial marriages also prove the case. After the initial shock of accommodating the Other in their midst, the "host" family quickly recognizes that the perceived differences are only superficial. In most cases, within months—if not days—such divergences become less and less apparent until, finally, there is acceptance and comfort. The rate of success in interracial marriages is at least as high as that in same-race unions (Chen, 1999).

Understandably, such inspiring, motivating realities are often overlooked when confronted with the Hindu caste system, the uniquely evil Nazi race laws, or the anti-Roma outbursts in East Europe. We have the examples of the genocide of the Native American populations and the forcible expropriation of land from the original inhabitants in countries around the world. It is still going on. In Australia, the Aboriginals have been relegated to the fringe of social, economic, and political life in what is regarded as a democratic society.

This discrimination is very destructive to the societies that foster it. In India, thanks to the caste system, a fractured Hindu society was unable to prevail over the invaders from Central Asia, Persia, and Afghanistan, not to mention Europe. The reason? The local elite considered the overwhelming majority of the population unworthy of defending their country and therefore excluded them from battle. The first line of defense for any country is a just society, in which every citizen has the motivation and opportunity to fight to preserve her or his liberty.

Today, although some scholars talk of "universal" values, what they actually mean is a new caste system—one in which societies are graded and boxed into a *vertical* categorization, with western society at the apex. Instead, what is needed is a *horizontal* view of society—one that accepts that each society has its pluses and its minuses, and therefore is equal in status and potential to any other. Unless the international educational system instills this truth in the minds of the young, our future will be as bleak as our past. The evil of religious extremism and a propensity toward exclusivism cannot be overcome except by those freed of notions of cultural superiority.

There is a phrase in Sanskrit: *Vasudhaiva Kutumbakam.* It means the whole world is one family—that regardless of the geographic, religious, or ethnic differences that persist in the world, at their core all human beings belong to the same family, and should regard and treat one another as such.

As mentioned earlier, many real-life sociological experiments prove this ancient truth. Children adopted as babies from poverty-stricken lands and brought up in homes in the West grow into productive citizens with a level of skill far in excess of that enjoyed by those they left behind in the country of their birth. It is not race that controls modernity and productivity but upbringing.

To use another example, India is correctly regarded as one of the poorest countries in the world. More than 200 million citizens of the Republic of India live in conditions that are at least as inhuman as those suffered by residents in certain sections of Sub-Saharan Africa. In particular, the two Indian States of Bihar and Uttar Pradesh are among the most backward territories in the world when it comes to education and social development. Those two states alone drag the rest of the country down by several percentage points on any international index (Planning Commission, 2004).

And yet, those who have lived all their lives in India's most backward states, Uttar Pradesh and Bihar, once they are able to emigrate to the United States, or even to more developed parts of India, become contributors to the economy almost immediately. Similarly, the same Indians who come from cities such as Kanpur and Patna, known for their filth and lack of public hygiene, adjust in days to the much higher standards of, for example, Singapore. In India, littering is almost a national sport. Yet few Indian citizens are guilty of littering in Singapore, which has stiff penalties against such behavior. What is the reason for such an adjustment in attitudes? Why has the litterbug of Patna become the model citizen of Atlanta? Clearly, their genetics haven't changed. So, it must be education, social environment, and the change in attitudes and perception that have been caused by the shift in location.

Sometimes a shift in location is not necessary, just a society-wide educational effort (and a good motivator). Surat in India was one of the dirtiest cities in the country, which is saying a lot. After an attack of bubonic plague in 1994, the city and its citizens cleansed themselves of most of the filth (Richardson, 1995). Today Surat has become livable. Other cities are looking to the future for educational motivation. Hyderabad has become much more clean and pleasant during the past decade. It has been a direct result of the successful effort of a regional politician to convert it into a world-class "cybercity" (BBC). If once-filthy Surat and Hyderabad can learn and adapt, so can the rest of India. If backward, illiterate India can learn and adapt, so can the rest of the world.

Indeed, what is the reason why India itself has become one of the fastest-growing economies of the world? Why has the country become a world-beater in information technology? And why is it rapidly developing into a biotech superpower?

Today, in cities and villages, in advanced states and those that are still laggards, a new type of Indian is emerging. They are confident of their ability to compete globally, and to help the international economy produce more, more cheaply, and more better. The initial success of a few pioneers in information technology has become self-reinforcing, and the confidence that it has generated has percolated into other sections of society. Slowly, expectations of what is possible are rising. Confidence in one's own ability to meet such expectations is growing. As a result, success is begetting success (NASSCOM, 1997).

Psychologically, it has been a long journey. Indians were told for years that this sort of success was genetically beyond their reach. That "defender" of liberty, Winston S Churchill, opposed freedom for India for decades, arguing that the different ethnic groups in the country, its stark poverty and the low educational standards, made it unfit for democracy. It is instructive to look through the wartime exchanges between President Franklin Delano Roosevelt of the United States and Prime Minister Churchill of the United Kingdom. While Roosevelt backed independence for the (then) 360 million people of the Subcontinent, Churchill was vehement that he would not agree to such a "catastrophe" (Quinault, 2001).

According to Churchill's logic, the liberty and the freedom that Allied forces were fighting the National Socialists to achieve were only suitable for the inhabitants of Europe, not the people of India. It makes sad reading to see such a lover of liberty—and a man who did so much against tyranny—to so oppose liberty for what was then, and is now, a sixth of the human race.

What was it in Churchill's education and upbringing that made him, and millions like him, regard human beings that were from cultures that were different from their own as being undeserving of freedom? Is there the danger that a similar "us and them" mindset is still being created in Europe by an educational process that puts western civilization at the apex of the human race—at the top of the human social pyramid?

We have seen the impact of a "vertical" view of human society (as distinct from the "horizontal") in history. We have seen the evil caused by fanatic schools in the Middle East that teach the young that they are superior to the Other and, being superior, that they have a right to violence to enforce their dominance on the rest of the world. The difference between one "vertical" education system and another is only one of degree, not kind. To the rational mind, there is more in common between the triumphalism of societal and historical pedagogy in, for example, France and the "madarsas" of Pakistan and Saudi Arabia than is acknowledged.

Despite Churchill's opposition, India became free on August 15, 1947. The founding fathers of the new republic rejected advice that they go slow on the introduction of democracy. They immediately instituted a system of universal adult franchise. The first election was conducted in 1952 and, since then, there have been many more. In that process as well, there was improvement in evolution.

Initially many voters were made to cast their ballots on the diktat of caste or other leaders. In the estimate of the writer, about 40% of votes in that first election were cast not because of free choice, but because of commands given to the voter by others. Even today, around 10% of the votes cast in elections in India are based on pressure from local elites. However, that means that fully 90% of votes in India are now free. Given the size and relative newness of the Indian democratic process, that figure is not disheartening. India has shown that, if there is commitment to the process and local education, poverty and backwardness need not condemn democracy to ineffectiveness and attenuation (Kalam & Rajan, 2002).

Any visitor who has been coming to India over a period of decades will sense the change that has been caused by democracy. In Bihar, for example, the powerful Bumihar community dominated over the far more numerous Yadavs and other backward communities. Even during the 1970s, a Yadav would not be allowed to sit in the presence of a Bumihar in several Bihar villages. And then, using their numerical strength, slowly the Yadavs began to assert their right to equal treatment. A political revolution took place by the 1980s, and a Yadav became the Chief Minister of the State. Since then, the feudal inequality that had been prevalent for thousands of years was banished. Social revolution has also taken place in neighboring Uttar Oradesh, again without bloodshed. In democratic India, the ballot and not the bullet has been the instrument of Revolution. Not exactly the catastrophe Churchill envisaged.

All over India, society has been transformed by the very democracy that Winston Churchill thought that Indians (and other "inferior" cultures) were incapable of. Sadly, his way of thinking is still present. In Germany, when the government introduced a measure in 2000 to bring in a limited 20,000 software programmers from outside the country (Tripathi, 2000), the conservative opposition party launched an effective campaign against such "dilution" of "racial purity" by inventing the slogan: Kinder Statt Inder (Children, not Indians [www.kinder-statt-inder.de]). Are there no children among the people of India? Are only German children "proper" children, and not those from India? It is astonishing that the politicians who invented this slogan are even today honored members of the European political scene, as are others who have used similar scare tactics against "Others."

Europe prides itself on its civilization. There is no doubt that Europe has a great cultural tradition. Many of the achievements of the modern age owe their origins to European—or more broadly, Western—scholarship and enterprise. Yet what cannot be forgotten is that it was from Europe that slave ships went to Africa to buy human beings, load them like cattle, and sell them to work in plantations—without any acknowledgment of their mutual humanity. It was also where the Holocaust took place—Europeans slaughtering other Europeans just because they belonged to a different faith. And it is the place that all too recently, during the splintering of Yugoslavia, introduced us to the term "ethnic cleansing."

Clearly, the record of the peoples of this particular continent is mixed (as with the record of most continents), and yet in almost every European school and university, what is taught implies that Europe is the fount of world culture and civilization. Within those narrow parameters, the accomplishments of the French, British, Italians, Greeks, or Germans—depending on location of the educational institution—are given preeminence in their respective locations.

Human civilization is a rope composed of many strands. The continent of Africa has made a great contribution to the world through its ancient scientific discoveries and its cultures—an influence that is still felt today, most evidently in music. Asia has had many great cultural streams, including the three that have endured for more than three millennia each: the Indic, the Sinic, and the Hebrew. All these strands cross over, interweave, and, when looked at from the right distance, become a single, strong rope tying us all together.

By teaching young Europeans that 99.9% of "civilization" is a thin, single strand spun from their continent, those responsible for such misinformation are creating the mindset that is the progenitor of the Skinhead and, in times past, was the creator of the brownshirt. World history is too precious to be looked at in this insular and selfish way. What is needed is to ensure that everyone learns a history that teaches the importance of each of the different strands that form the rope of World Culture, and how they are bound together. Just as a tree should not be mistaken for a forest, so should a segment of human civilization not be mistaken for the whole.

The emphasis given above on education in Europe is because of the reality that the colonial legacy of that great continent has resulted in its pedagogy and the direction of its educational "software" being adopted almost without change in several parts of the world, including India. Indeed recent efforts to "Indianize" the education system in India have been rebuffed, and the curricula of the schools has been sought to be returned to the West-anchored basis/bias that has been present since the days of Macauley, who sought to create in India a race of men British in mind though Indian in color. Thus, Europe has to take the lead in the horizontalization of education.

The problem in presentation isn't just one of geographical focus, but also of time period emphasis. In the 5,000 years of recorded human history, it is only in the last 500 years that western European countries have leapfrogged over the rest (and the United States is more recent still). Thousands of years ago, there were the flourishing civilizations of India, China, Israel, Persia, Greece, and Rome. Then followed the cultures of the Buddhists, Christians, and finally the Muslims. Even at the time when Britain colonized India, the country was far wealthier in terms of a stock of assets than its new master. And in terms of intellectual wealth, while many marvel at the statecraft of the Italian Machiavelli, a much more complete "handbook" was written by the Indian, Kautilya, 1,500 years before (Kautilya, 1987).

For a correct portrayal of human civilization, the entire 5,000 years of adequately footnoted human history must be taught. Instead, the focus is overwhelmingly on the past five centuries, with the previous 45 centuries appearing mainly as a brief prologue. What is the effect of such a distortion of human history? It is the creation of a mindset that regards itself as being on a higher level than others. This is as much an obstacle to social tranquility as similar feelings of caste superiority in India or religious exclusivism in the Wahabbi or Khomeinist faith.

An examination of history the way it is taught in Europe will show a dearth of information about perspectives not rooted in the misconception that the continent is the "navel" of the world (Ferguson, 2004). Small wonder that, even today, many European youth mature with the perception that normalcy dictates that their continent has a special place in world affairs, and indeed has had throughout human history. Hence it seems "natural" that problems in Sri Lanka or the Middle East can only be solved if Norwegians intervene there with their missionary belief in an instant solution.

Were the teaching of history to reach back 3,000 years at least, rather than simply a few centuries, then the periods during which India and China—to name just two examples—were ahead of every European country in development would also be factored into attitudes about the world. There would be a rounded view of the ebbs and flows of history, how today's empires can become tomorrow's scattering of fighting states. And how they can again come back to the fore.

There would also be a healthy respect for the true accomplishment of human beings, for example, for the survival of the people of Israel, who have maintained their heritage over millennia in the face of immense hardships. Indeed, had such a history been taught in European universities during the 1920s, the generation that accepted Adolf Hitler as their leader and followed his instructions may have not fallen into such a moral precipice.

What Hitler did was to prey on the attitudes and prejudices extant in much of European scholarship, which posits that the continent, and it's dominant religion, as the only deserving center of the universe—the glorious sun around which all else revolves. While many may reject this assertion, the reality remains that great and civilized people allowed themselves to fall under the control of a tyrant without parallel in world history. Worse, they approved of and helped him in the many despicable deeds that he subsequently undertook. It was the triumph of ignorance and its handmaiden hatred over knowledge and understanding.

That a cultured and highly civilized nationality allowed a Hitler to emerge from within itself is a stain not simply on an individual people but on all humanity. To avoid this, we need to ensure that the impressionable years of schooling every child not be distorted through (even inadvertent) theories of cultural or racial superiority; instead, they must learn the truth, that every human civilization—just like every human—has within it elements that are good and elements that are bad. By considering any one culture or heritage as "superior," we automatically assume all the rest to be inferior. We make the mistake of Winston Churchill, who regarded the people of India as unfit for democracy and self-rule. We make the mistake that some are making in Iraq today, of assuming that the Iraqi people are unfit to exercise sovereignty over their own geographical area.

Fortunately, in today's Europe and today's India attitudes are changing. Many are abandoning the dogmas of caste and race to accept the oneness of humanity. Hopefully, in time, the religious fanatics who seek to convert minds into vehicles for the propagation of terror will meet a like fate. For this process to be accelerated, what is needed is for an education process to be created that stresses the horizontality of society rather than posits an imaginary vertical view of the human race.

The time has come to end for good the sort of vertical approach that teaches, for example, that to eat food with hands the way people in India do is "uncivilized," even though in terms of hygiene, washing hands or washing cutlery should not make much difference. Similarly in these outdated teachings, the graceful—if scanty—dress of the Masai in Africa is given a lower rank in such a Weltanschauung than the layers of cloth worn by "modern" individuals—even in climatic conditions where a lighter form of dress would be more suitable. The impact of this vertical scholarship is so pernicious that, for example, several architects in India take pride in designing glass boxes that would make excellent sense in cold countries where sunlight is at a premium, but which create infernos in the tropical climate of Mumbai or most other Indian cities. Until the air-conditioning bills come due.

It is not just Europeans who are guilty of creating vertical views of cultures. It is amusing to hear some casteists in India talk of the "superiority" of their own tradition, and contrast this with the "backwardness" of countries in Africa. A more horizontal approach would show the many similarities between all of humanity. For example, the dress worn by an African Medicine Man—or a Shaman in the Americas—is similar to that worn by the *Velichappad* (medicine man) in Kerala, South India. And Kerala is the most educated part of India.

What is "civilized" and what is not is a matter of perception, With one exception: violence. Any recourse to violent means is uncivilized by definition, as human beings have no excuse to use means other than reason and persuasion to settle differences. The only case in which violence is justified is self-defense.

Defining elements are essential in the new horizontal curriculum for a true education in knowledge, understanding, and, ultimately, peace. The author sees, as a starting point, six essential lessons.

Lesson 1 in the education of peace is what we have already established, that all peoples and cultures stand on a horizontal scale, different from but equal to each other.

Lesson 2 shows us that force is the language of animals, reason the recourse of human beings.

Lesson 3 is a bit more philosophical. A human being is the psychological compound of three different layers: the material, the emotional, and the spiritual. There is often an interface between parts of these three layers. However, there are also vast areas of the psyche where the three operate in separate streams. Where we keep the emotional from the material, and the spiritual from the emotional, for example. What is needed is less a confluence of these than comfortable coexistence and coacceptance.

Lesson 3 in the education of peace teaches what in India is known as *Sanatan Dharma.* Loosely translated, this means that there may be many paths, but they all lead to the same destination. That there is more than one path to the Kingdom of Heaven, more than one path to God (Basham, 1975).

In this sense, the Jewish faith is an inspiration for the rest of humanity, for, if my understanding is correct, nowhere is it taught in the Jewish faith that one has to convert to Judaism in order to get salvation. Even if one follows another faith, one is still eligible to enter Heaven. "To each her or his own." It is perfectly legitimate to believe that only one faith can ensure entry into Heaven in the afterlife. What is impermissible is to deny the validity or the reason behind others having the same view on their own faiths.

A fitting example for this lesson is the life of Sri Narayana Guru, a saint who worked among the downtrodden of India more than a century ago. Sri Narayana himself came from an "untouchable" caste, a group regarded by "caste" Hindus as being so beyond the pale that it was regarded as polluting to even touch them. In India, it was the priestly (or Brahmin) caste that consecrated temples. Sri Narayana stunned orthodox Hindu society by consecrating several temples. When he was asked how he, as an "Untouchable," could consecrate temples the way only a Brahmin could, the Guru's reply was succinct: "I am consecrating temples for those who believe in my teachings. Those who believe in your superstitions and prejudices are welcome to not come to them."

A country where people of all faiths are not allowed to set up houses of worship, or where more than one faith is not allowed to be practiced, is an aberration that shames the entire human race.

It is the view of the author that the persecutions suffered by the Jewish people over millennia have earned for them the right to have their own state. The State of Israel is legitimate not just legally but morally as well. However, he would be the first to object were Israel to prevent those of other faiths from practicing their beliefs in the Jewish state, or deny them political and other human rights. He would object not because such an approach would militate against Christianity or Islam, but because it would go against the tenets and tenor of the Jewish faith, and of the civilized people that they are.

What is incomprehensible is that so many of those who are condemning Israel themselves practice the worst form of discrimination in the territories they control. *every* country, *every* society, needs to be subject to the same *universal* standards of tolerance and human rights. To demand it elsewhere while denying it at home is hypocrisy. The only point—and not simply a semantic one—is that such standards are *human* standards, not *Western* ones. The West has been as guilty of death and destruction as any other region, and cannot lay claim to a superior tradition. Indeed, by calling universal values "Western" values, certain cultural fanatics in Europe and the Americas inadvertently assist fanatics in Asia and Africa who seek to insulate their societies from such values.

I would like to refer to his theory of Indutva (Nalapat, 1999), which holds that every Indian is a compound of the Western, the Mughal and the Vedic traditions. She or he is thus simultaneously a child of the Judaeo Christian, the Muslim and the Hindu streams. It is the same elsewhere. We are all not just "globalized" in economics, but in the culture that runs through our psychic veins. And the sooner we accept this universalism in each of us, the better for the future of the world.

Some schools of thought hold that theirs is the only true path to God and to Heaven. It is, as mentioned earlier, the right of the followers of such faiths to believe so, and their view must be respected. What is impermissible in a society is to seek to impose any view on other human beings. In particular, to initiate the use of violence in order to promote a particular faith.

It is not accidental that in India, a land that has the second-largest Muslim population in the world, there are far fewer recruits to terrorist organizations than in countries such as Saudi Arabia and Pakistan (A. Sahni, personal communication, 2002). The reason lies in the millennial traditions of the land for tolerance of all faiths. Speaking personally, I have visited Christian churches, Muslim *dargahs*, and Hindu temples several times, and found solace and inner peace in all three. In a Muslim *dargah*, for example, which essentially is the tomb of a great saint, there is an atmosphere of serenity that is far removed from Wahabbi preachings of hate—preachings that make some variants of what is known as Wahabbism, the modern equivalent of National Socialism.

In India, Muslims, Hindus, and Christians join together to go to the great Hindu shrine of Sabari Mala, dedicated to Lord Ayyappa. Before climbing up the hill to the shrine, they worship together at the tomb of the great Muslim saint Vavar. Close by is a Christian church, where too many pilgrims visit. It is Indutva in action—just as all three traditions coexist peacefully within each Indian mind, so should the 1 billion Indians coexist peacefully with each other, whatever their faith. In a world where the chemistry of Indutva holds sway, all would be welcome in all religious places for, after all, God is in each of us. As the Indian epics say, the divine is as sugar mixed in water. We cannot see the sugar anywhere in the water, but we can taste the sweetness everywhere in the water.

Sadly, few even within India know of Sabari Mala. And none outside India. There are so many examples of religious intermingling and tolerance in the world, and yet so few are taught in schools and other institutions of learning. Textbooks are filled with wars, battles in which the youngster is steered to develop pride and create identity through victories and the humiliation and killing of the Other. What we need to fill them with are the true reports of situations in which human beings remained human beings, rather than descended to the level of animals. We need to see wars that were averted as the true victories.

In the past, continents have been discovered. Today, new planets are being discovered. Surely we can turn that unending quest for knowledge inward and discover the many examples within our own species of kindness and compassion. The whole world has been inspired by the example of Agnes Gonxha Bojacchiu, otherwise known as Mother Teresa. Her life is an example of compassion and inner beauty, but there are others in every city in the world with a similar inner beauty, and we need to locate these good human hearts and bring them to the attention of the world.

Lesson 4 in the education of peace is to ensure that each of the young in the world are taught examples of those who have risen above prejudice and looked at humanity as one, and worked among humanity as one. The Mother Teresas and the Albert Schweitzers have been joined in their idealism by thousands of others all over the world but we need to discover others from different regions and cultures. Heroism and sacrifice and also saintliness is not the monopoly of a geographic area.

For even in this, there is a vertical filter. Why is it that, in the Catholic Church, almost all the saints are of European stock? Were there no such individuals elsewhere, or is this part of the tunnel vision that has been created by the system of scholarship practiced in Europe? Each faith, and its followers, has to search their consciences to remove from their minds and their actions any perception that any set of human beings is "higher" than the rest. It is not only the Hindus who have a caste system that creates an artificial hierarchy based on birth. All such systems need to be eliminated. Only a horizontal view of humanity can ensure this.

The truth has to be taught to all. It has to become apparent that every culture, every people, have within them individuals of excellence and those who are destructive. That the flow of goodness is never a one-way street, going from one culture to another, but a shared pool in which each contributes. Unfortunately, despite the harsh lessons taught by history about the effects of past arrogance, even today there exists a triumphalism in certain parts of the world, a missionary instinct to convert others to a point of view that is not necessarily universal in its value.

Rather than pay mere lip service to the concept of One World, One Humanity, what is needed is to ensure that children in the sensitive years of 10–15 are given an education that emphasizes, through a horizontal Lessons for the Education of Peace, (1) the common strands in humanity and (2) the contribution made by different peoples and countries to world progress.

Indeed, the reality is that long ago it was Africa that was the lead continent, followed by Asia and then Europe. Today it is the turn of America. Tomorrow, it may well be Africa's turn again, once the much talked-about Asian century recedes. Let us not forget that until the Information Technology boom in the 1990s, India was widely perceived as backward. Today, the software skills and computing abilities of the billion-strong people of the world's largest democracy have earned it a different image. In the middle of the present century, the same transformation in perceptions may well take place in Africa. Those blinkered by a vertical view will be the last to know.

Indeed, to the clear horizontal mind, Europe's time is already fading. While both India and China were the largest economies of the world until the beginning of the 19th century, direct colonial rule in India and the overwhelming influence of foreign powers in China resulted in both countries slipping down the charts into the lower depths of the table of economic performance.

Even then, during the years when the country was ruled from outside, those parts of India that were under the control of native princes developed much more than the sections that were under colonial rule. And yet, in history books in several countries, the colonial experience has been glorified and the historical evidence falsified in order to justify the rule of one people over another: a situation that can never be justified by any individual who considers herself or himself to be a human being.

Lesson 5, then, is that individuals generally and severally need to be treated with respect and given the freedom needed to enrich their lives, whether culturally, spiritually, or materially.

After China and India recovered from their external control, beginning during the 1980s, China began racing ahead in economic growth, and is today on course to become the world's largest economy well before the midpoint of this century, if judged by purchasing power parity. Already, by the same standard, the Peoples Republic of China ranks just below the United States. As for India, it stands just a little below Japan, and is catching up rapidly. Thus, of the four top countries in the world in economic strength, three are from Asia, while the fourth has today more trade with Asia than with Europe.

The (re)emergence of India and China is scarcely mentioned in school textbooks in most countries, and yet it is an example of how a third of humanity can rise from the depths of poverty to economic betterment. Unfortunately, the way modern history is being taught in many regions of the world, youngsters in those regions believe that only their culture and civilization have progressed or are responsible for progress. Such a false view promotes the kind of arrogance and contempt for the Other that is the fundamental cause of conflict.

Each child must be taught explicitly that all cultures and peoples stand on a horizontal and not a vertical scale. That other cultures may be different but that does not mean that they are inferior. That economically empires come and go, but the people remain the same, some good, some bad, everywhere.

Indeed, it is unfortunate that several who claim to be opposed to the viewpoint of an Osama bin Laden—who seeks to impose his worldview on the rest of humanity no matter that few want it—themselves indulge in a triumphalism and in a cultural exclusivity that regards other manifestations of human progress with contempt.

The concept of *Vasudhaiva Kutumbakam* (the world is one family) needs to be fused to that of *Sanatan Dharma* (many paths, same destination) and taught to all, so that the feelings of difference and superiority that has been such a poisonous vertical influence on world history in the past do not recur. Looking at some of the views expressed by politicians in several countries—who call for their armies to be let loose in other countries so as to "civilize" them—the apprehension is that they have become too much like those they are opposing.

If modern India has taught us anything, it is that democracy can be a powerful force for peaceful change, for a transition not based on bloodshed. This is a lesson that needs to be repeated and re-repeated if we seek to create an education of peace. There is no way to ensure peaceful transition except through the introduction of democracy.

Lesson 6, is well proven in India: democracy is suitable for every human being, no matter what the culture or level of education. If it has worked in India, a land of myriad cultures and divisions, it can work anywhere else, including in Iraq, where the people have already endured too many decades of authoritarian rule to docilely put up with any more. Hopefully, international statesmen will follow the wishes of Franklin Delano Roosevelt rather than follow the path adopted by Winston Churchill.

In sum, what is needed is to universalize the core philosophy of the education system so that people of all countries see themselves as being part of the same ocean, rather than separate lakes where swimming in foreign waters is a dubious, even dangerous proposition.

We are each of us the superiors and the inferiors of each other, and are therefore equal. It is time for society to view itself as a horizontal river, imperceptibly flowing, eddying, and changing as one whole, rather than as a rigid, vertical totem. Rather than the elitism that created Nazism in the past, and Wahabbism and Khomeinism today, what is needed is a destruction of the prejudice that has so often made humans who thought they were gods into devils incarnate. The next generations can do it, but only with our help.

REFERENCES

Basham A. L (1975). *A cultural history of India.* Oxford: University Press

Chen, L. (1999). *Reflections on marriage to a Westerner.* Personal notes from interview with author.

Ferguson, N (2004). *Empire: How Britain made the modern world.* London: Penguin Books.

Holmes, B. (2005, February 26). Genetic 'map' shows patterns in human variation. *New Scientist.*

Kalam, A., & Rajan, Y. S. (2002) *India 2020.* New Delhi: Penguin Books.

Karin L. L. (2000). *Made in China: The story of adopted Chinese children in Canada* [Film]. Holiday Pictures, Canada

Kautilya. (1987). *The Arthashastra.* New Delhi: Penguin Books.

Nalapat, M. D. (1999) *Indutva*. New Delhi: Har Anand.

National Association of Software and Service Companies (1997). Available at www.nasscom.org

Planning Commission. (2004). *India Vision 2020*. New Delhi: Academic Foundation.

Quinault, R (2001, Summer). Churchill and Democracy. In *Finest Hour Journal, 111*.

Richardson, S. (1995, January). 1994—the Year in Science. *Discovery* [The Return of the Plague Special Issue].

Tripathi, S. (2000, May 2). European Affairs: Immigration. *Wall Street Journal Europe*.

CHAPTER 4

BIG DREAM/SMALL HOPE

A Peace Vision

Mohammed S. Dajani

"Talmeedai chachameem marbeen shalom ba'olam"
["Scholars expand peace in the world"]

—Mishnah

Palestinians and Israelis disagree over the peace issue because they view it in two diametrically opposed contexts—that is, with different beliefs, interests and values in mind. When competing actors—that is,Palestinians and Israelis—place the peace issue in their own conflicting contexts, decisions by policymakers to give more weight to one context than another typically determines the outcome of the dispute...pushing it more in the direction of war and conflict rather than in the direction of peace and conciliation. Putting Israeli security needs above Palestinian national needs resulted in making peace illusive since one party viewed its own values and needs above those of the other. One-sided total security in the long run is a theoretical and practical impossibility, unless the opponent is wholly *annihilated.*

   This study is divided into three parts. The first part looks at where are we today, (i.e., living the big dream). The second part looks at where we ought to be (i.e., living the small hope). The third part deals with the question of how we get there.? Through peace.

Educating Toward a Culture of Peace, pages 39–53
Copyright © 2006 by Information Age Publishing
All rights of reproduction in any form reserved.

In his classic book, *Stable Peace*, Kenneth Boulding defines the concept of peace as follows:

> The concept of peace has both positive and negative aspects. On the positive side, peace signifies a condition of good management, orderly resolution of conflict, harmony associated with mature relationships, gentleness, and love. On the negative side, it is conceived as the absence of something—the absence of turmoil, tension, conflict, and war. (Boulding, 1978, p. 3)

The political and economic environment in the late 1980s and early 1990s was charged with anger, hopelessness, tension, and anxiety, resulting in a wave of extremism and growing tendencies for radicalism, and thus precipitating an unpredicted dangerous situation in the region. For this reason, there was an urgent need to search for new options to defuse the crisis. Since the road of confrontation and violence failed to produce any tangible results for both conflicting parties, there was no other alternative but to search for new avenues and fresh approaches to meet the new challenges.

In 1991, the Madrid Peace Conference brought a glimmer of hope. It was followed 2 years later by the Washington Declaration signed and sealed by the two antagonists and witnessed by a superpower. This historic event inspired people to hope: "Finally, peace is attainable," they calmed their fears. However, since its early days in late 1993, the Oslo Peace Process lurched from one crisis to another with no light at the end of the tunnel. Thus, our life in the last decade had been a combination of despair and hope. When the waves of terrorism ebb, we are distraught with despair; when waves of terrorism subside, we are full of hope. But hope for what?

BIG DREAM/SMALL HOPE FRAMEWORK

In her book *The Vocabulary of Peace*, Shulamith Harevern maintains that the Oslo Accords brought an essential change: *"From now on, it is not automatically Jew against Arab and Arab against Jew; it is the Jews and Arabs who support peace, and those, Jews and Arabs both, who oppose it"* (1995, p. vii). Thus one main fruit of the Oslo Peace Process is the radical change in the identity of the protagonists. The identity of the two conflicting parties to the Middle East conflict has been transformed from being national in character (Arab-Israeli) to being more sociopolitical in character (pro-peace/antipeace).

The well-known Palestinian poet Mahmoud Darwish once wondered: "What is more important—a small hope or a big dream?" In my view, the Oslo Accords brought another essential change: *"From now on it is not Palestinians against Israelis and Israelis against Palestinians; but it is Palestinians and*

Israelis, who believe in the big dream, and those Israelis and Palestinians who believe in the small hope... "Thus as the peace process progressed, this identification has crystallized more into cultural/psychological character, which assembled in one camp those Palestinians and Israelis who are for the "Big Dream" in mortal combat with those in the other camp of the "Small Hope." But what is the big dream? What is the small hope? What is the big dream for Israelis? What is the big dream for the Palestinians?

For the Israelis, the big dream is to wake up one morning and find that Palestinians have disappeared in the desert and that only Jews live in the promised land of Eretz Israel in a purely Jewish state with the two rivers as its borders and unified Jerusalem as its capital. Among the early Jews who believed in this dream was Zeev Jabotinsky who advocated force to contain the Arabs of Palestine behind an "Iron Wall" of Zionist resolve, which they will be powerless to break down. He considered a "voluntary agreement" between the Jews and the Arabs of Palestine as "inconceivable now or in the foreseeable future." Israeli Prime Minister Golda Meir once proclaimed: "There is no such thing as a Palestinian people."

For the Palestinians, the big dream is to wake up one morning and find that all Israelis have departed and only Palestinians live in the Holy Land in an Arab state from river to sea as its borders and al-Quds el-Sherif as its capital.

THE BIG DREAM

Advocates of the "Big Dream" are those, at present in the majority, who struggle for the eventual triumph of their perception of good over evil as resembled by the other, and as a result seek to establish their state exclusively on the historic land of Palestine/Israel. In their effort to achieve their goal, the "Big Dream" camp demonizes the other and implements a highly nationalistic curriculum in its educational system that deligitimizes and demonizes the other. It promotes conflict education, which teaches the new generation the war philosophy of the old generation. It appeals to the emotional bondage of the people to the land and focuses on historical ties of the past. It denies the narrative of the other and ignores their history, culture, literature, and traditions.

In the big dream scenario, Israelis' morbid fantasy is expressed in the saying: "The only good Palestinian is a dead Palestinian!" On the other hand, Palestinian morbid fantasy: "The only good Israeli is a dead Israeli!"

The big dream vision is reflected in different aspects in both societies in conflict. In daily life, the "big dream" is reflected in building a negative mirror image of the other, divisiveness, demonization of the other, mistrust of the other, blaming the other, insecurity, broken hearts, shattered families, and vanished dreams. In both countries, the big dream advocates teach historical Palestine/Israel with all its total geography with maps including pre-1948 Palestine as the envisioned state of Palestine/Israel. In Palestine, Israel is viewed as a usurper state founded on the destruction of historical Palestine and the misery of its people; refugees would exercise their right of return to the state of Israel; politics and religion shape the character and tone of all other subjects such as civic education, language, history, literature, geography, and so on. Jerusalem is proclaimed as the capital of one nation at the expense of the other.

The media in both Israeli and Palestinian communities advance the big dream theme (Greenway, 2004, p. 7). Each echoes the popular messages: "We are victims; they are aggressors"; "Our victims are a terrible tragedy; their victims are statistics"; "Our actions are legitimate; their actions violate international law"; "Our aspirations are noble; their aspirations are despicable"; "Our cause is just; their cause is evil"; "We are peace lovers; they are war mongers"; "Our hands are clean; their hands are stained" (Wolfsfeld , 1995).

In evaluating Israeli and Palestinian education, one finds that the knowledge imparted through both Israeli and Palestinian textbooks reflect the "big dream" theme. They are hardly objective, truthful, or factual. Both Palestinian and Israeli textbooks instill enmity and hatred. They are biased, and include visual and verbal incitements, as well as negative stereotype images of the other. Both curriculums delegitimize and demonize the other, and fail to embody the principles of coexistence, peace, tolerance, multiculturalism, and diversity. Classes in Israeli and Palestinian schools and programs at universities do not include peace education courses.

The Center for Monitoring the Impact of Peace claims: "Palestinian textbooks instill hatred of Israel and Jews.... The PA has 'rejected international calls' to modify the Palestinian textbooks."[1] Similar views are echoed in the Israeli press: "The incitement to hatred of Jews and the destruction of Israel, which has always been part of the Palestinian school curriculum, was intensified" (Wein, 2000). Hillary Clinton (2000) claims: "A book that is required reading for Palestinian six graders actually starts off stating, 'There is no alternative to destroying Israel.'" The spokesman for Israeli settlers proclaimed: "We teach our children to respect life, while they teach that if you die with Jewish blood on your hands you go to heaven and are fed with grapes by 15 virgins" (Lamb, 2000, p. 26). Charles Krauthammer (2000) claims that since the signing of the Oslo Accords, the Palestinians had "intensified the propaganda, the anti-semitism, in their pedagogy and in their media" and that while Israel had "assiduously" changed its textbooks to prepare for peace, "on the Palestinian side, the opposite was happening." However, George Washington University Professor Nathan Brown (2001) finds such charges "inaccurate." He concludes: "While highly nationalistic, the Palestinian curriculum does not incite hatred, violence, and anti-Semitism." Similar views are stated in the Study on the New Palestinian Curriculum prepared by IPCRI (2003), which concludes: "The overall orientation of the Palestinian curriculum is peaceful.... It does not openly incite against Israel and the Jews. It does not openly incite hatred and violence."

Despite drafting a new curriculum, Palestinian education remains a source of conflict since it includes such words as "Palestine" and "Jerusalem" used in the new Palestinian textbooks, but without definition is interpreted by the other as a denial of a two-state solution. For instance, on one cover of a textbook on national education (grade 2, 2001) is a British Mandate stamp, which originally had Palestine written on it in English, Arabic, and Hebrew, and now has the Hebrew erased from it. Cities located in the State of Israel, such as Akka, Haifa, Nazareth, and Jaffa, are referred to in Palestinian textbooks as part of Palestine, which is interpreted as a denial of the existence of the State of Israel. Textbooks teaching the Arabic language in grade 6 include titles such as "Our Homeland Palestine" that shows a picture of the city of Akka, which the Oslo Agreement designates within proper Israel. Also, while Moslem and Christian religion, culture, and heritage is taught to students, Jewish religion is ignored, thus creating a rift with the other. Students are taught that "the [refugee] camp is not to be considered an original homeland for the Palestinian refugee, it is but a temporary place in which he was forced to live, and all Palestinians are waiting for the return of each Palestinian refugee to his city or village from which he was forced to leave." This position contradicts the spirit of the Oslo Accords. In an announcement addressed "To the Palestinian Leadership" in January 2001, over 30 Israeli peace activists, intellectuals, and politicians announced publicly that "we shall never be able to agree to the return of the refugees to within the borders of Israel, for the meaning of such a return would be the elimination of the State of Israel."[2] The leading figure in the Israeli peace movement, author Amos Oz, views the right of return to Israel of Palestinian refugees as a Palestinian demand to have "two states, both of them for Palestinian refugees."[3] Robert Mallay and Hussein Agha, whose article on Camp David Summit shed much light on the secret negotiations, wrote:

> The Palestinians, while maintaining the right of the refugees to return to the homes which they had lost in 1948, were ready to link the implementation of the resolution to a mechanism which would provide substitutes for the refugees and would restrict the number of refugees who would return to Israel itself. (2001, pp. 59–65)

In teaching Islamic education in grade 6, the focus is on "jihad rhetoric" and the lesson is that "the Moslem loves his country and defends it to stir national feelings to regain the homeland. Pupils are taught that it is their religious duty to be part of the struggle against occupation; however, this lesson is not balanced with any religious lessons on peace. Its nostalgic teaching of a vanished past has an anachronistic quality about the big dream textbooks. For example, a second-grade text reads: "A family takes a trip to Jaffa, smelling lemons and oranges along the way." This of course is the Jaffa of the past; current drivers along the way entering the city are more likely to smell the polluted air rather than smell oranges. This teaches Palestinians to yearn for a world in the past that does not exist anymore. Such education enforces fantasies of the big dream (Palestinian Ministry of Education, 2001, pp. 115–118).

On Israeli education, Maureen Meehan writes that "Israeli textbooks and children's literature promote racism and hatred toward Palestinians and Arabs." She asserts that

> Israeli school textbooks as well as children's storybooks, according to recent academic studies and surveys, portray Palestinians and Arabs as "murderers," "rioters," "suspicious," and generally backward and unproductive. Direct delegitimization and negative stereotyping of Palestinians and Arabs are the rule rather than the exception in Israeli schoolbooks.

Professor Daniel Bar-tal of Tel Aviv University studied 124 elementary, middle-, and high school textbooks on grammar and Hebrew literature, history, geography, and citizenship. Bar-tal concluded that Israeli textbooks present the view that Jews are involved in a justified, even humanitarian, war against an Arab enemy that refuses to accept and acknowledge the existence and rights of Jews in Israel (Bar-Gal, 1993, pp. 224–232; Bar-Tal, 1998, pp. 723–742; Meehan, 1999, pp. 19–20).

In the "Big Dream," Israelis maintain that hiding behind walls would provide them with the national security they seek. However, the historical experiences show the fallacy of this assumption. For instance, the Great Wall of China, built in 221 B.C. and stretching 2,550 miles across north China, failed to repel attacks from nomads to the north; the Constantinople Wall failed to protect the city and was eventually destroyed in the year 1453; the Maginot French defensive fortifications constructed in 1929-31 to act as protection against German invasion failed to prevent the German attack of 1940; the Barlev defenses along the Suez Canal crumbled and thus could not protect the Israeli western front in 1973; more recently, the 96-mile, 11.8-feet-high Berlin Wall, built in 1961, could not prevent East Germans to flee to West Germany and was finally torn down in 1989.

The lessons drawn from history are that great walls provide a false feeling of security without providing much protection. They symbolize failure in diplomatic communications and are no substitute for political solutions.

They also reflect a negative international image indicating lack of peace strategies. Thus while the "big dream" advocates call for building walls to separate them from the other, the "small dream" advocates call for building bridges of knowledge and understanding based on peace and justice.

THE SMALL HOPE

Advocates of the "Small Hope" are those, at present in the minority, who believe in the peaceful coexistence between the two peoples and call for the establishment of a two-state solution, living next to each other in harmony, peace, and security with Jerusalem as a shared capital for both. Refugees would exercise their right of return to state of Palestine politics and religion are discussed independently and separately and do not dominate the contents and nature of all other subjects.

The small hope advocates teach Israel/Palestine as two independent neighboring states with Palestine as West Bank and Gaza Strip while Israel's boundaries would reflect the 1967 borders with minor modifications; refugees would exercise their right of return to the State of Palestine in addition to being compensated; and politics and religion are discussed independently and separately without dominating the contents and nature of all other subjects. In the "small hope" vision, religion becomes a source of peace. The Bible says in Matthew 3:16: *"Blessed are the peacemakers: for they shall be called the children of god."* The Holy Quran states in Surah 47:35: *"Call for peace. And if they lean to peace, then leaneth thou too to it, and trust in Allah; verily he is the all-hearing, all-knowing."*

In the "small hope," society shows tolerance. As Joshua Leibman states, *"Tolerance is the positive and cordial effort to understand another's beliefs, practices, and habits without necessarily sharing or accepting them."*

The aim of the "small hope" is to build bridges for peace and justice with others, to help future generations make the right choice between war and peace, to make them realize that they do not have a monopoly over the truth, to give the ability to treat opinions and interests of the other with respect, to help solve problems through peace culture, to develop a sense of civic duty and personal responsibility for the fate of not just one's own country, but for the other (European Centre for Conflict Prevention, 1999; Galama, Anneke, & Tongeren, 2002).

In the world of the "small hope," Jerusalem would became the international City of Peace reflecting the multicultural, multiethnic, multireligious, and peaceful nature of the city.

In the education of the "small hope," both Israeli and Palestinian textbooks would not include negative images and adjectives of other; negative stereotypes in describing other; pejorative terminology. On the other hand, it would include narrative of other; positive features and traits of other; stories about friendship and cooperation between Israelis and Palestinians and a human, multidimensional, individual approach. The "small hope" Educational peace strategy aims at being:

1. *Democratic:* fostering independent and creative thinking. (For an assessment of the likelihood that the Palestinian education system would succeed in teaching the civic virtues necessary to democracy, see Rigby, 1995.)
2. *Peace-oriented:* focusing on the acceptance of the other and embodying mutual respect for the other.
3. *Nonauthoritarian:* avoiding placing any stress on authority and making manifest that truth is not absolute.
4. *Rational:* teaching students to think in a rational way, avoiding emotional decision making.
5. *Tolerant:* teaching students tolerance of the other.

The specific aim of peace education ought to focus on building bridges for peace and justice with the other. Its general objectives ought to focus on helping future generations make the right choice between war and peace, making each realize that they do not have a monopoly over the truth; giving each the ability to treat the other's opinions and interests with respect; helping one solve his problems through peace instruments; developing a sense of civic duty and personal responsibility for the fate of not just one's own country, but for the other.

In the society of the "small hope," there is no monopoly for one party over the truth as reflected in this wise Jewish folktale: Cohen and Levi both approached the rabbi in an attempt to resolve a festering dispute between them. After Cohen relates to the rabbi his side of the story, the rabbi pronounces to him: "You are right." Following Levi's statement of the facts as he sees them, the rabbi declares to him: "You are right." Once the two have departed, the rabbi's wife turns to the rabbi and asks: "But rabbi, how can they both be right?" To this question, the rabbi responds: "You are also right."

GLIMMERS OF HOPE FOR PEACE

International Initiative

The Road Map: Officially launched in June 2003, the Road Map for peace remains the only accepted political process for moving from a state of violence toward peace between Israel and the Palestinian authority. It has been endorsed and accepted by Israel, the Palestinian authority, and the Quartet led by the United States. Its main goal is the establishment of a Palestinian state, "independent, viable, and sovereign with maximum territorial contiguity." With regards to Jerusalem, the Road Map grants the Palestinians a political status equal to Israel; determines that the decision in the negotiations over the city's status will be with regard to "the political and religious interest of both sides"; emphasizing that Israel should reopen Palestinian institutions closed in East Jerusalem. As for settlements, it demands that Israel should immediately dismantle all the outposts and freeze all settlement activities, including natural growth. On security, the Road Map calls for security cooperation between Israel and the Palestinian Authority, with participation by "American security representatives." It demands that Israel cease its attacks on "Palestinian civilians" (Dimou, 2003, pp. 78–86). (For the text of the Road Map, see "The Road Map," *Palestine-Israel Journal,* Vol. 10, No. 2, 2003, pp. 115–119.)

Arab Initiative

The Saudi Peace Plan: Its main goal is the establishment of an independent Palestinian state based on the 1967 borders with East Jerusalem as its capital. It demands Israel to dismantle all its settlements and that Palestinian refugees be granted right of return for all the Arab states to establish normal relations with Israel.

Joint Palestinian–Israeli Initiatives

Ayalon-Nusseibeh People Initiative: People's Peace has been gathering momentum with tens of thousands of signatures from both Israelis and Palestinians supporting the peace process. Its main goal is seeking to find a viable, just solution to the conflict. It calls for the establishment of an independent Palestinian state maintaining that the borders will be set along the lines of the Saudi peace initiative with a 1:1 territorial exchange and calls for the City of Jerusalem serving as the joint capital of both states. (Dajani, 2004, pp. 7–14)

Beilen-Abd Rabbo Geneva Initiative: Israeli and Palestinian ex-officials announced on October 2003 that they had worked out an unofficial peace deal, known as the Geneva Accord, which they offered as a blueprint for formal negotiations. It calls for the formation of a Palestinian state in the West Bank and the Gaza Strip, the return of Palestinian refugees to that state, and the division of Jerusalem between the two states where "each side would govern its holy sites." (The Peace Coalition, 2004)

More than 50 Palestinian–Israeli intellectuals, initiated and signed on July 25, 2001, the joint Declaration for Peace "No to Bloodshed, No to Occupation," which stated in part:

> We refuse to comply with the ongoing deterioration in our situation, with the growing list of victims, the suffering and the real possibility that we may all be drowned in a sea of mutual hostility.... We implore all people of goodwill to return to sanity, to rediscover compassion, humanity and critical judgment, and to reject the unbearable ease of the descent into fear, hatred and calls for revenge.... In spite of everything, we still believe in the humanity of the other side, that we have a partner for peace, and that a negotiated solution to the conflict between our peoples is possible....

CONCILIATION AND FORGIVENESS

No doubt, there is an urgent need to invoke the spirit of reconciliation in order to reach a long, lasting peace. But reconciliation will be difficult to be reached if both sides to the conflict are not prepared to acknowledge their responsibility and guilt. Palestinians tend to distrust the term "reconciliation" as they feel it doesn't do justice to their pain and suffering. Hizkias Assefa (1999) argues that: "The central question in reconciliation is not whether justice is done, but rather how one goes about doing it in ways that can also promote future harmonious and positive relationships between parties that have to live with each other whether they like it or not." In *The Palestinian Exodux 1948–1988*, Palestinian Professor Rashid Khalidi raises the issues of responsibility and atonement in order to achieve reconciliation:

> We need truth so that the harm done in 1948 can be acknowledged by all concerned, which means facing history honestly, acceptance of responsibility by those responsible for their successors, and solemn atonement for what was done 50 years ago. We need truth also in order to clarify the limits of what can be done to right that injustice without causing further harm. Once these have been established, it should be possible to work toward attainable justice and therefore toward reconciliation. This is essential because our ultimate objective should be to end this conflict for good, which can only come from true reconciliation, based on truth and justice. (Khalidi, in Karmi & Cotran, 1999, pp. 221–243)

Professor of Political Science Munther Dajani of Al-Quds University expresses similar views in *The Palestinian Refugees: Old Problems—New Solutions*:

> At some point the Israelis must face the truth and begin the reconciliation process by accepting responsibility for injustices inflicted on the Palestinians

in general, and the refugees in particular. This will open the way to usher in the Palestinians as equal partners. While it is true that it has taken the Palestinians a long fifty years to finally accept the Israelis, it is my sincere hope that it will not take the Israelis another fifty years to accept the Palestinians...as partners in the peace process. (Dajani, 2001, pp. 243–244)

Nadim Rouhana argues that conflict reconciliation, as opposed to conflict resolution or conflict settlement, seeks to achieve a kind of relationship between the parties founded on mutual legitimacy. For this to occur, issues of justice, truth, and historical responsibility as well as the restructuring of social and political relations need to be addressed (Moughrabi, 2001).

Nur Masalha, in *Palestinian Refugees: The Right of Return*, states that "any genuine reconciliation between two peoples—as opposed to a political settlement achieved by leaders—can begin only by Israel taking responsibility for the displacement and dispossession of the refugees" (Masalha, 2001).

In my view for a lasting peace to be achieved, the Israelis need not acknowledge their central role in the historical dispossession of the Palestinians as a people, or that they should take collective responsibility for evicting the Palestinian people from their homeland. As a pacifist, I believe in forgiveness as echoed in the Christian Lord's Prayer: "Forgive those who trespass against us." Research shows that learning to forgive those who hurt us can have profound benefits. It helps to manage anger, cut stress, and improve relations. Forgiveness can be a powerful antidote to hate and bitterness. In her insightful article "The Power of Forgiving: Best Way to Heal a Heart," Lisa Collier Cool lists five steps to find peace: (1) Focus on the facts of the offense; (2) Don't condone it, but try to understand what led to it. Try not to take it personally; you aren't the only one to ever get hurt; (3) Focus on the offender's humanity, not just his hurtful behavior. (5) Forgive for yourself, not anyone else. And forgive in your heart. You needn't tell the offender (2004, p. 86).

WHICH ROAD TO TAKE?

While the Israeli and Palestinian masses dance to the tune of the maximalist big dream, radicalizing the discourse, few have opted for the less-taken road of the minimalist small hope pacifying the discourse. One such voice is the Israeli Daniel Barenboim, the well-renowned Israeli musician, who in inspiring words stated in his acceptance speech for the Wolf Foundation Prize reflected the theme of the small hope:

With pain in my heart, I ask today whether a situation of conquest and control can be reconciled with Israel's Declaration of Independence.

Is there logic to the independence of one people if the cost is a blow to the fundamental rights of another people?

Can the Jewish people, whose history is full of suffering and persecution, allow it to be apathetic about the rights and suffering of a neighboring people?

Can the State of Israel allow itself to indulge in an unrealistic dream whose meaning is an ambition to bring an ideological resolution to the dispute, rather than the aim of attaining a pragmatic, humanitarian solution, based on social justice?[4]

No doubt, security is a legitimate need for both sides and no security guarantee should be asked of one party at the expense of the other. Security concerns should be equal, mutual, and reciprocal on both sides.

CONCLUSION

In his *Proverbs for Paranoids*, American writer Thomas Pynchon writes that if you get people asking the wrong questions, you don't need to worry about the answers. That is why it is important for us to ask ourselves the right questions: What heritage and legacy do we want to leave for our grandchildren: conflict, hatred, bloodshed or peace, goodwill, prosperity, and security? Why don't we channel our pain and anger away from hatred and toward peace and conciliation? As in the parable of the Prophet Ezekiel, why don't we "revive the dry bones of peace, cloth it with flesh, lift it from dust and set it up as a joint concern." In their introduction to *Creating a Culture of Peace*, Gershon Baskin and Zakaria al Qaq write: "It is quite a considerable challenge to ask how do we influence, mold, create, lead our own societies to create a culture where our children, the next generation of Israelis and Palestinians, will really be able to live in peace. How can we play a role in paving that road so the challenges that will face the next generation will be smoother and easier than the ones we face today" (Baskin & al Qaq, 1999, p. 2).

If we have a strategy to achieve peace, what would it look like? A peace strategy should have two main targets: to bolster popular support for the peace initiative and to foster cooperation between the two negotiating sides. Significantly, it is not enough to base peace upon political and economic agreements, as was the case in the Oslo Peace process or the Egyptian–Jordanian–Israeli peace accords; it must be founded upon a culture of peace based on understanding, respecting and appreciating each other's values, perspectives, history, culture, tradition, religion, and aspirations. This conflict can be settled peacefully if both Palestinians and Israelis try to negotiate their differences rationally and sensibly, understand each other, listen to each other's arguments, defend their views steadfastly but without violence (UNESCO, 1997, p. 5). To move away from this culture of conflict, war, and violence both Palestinians and Israelis ought to get closer to each other, not away from each other. Konrad Adenauer was known for his dry humor. During his visit to the Hebrew University of Jerusalem, some students used the occasion to voice their protests against Germany. Adenauer's escorts urged him to pass on quickly, but he refused, saying: "Don't we want to get closer to each other?" (2001, p. 14). They need to grasp the opportunity of peace, it may not come back again! Peace is not a utopian dream but the hope at the end of the tunnel.

In Jewish culture there is the recognition that the child at the Passover festival may deliberately, naively, ask questions that would be seen as inappropriate if they came from an adult. Let me then be that child and ask the following questions: Do key terms such as "peace," "security," and "conciliation" mean the same thing to both Palestinians and Israelis? Do both people want peace, security, and conciliation or continued war, conflict, and bloodshed? Wouldn't it be much better to negotiate the establishment of a Palestinian state rather than to take it by force? And what is the future of such a state if established on the basis of force, hatred, and enmity? Here I am being a devout student of the lesson taught in the Book of Proverbs of the Hebrew Bible that instructs: *"Peace will not rise by force, but only through understanding"*; the Christian *Bible, which says: "Blessed are the peacemakers: for they shall be called the children of god"* [Mathew 3:16]; as well as the Muslim *Holy Quran*, which says in Surahs 47:35 and 8:61: *"Call for peace. And if they lean to peace, then leaneth thou too to it, and trust in Allah; verily he is the all-hearing, all-knowing."*

Let me close with these inspiring words of Indian writer Satish Kumar:

Lead me from death to life, from falsehood to truth.
Lead me from despair to hope, from fear to trust.
Lead me from hate to love, from war to peace.
Let peace fill our heart, our world, our universe. (Kumar, 1981)

NOTES

1. The Center for Monitoring the Impact of Peace, 2000, www.edume.org.
2. Israeli daily *Ha'aretz,* January 2, 2001.
3. Israeli daily *Yediot Aharonot,* August 3, 2000.
4. "A Renowned Israeli Musician Condemns the Israeli Occupation and Detonates His Prize to the Palestinian People," May 11, 2004. Barenboim remarks were met with a standing ovation by the audience during his acceptance speech for the Wolf Foundation Prize, which he received at the Knesset on May 9, 2004. The renowned musician has decided to donate his $50,000 prize to the Palestinian people aiming at encouraging the Palestin-

ian music. Daniel Barenboim was born in Buenos Aires in 1942 to parents of Jewish Russian descent. He started piano lessons at the age of 5 with his mother. In 1992 he became General Music Director of the Deutsche Staatsoper Berlin. In the autumn of 2000, the Staatskapelle Berlin appointed him Chief Conductor for Life.

REFERENCES

Assefa, H (1999). *People Building Peace. 35 Inspiring Stories from around the World.* Utrecht: European Centre for Conflict Prevention.

Baskin, G., & Al Qaq, Z. (Eds.). (1999). *Creating a culture of peace.* Jerusalem: Israel Palestine Center for Research and Information (IPCRI).

Boulding , K. (1978). *Stable peace.* Austin: University of Texas Press

Brown, N. (2001). *Democracy, history and the contest over the Palestinian curriculum.* Adam Institute.

Clinton, H (2000, September 26). Link P.A. aid to end anti-Semitism. *Jerusalem Post.*

Collier Cool, L. (2004, May). The power of forgiving: Best way to heal a heart. *Reader's Digest.*

Dajani, M. (2001) A Predicament in search of an innovative solution. In J. Ginat & E. Perkins (Ed.), *The Palestinian refugees: Old problems—new solutions* (pp. 243–244). Norman: University of Oklahoma Press.

Dimou, A. (2003). The road map peace plan. *DEFENSOR-PACIS,* Defense Analyses Institute, Issue 13, pp. 78–86. For the text of the Road Map, see: "The Road Map," *Palestine-Israel Journal, 10*(2), 115–119.

European Centre for Conflict Prevention. (1999). *People building peace. 35 inspiring stories from around the world.* Utrecht: European Centre for Conflict Prevention.

Galama, Anneke, & Van Tongeren. (Eds.). (2002). *Towards better peacebuilding practice: On lessons learned, evaluation practices and aid and conflict.* Utrecht, Netherlands: European Centre for Conflict Prevention.

Greenway, H. D. S. (2004, April 27). Leaving Gaza. *International Herald Tribune.*

Harevern, S. (1995). *The vocabulary of peace: Life, culture, and politics in the Middle East.* San Francisco: Mercury House.

IPCRI. (2003). *Analysis and evaluation of the new Palestinian curriculum: Reviewing Palestinian textbooks and tolerance education program.*

Khalidi, R. (1999). Truth, justice and reconciliation: Elements of a solution to the Palestinian refugee issue. In G. Karmi & E. Cotran (Eds.), *The Palestinian exodus 1948–1988* (pp. 221–243). Reading: Ithaca Press.

Konrad Adenauer Stiftung. (2001). *Konrad Adenauer for reconciliation and peace: Remembering the past to build the future.* Jerusalem: Author.

Krauthammer, C. (2000). *Is the Israeli/Palestinian peace process dead, and if so, what's next?* Available at www.aei.org

Lamb, C. (2000, October 15). Intifada: The next generation. *Sunday Telegraph,* p. 26.

Masalha, N. (2001). The historic roots of the Palestinian refugee question. In N. Aruri (Ed.), *Palestinian refugees: The right of return.* London: Pluto Press.

Moughrabi, F. (2001, Autumn). The politics of palestinian textbooks. *Journal of Palestine Studies,* Issue 121.

The Palestinian Ministry of Education. (2001). The Palestinian curriculum and textbooks. *Palestine-Israel Journal, 8*(2).

The Peace Coalition. (2004). *Geneva initiative: Peace is possible.* Ramallah: Author.

Rigby, A. (1995). *Palestinian education—The future challenge.* Jerusalem: Palestinian Academic Society for the Study of International Affairs (PASSIA).

UNESCO. (1997) *UNESCO and a culture of peace: Promoting a global movement* Paris: UNESCO.

Wein, B. (2000, October 26). Illusions. *Jerusalem Post.*

Wolfsfeld, G (1995). *The news media and peace process: The Middle East and Northern Ireland.* Washington, DC: The Brookings Institution.

Part II

GLOBALIZATION AND PEACE

CHAPTER 5

PEACE EDUCATION AND THE CONCEPT OF MANKIND

Dietmar Waterkamp

PEACE—A MAJOR TOPIC IN EDUCATION

Peace is a persistent topic of educational theory and practice. It does not enjoy a steady level of attention and interest, yet it is present all the time, and sometimes it comes to the fore more than at other times. When a war or a violent conflict comes into public perception or even into direct touch with a society, the topic dominates educational debates.

Peace is a key term for education, because it pertains to the basic conditions of human existence, of our being part of life as such, of our societal and political embedding, and of our relatedness to God. Each attempt to define "peace" demonstrates the extensive and pervading character of this concept, which no definition can fix. Sometimes, peace educators start a lesson by asking children to note their associations with this term, and a multitude of associations comes up. Peace can be seen as a behavior; it can be regarded as an attitude; it can be conceived as a specific relation among people; it can be defined negatively by its opposite, which might be identified as violence; it can be understood as the quality of relations among states and nations; it can be described as an inner and even hidden state of the soul. Each effort to understand the meaning of peace for the life of

Educating Toward a Culture of Peace, pages 57–71
Copyright © 2006 by Information Age Publishing
All rights of reproduction in any form reserved.

humans and nations reaches out to the basic problems and also to the basic values of human existence on this planet: to poverty and wealth, to justice and injustice, to ecology and the preservation of nature, to the relation of the sexes, to health and disease, to education and rationality, to hopes and to mankind's destiny, to the genius of humankind and the ruthlessness of men, to the conscience as an inner voice of all humans, to homeland and alienation, to secularness and faith, to the respect of life and power over life, to love and hate.

Not less diverse may the answers be that are given to the question of how we look at our relation toward peace, and which relation we want the students to have toward peace. What is our aim with respect to peace? Is it to keep peace, which means to control our behavior in an appropriate way? Is it to appreciate and love peace, which means to cultivate and strengthen our feelings in this respect? Is it to understand peace, which means how it is established and how it is destroyed? Should we give priority to the development of our inner attitudes or to the intervention into events among people around us or even into politics, shall we regard peace as an absolute value or as a value that competes with others?

There is not only one consistent answer to all these questions, and therefore we find a variety of approaches for peace education that cannot be brought into a system. This is the nature of this word, which is among the most basic words of mankind that speak to us like a big promise, like a big "nevertheless"—against all experiences and indications. Other words of the same weight are truth, justice, grace, God.

Obviously, peace is more difficult to have than non-peace. That is why the term is appealing us permanently. The idea of peace is a call to accomplish something that is not given us naturally. To come closer to peace implies to transgress our nature. It means to widen oneself into something new, something unknown. Therefore, the need for education is embedded in the idea of peace. Peace demands an effort of education, first of all self-education. Without preparedness to widen oneself, peace cannot be won or maintained. Peace requires to overcome selfish intentions, to leave behind feelings like revenge, like strengthening the ego at the expense of others, like the desire to possess other people's wealth, feelings like the wish to have the final say and like triumph. So, peace has got an affinity to education insofar education implies surmounting oneself.

In accordance with the variety of approaches to the idea of peace, a divergence of theoretical and practical efforts exists in education, which all intend to strengthen the readiness for peace. The Norwegian peace educator Birgit Brock-Utne (1995) emphasizes the difference of teaching about peace and teaching for peace. The former endeavor depicts cognitive components and value perspectives inherent in the idea of peace, whereas the latter also comprises the readiness for action (p. 56).

All of these three aspects may be regarded as constituent of peace education. Each of them can be emphasized in a different way. They obviously have affinities to different situations or fields of education. The cognitive component is in the center of school education, the value dimension might also be touched in school education, yet it plays a stronger role in religious educational settings and in philosophical education in contexts of adult or higher education, whereas the readiness for action prevails in specific educational settings for youth and adults outside formal teaching arrangements. These differences point at the difficulty to provide for a comprehensive peace education in one institution and to attain the goals of peace education in total.

For school education, extensive curricula have been developed that insert aspects of peace education into almost all subject curricula. An excellent example for this is the "School of Peace" (Friedensschule) at Heidelberg, which was advised by Professor Hermann Röhrs. For the biology curriculum, for example, Röhrs recommended to discuss the ethical principle of Albert Schweitzer, "I am life which wants to live, amongst life that wants to live." Another topic should be the discussion of ethological theories on the "biological trap" of mankind, that means our genetic heritage of aggressiveness. In sports, games requiring cooperation instead of competition should be introduced to balance our competition-oriented practices in sports (Röhrs, 1983).

A more specific approach of enriching school curriculum with respect to peace education has been demonstrated by Karin Utas Carlsson from the Malmö School of Education in Sweden. Her program aims at the level of behavior, and for this she stresses reflexivity and self-competence. Carlsson brings forward a behavior-related definition of peace as opposite to violence (1999, p. 197) and concentrates peace education on violence prevention and conflict resolution. The methodology of the program is built on classrooms methods, mostly oral methods, such as brainstorming, guided imagery (phantasy exercises), role-played sketches, case studies taken from literature and also writing notebooks, visionary essays, and others. Video films (e.g., about Romany people [the Gypsies]) are introduced and talked about. Negative behavior such as bullying, which is to be avoided, is produced in role plays and than discussed.

As for the value perspective in education, many discussions end up in open questions, in an undecided situation. Obviously, there is no definite ethical standpoint from which necessary behavior can be clearly deduced. Yet, there are decisions in specific situations—for or against. A permanent problem in value discussions refers to the question if and eventually when the use of violence is legitimated. Does a "just war" or even a "holy war" really exist? If a consequent position of nonviolence is held in accordance with the basic ethical belief of Gandhi, for example, believers will know that they have to prove a great ability of suffering or even martyrdom. Sometimes it is said that those who strictly pursue the principle of nonviolence should not interfere into politics but restrict this principle to their personal lives (Buddrus/Schnaitmann, 1991, p. 338). Nevertheless, within the philosophy of Gandhi, which comprises the ideas of truth, nonviolence and morality in ends and means, there are incentives for productive political action (Bose 1995). Sometimes, it is also said, that in the present time of atomic weaponry any war or violent action is obsolete and can no longer be justified. This is obviously a serious argument, because for the first time in history humankind as a whole is being threatened. Whereas up to the present, mankind felt that it has in common the ability to kill, it now feels that it has in common to be threatened by an unnatural death. This situation conveys the awareness that mankind as such is mortal. So far we do not know which impact this knowledge will have on humans in the long run. It might change our ethics (Arendt, 1970).

As far as the dimension of readiness for action is concerned in peace education, it reveals the great difference between peace education that aims at preventing conflicts or strives for reconciliation after a conflict, and peace education that is undertaken in the midst of a conflict. Whereas peace education conducted more or less remote from an acute conflict most of the time relies on examples that do not embody the learners' personal infliction, this is different when peace education includes encounters of members of conflicting parties. This is not only a challenge for knowledge and understanding, but it questions the involved persons deeply. This is to be felt, for example, in encounters conducted by groups of Jewish Israelis and Arab Israelis in the Peace School of Neve Shalom/Wahat al Salam in Israel (Halabi/Phillips-Heck, 2001). The Jerusalem Link was formed in 1994 as a coordinating body of two independent women's centers: Bat Shalom on the Israeli side and the Jerusalem Center for Women on the Palestinian side, who decided to establish common talks (Bahdi, 2003).

THE CONCEPT OF "MANKIND"—A FRAME
FOR TEACHING PEACE

This chapter intends to contribute to the reasoning about peace education and abstains from recommendations for the practice of peace education. Reasoning undertaken here is inspired by the author's commitment to the academic field of comparative education. Not few comparatists regard efforts for international understanding and for peace as practical emanation of the scholarly research on international relations in the field of education. As mentioned before, the understanding of peace varies with situations, the concept needs interpretation and legitimisation (i.e., it needs to be rooted in some idea that gives hold to it). Gandhi, for example, grounded his understanding of peace in a specific concept of truth, which was something absolute. Also a divine command such as the prohibition of killing a human being or killing at all can serve as an absolute frame for the conceptualization of peace. Here I suggest the concept of mankind as something absolute toward which the reasoning about peace and peace education can be orientated. The concept of mankind has got the capacity to be a guiding philosophical concept for the field of education in general and in particular for comparative education, because the unity of mankind can be regarded as the ultimate goal of our internationally connected scholarly efforts. A guiding concept is more than an analytical tool, it is both of empirical and normative significance. It names an absolute value and at the same time depicts a tendency or even force that impinges on reality in a way that is accessible to empirical observations.

To declare mankind an absolute idea needs further clarification. Even more, it is necessary to concede that the concept of mankind has been disputed among philosophers and sociologists. Resuming this concept sounds like replicating former ideas of establishing a new morality—for example, the religion of humanity, which was invented by Auguste Comte after the French Revolution (Wright, 1986). Indeed, not few intellectuals dislike the notion of mankind because of its metaphysical or religious connotations. A philosopher of mankind in Germany's 19th century was Karl Christian Friedrich Krause. Even during his lifetime, his metaphysical philosophy has remained almost unknown in Germany (Krause, 1851). Despite his being a disciple of Kant, he did not find much response to his bold, comprehensive vision and had an unlucky career. It seemed as if "mankind" could not become a serious object of philosophical thinking. Surprisingly, some of Krause's philosophical ideas experienced posthumous discovery in the liberal intellectual movement of *krausismo*, which was influential for educational thinking in Spain, and from there it spread with even more vigor to Latin America. This fact stands for the continuous appeal of this concept.

A glance at the *German Dictionary on the History of Philosophy* (Bödeker, 1980) teaches how controversial the term has been among 20th-century philosophers and sociologists. Oswald Spengler, for example, permitted the term "mankind" only to be a zoological concept. Sociologist Gumplowicz felt "mankind" not to be a sociological term. Political philosopher Carl Schmitt added that it was a political concept neither, and Arnold Gehlen even denied its capability to be a moral concept. Other philosophers such as Max Scheler or Wolfgang Schulz attached philosophical importance to this concept. Among these thinkers existed a distinction between "rightists" and "leftists" to a certain degree, yet perhaps the division between "secular" and "religious" was even more obvious with respect to this question.

Nevertheless, in recent years it was the French philosopher Edgar Morin who renewed this concept (Morin, 2001). In an essay written on request of the UNESCO and first published in 1999, Morin emphasized the entirety of mankind. When he looked upon mankind as one species and one race, his view resembles thoughts of Immanuel Kant expressed in his treatise "Perpetual Peace: A Philosophical Sketch" from 1795 (Reis, 1991 pp. 92–130). For Morin (1992, 2001), mankind is one entity, because all humans rely on the globe, on the planet earth, which nourishes and shelters them. Mankind acquired a planetary consciousness, he said. This originates the idea of a planetary citizenship, which is being more and more developed and accepted. It is the base of a new ethics, which is bound to the triad of "individual–society–species." Each unit of the triad is a means and an end to both others at the same time. Whereas sociological thinking is mostly bound to the relation between individual and society, philosophical thinking, especially ethical thinking, also considers the species, which leads to the triad or triangle as basic pattern of thinking. It certainly heightens the complexity of thinking, yet it might help to solve problems which remain unsolved when thinking is bound to the duality of individual and society, such problems as peace, preservation of the environment on earth, the definition of human life's dignity and life as a whole. It coincides with these ideas that some law philosophers examined the possibility of establishing mankind as a legal personality, although this effort still encounters big difficulties (Baslar, 1998, pp. 70–78. Stöcker, 1992).

"Mankind" as a guiding idea for education has got an absolute character, although we are far from spelling its contents. Mankind is our fate, we do not know from where mankind comes and where it goes to. We are unable to think a world without mankind—this is a fact that makes the concept of mankind an absolute idea. Any attempt to think a world without mankind or to imagine the last moment of any human being's existence in the universe leads us to absurdity and desperation. Although some philosophers thought that their equals should endure such an imagination—we can't live with that. In the beliefs of Judaism and Christianity, God needs mankind and even strives to gain the hearts of men.

It is due to the character of the educational endeavor as such that educational thinking needs to start from an absolute idea. This connection is obscured when education is conceived as a means for external goals. Up to nowadays, education was often seen as a means for accomplishing national cohesiveness and identification. It was also seen as a means to strengthen the economic power of a nation. On the other hand, it was also perceived as a potential way of fostering peace and international understanding. The international and globalized goals seem to be free of nationalistic or culture-centred motives, yet critics say that these are still imbedded in apparently all-embracing political goals. The debate is more on political goals than on the basic understanding of education. The assumption always seems to be that education does not bear its aims itself, but is instrumental for aims that are set at another level. Yet, it was already John Dewey who opposed the understanding of education being driven by aims from outside. The instrumental view on education is a heritage of the nation-based approach, which for long prevailed in education and even more in comparative education. It resulted from the educational ambitions of the states.

The very general and seemingly abstract idea of mankind can serve the function of providing educational thinking with an independent starting point. This is a very formal way of looking at it. Yet, from a formal point of view, it can be assumed that a starting point that allows for independence of educational thinking might be a promise to discover the heart of the educational endeavor as such. At least, great thinkers on education such as Comenius and Pestalozzi encouraged us with this rather formal view. Their educational thinking was directed toward humanity and mankind, and still is effective for educators. It is true that their wide-reaching hopes have not been fulfilled up to now. Yet, we might wonder if effectiveness in terms of impact on a great multitude of people is the true criterion for education and pedagogy.

For many, it is indisputable that education must be valuated by its effects. However, when it comes to education for values and to educating basic attitudes, educators are rather uncertain about long-lasting effects. Education is not the only human activity. The only thing the educator can be sure of is the change in his or her own attitudes. By reflecting on one's own educational experiences, educators help themselves to understand human beings in a deeper way. This fact gives hope for some effectiveness in the education process, because eventually, educators' attitudes educate more than their words do. Their activities emanate from their pedagogical attitude. This is true, although educators do not want to be imitated and cannot foresee their impact on people within their area of responsibility.

Relating to mankind as a guiding idea implies an idea of peace without talking about it. Talking about peace also needs talking about war. Pleading for peace also means talking against something. Talking against something is not at the heart of education, it happens in situations of fear and distress. Talking about mankind means taking steps forward to discover an unknown world of commonalties among beings who turn out to feel and act similar to us. The idea of mankind forms a positive framework for teaching peace.

THE NOTION OF A "UNITY OF MANKIND"

Which are the contents of the notion of mankind that makes it a key concept for educational philosophical reasoning and especially for the academic field of comparative education? In this chapter, this question can only be answered tentatively. When Morin emphasized the entirety or wholeness of mankind, this seemed not to be enough to beat educational sparks out of it. In the 20th century, a comprehensive philosophy of mankind was created by the French biologist, palaeontologist, philosopher, and theologian Pierre Teilhard de Chardin. Teilhard also took up a Kantian thought. He deepened Kant's discovery of the connection between the global nature of the earth and the pressure on men to keep peace. Kant wrote about "all men": "Since the earth is a globe, they cannot disperse over an infinite area, but must necessarily tolerate one another's company." He spoke about the "right to the earth's surface" that the human race shares in common (Reiss, 1991, p. 106). It is a true philosophy of globalisation that the global nature of the earth in the long run urges more and more peoples to acknowledge each others' rights on the piece of the surface of the earth where they traditionally live. Teilhard sharpened this idea by comparing the globe to a vice that grips the rapidly growing mankind firmer and firmer. After the earth in former times had invited men to expand, it nowadays compresses mankind. The compression heightens the complexity, yet heightening the complexity is the way to unite mankind. The globe exerts a regime of interdependence, which will result in a new type of sphere covering the earth: the so-called noosphere. This is a type of collective brain, because it is the growth of the brain that drove and drives the evolution ("cerebralization") (Teilhard de Chardin, 1942/1964, 1949/1969, 1950/1963).

These are philosophical thoughts on mankind and globalization, which point at the chance to go beyond the idea of the entirety or wholeness of mankind and to face a process of unification of mankind. The idea of the unity of mankind has more potential for stimulating educational thinking than the idea of wholeness, not only because it brings educators closer to the imagination of cooperation and sympathy among men, but above all because it directs the attention to the future of mankind. The process of compression, growing interdependence, and increasing reflectivity is so powerful that we have to direct our comprehension to the future in order to keep up with it. Future orientation without fear is of high educational value. Future does not only mean a change in conditions of our living, but in ourselves.

To name these ideas "philosophical" does not deny their reflecting scientific observations. In the case of this topic, even ethnographic research confirms the idea of a unity of mankind in a special way. When German anthropologist Adolf Bastian in the year 1899 stated the "principle of the psychic unity of mankind" at first time, he resumed the observations from newly discovered small societies who showed the basic human feelings and attitudes such as love, sadness and grief, joy, hatred, and fear, and revealed the same intellectual capacities as were known from peoples with much more differentiated technologies such as, for example, the Arabs, the Chinese, the Indians, and the Europeans (Bastian, 1899). The insight of all humans to be in principle capable of high intellectual achievements was not self-understanding. Many groups of humans believed to be humans as such and to occupy the center of the world. When men from a distant continent first encountered an unknown people, the appearances of people and cultures were so different that they did not believe in commonalties of peoples. A history of crime and pain passed by, until the incoming group acknowledged the par of the indigenous people, and still we are not sure that this insight has been acknowledged.

Ethnographers teach us about commonalties among children in many cultures. One is, for example, the ability to draw, paint, and sculpture. Other common traits in upbringing children are the joy of playing, the joy of physical exercise, the joy of playing music and dancing, the concern that each offspring should learn the abilities necessary to make their own living and to prepare young people for parenthood (e.g., Engel, 1968). As for the field of ethics, ethnographers tried to give evidence of the fact that all human groups know basic ethical commands, which are apparently rooted in a conscience (Cathrein, 1914).

The processes within mankind described so far with reference to Morin and Teilhard do not necessarily lead to solidarity and sympathy within mankind. They have got the potential to bring about peace in the long run, which means not more and not less than the absence of wars. Teilhard yet believed that mankind still is in an embryonic state of development, and in later stages will be united by a new quality of love. The consciousness and feeling of solidarity and sympathy has been named in Christianity—and not only there—sisterhood and brotherhood of men. Sympathy, love, sisterhood, and brotherhood—all are strong energy in education. The notion of sisterhood and brotherhood comprises more than just the idea of a common nature of all humans. Also, it does not restrict itself to the fact that all people on earth will share a common fate, because all of them depend on the conservation of natural sources for life, and all will be affected by wars with mass destruction weapons. Such an idea of unity results from fear, because all people are threatened the same way. However, it is not able to constitute an active, sympathetic attitude toward other people and perhaps even not a feeling of solidarity, because eventually each group of people might think of its own rescue first.

Two examples from the history of education shall be given here that reveal the educational stimulus originating from the belief in sisterhood and brotherhood of men.

After Pestalozzi had taken very poor and neglected children into his farm called Neuhof to provide them a home and to teach them how to ensure their living, he wrote his first piece of educational writing entitled "Fragment from the History of the Least of Mankind." In this, he gave portraits of several children, of the state in which they came in, of how they behaved and how they developed. Although some of them looked to be the least ones of mankind when they arrived and behaved mean, it turned out that each of them expressed a need and showed an ability from which Pestalozzi could start (1777/1945).

Another example are the missionary activities of the Moravian Brothers, which is a church whose most famous bishop was Johann Amos Comenius, and which in the 18th century was refounded by the Duke of Zinzendorf in the state of Saxony in Germany. In their belief, the notion of brotherhood of mankind was a driving force. It is linked to the Christian belief that Jesus became brother of all people. The missionaries sailed to very distant shores to unknown peoples, where they were convinced to meet sisters and brothers who were native people. In their belief, these people were loved by Christ through brotherly love. They, living in the presence of Christ, tried to do the same. The missionaries went there as craftsmen who lived on their own hands' work. They diligently asked the natives whether they could stay or not. They founded schools and hospitals and preached. The sustaining success of their educational work among the natives, which still is existent in some of these countries, resulted from their basic attitude. There are many examples which show that they did not feel superior to the natives, they bought slaves out of slavery to be able to teach them, and they had marriages between whites and blacks, blessed by the Duke personally, and some former slaves received important tasks in church and in schools, even in Europe. Perhaps this idea of human brotherhood is the deepest and—in terms of the educational stimulus—strongest idea of mankind that was put into practice (Klink, 2003).

Whereas it is hard to find the idea of unity of mankind clearly expressed in the Greek antiquity and even with Cicero (Baldry, 1965), it is to be found in Judaism and Christianity (Greenberg, 1971; Moltmann, 1971). In this connotation, it does not remain an abstract normative, but is a conviction full of empathy and comprises a feeling of love. The precondition is modesty and thankfulness as for one's own personality. With respect to the missionary activities of the Moravian Brothers, this belief brought about surprising results in terms of conveying literacy and schooling, although these were not the primary aims. These results may still be observed with the people on the islands of the Nicobares, with parts of the Aborigines in Australia, with Inuit in Greenland and in Labrador, with Indians in Pennsylvania, with black people in Surinam, and with people in Tanzania and other places. The sense of brotherhood among all humans proved to be an attitude, which has a strong pedagogical potential.

The recalling of Christian beliefs and ideas in this context shall not mean that other religions or philosophies did not produce unitarian ideas about mankind. In some cases, these ideas were stimulated by the confrontation with Christian ideas. The Indian scholar of comparative religion J.G. Arapura (1971), who was a university teacher in Canada, stated that Asian thinkers and Asian religions had a latent consciousness of the unity of mankind, which was activated and also received a new direction by the influence of Christianity in the 19th century (Arapura, 1971). He also reminds us of the difference between the ideas of unity of mankind and of unity of all being. Universality in this context is limited to men, which in fact sometimes is regarded as an unjustified limitation. In Arapura's opinion, no one brought forward the idea of the unity of mankind in early times as passionately as the apostle Paul did.

Danish theologian, philosopher, pedagogical thinker, and writer Nicolai Frederic Grundtvig created the motto "Man first—then Christian." Another version of this was: "No man—no Christian." It implied the acknowledgement of non-Christian beliefs and ideas of God that existed and exist in mankind as fragments of the truth that on earth never will be fully completed. All men and human groups in history, Grundtvig was convinced, have experienced the "big disaster" and can understand what the Good Book tells about the disobedience of Adam and Eve. At the same time, the motto was meant to be a message for Christian believers, which said that going deeper into the Christian belief results in approaching the idea of being a human in the true sense (Röhrig, 1991, pp. 56–60; Thodberg/Thyssen, 1983, pp. 310–312). Grundtvig, who deeply loved his own Danish people and believed in its unique mission in the world, nevertheless gave an example of how a European thinker exceeded Eurocentrism.

For comparative education, an appeal to put the notion of mankind into the center of theoretical thinking is not fully new. However, it was only one scholar within this academic field who made a suggestion to go this way. It was Robert Ulich, a Harvard professor from 1934 to 1971. His article was inspired by the activities of the Council for the Study of Mankind, which had been created by Gerhard Hirschfeld. When he concluded it by saying: "Everyone who works on himself opens the door for humanity, and whoever cares for humanity enters deeper into self, and thus helps to balance the ambivalence that has been part of man through the centuries" (1968, p. 33), he appealed to educators to deepen their attitudes as educators toward a rich notion of brotherhood, of respect for every human, of sympathetic feeling and intellectual understanding of those they take responsibility, children and adults as well.

IMPLICATIONS FOR EDUCATION

Introducing the notion of the unity of mankind or even brotherhood of mankind to educational reasoning allows starting educational thinking and activities from commonalties, not from differences. At the beginning is the idea that each human being makes and is a unique contribution to mankind. In Christian belief, Christ was one of the least. The educator who pursues the idea of mankind searches for the unique contribution that each human wants to make and that each individual is able to make—not only strong and healthy people, but also handicapped ones, even not yet born ones and even criminal ones, although this is not easy to say. Pestalozzi (1781/1927), who searched for ways of educating the "least," outlined ideas of pedagogy for criminals. Each human makes a contribution to the physical appearance of mankind and also to the soul, mind, and spirit of mankind. Unity of mankind is not only meant in the sense of entirety of mankind, not only in the sense of commonalties among humans, but also in the sense of solidarity, which bases itself on a feeling of our similarity that will exist even if our appearances and our fates differ.

The notion of the unity of mankind includes far-reaching implications. It replicates the sense of the famous quotation of Terence: *Homo sum, humani nihil a me alienum puto.* This means that in principle, each human can acquire the intellectual achievements that were brought about by any other group of people elsewhere on earth, remote in terms of time and space, and make them fruitful for own intellectual projects. What missionaries of the Moravian Brothers experienced with thankfulness was the fact that their own children born among indigenous people easily learned their language, which for the adult missionaries was much harder to do. The indigenous languages were much stranger to the missionaries than the European ones, yet the strangeness did not count for their young children. Chomsky taught that a universal grammar exists beneath the grammar by which people construct phrases. Perhaps this explains the amazing ability of all newborn humans to learn any human language (Huck/Goldsmith, 1995). Even if the theory of "innateness" is not shared by all linguists, it is important that the formal grammar structures are independent from the principles that allow us to connect forms and meanings. Linguist Eric H. Lenneberg from Harvard University stated in 1967 that languages of all cultures—those who live on Neolithic technological level and also those on a modern scientific level—rely on similar principles (Lenneberg, 1967, p. 323). Preceding Chomsky, Danish linguist Otto Jespersen pointed at some more commonalties such as the similarity across cultures in the first simple words spoken by children, the tendency of augmenting the amount of words in nearly all languages, the fact that each language implies the function of naming—of attributing names—and also the fact that in many cultures, children try to create secret language systems (Jespersen, 1954, p. 193ff).

Unity of mankind also means that in principle, each human can discover feelings within their own soul that he or she observes with other people—may they be very distant in terms of cultural habits. A practical outgrowth of this reasoning is to humanize our curricula in the sense of the unity of mankind. The objective of this is not to provide a museum-like glance at other cultures, but to make active use of intelligent creations from other groups of people, for example, in the fields of counting and mathematics, of grammar and language, of scripts, of technical inventions, of games and exercises, arts, dances, and music. In all human societies, children grow up with animals. How children in different societies are accustomed to live with animals can teach children in other societies. No child in the world can avoid learning about death. How children in different cultures are made familiar with this fact can be beneficially studied with respect to talks with children in their own society. As for human aggressiveness, the science of human ethology points at rituals and games in different cultures that serve as positive substitutes (Haug-Schnabel, 2001). To give a curriculum a spirit of humanness in the sense of the unity of mankind is a prerequisite for sustainable education for peace.

REFERENCES

Arapura, J. G. (1971). The effects of colonialism upon the Asian understanding of man. In J. R. Nelson (Ed.), *No man is alien: Essays on the unity of mankind* (pp. 109–128). Leiden: Brill.

Arendt, H. (1970). *Macht und Gewalt.* München/Zürich: Piper Verlag.

Bahdi, R. (2003). Security Council Resolution 1325: Practice and prospects. In *Refuge. Canada's Periodical on Refugees, 21*(2), 41–51.

Baldry, H. C. (1965). *The unity of mankind in Greek thought.* Cambridge, UK: University Press.

Baslar, K. (1998). *The concept of the common heritage of mankind in international law* (Developments in International Law, Vol. 30). The Hague: Martinus Nijhoff.

Bastian, A. (1899). *Zur Verständigung über Zeit- und Streifragen in der Lehre vom Menschen* (Lose Blätter aus Indien. Nachtrag VII). Berlin.

Bödeker, H. (1980): Menschheit, Menschengeschlecht. In J. H. Ritter & K. Grunder (Eds.), *Historisches Wörterbuch der Philosophie* (Vol 5, cols. 1127–1137). Basel.

Bose, A. (1995). Mahatma Gandhi's principles of peacemaking. In H. Löfgren (Ed.), *Peace education and human development: To Professor Åke Bjerstedt. A book of homage* (pp. 44–54). Lund: Lund University, Malmö School of Education.

Brock-Utne, B.(1995). Peace education at the end of a millenium. In H. Löfgren (Ed.), *Peace education and human development: To Professor Åke Bjerstedt. A book of homage* (pp. 55–75). Lund: Lund University, Malmö School of Education.

Buddrus, V., & Schnaitmann, G.W. (Eds.). (1991). *Friedenspädagogik im Paradigmenwechsel. Allgemeinbildung im Atomzeitalter. Empirie und Praxis*. Weinheim: Deutscher Studienverlag,

Carlsson, K.U. (1999). *Violence prevention and conflict resolution. A study of peace education in grades 4–6*. (Studia Psychologica et Paedagogica Series Altera CXLIV). Lund: Malmö School of Education.

Cathrein, V. S. J.(1914). *Die Einheit des sittlichen Bewußtseins der Menschheit. Eine ethnographische Untersuchung. Erster Band: Die Kulturvölker. Die Naturvölker Europas, Asiens und Afrikas* (nördliche Hälfte). Freiburg.

Engel, H. (1968). *Musik der Zeiten und Völker. Eine Geschichte der Musik von den Anfängen bis zur Gegenwart*. Wiesbaden.

Greenberg, M. (1971). Mankind, Israel and the nations in the Hebraic heritage. In J. R. Nelson (Ed.), *No man is alien: Essays on the unity of mankind* (pp. 15–40). Leiden: Brill.

Halabi, R., & Phillips-Heck, U. (Eds.). (2001). *Identitäten im Dialog. Konfliktintervention in der Friedensschule von Neve Schalom/Wahat al-Salam in Israel* (Schriftenreihe des Deutsch-Israelischen Arbeitskreises für Frieden im Nahen Osten e.V., Band 36). Schwalbach: Wochenschau Verlag.

Haug-Schnabel, G. (2001). Die ‚Natur des Menschen’ und die Beachtung des humanitären Völkerrechts. In J. Hasse, E. Müller, & P. Schneider (Eds.), *Humanitäres Völkerrecht. Politische, rechtliche und strafgerichtliche Dimensionen* (Demokratie, Sicherheit, Frieden, Vol. 133, pp. 178–194). Baden-Baden: Nomos..

Huck, G. J., & Goldsmith, J. A. (1995). *Ideology and linguistic theory: Noam Chomsky and the deep structure debates*. London: Routledge.

Jespersen, O. (1954). *Mankind, nation and individual: From a linguistic point of view* (2nd ed.). London.

Klink, C. (2003). Das menschheitliche Bildungsverständnis in der Mission der Herrnhuter Brüdergemeine. Weltgesellschaft, Globalisierung und Menschheit im pädagogischen Sprachgebrauch. *Katholische Bildung, 104*(7-8), 301–311.

Krause, K. C. F. (1851). *Urbild der Menschheit. Ein Versuch. Zweite unveränderte Auflage.* Göttingen.

Lenneberg, E. H. (1967). *Biologische Grundlagen der Sprache*. Frankfurt: Suhrkamp.

Löfgren, H. (Ed.). (1995). *Peace education and human development. To Professor Åke Bjerstedt. A book of homage.* Lund: Lund University,Malmö School of Education.

Moltmann, Jürgen (1971). Man and the son of man. In J. R. Nelson (Ed.), *No man is alien: Essays on the unity of mankind* (pp. 203–224). Leiden: Brill.

Morin, E. (1992). *Einen neuen Anfang wagen. Überlegungen für das 21. Jahrhundert*. Hamburg: Junius.

Morin, E. (2001). *Die sieben Fundamente des Wissens für eine Erziehung der Zukunft*. Hamburg: Krämer.

Pestalozzi, J. H. (1777/1945). Bruchstück aus der Geschichte der niedrigsten Menschheit. Anrufung der Menschlichkeit zum Besten derselben. In P. Baumgartner (Ed.), *J. H. Pestalozzi, Werke in acht Bänden. Gedenkausgabe zu seinem zweihundertsten Geburtstag* (Vol. 1, 77–83).

Pestalozzi, J. H. (1781/1927). Fragmentarischer Entwurf zu "Arners Gutachten." In J. H. Pestalozzi, *Sämtliche Werke. Hrsg. von Artur Buchenau, Eduard Spranger, Hans Stettbacher* (Vol. 8, pp. 371–397).

Reiss, H. (Ed.). (1991). *Kant: Political writings*. Cambridge, UK: Cambridge University Press.

Röhrig, P. (Ed.). (1991). Um des Menschen willen. Grundtvigs geistiges Erbe als Herausforderung für Erwachsenenbildung, Schule, Kirche und soziales Leben. Dokumentation des Grundtvig - Kongresses vom 7. bis 10. September 1988 an der Universität zu Köln. Weinheim: Beltz.

Röhrs, H. (1983). *Frieden – eine pädagogische Aufgabe*. Braunschweig: Westermann.

Stöcker, W. (1992). *Das Prinzip des Common Heritage of Mankind als Ausdruck des Staatengemeinschaftsinteresses im Völkerrecht. Diss*. Zurich: University of Zurich.

Teilhard de Chardin, P. (1949/1969). *Die Entstehung des Menschen*. München: Beck.

Teilhard de Chardin, P. (1942/1964): Der Ort des Menschen im Universum. In P. Teilhard de Chardin, Auswahl aus dem Werk. Mit einem Nachwort von Karl Schmitz-Moormann. Wien-St.Pölten 145–175. (Lecture held in Beijing on November 15, 1942)

Teilhard de Chardin, P. (1950/1963). Über die wahrscheinliche Existenz eines, Ultra-Humanen' im uns Vorausliegenden. In P. Teilhard de Chardin. Werke, vol 5. Olten and Freiburg 357–370.

Thodberg, C., & Thyssen, A. P. (Eds.). (1983). *N.F.S. Grundtvig—Tradition und Erneuerung. Grundtvigs Visionen von Mensch, Volk, Erziehung und Kirche, und ihre Bedeutung für die Gegenwart*. Kopenhagen: Danske Selskab.

Ulich, R. (1968). The ambiguities in the great movements of thought. In R. Ulich (Ed.), *Education and the idea of mankind* (pp. 3–33). Chicago: University of Chicago Press.

Wright, T. R. (1986). *The religion of humanity: The impact of Comtean positivism on Victorian Britain*. Cambridge, UK: Cambridge University Press.

CHAPTER 6

ECHOES FROM THE PERIPHERY

Challenges to Building a Culture of Peace Through Education in Marginalized Communities

Erwin H. Epstein

Governments' provision of schools is commonly done in the name of a predominant ideology. Capitalist countries profess to build schools in good part to prepare citizens for political participation in the policymaking process and the marketplace. Socialist and some authoritarian governments place greater emphasis on the provision of education to equip citizens with skills needed by, and an attachment to, the collective whole. As a government uses schools to spread its form of political culture and values, education becomes an instrument of globalization, incrementally penetrating into communities remote from the cultural mainstream and displacing indigenous worldviews and practices. Such penetration raises critical questions about a government's use of education in promoting or, conversely, retarding a culture of peace.

The displacement of indigenous cultures is accompanied by social class reproduction, human capital production, and national economic development. Indeed, a considerable body of comparativist literature has been

Educating Toward a Culture of Peace, pages 73–91
Copyright © 2006 by Information Age Publishing

devoted to discerning the differential influence of schools and family background on both societal development and individual behavior. As nations intensify political and economic investment in access to education, the content and organizational contours of education become more universalistic, resulting in an expanding compression of consciousness throughout much of the world.

Yet despite the reach and importance of education in this process of transforming lives, its impact is often misinterpreted. My purpose is to shed light on the role of education in globalization by showing how schools penetrate the cultures of traditional societies, but also by showing why this process has been poorly understood. In viewing the impact of education, my emphasis is on the commonplace misapplication of theory in interpreting the role of education in globalization and, by extension, building or opposing a culture of peace.

GLOBALIZATION

Globalization is an accelerated compression of the contemporary world and the intensification of consciousness of the world as a singular entity. Compression makes the world a single place by virtue of the power of a set of globally diffused ideas that render the uniqueness of societal and ethnic identities and traditions irrelevant except within local contexts and in scholarly discourse (Robertson, 1987). Globalization intensifies the growing complexities of interconnectedness and interdependence of people and institutions throughout the world, and many scholars have observed what appear to be ineluctable worldwide influences on local settings and responses to those influences (Sklair, 1997). Such influences touch aspects of everyday life. For example, structural adjustment policies and international trading charters, such as the North American Free Trade Association (NAFTA) and the Asia Pacific Free Trade Agreement (APEC), reduce barriers to commerce, ostensibly promote jobs, and reduce the price of goods to consumers across nations. Yet they also shift support from "old" industries to newer ones, creating dislocations and forcing some workers out of jobs, and have provoked large and even violent demonstrations in several countries.

The spread of democracy is part of globalization, giving more people access to the political processes that affect their lives, but also, in many places, concealing deeply rooted socioeconomic inequities as well as areas of policy over which very few individuals have a voice. Even organized international terrorism bred by Islamic fanaticism may be viewed by some as an oppositional reaction, an effort at *deglobalization*, to the pervasiveness of Western capitalism and secularism usually associated with globalization.

Influences of globalization are multidimensional, having large social, economic, and political implications. The massive spread of education and of Western-oriented norms of learning at all levels accompanying democratization in the 20th century can be considered a large part of the globalization process (Benavot, Cha, Kamens, Meyer, & Wong, 1991, pp. 85–101; Ramirez & Boli-Bennett, 1987, pp. 2–17).

As the major formal agency for conveying knowledge, the school features prominently in the process and theory of globalization. Early examples of educational globalization include the spread of global religions, especially Islam and Christianity, and colonialism, which often disrupted and displaced indigenous forms of schooling throughout much of the 19th and 20th centuries (Epstein, 1989, pp. 1–23; White, 1996, pp. 9–25). Postcolonial globalizing influences of education have taken on more subtle shapes.

In globalization, it is not simply the ties of economic exchange and political agreement that bind nations and societies, but also the shared consciousness of being part of a global system. That consciousness is conveyed through ever-larger transnational movements of people and an array of different media, but most systematically through formal education. The inexorable transformation of consciousness brought on by globalization alters the content and contours of education, as schools take on an increasingly important role in the process.

Naturally, sectors of society most remote from the sociopolitical mainstream are at once the most distant from processes of globalization and the most susceptible to profound change when it is experienced. Holding social and political values that are the least consistent with the values imbued by globalization, these sectors at the point of departure have the longest path to travel and the most to relinquish in terms of primordial culture. Moving from a traditional way of life, globalization surely represents for such people the most profound transformation of all. Although globalization transcends national boundaries, it often, paradoxically, accompanies nationalism. As schools inculcate national values and allegiances, they also teach ideas and knowledge shared by people outside their own country. Learning from and about the outside world in communities at the margins of mainstream society is not a simple process of gaining objective knowledge, but involves cultural displacement and has large implications for building or impeding a culture of peace.

STIMULUS GENERALIZATION THEORY

A genuine grasp of the impact of change on social and political culture requires going beyond the macro level of society and delving into the micro level of individuals, that is, examining psychological processes. As a primary agent of change, this is especially true of the school. Introducing modern schools in traditional societies forces adjustment in the community's social, economic, and cultural environment and sets in motion a socialization process that alters fundamentally children's consciousness of their social and cultural condition and undermines their indigenous identity and sense of belonging. In viewing this process, accounts of how schools induce change in traditional societies often make micro-level assumptions derived from *stimulus generalization theory*, which posits that a conditioned response will be elicited not only by the stimulus used in conditioning, as predicted by basic stimulus–response behavioral assumptions, but also by a variety of similar stimuli (Hull, 1950, pp. 221–228; Murdock, 1949). Stimulus generalization theory sheds light on reinforcement mechanisms linking a primary group, most notably the family, with secondary groups, represented especially by the school, in the socialization process.[1] This theory, as I will show, has been used to explain a wide range of findings on differential social outcomes of education. Yet it fails to explain the school's globalizing impact at the periphery of the world system.

As applied to education, stimulus generalization theory would predict that the more children are attached to primordial ethnic values and the more ethnically homogeneous they are, the less likely schools will be to succeed in socializing them to nationally oriented allegiances and behaviors. Robert A. LeVine, using stimulus generalization theory, reasoned that the fewer the stimulus elements common to the distal political environment and the proximate family environment, the less likely individuals are to extend their family response patterns to the political sphere of action (1960, pp. 51–58). In regard to how education influences social change, this suggests that the school, which embodies stimulus elements derived directly from the distal mainstream political culture, will have limited impact on children from indigenous societies by virtue of having to overcome overwhelming contrary response patterns emitted in the proximate family environment. Only under the rare condition in which a village school conforms to the stimulus patterns of the indigenous community will the school contain the psychological elements needed to have a significant modernizing impact (Foster, 1962, pp. 127–135; Hagstrom, 1968; Nash, 1965, pp. 131–145). Yet such schools, by virtue of depending for their impact on having stimulus elements in common with the family environment, are unlikely to alter the consciousness of their charges and produce the kind of change favorable to mainstream political culture that is sought by governments.

Stimulus generalization assumptions have been applied widely in educational research to explain differential socialization consequences. Children from low-income families achieve poorly, because the stimulus elements at home are not consistent with stimulus elements in the school environment. Conversely, children from high-income families, where the stimulus elements of home and school are isomorphic, score well. Stimulus generalization theory plausibly reached its zenith in the classic report of James Coleman and colleagues, *Equality of Educational Opportunity* (1966), which attributes achievement differentials to socioeconomic status, with lower status children possessing attitudes and values less compatible with school culture.

Stimulus generalization assumptions have also guided findings on children's resistance to schooling. Most countries have laws compelling parents to send their children to school until a specified age, even where cultural or socioeconomic incompatibility creates a hiatus between values of school and of family, commonplace in socially stratified societies throughout the world. Where incompatibility exists, parents cannot simply decline education for their children as an option, and compulsory education forces a wedge between values of the school and values of the family. It is not to be assumed that children meekly adapt to the school's values in such circumstances. Rather, it is common for children from home environments containing stimulus elements incompatible with formal school learning and structure to devise methods of resistance to formal education (Everhart, 1983; Foley, 1991, pp. 532–551; Luykx, 1996; MacLeod, 1995; Willis, 1977). Resistance to schooling takes many forms of opting out, from violent disruption to sullen passivity. Such resistance has serious consequences for countries that rely on education to promote a spirit of nationalism to bind together disparate national population sectors. Resistance to schooling reduces the ability of the state to engender social cohesion through patriotic appeals.

Stimulus generalization theory holds that before entering school, a child becomes conscious of the political world as mediated by a variety of social groups. Within these, the child learns to accept certain predispositions toward authority and limits of submissiveness and dominance. Somewhat later in development, the child learns to distinguish between membership in primary groups and other groups whose members are not in intimate and frequent contact. How a child learns to have a national consciousness or identity depends in good part on whether the norms of behavior and expectations of primary groups are consistent with those of more socially distant, impersonal secondary groups, and with the larger society overall. When these are consistent, primary socialization tends to play a binding role in shaping the individual's national identity, and the school may function as an extension of the family in achieving that objective (LeVine, 1960, pp. 291–296). If, however, there is an incongruence of norms and values between the larger society and the child's primary groups, the child may find it difficult to generalize from allegiances and behavioral patterns learned within family or tribe to national political objects and symbols.

When such instances of incongruence are common in a society, the school is often mandated to perform a resocializing function. This may occur, for example, when children of immigrants or those who belong to unassimilated ethnic groups are suddenly exposed to the national cultural mainstream. It may also occur when the society experiences abrupt social change, as in war, conquest, or revolution—circumstances that shatter the congruence between community (*Gemeinschaft*) and society (*Gesellschaft*).

In transitional societies, discontinuities between the political values of family and local community on the one hand, and of nation on the other hand, are likely to arise with an influx of schools. The school, as the agent of government and the larger society, forces a wedge between home and child by reorienting the child to national political realities that are incongruous with values of the local community. Ironically, coercion in the form of compulsory education is often used to inculcate noncoercive democratic values. Yet, however ironic this may be, and however disorienting schooling may be to children exposed to abrupt social change, this resocialization process may be critical to the life of a country struggling to unify unassimilated ethnicities or urban and rural subcultures, and seeking to define its national character.

A collective sense of nationality is critical for binding a nation together. It emerges as nationalism as national character becomes the predominant measure of collective power. National character can be associated with ethnic or civic features, or both (Ignatieff, 1993). When ethnicity defines national character, nationalism may be driven by charismatic leadership, often combined with primordial or socially constructed cultural features. In the extreme, ethnic nationalism degenerates into a "metaphysics of racism" (Morganthau, 1955), a condition that undermines peaceful social relations. By contrast, when defined by a people's civic orientation, nationalism arises from a shared sense of rules, procedures, and values based on law. Civic nationalism is generally more characteristic of culturally heterogeneous countries. Civic nationalism is predominant in the Western world, where children learn the political culture in school—as a civic duty and expectation—not because of any primordial yearnings or wish to elevate particularistic ethnic values.[2] Nationalism of this type, when encompassing a wide array of in-country national groups, can be the foundation of a peaceful culture.

A FILTER EFFECT THEORY

Scholars have long observed instances of educational expansion contributing to political instability (Abernathy, 1969; Young, 1976). Stimulus generalization theory holds, as I have described, that if there is an incongruence of norms and values between the larger society and a child's primary groups, the child will find it difficult to generalize from allegiances and behavioral patterns learned within family or tribe to national political objects and symbols. This theory has grave ramifications for education, because it suggests that the more pupils are attached to particularistic ethnic values and the more ethnically homogeneous they are, the less likely schools will be to succeed in socializing them to nationally oriented allegiances and behaviors. This implies a reduced efficacy in the school's ability to inculcate values associated with civic nationalism. By extension, relative deprivation theory suggests that individuals outside the cultural mainstream will display rising discontent and contribute to political instability by virtue of, among other things, their lesser access to schools (Monchar, 1981, pp. 1–12; Runciman, 1966; Williams, 1975).

Nevertheless, stimulus generalization theory is of limited value in explaining schoolchildren's sense of nationality in communities newly experiencing abrupt change, a condition widely found in economically developing countries. From data I conducted in Peru, St. Lucia, and Puerto Rico, I found that pupils whose families have fewer stimulus elements in common with the larger society actually displayed more acculturative tendencies, a result directly contrary to what stimulus generalization theory would predict. In other words, children attending schools more distant culturally from the national mainstream actually had more favorable views of, and expressed a stronger attachment to, the nation—its history, traditions, language, and way of life—than children in schools closer to that mainstream.

As a specific example, I showed that in regard to Quechua and Aymara-speaking schoolchildren in the Puno area of Peru, near Lake Titicaca and bordering Bolivia in the high Andes, the more rural the schoolchildren the more likely they were to display attitudes favorable to acculturation (Epstein, 1971, pp. 188–201; 1982, pp. 280–300). Indeed, more acculturated children—those in more densely populated areas and more exposed to the trappings of mainstream Peruvian and globalized cultures—displayed less attachment to national symbols than children living in more remote and sparsely populated areas.

My results for the Caribbean island country of St. Lucia were similar to those for the Peruvian highlands (Epstein, 1997). The findings are based on a survey I conducted in 1968, one year after the island gained autonomy in the form of "associated" statehood with Britain. St. Lucian "mainstream" culture is essentially British, with the government and civil infrastructure modeled on the mother country's institutions. Those institutions are most evident in Castries, the island's capital and principal city. Although Castries schoolchildren are the most acculturated to British ways, they displayed the weakest allegiance to British nationhood. Indeed, the more rural and culturally distant children were to Castries, the stronger was their sense of British nationality.

Puerto Rico represents a somewhat different acculturative environment than Peru or St. Lucia. However, I reported the same acculturative tendency in the island commonwealth of the United States (Epstein, 1967, pp. 133–143). In Puerto Rico, acculturation is with North American norms and values. Schoolchildren in private schools in which English is the medium of instruction are the most acculturated students. Yet when I compared attitudes of private and public school children, pupils in these private schools were less inclined to identify with North American culture than children in the public schools, where Spanish was the medium of instruction for most subjects.

Clearly, the results of my research cannot be explained by stimulus generalization theory. Indeed, that theory would predict directly contrary results—that children more remote from the dominant cultural mainstream would display less acculturative tendencies. How, then, can these findings be explained, and what implications do they have for understanding the role of the school in building a culture of peace?

Schools Sanitize Reality

It is important to note that the children closer to the mainstream that I surveyed were nevertheless not at the mainstream center. In observing the difference between center and periphery, I refer to cultural, if not physical, distance. All three societies were experiencing abrupt and pervasive social changes at the time I conducted my studies. Although these changes were pervasive, they were felt most palpably not at the remote margins, but in the towns and regions closer to the center. It is nearer the center, after all, where the institutions (such as law enforcement, employment, and welfare agencies; medical clinics; and businesses) that represent the mainstream are newly prevalent and most powerfully challenge traditional community values. As people move from the periphery toward the center (in a cultural if not physical sense), they are, moreover, exposed more to media of information beyond the confines of the school. In Peru, such people would be found more in the towns, especially in the highlands, where Spanish as well as Quechua or Aymara are widely spoken. In St. Lucia, they would be mainly in Castries, the capital, and, perhaps, Vieux Fort, the second city— where Patois is still spoken but where English is pervasive. In Puerto Rico, those children would be largely in the private-school enclaves of San Juan, where children and parents are bilingual in Spanish and English and come most in contact with North American ways.

I contend that it is easier for children living in more remote areas to accept myths taught by schools regarding the cultural mainstream. By contrast, children living closer to the mainstream cultural center—the more acculturated pupils—are more exposed to the realities of the mainstream way of life and, being more worldly, are less inclined to accept such myths. It is not that schools in different areas teach different content; in all societies that I studied, schools, whether located at the mainstream center or periphery, taught an equivalent set of myths and allegiances to national symbols. Rather, it is that schools at the margin are more effective in inculcating intended political cultural values and attitudes—because they operate in an environment with fewer competing contrary stimuli. Children living in more traditional, culturally homogeneous and isolated areas tend to be more naive about the outside world and lack the tools and experience to assess objectively the political content that schools convey. Children closer to the center, by contrast, having more actual exposure to the dominant culture, are better able to observe the disabilities of the dominant culture—its level of crime and corruption, its reduced family cohesion, its heightened rates of drug and alcohol abuse, and so on. That greater exposure counteracts the favorable images all schools convey about the cultural mainstream, and instead imbues realism—and cynicism—about the myths taught by schools. It is at some distance from the periphery—but not at the periphery itself—where we are likely to find resistance in some form to schooling.

The myths that schools teach may glorify indigenous people as well as the dominant culture. However, even when people at the periphery are glorified, it is often done in a way to induce children to embrace the center and repudiate their own culture. For example, in 1974 the ruling military regime in Peru redefined "Indian communities" as "peasant communities," and schools celebrated St. John's Day (June 24) as the "Day of the Peasant" instead of the "Day of the Indian" as part of the government's campaign to emphasize the dignity of work and manual and peasant labor as a patriotic activity. The government appropriated indigenous symbols to convey a unique sense of identity. It referred to its development plans as "Plan Inca" and "Plan Tupac Amaru" to invoke images of Peru's Indian past, and, in 1975, the most common Indian language, Quechua, was made an official language along with Spanish, to be taught in schools and used in court proceedings (Werlich, 1977, pp. 81–82).[3] Elevating the status of Indian symbols such as language, especially in schools, served two purposes: it provided unique markers of nationality to which all Peruvians could claim an affinity and it encouraged the social, political, and economic integration of the indigenous population.

Stress on native language instruction was aimed not, however, at strengthening a sense of Indian ethnicity, but at expediting literacy in

Spanish. The government viewed Indian language as the preferable medium for "easing" children at the periphery into mainstream education, until they were sufficiently comfortable to be taught Spanish and learn most subjects in that language (Chiappo, 1973, pp. 26–37; Drysdale & Myers, 1975). As such, rather than blending stimulus elements of the periphery and center to reduce the cultural distance that Indian children have to negotiate, schools actually used indigenous symbols as part of the filtering process to expedite the displacement of indigenous culture.[4]

Additional evidence of the filter-effect theory comes from David Post, who found that in Peru Quechua-speaking male secondary-school leavers who more frequently read newspapers had lower earnings expectations than those who were less frequent newspaper readers, indicating a greater realism of individuals more in touch with the larger world (Post, 1994, pp. 271–295; Portocarrero & Oliart, 1989). Post (1994) shows that imagined benefits of indigenous boys with some education decline rapidly if they are even minimally connected with mass media. In effect, the mass media expose youths at the periphery to the reality of the social and political world, displacing the mythologized images conveyed by schools. Here, it is not the school that moves children from the periphery and away from primary-group influence, but exposure to reality by the mass media. Post shows, moreover, that the effect of good grades in enhancing students' faith in the larger social system is most pronounced in the indigenous population, whose home language is Quechua rather than Spanish and who are the most marginalized and isolated from the social and political reality of mainstream culture. Mary Jean Bowman (1982) reported similar findings in Japan in regard to views of marginalized rural youths, who have unrealistically high expectations of future salaries compared to their urban peers having more links with informal information networks.

Theory Complementarity

Earlier I suggested that relative deprivation theory extends the range of implications of stimulus generalization when interpreting schools' efficacy in inculcating values associated with civic nationalism. It does this by predicting rising discontent and political instability among people at the periphery by virtue of, among other things, that sector's lesser access to the center's institutions, most particularly schools. However, relative deprivation theory is a far better fit with filter effect theory, which adds the essential element of felt need. That is, when looking at the periphery it is not enough to discern degrees of congruence of cultural stimuli, as between primary and secondary groups, in predicting outcomes; it is important also to know how stimuli are affected by changes in the conditioning environment.

By adding felt need as an essential element in the set of cultural factors accounting for behavior, filter effect explanations emphasize environmental dynamics. By contrast, stimulus generalization looks only at the compatibility of cultural stimuli among socializing groups, and as such fails to account for how those stimuli are processed under conditions of change. Filter effect theory can explain the complacent acceptance and passivity of children at the periphery by virtue of their controlled (by the school) exposure to an otherwise disturbing reality; not having the means (mass media, wide social networks, etc.) to "feel" (become conscious of) the benefits of which they are deprived, they feel undeprived. By contrast, stimulus generalization theory emphasizes the distance between stimuli at home and at school, and can only predict resistance and rebellion, outcomes not borne out by research on children at the periphery. Filter effect theory, by emphasizing the tight control exercised by the school over knowledge exposure at the periphery, predicts instead quiescence, though quiescence that progressively turns into resistance as children become acculturated into the mainstream, and the school's power to sanitize images of the mainstream culture is reduced.

The emphasis on "*relative*" is what makes relative deprivation theory complementary to filter effect theory. The school at the periphery works to keep deprivation nonrelative—not by furnishing the skills and knowledge needed for good jobs, and thus narrowing the socioeconomic gap between periphery and center, but by reducing the felt need for the benefits enjoyed at the center. A Marxian approach to interpreting the school's control over images of reality in children at the periphery would be to explain quiescence in terms of the inculcation of false consciousness. The filter effect interpretation is similar, except that the emphasis is on control under a condition of isolation rather than on the iron grip of capitalism over schools and other institutions. However, contrary to a Marxian interpretation, the filter effect theory would predict a reduced efficacy for the school as the peripheral community is globalized, regardless of the strength of capitalism (though many would argue that globalization is concomitant with the spread of capitalism), even as the school participates in and advances globalization. Both Marxian and filter effect interpretations hold that it is not absolute deprivation that elicits defiance, but an awareness of deprivation and a sense of deserving the benefits available at the center, conditions absent at the periphery and contained by the school, at least in the initial stage of globalization.

Awareness of deprivation is a key element here. As a concept it derives from social comparison theory, a corollary to relative deprivation theory. Simply put, individuals become resentful when they come to recognize inequalities between themselves and others in the distribution of goods in society (Festinger, 1954, pp. 117–140; Hyman, 1942; Stouffer et al., 1949; Thibaut & Kelley, 1959). Research showing the behavioral outcomes of individuals' comparison of one's self or one's own group to others is among the best documented in the social psychology literature (Austin, McGinn, & Susmilch, 1980, pp. 426–441; deCarufel, 1979, pp. 847–857; Messe & Watts, 1983, pp. 84–93; O'Malley, 1983, pp. 121–128; Ross & McMillan, 1973, pp. 437–449). Of particular interest here are studies showing that relative deprivation can be influenced by both the perceived likelihood of obtaining an outcome under existing circumstances and the subjunctive probability of obtaining that outcome under alternative, hypothetical circumstances (Folger, Rosenfield, & Robinson, 1983, pp. 268–273).

How do social comparison and relative deprivation theories relate to the impact of schools at the periphery? Stimulus generalization theory, as I have shown, fails to explain this impact, however robust it may be, especially when tied to social comparison and relative deprivations theories, in explaining the school's impact at the center. Clues may be found in a study by Deborah A. Prentice and Faye Crosby on the social structure of work and home environments. Drawing on the work of Crosby, Muehrer, and Loewenstein (1988) regarding the importance of context for feelings of deservedness and deprivation, Prentice and Crosby found that managers in a large corporation in Connecticut compared themselves differently with referents at home compared to work.

> At work, people have an abundance of others with whom to compare themselves. They have coworkers who have similar responsibilities and who likely have received similar training, and they have superiors against whom they can judge their potential for advancement. They also have objective measures of how much their co-workers put into the job, in terms of hours worked and amount and quality of work accomplished, and of what rewards these comparison people are receiving, in the form of promotions, salary increases, or special praise. Thus, they have all the information necessary to compare themselves, in some sense objectively, to other, relevant people.... At home, on the other hand, there is no readily available comparison group. (1987, pp. 165–182)

At the periphery, where the home is the primary institution and the school is newly introduced, children have no readily available comparison group. Isolated from the outside world, their exposure to mainstream culture is filtered by and through the school, filtered to distort the image of how distribution of benefits in that world is done. The school, in the service of the dominant society, strives to draw peripheral children into the mainstream by making them feel part of the nation. It does this by teaching them myths that, once believed, entice them to love and embrace national "heroes" and symbols and the image of a just society. Children are taught knowledge and skills that have little meaning within the immediate community environment but have imagined value in a society that they are persuaded is available to them and in which they will participate upon reaching adulthood. In other words, not having direct exposure to external realities, they are effectively taught to compare themselves favorably to imagined groups in the world outside the periphery. Without the felt presence of a privileged group with whom to compare, children at the periphery have no sense of being deprived of society's benefits. By thus combining filter effect theory with social comparison and relative deprivation theories we can explain children's embrace of mainstream culture and the role the school plays in expanding globalization at the periphery. This explanation, I contend, is more robust than stimulus generalization theory in accounting not only for the inclination of schoolchildren at the periphery to embrace more strongly national symbols and display national allegiance, but also for their being more motivated to achieve academically. Material resources, to be sure, may be important in the school's influence on how children embrace symbols and achieve academically, but at the periphery, I contend, the binding influence is the ability of the school to control children's awareness of the outside world. It is this ability that makes the role of the school so critical in building a culture of peace at the periphery.

CONCLUSION

Prevailing explanations of the school's role in globalization are cogent for much of the industrialized world, but not at the periphery. We recall that globalization is both an accelerated compression of economic and political forces and the intensification of consciousness of the contemporary world. There is reciprocity in this definition, because it implies both compression (of economic and political reality) and expansion (of consciousness of that reality). The school plays a fundamental role in both aspects of globalization: by conveying the skills commonly needed for participation in the economic and political spheres at the center and bringing knowledge of those spheres to the periphery. It is the second part—inducing a consciousness of the center's economic and political reality—that is most crucial in the expansion of globalization, because, as Edward Shils puts it, the center's centrality

> has nothing to do with geometry and little with geography. The center, or the central zone, is a phenomenon of the world of values and beliefs.... The central zone partakes of the nature of the sacred.... The center is also a phe-

nomenon of the realm of action. It is a structure of activities, of roles and persons, within the network of institutions. (1975, p. 4)

However much reciprocity is contained in the definition of globalization, there is no symmetry in the globalization process; in the world system the center expands at the cost of the periphery, and much of that expansion is attributable to the school. The dominant psychological theory explaining the efficacy of education—stimulus generalization theory— would predict discontinuities between what schools teach and what children are willing to learn in communities at the periphery, and that children in those schools would resist and rebel against such instruction. I have shown, however, that research findings are contrary to what stimulus generalization theory would predict, and that we must look for a proper explanation elsewhere. I have offered a new theory—a filter effect theory—in association with relative deprivation and social comparison theories to explain children's embrace of the combination of myths and quasi reality taught by schools at the periphery. Indeed, it is at what Wallerstein calls the semi-periphery—between the center and the periphery—where children are likely to be most resistant to formal instruction. Here children have exposure to the center's reality through direct experience and alternative means of information about that reality, and, unlike at the periphery, are in a position to assess the contradictions between schooled myths and hard observation. At the semi-periphery they can see the usually vast gap between their own economic and political powerlessness and the privileges of elites at the center, and, most importantly, the enormous obstacles to narrowing that gap notwithstanding the promises held out to them for doing so by the school.

It is by getting children to believe the myths about the center and to "buy into" the center's structure that schools assist in globalization at the periphery. Expanding globalization here involves a traditional society's relinquishment of its culture and traditions in favor of behaving and believing more like people at the center and accommodating to their institutions and cultural trappings.

Consider Laura Rival's (1996, pp. 153–168) account of schooling in the Huaorani villages of Ecuador. As soon as the state grants a school to a village, that village appears on the country's map. As that happens, Huaorani villagers, now recognized as citizens, are faced with new obligations and administrative formalities. They must vote, get birth and marriage certificates, and own identity cards. As a new public sphere is created, a new division of labor based on a redefinition of production, based on agricultural rather than hunting, is introduced. This new division of labor, presented as rational and progressive, is reinforced in teachings dedicated to changing concepts of work, production, and gender. Children are taught, for example, that agriculture creates abundance and welfare through hard labor and represents an evolutionary stage superior to that of hunting, and if their parents intensify horticultural production, food will be more nutritious and varied. In this way schools move children from their natural environment and *de-skill* them with regard to forest knowledge. As the village environment is transformed from forest into large, grassy places and dispersed plantations, children's knowledge of the primary rainforest and its resources is incrementally eroded.

For the Huaorani, the school demands a change in villagers' traditional connection with their environment, requiring a fundamental alteration in social relations. The knowledge children learn is *decontextualized,* separated from the group's traditional activities of hunting, gathering, chanting, and crafting artifacts. Weaned away from context-specific activities, children change their concept of personal autonomy and collective sharing of natural abundance, and take on a modern identity, fundamentally at variance with the traditional group. Concurrently, parents and village elders lose much of their authority as arbiters of culture and sources of normative behavior for their children.

Thus, at the periphery, myths taught by schools about mainstream society come to displace in children's consciousness myths about their indigenous past taught in traditional, less formal ways by parents and elders. Myth displacement is an important part of resocialization that allows globalization to take place. This process of transformed consciousness creates the conditions of susceptibility to world forces. The school often becomes the leading authority in the village, interpreting a new social reality and filtering out unflattering images of the dominant culture and the exogenous world. Children learn to be citizens of a nation—to participate with others in the polity, obey laws, function in the marketplace, and render allegiance to the state. Abetted by the school, globalization cuts the pillars of normative thought and behavior from the traditional village and expands into the periphery.

As communities become more "mainstream" they also become more conscious of the disabilities of mainstream culture. The school is a major instrument in the cultural displacement process, but, paradoxically, its power to mold images and attitudes (though not necessarily its effectiveness in teaching objectivized content) weakens as acculturation advances. Hence, the school works, in a sense, against its own interests. It conveys myths that are believed for a while, building through them an attachment to mainstream and global values. Yet it is an attachment that is severely challenged as progressively acculturated communities discover that they have been deceived, that they have relinquished sacred and time-honored traditions in the belief that the myths about mainstream society that they have been taught by schools were, after all, only myths.

In brief, it is an almost universal mission of schools in peripheral communities to generate national cohesion by teaching an attachment to mainstream society. Yet that mission encourages schools to create and use myths to transform consciousness and displace traditional cultures. Myth teaching, however necessary to promote national unity, is an education of deception. Upon becoming aware of having been duped, once compliant communities may become resentful and resistant. Those who view schools as building cultures of peace ignore at their own peril this dilemma in marginalized communities.

NOTES

1. Theories that explain school effects based on cultural discontinuities derive from or are otherwise similar to stimulus generalization theory. See Garcia (1999, pp. 1072–1091).
2. My discussion here is based on Anthony D. Smith's distinction between civic-territorial and ethnic-genealogical models of the nation. See Smith (1991, pp. 81–84).
3. Peru, *El Proceso Peruano, Lecturas* (Lima: INDICE, 1974).
4. History is replete with examples of dominant groups imposing their own languages at the cost of ethnic vernaculars. See, for example, Petherbridge-Hernandez and Latiner Raby (1993, pp. 31–49). However, using the vernacular as a temporary device of political socialization among repressed minorities is not an unknown policy. For example, the Soviet Union promoted Yiddish-language schools as a replacement for Jewish religious education. The purpose of such schools was not to perpetuate Jewish ethnicity, but to convey more efficiently proletarian consciousness and the "Spirit of Communism." See Epstein (1978, pp. 223–254).

REFERENCES

Abernathy, D. B. (1969) *The political dilemma of popular education*. Stanford, CA: Stanford University Press.

Austin, W., McGinn, N. C., & Susmilch, C. (1980). Internal standards revisited: Effects of social comparison and expectancies on Judgments of fairness and satisfaction, *Journal of Experimental Social Psychology, 16*, 426–441.

Benavot, A., Cha, Y.-K., Kamens, D., Meyer, J. W., & Wong, S. Y. (1991). Knowledge for the masses—World models and national curricula, 1920–1986. *American Sociological Review, 96*(1), 85–101.

Bowman, M. J. (1982). *Educational choice and labor markets in Japan*. Chicago: University of Chicago Press.

Chiappo, L. (1973). Liberación de la educación, *Participación, 2*, 26–37.

Coleman, J. S., et al. (1966). *Equality of educational opportunity*. Washington, DC: U.S. Government Printing Office.

Crosby, F., Muehrer, P., & Loewenstein, G. (1988). Relative deprivation and explanation: Models and concepts. In J. Olson, M. Zanna, & P. Herman (Eds.), *Relative dDeprivation and assertive action.* Hillsdale, NJ: Erlbaum.

deCarufel, A. (1979). Factors affecting the evaluation of improvement: The role of normative standards and allocator resources. *Journal of Personality and Social Psychology, 37,* 847–857.

Drysdale, R. S., & Myers, R. G. (1975). Continuity and change: Peruvian education. In A. F. Lowenthal (Ed.), *The Peruvian experiment: Continuity and change under military rule.* Princeton, NJ: Princeton University Press.

Epstein, E. H. (1967). National identity and the language issue in Puerto Rico. *Comparative Education Review, 11*(2), 133–143.

Epstein, E. H. (1971). Education and *Peruanidad:* Internal colonialism in the Peruvian highlands. *Comparative Education Review, 15*(3), 188–201.

Epstein, E. H. (1978). Ideological factors in soviet educational policy toward Jews. *Education and Urban Society, 10*(2), 223–254.

Epstein, E. H. (1982). Peasant consciousness under Peruvian military rule. *Harvard Educational Review,* 52(3), 280–300.

Epstein, E. H. (1989). The peril of paternalism: The imposition of education on Cuba by the United States. *American Journal of Education, 96*(1), 1–23.

Epstein, E. H. (1997). National identity among St. Lucian schoolchildren. In J. M. Carrión (Ed.), *Ethnicity, race and nationality in the Caribbean* (pp. 338–363). San Juan: Institute of Caribbean Studies, University of Puerto Rico.

Everhart, R. B. (1983). *Reading, writing and resistance: Adolescence and labor in a junior high school.* Boston: Routledge and Kegan Paul.

Festinger, L. (1954). A theory of social comparison processes. *Human Relations, 7,* 117–140.

Foley, D E. (1991). Rethinking school ethnographies of colonial settings: A performance perspective of reproduction and resistance. *Comparative Education Review, 35,* 532–551.

Foster P. J. (1962), Ethnicity and the school in Ghana. *Comparative Education Review, 6*(2), 127–135.

Garcia, E. E. (1999). Reforming education and its culture, *American Behavioral Scientist, 42*(6), 1072–1091

Hagstrom, W. O. (1968) Deliberate instruction within family units. In A.M. Kazamias & E.H. Epstein (Eds.), *Schools in transition: Essays in comparative education* (pp. 262–279). Boston: Allyn & Bacon.

Hyman, H. H. (1942). The psychology of states. *Archives of Psychology,* No. 269.

Ignatieff, M. (1993). *Blood and belonging: Journeys into the new nationalism.* New York: Farrar, Straus, & Giroux.

LeVine, R. A. (1960a). The internalization of political values in stateless societies. *Human Organization, 19,* 51–58.

LeVine, Robert A. (1960b). The role of the family in authority systems: A cross-cultural application of stimulus-generalization theory. *Behavioral Science, 5,* 291–296.

Luykx, A (1996). From *Indios* to *Profesionales:* Stereotypes and student resistance in Bolivian teacher training. In B. A. Levinson, D. E. Foley, & D.C. Holland (Eds.), *The cultural production of the educated person: Critical ethnographies of schooling and local practice* (pp. 239–272). Albany: State University of New York Press.

MacLeod, J. (1995). *Ain't no makin' it: Aspirations and attainment in a low-income neighborhood.* Boulder, CO: Westview Press

Messe L. A., & Watts, B. L. (1983). Complex nature of the sense of fairness: Internal standards and social comparison as bases for reward evaluations. *Journal of Personality and Social Psychology, 45,* 84–93.

Monchar, P. H. (1981). Regional educational inequality and political instability, *Comparative Education Review, 25*(1), 1–12.

Morganthau, H. J. (1955). *Politics among nations: The struggle for power and peace.* New York: Knopf.

Nash, M. (1965). The role of village schools in the process of cultural and economic modernization. *Social and Economic Studies, 14*(1), 131–145

O'Malley, M. N. (1983). Interpersonal and intrapersonal justice: The effect of subject and confederate outcomes on evaluations of fairness. *European Journal of Social Psychology, 13,* 121–128

Petherbridge-Hernandez, P., & Latiner Raby. R. (1993). Twentieth century transformations in Catalonia and the Ukraine: Ethnic implications in education. *Comparative Education Review, 37*(2), 31–49.

Portocarrero, G., & Oliart, P. (1989). *El Perú Desde la Escuela.* Lima, Peru: Instituto de Apoyo Agrario.

Post, D. (1994). Through a glass darkly? indigeneity, information, and the Image of the Peruvian university. *Higher Education, 27,* 271–295.

Prentice, D. A., & Crosby, F. (1987). The importance of context for assessing deservingness. In J.C. Masters & W. P. Smith (Eds.), *Social comparison, social justice, and relative deprivation: Theoretical, empirical and policy perspectives* (pp. 165–182). Hillsdale, NJ: Erlbaum.

Ramirez, F. O., & Boli-Bennett, J. (1987). The political construction of mass schooling: European origins and world-wide industrialization. *Sociology of Educatioin, 60,* 2–17.

Rival, L. (1996) Formal schooling and the production of modern citizens in the Ecuadorian Amazon. In B. A. Levinson, D. E. Foley, & D. C. Holland (Eds.), *The cultural production of the educated person: Critical ethnographies of schooling and local practice* (pp. 153–168). Albany: State University of New York Press.

Robertson, R. (1987). Globalization theory and civilizational analysis. *Comparative Civilizations Review, 17.*

Ross, M., & McMillan, M. J. (1973). External referents and past outcomes as determinants of social discontent. *Journal of Experimental Social Psychology, 9,* 437–449.

Runciman, W.G. (1966). *Relative deprivation and social justice.* Berkeley and Los Angeles: University of California Press.

Shils, E. (1975). *Center and periphery.* Chicago: University of Chicago Press.

Sklair L. (1997) Globalization: New approaches to social change. In S. Taylor (Ed.), *Sociology: Issues and debates* (pp. 321–345). London: Macmillan.

Smith, A. D. (1991). *National identity.* Reno: University of Nevada Press.

Stouffer, S., et al. (1949). *The American soldier: Adjustments during army life* (Vol. 1). Princeton, NJ: Princeton University Press

Thibaut, J. W., & Kelley, H. H. (1959). *The social psychology of groups.* New York: Wiley.

Werlich, D. P. (1977). The Peruvian revolution in crisis. *Current History, 72,* 81–82.

White, B. W. (1996). Talk about school: Education and the colonial project in French and British West Africa. *Comparative Education, 29*, 9–25.

Williams, R. M., Jr. (1975). Relative deprivation. In L. A. Coser (Ed.), *The idea of social structure: Essays in honor of Robert K. Merton.* New York: Harcourt, Brace.

Willis, P. (1977). *Learning to labour: How working class kids get working class jobs.* Westhead, UK: Saxon House

Young, C. (1976). *The politics of cultural pluralism.* Madison: University of Wisconsin Press.

CHAPTER 7

MOROCCAN DELINQUENT BOYS IN DUTCH SOCIETY

Hans Werdmölder

INTRODUCTION

In October 2004 Moroccan boys made headlines again in the Dutch media. A small group of young Moroccans had terrorized a young Dutch family in such a way that they had been forced to flee their own home. This was not the first time families had been forced to leave their neighborhood as a result of the annoying and criminal behaviour of Moroccan youngsters. A year before, all Dutch newspapers, radio, and television also covered an incident involving a group of Moroccan boys between 15 and 18 years old who had hung puppets on a lamppost and a tree, with a noose around the neck. The puppets were wearing plates with the names of some local policemen on it. Only one week before that incident, also in Amsterdam, a group of Moroccan boys and one Tunisian boy had kicked to death a female drug addict. Supposedly, but proved wrongly afterward, she had stolen a can of beer. As the woman shouted the word *kutmarokkanen* ("fucking Moroccans"), she was kicked over and over again. She died as a result of her injuries. Almost a year ago a municipal alderman had introduced the nasty, abusive word in an informal chat with the mayor of Amsterdam. That chat happened to be recorded and the alderman had to make his apologies.

Educating Toward a Culture of Peace, pages 93–108
Copyright © 2006 by Information Age Publishing

In May 2003, a number of Moroccan boys had disturbed the traditional May 4 ceremony to the memory of those fallen during World War II. At three different places in Amsterdam, incidents involving Moroccan youths had been reported. One incident concerned Moroccan boys who were screaming "joden moeten we doden" ("we should kill the Jews"). At another place Moroccans were playing soccer with the wreaths and the bouquets of flowers, which had been laid down at the monument. At a third place, the monument to the memory of homosexuals who had died in World War II, Moroccan youngsters had been yelling during the traditional two minutes of silence. People were shocked again.

So far, the above events have been the culmination of a long list of incidents in which Moroccan boys have been involved. Native Dutch people have been wondering, what has happened with these Moroccan youths? Why are they showing this kind of criminal behavior? Why do they hate us? Why are they using such abusive language, not only to describe young Dutch women, but in their relations with elderly people? Why are they ignoring the Holocaust and do not want to be instructed about this important piece of European history? From their own perspective, the young Moroccans have been (and still are) complaining about too much police attention, discrimination, and stigmatization in Dutch society.

Having observed the behavior of Moroccan delinquent boys for a period of more than 20 years now, the recent incidents have been a shock for me too (Werdmölder 1990, 1997). Having studied immigration patterns in the United States and other countries, I had been expecting to observe that in the end Moroccan youngsters would integrate and assimilate into Dutch society. I believed that those Moroccan boys who were born and raised in the Netherlands would participate much more in important institutions, as a consequence of which it would be easier for them to integrate into Dutch society and their high share in criminal statistics would drop accordingly. However, this seems not to have been the case for Moroccan boys in the Netherlands. In this chapter I argue that their delinquency, their antisocial and even radical behavior is best understood within the theoretical framework of what I call the "internalized culture conflict."

MOROCCANS IN DUTCH SOCIETY

Today, the Netherlands has a population of 16.3 million inhabitants. The Moroccans, as one of the ethnic minority groups living in the country, counts approximately 316,000 persons. At this moment, half of the Moroccan community (48%) lives in one of the four larger cities in the western part of the Netherlands: Amsterdam, Rotterdam, The Hague, and Utrecht.

At the turn of the past century, one out of six inhabitants of Amsterdam below age 20 is a person with Moroccan roots (CBS, 2003).

In Amsterdam, a city of 739,000 inhabitants, 39% of the local population belongs to one of the ethnic minority groups. At this moment, there are living some 174 nationalities in Amsterdam; 63,000 of them have a Moroccan background. A similar pattern can be observed in the other larger cities, such as Utrecht, The Hague, and Rotterdam. The ethnic minorities in these cities tend to be concentrated in areas characterized by cheap and mostly subsidized housing. However, these areas can neither be characterized as "no-go areas," nor can these "ethnic enclaves" be compared with, for instance, the *bidonvilles* in France or the ethnic slums in American cities.

A majority of the Moroccans living in the Netherlands, some 70%, are descendants of Berber-speaking tribal groups in the northern and northeastern parts of Morocco. This part of the so-called North African Maghreb has been an economically underdeveloped and hardly accessible area. Various Berber tribes, who also speak different languages, populate the Maghreb area, also known by the name of "Rif." The Rifians have a reputation for being proud, hospitable, and independent. They regard themselves as men of honor. They are also well known for their fighting spirit (Hart, 2000; Seddon, 1981). During the Spanish war in the 1930s of the last century, as the northern part of Morocco still was a Spanish protectorate, many Rifians were fighting on the side of General Franco. More than 70,000 Moroccans have been fighting in World War II, as part of the French army (Klinkert, 2003). Like other Moroccans, the people from the Rif are traditional Muslims.

The first Moroccans arrived in the Netherlands as so-called "guest laborers." In the second half of the 1970s family reunification programs were underway. This process has now practically come to an end. In practice, family reunification meant that on average one Moroccan family brought over five to six children. Present-day immigration is largely a result of marriage patterns, in which Moroccans bring over their partners from Morocco—so-called "import-brides." Two out of three marriages of second generation Moroccans are with an "import-partner." Intermarriage of young Moroccans with Dutch partners is almost nonexistent (Hooghiemstra, 2003).

In the mid-1980s, a large section of the first-generation Moroccans became unemployed. In this period Dutch industry was going through an important phase of reorganization, which had far-reaching implications for the low-skilled, migrant workers. Many of the companies involved (Ford, Daf, Hoogovens) chose the easier option of placing workers in the disability pension system (WAO) rather than firing them. For the workers, this also turned out to be a better option. The disability pensions were far higher than the unemployment benefit they would otherwise receive. However, the long-term unemployment of Moroccan workers has had important consequences for the Moroccan community as a whole, in particular isolation and withdrawal from the ongoing developments in Dutch society. In 1991, 46% of the Moroccans between ages 15 and 24 in the Netherlands were still unemployed (Roelandt, Roijen, & Veenman, 1992, p. 109).

In 2001, 27% of Moroccans ages 15 to 64 are still dependent on the social benefit system, and half of them are dependent on the disability pension system (CBS, 2003, pp. 106–111). Due to the rise of the economy in the second half of the 1990s the unemployment rate for young Moroccans (under 30 years of age) has been decreasing. Although their share in the total population has increased to more than 10 %, their unemployment rate has decreased from 25% in 1994, to 12% at the end of the last century (still twice as high as the native population). At this moment unemployment is rising again, due to the downturn in the Dutch economy. Most of the jobs are based on temporary contracts, so-called "dead-end jobs" (Storm & Naastepad, 2003).

The education profile of the Moroccans is not very good, although it has increased proportionally since the end of the 1980s. Still, 57% of the Moroccans in the age bracket of 15 to 24 years have only a certificate with primary education. In 2002, 18% of the Moroccan pupils between age 15 and 34 have left secondary school prematurely (i.e., without a degree) (SCP, 2003, p. 125). The dropout has shown a proportional decrease, but this figure is still far too high. In the four larger cities, the segregation of the ethnic minority part of the pupils visiting primary and secondary schools at the lower educational level is almost complete.

What can be said about the position of Moroccan women? Most women have a very dependent position. Among the different ethnic groups in the Netherlands the participation of Moroccan women on the Dutch labor market is the lowest; only 22% of the Moroccan women had a (part-time) job. In 2003 the figure of abortion among Moroccan women was five times as high as among Dutch women (Wijsen, 2004, p. 16). Half of the abortions involved young unmarried Moroccan women, in most cases as a consequence of the unsuccessful use of birth control pills.

Migration to another country and starting a new life there inevitably hurts. The Moroccan adventurers of the 1960s are now in the age bracket of 55 to 60 years. Most of them are unemployed; they pass their time in a teahouse, longing for Morocco. Many stay in the Netherlands, but only because their children and grandchildren still live there. There is a feeling of loss and longing, which are typical characteristics of a migrant community. One older Moroccan man told me once: "With my body I am staying in Holland, with my head I am living in Morocco."

The integration of young Moroccans in Dutch society faces many difficulties. Many Moroccans find themselves in a marginalized situation. This may be a depressing conclusion; on the other hand, one can also observe a lot of ambition and creativity in the Moroccan community. As the Dutch Morocco watchers Herman Obdeyn and Paolo de Mas argue in their essay *The Moroccan Challenge* (2001), second-generation Moroccans are now taking over the stick from the first generation.

DELINQUENT MOROCCAN BOYS IN DUTCH SOCIETY

In 1989, the first incidents involving delinquent Moroccan boys came to the attention of the general public. In that year a so-called "secret report" of the municipal authorities in Amsterdam had been published in a newspaper. The report mentioned the existence of some 200 to 300 delinquent Moroccan boys. Stealing and robbing, they were making the inner city of Amsterdam unsafe (Loef, 1989; Werdmölder, 1989).

From that moment onward, delinquent and antisocial Moroccan boys have been in the news more or less permanently. They were annoying Dutch girls in swimming pools, they were threatening homosexuals, they made trouble with tourists in the seaside resort of Zandvoort, and they were running drugs in Rotterdam. "They think badly about us, so we are behaving badly," one of them told me. A striking detail in this continuing public debate is that the parents of the delinquent Moroccans remain outside the media coverage. They prefer to remain silent, although they are confronted with most of the problems. When asked about the behavior of their sons, they feel ashamed. According to some older Moroccans, these youths are bewitched.

In a large-scale survey study, Junger stated that one in three Moroccan youths (34%) between the ages of 12 and 18 has been in trouble with the law at least once, for the Turkish boys this was 22% and for the Dutch youths originating from the same neighborhoods this was 15% (Junger, 1990, p. 40). Moroccans showed the highest arrest rates, the type of criminality usually based on thefts, burglary, mugging, and prostitution. Young Moroccans also got easily hooked on gambling and hard drugs. This type of criminality is typical for young and uprooted migrants—one may call them "quality of life offenses."

At the end of the 1990s, the criminality rates among Moroccan youths still seemed to be a big problem. However, it is no longer a problem of the big cities in the Western part of the country alone; each Dutch town with a relevant Moroccan community is faced with the phenomenon of uprooted Moroccan boys. Survey studies and in-depth research in the 1990s confirmed the conclusions of the 1980s (Driessen, 2002). Moroccan boys are overrepresented in the catagory of regular crime (three offenses in one year, and also criminally active in the year before). From every 1,000 persons Moroccans score 18.6 offenses in the crime rates, in comparison the number of offenses among Dutch-autochthonous youth is 2.0 and among Turkish youth it is 3.4 (Willemse & Backbier, 2002) Today, some 10,000 registrated Moroccan boys are involved in delinquent behavior daily, partly drug-related crime. At last, Moroccan boys are also overrepresented in the judicial institutions for juvenile offenders.

However, what concerns people most is not only their criminality, but moreover their antisocial behavior. After September 11, 2001, more incidents are registered in which the Moroccan boys stand against Dutch society. The incidents do not only take place in the street, but also at schools. At some schools, not all of them, Moroccans and native Dutch youths are irritating each other by wearing special clothes. Right-wing youths have short haircuts and wear high boots with white or red bootlaces. They also wear Lonsdale shirts, a brand with a right-wing connotation in the Netherlands. The shirts, worn under a bomber jacket, are visible through the middle letters of LONSDALE, which happened to be the same letters as the former German Nazi-party NSDAP (read P for L). For that reason, Lonsdale has a right-wing and racist reputation. In order to restore their image, the trademark introduced a new slogan: "Lonsdale loves all colors." Moroccan boys, from their side, wear jackets with fur collars. They have buttons on their clothes with the Islam fighter Osama bin Laden and on their trendy jacket one can notice the little Moroccan flag.

The antisocial and criminal behavior of the Moroccan boys are unique in comparison to other ethnic youth groups in Dutch society. Their criminality is not only more than proportional, but it is also very provocative, aggressive, and intimidative. These so-called quality-of-life offenses are mostly directed toward Dutch autochthonous people. Among them are also vulnerable groups such as Jews, homosexuals, and young women.

POLITICAL TURMOIL AFTER 9/11

September 11, 2001, has changed the political and social climate regarding migrants in the Netherlands. After that devastating moment the media have aroused the public with articles, discussions, and news about Islam, in particular about the so-called "threat of Muslim fundamentalism" (Van den Brink, 2004). They have also annoying questions to young Muslim women why they wear a headscarf. Of course, this is not a neutral question. More and more Moroccans have the feeling that they have to defend themselves, especially in respect to their Muslim background and the criminal behavior of some of their young countrymen.

People in the Netherlands have rather mixed feelings about Islam, from one side there is curiosity and from the other side there is fear. The case of the Moroccan imam El Moumni seemed to be a central turning point. Because of his hate speech, this imam had been forbidden to preach any longer in Morocco. Nevertheless, he was invited by a mosque organization in the city of Rotterdam to become their imam. In one of his speeches, which was recorded, El Moumni argued that Western society was a civilization without morality, in which it was accepted that homosexuals can marry with each other. He also preached that homosexuals were less than pigs. This so-called *fatwa* was followed by the reaction of the late politician Pim Fortuyn, who was not only a cultural-nationalist but also a practicing homosexual. Fortuyn's argumentation runs as follows. In the Netherlands, Imam El Moumni can preach as he thinks. In Western society, there is freedom of speech—one of our central human rights. For that reason, he may say that I am less than a pig. "But I am telling you," said Fortuyn in an interview in a daily newspaper, "the Islam is a backward culture" (Pels, 2003, p. 214). After giving this interview, Fortuyn was forced to leave his party (*Leefbaar Nederland*—leefbaar is liveable in Dutch, with a strong base in local city councils).

After being thrown out of *Leefbaar Nederland*, Fortuyn started his own party: *Lijst Pim Fortuyn* (LPF). Only nine days before the national elections of May 15, 2002, a left-wing environmental activist assassinated Pim Fortuyn. His funeral became a national event. Nevertheless, the elections were held and the results were dramatic. The ruling center-left "Partij van de Arbeid" lost nearly half of its parliamentary seats. The late Fortuyn's LPF came from nothing to 26 seats in the Dutch Parliament, becoming the second largest party—a fact that raised the world media's attention.

The populist Pim Fortuyn became very popular in the Dutch media by slogans like "One should say as one thinks" and "The Netherlands are full." He also criticized the Dutch government for the uncontrolled influx of migrants. He did not advocate, however, throwing out immigrants who were already in the Netherlands, but his argument was 'they must accept the country's norms and values." The sudden rise of the flamboyant and charismatic Pim Fortuyn and his support all over the country was a shock for the left- and right-wing establishment in Dutch politics (Pels, 2003, pp. 214–276).

Fortuyn's outspoken views on issues of race and culture, high criminality among Moroccan and Antillean youths, and his antiestablishment stance attracted not only the votes from native Dutch people, but also from the new migrant population as well. The local Hindustani movement, consisting largely of migrants from Surinam, advised its members to vote for the LPF. After renewed elections in 2002, the LPF was eliminated to only seven seats (Storm & Naastestad, 2003, pp. 131–151).

On November 2, 2004, the Dutch society was vehemently shocked again by the brutal and ritual murder of the filmmaker, social commentator, and maverick Theo van Gogh. Van Gogh was found slayed on the street. The murderer had pricked a knife on his body with a political-religious pamphlet. In this pamphlet it was stated that the assassination was a revenge on his provoking insults to the Islam—he had called them "geitenneukers" ("goat fuckers")—and the ultimate consequence of the making of the film *Submission, Part 1.* This short film was made in collaboration with a Somali-born member of the Dutch Parliament, Ayaan Hirsi Ali. The suspect of the murder is a 26-year-old Dutch citizen of Moroccan origin and a member of a radical Islamic group. The reactions on the brutal murder were vehement. Everyone, also the Muslim community in the Netherlands, was very shocked. But there were also people who argued that the brutal murder of Theo van Gogh was the sad and ultimate consequence of his continued efforts of insulting the moslims. Many politicians and commentators condemned the attack in unequivocal terms. Dutch Deputy Prime Minister Gerrit Zalm even described the murder as a "declaration of war." On the streets there was not the usual silent protest, the day after the murder a very loud protest was organized on the central Dam Square in Amsterdam.

The consequences of this political turmoil and the overall discussions in the Dutch media are far reaching. As a reaction to the multicultural and liberal stance of the official authorities and intellectuals in the past years, ordinary Dutch people are no longer hiding their real feelings. Most Dutch people think negatively about the ideal of a multicultural society. The blunt message of the people on the streets is: "Think as we think" and "Behave yourself like we do." In this respect, the slogans of the late politician Pim Fortuyn, the public presentation of the shocking film, and the assassination of Theo van Gogh did not help to bring the Moroccans and the Dutch together.

ACCOUNTING FOR THE BEHAVIOR

Why are Moroccan boys behaving in this negative way? First, the marginalization of Moroccan youths in Dutch society is a breeding ground for their criminal behavior. Most Moroccan boys grow up in families with many problems. According to the Commission for Moroccan Youths, who conducted research in 1998, the number of problematic Moroccan families can be estimated at some 3,500 (Commissie Marokkaanse Jeugd, 1998). This does not imply that every Moroccan boy who is not participating in important institutions of their own community and Dutch society will become a criminal. The chances on criminal behavior are only higher. For the Moroccan youngsters who are marginalized, who have left school and who are without a job, criminality (stealing and mugging) is their way of life. Earlier, I have coined this type of criminality among young migrants as "uprooted crime" (Werdmölder & Meel, 1993, p. 272).

The criminal and antisocial behavior of Moroccan boys is often directed toward Dutch people, especially to those persons who are typically representative of Dutch society. There is more than one explanation for this attitude. First of all, there is much discrimination in Dutch society. Moroccan boys find it hard to find a decent job, because of the overall negative attitude toward them. One can also observe discrimination in public life, partly the result of the fact that Moroccan boys have "a bad name." Their negative attitude is, so to speak, also a reaction of a discriminating society.

On the other hand, there are some explanatory elements within the Moroccan community. Cultures differ, also in the way they react toward the dominant Dutch culture. Moroccan, Turkish, Surinam-Creole, or Indonesian people have also different answers to important and relevant questions. Of course, one cannot argue that Moroccan youngsters are criminal because they happened to be Moroccan. Their criminal behavior, however, can be distinguished from the criminality of, for example, Antilleans, Turkish, or Surinam-Creole youths in Dutch society (Werdmölder & Meel, 1993).

First of all, the Moroccans in the Netherlands are a fragmented community, which means that they have a lot of distrust and jealousy within their own group. The Moroccan-Riffian people, as stated earlier, have a tradition of being proud and independent. They also have a high fighting spirit. This typical attitude, which should not only be explained negatively, can be observed among children of the first generation of Moroccans as well. There are also many incidents in which "honor" is involved. Young Moroccans do not want to lose their face in public. They feel that they have to react when they are put in a position that is beyond their own control. In this respect, honor can be a part of their delinquent behavior. Lastly, this generation is also influenced by the anti-Western propaganda of Arabic websites and the Internet.

These Moroccan boys have grown up and are influenced by Dutch society as well. They have been penetrated by the Dutch culture, *pénétration hollandaise* as the French will call it. One can even observe this new phenomenon by traveling in Morocco. The young Dutch-Moroccans behave in a different way; they are more open, brutal, and assertive—all more or less typical behavior for Dutch youngsters. Older Moroccans say: "They have no respect." But in Dutch society as well, people say they have no respect, not for the Dutch police, not for their Dutch teachers, and so on. Moroccan boys have a problem with Dutch authority and don't want to be corrected by officials.

Moroccan parents attach much value to a modern education for their children, but they also want to preserve their cultural and religious values.

In this process of socialization they are supported and controlled by their Moroccan network and community in the Netherlands as well as in Morocco. On the other hand, at school, by watching television and hanging out on the streets, Moroccan children are influenced by values and norms—such as autonomy, independence, a more open and assertive way of behavior and Western style of relations between men and women—which are very different from those in their home setting and community. The behavior of Moroccans is more group and family oriented. Their attitude to society is always related to what others will think, especially members of the family, friends, villagers, and colleagues.

These children are, according to anthropologist and pedagogue Lotty Eldering (1998), "socialised in various settings in the Netherlands and Morocco, which sends them mixed messages about their role and their identity." Therefore, in the case of Moroccan boys in the Netherlands we cannot speak any longer of Moroccans, but about Dutch-Moroccans. Many of them have formed a new identity, which combines elements of two very different and contrasting cultures. This may result in feelings of tension, but it can also lead to creativity. In some cases, it will also result in antisocial behavior and criminality. In this respect, I have coined the term *internalized culture conflict.*

The so-called "liminal position" of young migrants is often described as "living between two cultures." Liminal positions are neither here nor there. They have "betwixt and between positions," assigned by different social structures and cultures (Turner, 1969, p. 95). Moroccan youths react in a different way to personal tensions, daily intercultural confrontations, and racial discrimination. The first possible answer to the constant pressure of Dutch society is a creative one. The second-generation Moroccans who participate well in Dutch society are very ambitious. They are profiling themselves in different cultural and social niches of Dutch society. They are already successful in Dutch literature (there are already more than 10 Moroccan novelists), in sports (soccer and fighting sports are very popular), in film (*Shouf, Shouf Habibi* is a very popular movie of a Moroccan multiproblem family in the Netherlands), in the theatre, and in the world of fashion. Moroccans are very well organized on the Internet (Maroc.nl, Magheb.nl, Mocros.nl), and at my own law faculty one can observe many university students with a Moroccan, female background. At last, they can also be successful in criminality. Some of them earn a good living by selling and running soft drugs.

Their "liminal position" can also result in intercultural conflicts, as a form of "soft resistance" to the dominant Dutch society. There is a group of Moroccans who don't want to assimilate in Dutch society. They do not want to become "cheeseheads" ("verkazen," making them as flat as cheese). They wear modern or traditional headscarves, they are painting their hands with Moroccan figures, they sometimes have Osama bin Laden pictures on their cell phones, they go to their own concerts and they will marry persons of their own kind. Since 9/11 more and more young migrants find their new identity in the fact that they are Muslims. Their religious conviction can be based on a modern and tolerant interpretation of the Koran, but it can also be based on a more radical and fundamentalist variant. Their identification with the Islam is even more important than their Moroccan or Turkish background. Some years ago, Dutch researchers have asked the young Moroccans to whom they really belong. The answers were, in the following order: Muslim, Moroccan, Rotterdammer (citizen of the city Rotterdam), and at last Dutch citizen (Phalet, van Lutringen, & Entzinger, 2000).

At last, the most opposite reaction as a result of this "liminal position" is "full resistance." Moroccan boys are not only influenced by Dutch and Moroccan culture and society, they also react by the codes and norms of the dominant street culture. This is the most negative side of what I have called earlier "the internalized culture conflict." One Moroccan pupil said to his schoolteacher, "You are the boss in school. But outside we are the boss." Uprooted Moroccan boys do not want to be controlled by Dutch supervisors. Sometimes, in the streets, you see them thinking: "I hate you, before you are going to hate me." It is interesting to observe that their behavior changes when they are in Morocco. Already in the airplane, flying with *Royal Air Maroc*, their behavior is already corrected by the air hostesses. Nevertheless, also when they are staying in Morocco, some of them still get involved in conflicts.

The attitude of "full resistance" can also lead to a real cultural clash. Some better-educated young Moroccans in the Netherlands can find a refuge in extremism and Islam fundamentalism. Mohammed B, the suspect of the assassination of filmmaker Theo van Gogh, was such a "born-again Muslim": a young man with a Moroccan background, a second-generation migrant, well educated, frustrated by personal experiences and heavily influenced by religious Muslim-fanatics. His radicalization did not take place in Morocco, but in the Netherlands. Reading his personal biography, I was struck by the notable similarity with the personal story of the so-called "twentieth hijacker," who is considered as the presumed missing link of the 19 terrorists who hijacked the airplanes in their coordinated suicide attack on 9/11. The real name of the "presumed hijacker" is Zacarias Moussaoui, a French-born Moroccan and well-educated young man who radicalized in France. Staying in London he came under the influence of the appeal of extremists of the *Wahhabism*, the state religious ideology of Saudi Arabia (Moussaoui, 2003).

APPROACHING THE PROBLEMS

Many educational and prevention projects have been developed to solve the problems with this particular group of delinquent Moroccan boys. The first one ringing the alarm-bell was the municipal police of Amsterdam. Police officers have been very active in getting Moroccan kids off the streets. Some of them got a job after mediation by idealistic police officers. Others are participating in special projects, such as the program *Beware, Watch Out.* Moroccan boys who are patrolling the streets, with on the backside of their blue jackets the text *Beware, Watch out.* In order to get a better understanding with the local community, the police have been organizing meetings with the imam, the parents of the boys, and they have also visited schools. In Amsterdam, the police have installed their own "peace corps," a branch of voluntary policemen that will be activated in case of demonstrations and manifestations. In reaction to these nontypical policing and social initiatives, the Amsterdam police argued: "The social workers are doing nothing, so we had to play the ball."

Regarding the reception and resocialization of the category of serious delinquent boys, one of the most challenging programs is the Glen Mills School's approach. The objective of this American-style approach is to restructure antisocial behavior of youths in the age bracket of 12 and 18 years into prosocial behavior, within a minimum period of 18 months. The basic assumption of the Glen Mills School is that youth are not bad, but have done bad things. Six status levels with their own privileges stimulate youth to rise in the hierarchy. The program is fully attached to changing the attitude of the social delinquent boy into a *bull,* a so-called "positive student." Through stressing tolerance and a positive group culture, the Glen Mills School tries to restructure the negative norms and values from the street that boys know from the past. The most important elements in achieving this goal are peer pressure, positive normative culture, confrontations, hierarchy, student participation, participation in a clear and structured program from early in the morning to late at night, and good education. The most striking aspect of this program is that the boys are not corrected by social workers, but by their own kind (Hilhorst & Klooster, 2004).

In the Netherlands this special "school" started as an experiment and has been operative for 5 years now. The Glen Mills School has settled in a former military barrack in the Eastern part of the Netherlands. They call themselves "a school for winners." The school emphasizes the value of the absence of fences and barred windows. This enables students to learn to take responsibility for themselves and for others. Nevertheless, innumerable measures are taken to ensure that the boys do not run away. Three out of four students in Glen Mills School has a migrant background, and one-fourth of the population has a Moroccan background. Some of the students acted in the film *Cool!*, a movie about life in Glen Mills School and made by the late Theo van Gogh.

A youth receives follow-up supervision for 18 months after leaving the school. The objective of the follow-up supervision is to help youths integrate into Dutch society as rapidly and as adequately as possible. Former students believe that this approach is a tough program, which is experienced as rather difficult, especially during the first 6 months. According to an internal evaluation from the Process Supervision Unit, it can be stated that of 117 former students an estimated 56% are doing well; 18% are struggling and 26% have probably relapsed (Hilhorst & Klooster, 2004, p. 66). Some Dutch researchers are more critical about the Glen Mills School initiative because they think that the project is not able to remove the criminal elements in their neighborhood.

Finally, there are local projects in which delinquent and problematic boys are returning to Morocco. During some weeks they visit local projects, youth institutions, and youth homes at several places. The general idea behind these kinds of local initiatives is that Moroccan-Dutch boys will think about their better prospects and chances when they are confronted with the life of Morocco-born youngsters ("En nu iets positiefs Twee," 2002).

CONCLUSION

The Moroccans have settled permanently in Dutch society. The Moroccans in the Netherlands can be seen as a divided and fragmented community. There is little social cohesion. Both the first- and second-generation Moroccans remain very much connected to heir homeland, also when they have been born and raised in the Netherlands.

Despite the strong motivation to become successful in Dutch society, a part of second-generation Moroccans finds themselves in a marginalized position. Of course, many of them are facing the problem of discrimination in Dutch society as well. Most of them grow up in so-called multiproblem families. When Moroccan boys have no harmonious family life, they feel as if they are in conflict with the host society as a whole. They become criminal, are using drugs, or get a living in trafficking drugs. Moroccans are also overrepresented in youth institutions. The incidents in which the Moroccan youths are involved catch the attention of the media, much to the annoyance of the successful Moroccans. However, they cannot be considered fully as Moroccans. They are so to speak "Dutch-Moroccans."

In this chapter, I have argued that the young Moroccans in Dutch society have "betwixt and between" feelings, as the result of the challenges to become part of two very different cultures. For many young Moroccans integration in Dutch society has become a personal struggle. They don't want to become Dutch, but they are no longer Moroccan either. For this personal struggle, I have coined the term *internalized culture conflict*. This conflict has resulted in much creativity, a strong ambition to become successful, but also in stress and personal failure. The most negative answer to their "liminal position" is antisocial and criminal behavior.

The challenge will be how to successfully integrate these problematic Moroccan youngsters in Dutch society, without giving them the feeling that they have to become "flat Dutch." With respect to the criminal and antisocial behavior among some of the Moroccan youth, a hopeful and also criticized initiative is the establishment of the Glen Mills School. The objective of the Glen Mills School's approach is to restructure antisocial behavior of criminal and antisocial into prosocial behavior.

NOTES

I would like to thank Jeroen Gutter for his helpful comments in revising the English text.

REFERENCES

Brink, van den, G. (2004). *Tekst, Traditie of Terreur? Naar een Moderne Visie op de Islam in Nederland* [Text, tradition or terror? Towards a modern vision on the Islam in The Netherlands]. Utrecht: Forum-essay.

Centraal Bureau voor de Statistiek (CBS). (2003). *Allochtonen in Nederland* [Allochtonous people in The Netherlands]. Den Haag.

Commissie Marokkaanse Jeugd. (1998). *"Samen vol vertrouwen de toekomst tegemoet." Perspectieven voor de Marokkaanse jeugd in de Nederlandse samenleving in de XXIe eeuw* ["Togetherwith full confidence towards the near future." Perspectives for the Moroccan youth in Dutch society in the 21st century]. Den Haag: Ministerie van Justitie.

Driessen, F. M. H. M., et al. (2002). *"Zeg me wie je vrienden zijn." Allochtone jongeren en criminaliteit* ["Tell me who your friends are." Allochtonous youths and criminality]. Utrecht: Bureau Driessen.

Eldering, L. (1998). Mixed messages. Moroccan children in the Netherlands living in two cultures. In Y. Zou & E. Trueba (Eds.), *Ethnic identity and power: Cultural contexts of political action in school and society* (pp. 259–282). Albany: State University of New York Press.

En nu iets positiefs Twee [Something positive now, two]. (2002). Working paper. Den Haag.

Hart, D. M. (2000). *Tribe and society in rural Morocco*. London: Frank Cass.

Hilhorst, N., & Klooster, E. (2004) *Programma-Evaluatie van de Glen Mills School* [Evaluation Program of the Glen Mills School]. Amsterdam: DSP-groep BV.

Hooghiemstra, E. (2003). *Trouwen over de grens. Achtergronden van partnerkeuze van Turken en Marokkanen in Nederland* [Marriage beyond the borders. Explanations for partner choice among Turks and Moroccans in The Netherlands]. Den Haag: SCP.

Junger, M. (1990). *Delinquency and ethnicity. An investigation of social factors relating to delinquency among Moroccan, Turkish, Surinamese and Dutch Boy.* Boston: Kluwer.

Klinkert, W. (2003). De Marokkaanse militaire bijdrage aan de strijd tegen Nazi-Duitsland in Europa 1940–1945 [The Moroccan military contribution to the battle against Nazi-Germany in Europe 1940–1945]. *Militaire Spectator, 172.*

Loef, K. (1989). *Marokkaanse daders in de Amsterdamse binnenstad* [Moroccan culprits in the center of Amsterdam]. Amsterdam: Rapport Bestuursinformatie Amsterdam.

Moussaoui, A. S. (2003). *Zacarias, my brother. The making of a terrorist.* New York: Seven Stories Press.

Obdeijn, H., & DaMas, P. (2001) *De Marokkaanse uitdaging. De tweede generatie in een veranderend Nederland* [The Moroccan challenge. The second generation in a changing Netherlands]. Utrecht: Forum-essay.

Pels, D. (2003). *De geest van Pim. Het gedachtegoed van een politieke dandy* [The spirit of Pim. The ideas of a political dandy]. Amsterdam: Anthos.

Phalet, K., van Lotringen C., & Entzinger, H. (2000). *Islam in de Multiculturele Samenleving. Opvattingen van jongeren in Rotterdam* [Islam in a multicultural society. Opinions of youths in Rotterdam]. Utrecht: Ercomer.

Rapportage Minderheden. (2003). *Onderwijs, Arbeid en Sociaal-culturele integratie* [Report on ethnic minorities. Education, labor and sociocultural integration]. Den Haag: Sociaal Cultureel Planbureau.

Roeland, T., Roijen, J. H. M., & Veenman, J. (1992). *Minderheden in Nederland* [Ethnic minorities in The Netherlands]. ISEO. Den Haag: SDU.

Seddon, D., (1981). *Moroccan peasants. A century of change in the Eastern Rif 1870–1970.* Folkestone: Dawson & Sons.

Storm, S., & Naastepad, R. (2003, March–April). The Dutch distress. *New Left Review, 20,* 131–151.

Turner, V. (1969). *The ritual process; Structure and anti-structure.* Chicago: Aldine.

Werdmölder, H. (1989). Een taboe doorbroken. Marokkaanse jongeren en criminaliteit [Breaking a taboo. Moroccan youths and criminality]. *Intermediar, 25,* 17–23.

Werdmölder, H., & Meel, P. (1993). Jeugdige allochtonen en criminaliteit. Een vergelijkend onderzoek onder Marokkaanse, Turkse, Surinaamse en Antilliaanse jongens [Allochtonous youths and criminality. A comparative research among Moroccan, Surinam and Antillean youths]. *Tijdschrift voor Criminologie, 34,* 252–276.

Werdmölder, H. (1997 revised translation) *A Generation Adrift. An Ethnography of a Criminal Moroccan Gang in the Netherlands.* The Hague and Boston: Kluwer Law International, London.

Werdmölder, H. (2005). *Marokkaanse lieverdjes. Crimineel en hinderlijk gedrag onder Marokkaanse jongeren* [Moroccan sweethearts. Criminal and anti-social behavior among Moroccan boys]. Amsterdam: Balans.

Willemse H.M. and Backbier E.H.F. (2002) 'Etnische Bortingen met de Strafwet' (Ethnic Confrontations with the Penal Statute'), in: *Justitiele Verkenningen* (28), pp. 38–39.

Wijsen, C. (2004) *Jaarverslag Landelijke Abortus Registratie 2003.* (Yearly Report of National Abortion Registration 2003) Utrecht: Rutgers Nisso Groep, juni.

CHAPTER 8

GLOBALIZATION AND THE CULTURE OF PEACE IN THE MIDDLE EAST

A Case Study

Faisal O. Al-Rfouh

The notion of globalization entails two aspects of change: a quantitative dimension and a qualitative one. Quantitatively, globalization refers to an increase in trade, capital movements, investments, and people across borders. Qualitatively, globalization represents changes in the way people and groups think and identify themselves, and changes in the way states, firms, and other actors perceive and pursue their interests. Anthony Giddens and John Tomilson have described globalization as a multidimensional process. It is best "understood in terms of simultaneous, complex related processes in the realms of economy, politics, culture, technology and so forth" (Tomilson, 1999, p. 16).

A more sophisticated version of the broad school of globalization critics has opined that "deterritorialization" of culture is occurring due to the

Educating Toward a Culture of Peace, pages 109–128
Copyright © 2006 by Information Age Publishing
All rights of reproduction in any form reserved.

hybridization of cultures. Global mass media and communication technologies are accelerating this process. The global culture that is emerging is complex and deterritorialized rather than simplistic and monolithic. This complexity exists because culture is not linked to local nation-states but is deterritorialized, which in turn, links to a cultural process of enforced propinquity and cosmopolitanism (Tomilson, 1999, p. 16). Giddens (1999, p. 10) also perceives globalization as a "political, technical and cultural as well as economic" process.

ASPECTS OF GLOBALIZATION

Globalization, as such, entails three interconnected elements: (1) the expansion of markets; (2) challenges to the state and institutions; and (3) the rise of new social and political movements. These elements do not represent either alternative definitions or competing theories but reflect different aspects of Globalization.

The first aspect of globalization is symbolized by the expansion of markets in terms of the transformation of global economic activity. Technological change and governmental deregulation have permitted the establishment of transnational networks in production, trade, and finance, which is termed a "borderless world" by Ohmae (1991). In trade, globalization refers to the fact that the quantity and speed of goods and services traded across the globe has increased, and so too has the geographical expanse of participants, the strength and depth of institutions that facilitate trade, and the impact of trade on domestic economic arrangements.

The second element of globalization is political. Some people have expressed the opinion that a new "global politics" is emerging that, like the "borderless world economy," is characterized by a global political order in which states' political boundaries become much less important (McGrew & Lewis, 1992). Even without subscribing to the view that all politics have become "global," several important changes can be discerned in political power and authority. These changes have taken place owing to technological advances in communication and to policy changes as governments and other actors revisualize their interests and their legitimate domain of authority.

"Global issues"—like human rights, environmental degradation, the fast pace of depletion of natural resources, proliferation of small arms, international terrorism, drug-trafficking, and weapons of mass destruction—require countries to coordinate policymaking at levels above the nation-state. The nature of these developments is such that no one country can effectively regulate on its own. Likewise, economic globalization requires new forms of regulation. For this reason, the globalization of politics describes a shift in decision making up to either the regional or the international level.

Globalization affects more than markets and states. It is metamorphosing the lifestyles of people across the globe and casting influence on their culture and values. New communications systems mean that media, music, books, international ideas, and values can all be dispersed in a global and essentially instantaneous manner. This is producing what some describe as a "global culture." Concurrently, globalization is producing very different kinds of reactions and cultures, thereby culminating in a strong reassertion of "counter" national or religious identity. A common feature of both Westernization and reactions against it are groups and movements organizing themselves using new technologies and new ways of connecting across borders.

Common to all elements of globalization is the sense that activities hitherto undertaken within national boundaries can be momentarily undertaken globally or regionally—to some extent "deterritorialized." "Globalization denotes the expanding scale, growing magnitude, speeding up and deepening impact of interregional flows and patterns of social interaction" (Held & McGrew, 2001). This definition is not limited to the economic dimension, as is for example the understanding of the term utilized by the ILO's Task Force on the Country Studies debate (Torres, 2001). There is no denying the fact that the globalization process, along with the economic dimension, involves a number of key noneconomic forms of social interaction relating to culture and governance.

Globalization is said to envisage new patterns of governance, either in the shape of detached markets or private, "sovereignty-free actors" such as multinational corporations, transnational societies, and international organizations. While globalization is no longer expected to render states outmoded, some observers still feel that political authority within the international system is becoming more dispersed. As Susan Strange says, "the reality of state is not the same as it once was" (1995, pp. 55–74). It goes without saying that the national governments are sharing powers, including political, social, and security roles at the core of sovereignty with businesses, with international organizations, and with a multitude of citizens groups.

Undoubtedly, globalization is a multidimensional process, entailing both economic and noneconomic aspects. However, the current testimony substantiates that there is better economic globalization than other forms of noneconomic globalization. *Ipso facto* globalization refers to processes that potentially encompass the entire globe. Viewed in a broad perspective, there are three approaches to determine levels of economic integration of a country. First, by examining the extent of institutional convergence or harmonization across countries; second, by focusing on the prominence of the flows compared with the domestic ones; and third, by evaluating the outcomes of integration in terms of converging prices of goods, services, and factors.

Convergence or harmonization of native economic institutions curtails hurdles or transaction costs to transborder economic flows. The latest trends in regional and global trade, fiscal, and investment agreements indicate endeavors to minimize transaction costs of cross-border flows. Harmonization or convergence therefore constitutes a *sine qua non* for globalization.

According to one opinion, the nation-state's authority will be minimized in terms of policy options in the economic realm. There is also possibility of economics determining security considerations in the emerging "New World Order." In this respect globalization entails the potential of heralding the collapse of both the Westphalia system and the welfare state. The second perspective, in contrast, views status quo for the state. Undoubtedly, the existing mechanism of economic policy, perhaps with some modifications, is adequate to deal with the challenges emanating from globalization. Moreover, the security imperatives of international relations will continue to retain their salience. The third perspective is that the state will neither shrivel away nor remain static. Rather, the states will rearticulate themselves by exuviating some political and economic functions and adopting new ones. Also, though national security considerations will remain important, a new perspective on security will evolve.

There also prevails a view that the Westphalia system is on the wane and the world is heading toward some kind of a new political order that resembles the medieval period. For the protagonists of this view, the arrival of a "borderless world" is at hand. This global village will be governed by supranational institutions and the European Union is generally cited as a probable model. Others suggest that the new governance institutions will resemble an order with governance at both the subnational and the supranational levels and citizens having loyalties to multiple jurisdictions.

Since the ability of the state to influence economic process is predicted to greatly diminish, what policies should be adopted to enhance the welfare of the citizens, particularly the ones that no longer have a 'voice', cannot 'exit', and have little hope of successfully employing 'loyalty' to change the system from within? O'Brien (1992) has argued that globalization is an inexorable force, merciless to those who defy its logic. It is reasoned that the Westphalia system of security-conscious states will yield a place in a New World Order where economies will override politics. It is suggested that national security will not remain a critical factor in international relations. As Kienchi Ohmae has observed:

> Under cold war assumptions, government officials fall back on arguments that countries have to be prepared for emergencies—that is, wars. Inefficient

industries are subsidised in the name of national security.... Meanwhile, Singapore and Hong Kong don't worry about ifs. In theory, Singapore can't exist because it has no insurance, either in the form of military or strategic industries. Yet, it enjoys current prosperity. I believe that the Singaporean solution is the right one, because in the global economy, economic linkage increases security. (1991, pp. 13–14)

According to Bruce Russett (1993), since globalization processes have led to the spread of democracy, and democracies almost never fight each other, national security will be relegated to economic issues. However, the recent expansion of NATO, the ongoing strife in the Balkans, the continuing stalemate in the Middle East, the uncertain situation in Afghanistan, and political instability in post-Saddam Iraq, and so on, suggest that security considerations remain important in international relations. The recent controversies in the United States involving the sale of dual-use technologies to China suggest that many policymakers vigorously oppose the idea that commercial considerations should have predominance over national security issues.

Tyson (1991), Carnoy, Castells, Cohen, and Cardoso (1993), and Pauly and Reich (1997, pp. 1–30) have qualms over globalization, whether governments have actually become so powerless compared to the multinational corporations (MNCs) and financial markets, and whether the "stateless corporation" has indeed arrived. For them the state-centered Westphalian model still retains tenacity, governments continue to remain powerful in the economic sphere, and national origins of MNCs remain significant for both business strategy and public policy. According to Richard Falk:

> The policy orientation of the state has been pulled away from its territorial constituencies and shifted outwards, with state action characteristically operating as an instrumental agent on behalf of non-territorial regional and global market forces... this partial instrumentalisation of the state was evident in the Gulf War, properly regarded as the first post-modern war, where the extraordinary mobilisation of military capabilities was responsive to serve global market anxieties about the price of oil and the future control of Gulf reserves. (1997, p. 129)

Another group of experts holds the view that given the pressures from the processes of globalization, states would be unable to do business-as-usual. They will not break down either; rather, they will rearticulate themselves by modifying their institutions and policies. Besides, national security considerations will remain critical in international relations, the notion of security itself will be reformulated and acquire new dimensions.

In a globalizing world, developed countries, particularly the United States, are increasingly manifesting tendencies of dependence on international institutions to probe the domestic details of politics, norms, values, and organization within states. In the 1990s, this proclivity was discernible not only in international finance but also in areas as separate as trade and security. In international trade the requirements of a more global trading order have culminated not just in the establishment of a more powerful international organization, the World Trade Organization (WTO), but led to the negotiation of rules and standards in matters previously considered clearly "domestic" and not international.

In the domain of global security, international institutions are increasingly evincing interest in what happens within states, in contrast to addressing what goes on between states. The shift of emphasis has taken place because governments now face a threat from conflicts that entail spillover effects, engulfing adjacent countries and even regions. The new threat of spreading conflicts has resulted partly as the outcome of the end of the Cold War, which contained warring parties within an elementary balance of power. Equally important is the fact about the new threat is due to the ease with which belligerents, arms, refugees, aid agencies, propaganda, and reporting can cross borders and regions. The deep penetration of global communications, travel, and cross-border activities facilitate quickly spreading violence and instability. Most recently, the apprehension of spreading conflict has catalyzed international intervention in Cambodia, the former Yugoslavia, Somalia, Rwanda, Haiti, and Afghanistan. These interventions are seen as "the growing willingness to address, rather than ignore, fundamental problems within the borders of war-torn states." In the early 1990s, there was much talk of a "new interventionism" engaging security institutions in domestic issues of human rights, democracy, and governance.

GLOBALIZATION AND THE MIDDLE EAST

In the post–Cold War period, the world order appears to be moving toward a tri-continental model veering round three core continental powers:

- The United States and the American continent, starting with the North American Free Trade area (NAFTA) and gradually moving South.
- The European Union (EU) with its eco-magnetic power attracting a Europe that extends from the Atlantic to the Urals, within the EU, the French–German couple stands as the moving force.

• The Asia-Pacific region, evolving around Japan, which is trying to assert itself politically by searching for a status appropriate to its economic capabilities (Hitti, 1994, p. 86).

The rivalry over regional influence has been shaping up among the three contenders. For instance, during the Arab–Israel peace process held on January 1992, in Moscow, the European Union charged the United States, which had tried to keep the EU outside the Committee on Disarmament and Arms Control, wanting to run the show itself. However, the Israeli distrust of the EU and pro-Israel tilt in the American approach could be other factors to be kept in view in this regard.

Endowed with vast economic resources and the high absorption capacity of its markets, the Middle East has emerged as the nerve center of such a rivalry, thereby paving the way for geoeconomics to command precedence over geopolitics. Availability of oil and natural gas in the Middle East, particularly in the Persian Gulf countries, and heavy dependence of Europe, the United States, countries of East Asia, and rest of the industrialized countries on Gulf oil can be said to have given credence to geoeconomics enjoying precedence over geopolitics. The United States, West European, and East Asian countries in particular and the world economy in general are becoming steadily more dependent on imports of Gulf oil and gas. It is not ingenuously a subject of direct imports, but of imports of manufactured goods from Europe and Asia that are dependent on Gulf oil for energy. Oil prices not only continue to remain erratic, but are also registering a phenomenal hike in prices. With its domestic oil production declining, there seem no near-term prospects that the United States could reduce its growing dependence on energy imports. Following Table 8.1 shows the increase in oil imports from the Gulf countries by the United States, Western Europe, and Japan.

It can be observed from Table 8.1 that during 1982–87, the percentage of total net oil imports by the United States from the Gulf region ranged between 10–18% per annum, which rose to 28% in 1991 and in 2003 it was 22%. Though the west European countries have shown a declining trend in their share of oil imports from the Gulf region from 45% in 1990 to 42% in 2000 and 30% in 2003, yet the western Europe meets about one-third of its energy requirements by imports from the Gulf region. It is also discerned from Table 8.1 that Japan is fast becoming heavily dependent on oil imports from the Gulf region, from an average of 60% per annum during the 1980s, to 70% in 1995 and 76% in 2003.

According to broad estimates, the volume of Gulf oil exports will more than double by 2020 (Cordesman, 2000). A shift is also becoming discernible in Gulf oil exports from a U.S.- and European-oriented market to one focused on Asia. As bulk exports from the Gulf ports to their respective

Table 8.1.   Net Oil Imports from the Persian Gulf Region

	As % of Demand			As % of Total Net Oil Imports		
	US	W. Europe	Japan	US	W. Europe	Japan
1982	10%	NA	58%	16%	NA	60%
1983	10%	NA	60%	10%	NA	60%
1984	10%	NA	61%	11%	NA	61%
1985	10%	NA	58%	7%	NA	59%
1986	10%	NA	58%	17%	NA	58%
1987	9%	NA	59%	18%	NA	60%
1988	9%	NA	57%	23%	NA	58%
1989	9%	NA	64%	26%	NA	63%
1990	12%	29%	66%	27%	45%	65%
1991	11%	27%	65%	28%	41%	64%
1992	10%	26%	67%	26%	42%	66%
1993	10%	29%	70%	23%	47%	69%
1994	10%	25%	70%	21%	45%	69%
1995	9%	23%	71%	20%	44%	70%
1996	9%	22%	69%	19%	41%	70%
1997	9%	23%	76%	19%	44%	75%
1998	11%	26%	76%	22%	47%	77%
1999	13%	22%	73%	25%	43%	74%
2000	13%	22%	75%	24%	42%	75%
2001	14%	18%	76%	25%	33%	76%
2002	12%	16%	74%	22%	29%	74%
2003	12%	17%	78%	22%	30%	76%

Source: *Persian Gulf Oil and Gas Fact Sheet*, September 2004, available at http://www.eia.gov/emeu/cabs/pgulf/html

destinations in Asia and elsewhere is transported through sea-lanes of communications (SLOCs) of the Indian Ocean like the Strait of Hormuz, the Malacca Straits, and other waterways, the presence of a powerful navy is required for ensuring safe and uninterrupted flow of oil through the strategic waterways of the Indian Ocean. The United States, having massive naval presence in the Indian Ocean, enjoys strategic advantage over other great powers vis-à-vis the Gulf region.

Two aspects of the 1991 Gulf crisis and the Gulf War II could be regarded to be an American attempt to gain an upper hand over other rivals. The first is the competition over oil and second has been U.S.

attempts to stem the proliferation of WMDs. The U.S. image as the principal security guarantor and balance holder in the Gulf is of a strategic advantage in the new competition over resources. As the U.S. has a strong influence over OPEC policies, the international oil regime has been deeply penetrated by the United States through the Middle East. The 1991 post–Gulf crisis opened up gigantic opportunities for reconstruction in the Gulf. According to one assessment, around $79 billion were to be spent on oil infrastructure in the Gulf in the years to come (*Al Hayat*, 26 January 1992).

The U.S. image as the sole guarantor of stability and that of a conflict manager with the competence to resolve the Arab–Israel conflict enhanced its regional clout. In the process, the Middle East became more responsive and vulnerable to American demands and interests. Countries apprehending a high level of threat are turning to the United States for security arrangements and arms assistance. The Gulf Cooperation Council (GCC) members are the biggest clients of the U.S. arms. While the U.S. presence is strongly felt from the Suez to the Persian Gulf, specifically on its Arab shores, the periphery of the Middle East is forging relations with the two other major powers—France and Germany.

Proliferation is a growing regional threat. Iranian and Iraqi efforts to create chemical, biological, and nuclear weapons, coupled with their development of long-range missile forces, had a potentially destabilizing effect on the region. This confronted Washington with the need to try to restrain any new capabilities, find ways to encourage arms control, and develop counter-proliferation capabilities to deter the use of weapons of mass destruction and defend its forces and allies against such attacks. The U.S. involvement in Gulf War I and II have been designed to dismantle Iraqi capabilities of manufacturing WMDs. However, the American-led coalition attack on Iraq in 2003 has been able to dislodge Saddam Hussein from power but without finding any evidence of WMDs in Iraq. This has given rise to more instability inside Iraq and potential for regional tension.

The threat of proliferation portends the greatest military challenge to the security of the region. The U.S. assumes it as the greatest challenge to its military capabilities to deter and win a conflict in the region without unacceptable losses to itself as well as its allies and damage to the global economy. Iraq is under American control for the time being. However, Iran has been actively seeking acquisition of biological, chemical, and nuclear weapons. Apart from having obtained long-range missiles, Iran is developing a missile booster that could be used to create an ICBM that could launch a warhead against the United States. Chemical weapons were used against each other in the Iran–Iraq War. According to ACDA reports, Iran imported an average of over $3 billion a year in constant 1993 dollars. It cut these imports to $1.6 billion in 1989, raised them to $2.0 billion in

1990 and $2.2 billion in 1991, cut them to $369 million in 1992, and spent $1 billion in 1993. These data are scarcely an indication of a massive Iranian build-up (Cordesman, 2000).

Toby Dodge (2002, p. 7) has opined that the Middle East has become the *bete noire* of those trying to gauge the spread of globalization by identifying economic integration, zones of peace, and the growth of rationalistic liberal sentiment. Some acts of radical Islamic groups are generally used as examples of a region constrained by the dominance of religion, untouched by the positive effects of Globalization and the end of the Cold War. Despite convincing arguments that place the ascent of Islamic radicalism in its sociological, historical, and, ultimately, secular context, it is easier to play down archetypes that characterize the Middle East as unchanging, irrational, and dominating by Islam. However, a closer look at the region for the past three decades, especially in the post–Cold War era, shows that states and societies are striving to deal with changing strategic, economic, and political scenarios. According to Toby Dodge, interpretations of Globalization that originate in the Middle East see it not as a universal and multicausal process, but as the rejuvenation of Western, specifically American, dominance in the post–Cold War world. Globalization is considered to have brought in its wake greater vulnerability to political and economic actors external to the region (Dodge, 2002, p. 8).

Some countries of the Middle East are reeling under heavy indebtedness. These countries, having a large or relatively large population, seem to be responsive to economic reforms. The Arab world, having an average population increase of 3% per year, is confronted with the acute demographic problems. The indebtedness of certain Arab countries, which amounted to $142 billion in 1989 with a yearly debt service of $14.1 billion or 33.2% of the export earnings of these countries (Arab League, 1992, pp. 5, 13), have increased the pressure on the one hand and added to the incentives on the other hand for economic reforms. Within the Arab world itself there is "north" and "south" division on economic lines. The gap remains wide between the north, comprising nine oil-producing countries with small populations (except Algeria and Iraq), and the south, which encompasses the remaining 12 countries. The GDP of the Arab "north" reached $300 billion in 1990 compared to a GDP of only $119 billion of the Arab "south" (Arab League, 1992, pp. 39–40).

The failure of the "socialist" model in the erstwhile Soviet Union built up pressure on the Arab countries—Egypt, Tunisia, Algeria and Iraq—that had adopted an 'eclectic socialism' based on a coercive interventionist policy to cast off socialist policies. These countries gradually moved toward liberalizing their economies. The Economic and Social Council meeting of the Arab League in February 1992, as well as certain resolutions adopted by the Council (Arab League, 1992, pp. 164–166), called for structural economic reforms, along with the lines of privatization. It was an indication of the overwhelming support that reforms were gaining at the regional level. Indeed, both the market economy and privatization represented the future in the Arab world (Arab League, 1992, pp. 168–169). However, this phenomenon was not confined to the Arab part of the Middle East, although it was at work from Morocco to Oman.

PEACE AND STABILITY IN MIDDLE EAST

Peace and stability in the Arab part of the Middle East has been contingent upon Islam and Arab nationalism. However, the external intervening factors have been instrumental in creating fissures within the Arab world, and coupled with the factor of Israel, peace and stability has been elusive to the region. The process of globalization entails the potential of cementing those fissures and usher in an era of peace and stability in the region, provided globalization does not violate the basic tenets of Islam and Arab national feelings. It is a complex situation riddled with subtleties, which needs to be understood in order to comprehend the full gamut of the twin phenomena of peace and stability in the Middle East.

The three instruments of transformation—liberalism, capitalism, and nationalism—that together brought the unraveling of the Soviet geopolitical empire appeared to be coming from two different places and heading for different ends. Nationalism is seen in terms of the revival of primitive loyalties. Westernization, encompassing liberalism and capitalism, is perceived as the appeal to adopt utilitarian values. Each has a device of reference with different sets of priorities. They are not contradictory by definition. However, the possibility of their locking horns with, in the transitional phase that most of the developing countries are undergoing, cannot be ruled out.

Francis Fukuyama (1989, pp. 4, 18) saw the "end of history" after the ascendancy of the Western way of thought. But what has come forth triumphant is one Western mode of thought over another. They are both Western in terms of pertaining to the same cultural heritage and tradition. This was a rivalry within the same frame of reference of utilitarian values. While Marxism–Leninism was ousted by liberalism and capitalism, the latter failed to undo another frame of reference, which incorporates ethnicity, religion, and nationalism. The outcome of the competition between the two remains to be seen wherever there exists such an encounter.

American triumphalism mirrors a deep-seated tradition of sanguinity that discerns the evolution of the world in linear terms. William Pfaff (1989, pp. 50, 52) characterizes American civilization as one "for which optimism has been a historical necessity." Though Communism as a system of governance is currently not in vogue, the totalitarian tendencies are emerging and may rise under different names, but with the same power of disruption. According to Jack A. Goldstone (1982, p. 203), any ideology that highlights a potent unease between good and evil, lays stress on the importance of withstanding evil in this world through active remaking of the world, and sees politics as simply one more battlefield between good and evil may serve as the foundation for a revolutionary ideology. Integral nationalism and religious fundamentalism are two facades of this phenomenon.

Emergence of nationalism as a political ideology is a phenomenon of recent origin in the Middle East and until 1900 it was still inchoate. However, the rise of nationalism at a faster pace has proved to be both a productive and a noxious force in the Middle East. For instance, reform and modernization have been the first goals of the several indigenous Middle Eastern nationalist movements. The endeavors of these movements to reform and modernize have contributed to the civil and social betterment of the people of the region. However, ethnocentrism, irredentism, and national sovereignty have also been integral parts of the nationalist programs; and these aspects of nationalism have often been the cause of conflict and upheaval. Antagonism between Turkish versus Arab nationalism within the Ottoman Empire, Zionism versus Arab nationalism, and Turkish, Arab, and Iranian nationalism versus European colonialism have been instances of this.

It goes without saying that the rise of true nationalism, in the Middle East in general and the Arab world in particular, took place with the ascent of Islam. The narrow blood and tribal ties were swapped with a broader religious patriotism under the aegis of Islam. The Arabs were united into one great community of the faithful, the *Ummah*, or the nation of Islam (*Quran* 3:110). Islam was the prime mover of national life and political unity on the Arabian Peninsula. Expansion of Islam and Arab power roved instrumental in instilling a feeling of distinctness among the Arabs as they came into contact with other races and cultures. This feeling, which in modern parlance can be equated to national consciousness, was overridden by the Islamic religious paradigm of what is equivalent to a nation based on the concept of brotherhood of believers (*Quran* 49:10). Islamic nationalism thus transcends geographical and ethnic barriers, which constitute the basis of the modern Western notion of nationalism. Under the Ottoman Empire, Muslim Arabs prided in Turkish power and prestige. The Arabs approved of Turkish rule steadily because the Turks were Muslims. Until later, in the 19th century, the Ottomans did not attempt to "Turkify" the Arabs, keeping in consonance with the early Muslim administrative practice based on religion—the millet system, which respected the autonomy and integrity of each religious community. It was religion and language that preserved the national unity of Arabs, despite living under Turkish rule.

During the decades of the 1950s and 1960s, the activities of the states in the Middle East expanded to embody practically the whole spectrum of public sphere of activity. In this regard, autonomous civil society organizations were metabolized directly into the state apparatus (Crystal, 1995, pp. 59–63), co-opted by the state (Muslih, 1995, pp. 56–58), or were outrightly banned (Ibrahim, 1995, pp. 39–44). In the wake of these developments, civil society weakened and dissent was driven underground and radicalized as licit means of its expression were cut off. However, the increasing retraction of the state from the public sphere from the mid-1970s onward—an international phenomenon spearheaded in the West by the economic policies of the United States, and in the Third World by the economic restructuring policies of the International Monetary Fund (IMF) and the World Bank—paved for the rapid expansion of civil society. According to one assessment, the number of Arab nongovernmental organizations rose from less than 20,000 in the mid-1960s to over 70,000 in the late 1980s. A large cadre of political parties accounted for some of the growth: 46 in Algeria, 43 in Yemen, 23 in Jordan, 19 in Morocco, and 18 in Egypt (Norton, 1995, pp. 1–25).

The decade of the 1990s saw a mushroom growth of professional syndicates in some the countries of the Middle East. The emergence of these syndicates assumes significance in view of the fact that they enjoy a high level of socioeconomic homogeneity, education, and financial independence. Besides, they tend to be organized on the regional level and to be networked cross-regionally and internationally. This networking provides a certain level of protection against the forces of state oppression. Another benefit accruing to these syndicates is that they are located at the nucleus of the economic system as well as in institutions of strategic importance, which makes it difficult for the ruling elites to practically put them down.

Civil associations have played a crucial role in maintaining the social fabric of the society during crises—be it in Lebanon during the civil war, 1975–90; in Palestine during the *Intifada*, 1987–90; in Kuwait during the Iraqi invasion and occupation, 1990–91; or in Turkey in the aftermath of the 1999 earthquakes. The channels of contacts they forge provide material and moral support to citizens both at home and abroad. However, their potential political role is still unclear. In the West the role of civil organizations is strongly propagated as a harbinger for democratization (*Al-Ahram*, 12 April 2000).

However, these expectations have not been corroborated in the Middle East. Optimistic analogies based on Western perceptions have been ambiguous, as the staggering international inputs into the Middle East political system have radically gnarled the development process in the region. Western democracy, in contrast, developed free from such foreign influences. In the Middle East generally, independence was interpreted in terms of independent sovereign states, which came into being with overt or covert support of Western imperialist forces. In that eventuality, Europeanized elites who found themselves at the helm of affairs in the newly independent states were opposed to domestic political culture and the political dynamics that it validated indigenously.

The political elites of the post-Ottoman Middle East had consummated political power through overt and/or covert collaboration with Western powers. Economic and strategic dependence on the West tied regional political developments to the global economy of the developed world. The steady regional tension, a by-product of hostilities ingrained in the region by the imposition of the nation-state system (e.g., Arab–Israeli; Iraq–Iran; Kurdish uprising in Syria, Iraq, Iran, and Turkey, etc.), provided new, fertile ground for foreign intervention in the Middle East politics. Reflecting the level of violence miasmatic in Middle East politics, between 1948 and 1991, interstate and intrastate conflicts resulted in over 2.2 million casualties in the region. More than 3 million people were displaced, and more than $1.4 trillion was spent on armaments (*Al-Ahram*, 8 August 2000).

Ibn Khaldun, the 14th-century Muslim philosopher, emphasized honor and *asabiyya* or solidarity as key to the social cohesion with ties to Arabia, North Africa, and Spain. The *asabiyya* or solidarity that Ibn Khaldun perceived as a manifestation of civilization has turned in modern times into hyper*asabiyya*, a devotion to one's group that degenerates into hostility to another group. And that honor, once signifying an eagerness to defend the weak, is now synonymous with cruelty to the innocent other. Globalization and modern dislocations have contributed to these contortions in understanding what loyalty and honor stand for. False honor and revenge, popular impulses in the Western world, have crept into developing countries, including the Middle East region as well.

Islam has played the role as a force of community and social justice in the Middle East. The enlargement of state power has often excluded the people it is supposed to represent. Colonialism, socialism, and nationalist attempts to define a "modern" and secular society have wrought the destruction of the society. Under these circumstances, Islam has emerged as the sole legitimate indigenous sociopolitical force in the region for the majority of its people. The future political culture of the Middle East will be shaped by the relationships between the formal doctrines of Islam and the ways in which Muslims live in the modern world. Islam is not just a religious system; it is a complete way of life for the individual, society, and state. It does not recognize national, racial, or linguistic boundaries. It conceives of both God and his message as universal and does not permit a separation between the secular and the religious.

The primary political unit in the Muslim world today is the nation-state, but the corresponding conceptual unit in Islamic law is the *Ummah*, the Islamic community. This community is the brotherhood of all Muslims, and it transcends national barriers. In the past it has sometimes been a single political unit, although today it is primarily a religious and cultural one. The *Ummah* is held together by several basic tenets, including a common belief in *Tawhid*—the oneness and perfect unity of God, the exemplary practice of the Holy Prophet, the *Holy Quran*, the Shariah, and a variety of other common cultural patterns. The *Ummah* has functioned much like Christianity in Europe by providing a binding force that has allowed the Middle East to present a unified front to counter external interference. The *Ummah* has also been a fundamental force in the creation and development of the Islamic Empire and in the most recent attempts at Pan-Arabism.

The community concept of the Ummah, however, is incongruous to the reality of the modern nation-state. The Middle East has rarely acted as a single political unit. Early Arab conquests resulted in the incorporation of different racial, linguistic, and cultural groups within the expanding territorial sphere of Islamic brotherhood. The building of the Arab and Ottoman Empires led to assimilation of a great number of people who were not Muslims. European expansion in the 19th century also played a pivotal role in injecting Western ideas and practices into the bloodstream of the Islamic Middle East. The tangible outcome of these complex historical developments has been a diversification within the Islamic world, resulting in the emergence of several nation-states displaying marked differences with one another.

The concept of equality, like *Ummah*, also wields influence in shaping Islamic politics. Equality before God becomes, theoretically, equality in all situations. Of course, racial, class, and gender distinctions exist in Middle Eastern states as they do elsewhere. Nonetheless, the theoretical equality of all Muslims leads to awareness that all people have certain rights. In practice, however, non-Muslims have traditionally been considered unequal to Muslims because they reject the rule of God.

Compatibility between the Western modernization process and the social values of Islam has been a major problem in the Middle East today. Adoption of Western penal codes and family law created a serious problem for Middle East society. However, a more serious problem is generated in the wake of adoption of certain controversial Western social values. Turkey managed the situation by divesting the Shariah, the religious courts, of their secular authority, resulting in the first real separation of church and state in an Islamic society. In addition, it opened the door to government control and led the latter to assume the prerogative of changing the social structure whenever its need and desires run counter to the tenets of Islam. Some militant groups in Turkey advocate a return to some degree of

Islamic law. While not averse to modernization and material progress, they are distraught by what they perceive as the Western social evils accompanying the process of modernization.

The politico-strategic discourse in the Middle East, since the end of World War II, has been characterized by four major developments. The first was the creation of the State of Israel as a Zionist entity on the territory of Palestine in 1948. This ushered in strong sentiments of military-centered nationalism, and the entire region was embroiled in war. Following the defeat of the Arab military forces in the June 1967 Arab–Israel War, it became apparent that the military nationalists had failed to provide answers to the most pressing issues of the region, including social and economic disparities, Israeli occupation of more Arab territory, and the questions of civil society. The second important development was the Camp David peace accord between Egypt and Israel in 1978. The next turning point was the 1982 Israeli invasion of Lebanon. The inability of any Arab government to successfully respond to the Israeli invasion led to the growth of an alternative nucleus of power throughout the region in the diverse miens of radical Islam. Finally, the devastation and structural changes slammed by the 1991 Gulf Crisis and the subsequent Madrid and Oslo peace processes have forever transformed the political panorama of the entire region.

In an era of globalization, there is sufficient enthusiasm for the economic reforms in the Middle East, whereas there is reluctance for participatory democracy. However, the democratic principles of the alternation to power remain odium to the mostly predominant authoritarian regimes. However, a gradual process of political liberalization is becoming discernible in the Middle East, mainly in the increasing levels of tolerance to the media, the growing activities of political groupings and civic associations, the establishment of *Shura* Councils and the Organization of parliamentary elections, and so on.

With regard to relationship between economic liberalization and democracy, some apologetics contend that democracy does not lead to economic prosperity. According to them, it is more significant to begin with restructuring before adopting any liberal policies, which could otherwise thwart reforms. South Korea's example is cited as an illustration in this regard. It has been argued that the pattern of democratization in the Middle East today suggests that the state has moved tactically toward political liberalization in the face of "economic necessity" (Cantori, 1991, p. 2).

In the absence or weakening of civil society, the Islamist populist groups have emerged as the most organized and the strongest groups. The apprehensions about the potential of the Islamist groups can be said to be derailing or delaying the democratic process by neutralizing non-Islamic groups.

The Arab world seems to be caught in the whirlpool of a debate entailing questions like: should the formula of "one man, one vote, one time" as covertly espoused by some Islamists be accepted? Will electoral politics temper and moderate absolutist tendencies (Fuller, 1992)? What are the implications of an Islamist electoral victory in a bireligious or biethnic state? This debate is also influenced by what Egyptian philosopher Fouad Zakaria calls the "double alienation," which certain Westernized intellectuals suffer from. The first group endorsed the imposition of Western democracy in an arbitrary manner on a traditional Muslim society. The second group, perhaps commanding a larger following, with a fetish for the past, seeks to emulate the "democracy" of the righteous capabilities. Viewed in a broad perspective, this group makes a complete rumination of the complex set of elements that are the products of 14 centuries, which make up the distance between the model and the call for its implementation.

The cultural element of the debate cannot be neglected. Islam as a religion and a state allows for a variety of interpretations, thus creating another debate within the Islamist constituency. Modernist interpretations of political Islam accommodate the Western concepts of democracy, party politics, and pluralism. Whereas modernists harmonize the Shura with democracy, fundamentalists consider that the Shura system does not certainly suggest falling for the views of the majority. Indeed, it calls for only an ad hoc, nonbinding and limited form of political participation. It does not imply an institutionalized and permanent structure of consultation. Fundamentalists reject democracy as an alien concept on theological grounds. Democracy is based on the sovereignty of the people, whereas Islamic rule is based on the governance of Allah or God, in the case of Sunni fundamentalism or *Vilayat al-Fagih* (the rule of the highest jurisprudence) of Shia fundamentalists (Shatta, 1992, p. 14). This denotes the moral superiority of the fundamentalists vis-à-vis others.

Envisaging societal change in the Middle East involves a number of destabilizsing forces. High levels of population growth and a lack of economic diversification have cut real per capita income by more than 40% since the height of the oil boom in the early 1980s. Hyperurbanization is breaking down the traditional social structure. A lack of relevant education, welfare and a weak work ethic, and dependence on foreign labor has left some Gulf countries without new jobs for many of its young men and women. Direct and disguised unemployment are high, often in excess of 25%, in nations undergoing a youth explosion and where more than 60% of the population is under 25 years of age. Undoubtedly, there are no immediate signs of major political and social unrest in the southern Gulf, but there are powerful structural problems.

The ability of Gulf countries to finance the massive increase needed in Gulf oil production capacity, while simultaneously addressing the growing economic problems they are encountering because of major increases in population, declines in per capita oil wealth, and the failure to diversify their economies. The free market may be able to provide the capital that the Gulf needs. At the same time the Gulf states should make the required investments, allow foreign and private investment, reform and diversify their economies, and consider efforts to limit population growth.

CONCLUSION

The phenomenon of globalization has become a predominant factor in domestic and external policies of a country throughout the globe, including the countries of the Middle East. Globalization is a multidimensional and complex process. It is generally construed in terms of economic liberalization and emphasis on political reforms. In the context of the Middle East, economic aspects of globalization have become more pronounced, while political and cultural aspects continue to be the subject of serious debate for the historical, religious, and cultural reasons deeply ingrained in the background of the region. Peace and stability have usually eluded the Middle East because of the perennial nature of Arab–Israel hostilities and machinations of great powers, particularly that of the United States. Adoption of Western/American political and cultural models in the guise of globalization by the countries of the Middle East is considered a new form of Western/American domination of the region. The political model purely based on Islamic tenets, as advocated by the Islamists, is creating apprehensions among the ruling elites of the Middle East for fear of their losing power and the viability and acceptance of such a model by the international non-Islamic community in general, and West and the United States in particular. The Middle East is heavily dependent on the West and the United States for its technological and defence requirements.

A state of confrontation is not good for either side. Hence what is required is the initiation of negotiations for sorting out the outstanding problems and give peace a chance. The United States can persuade Israel to settle its disputes with neighboring Arab countries and withdrawal of the occupied Arab territories. This will help both Israel and its Arab neighbors to increase their mutual economic interaction, attract investment, and thereby help raise the standards of their respective populations. There is a dire need to make the entire region of the Middle East an "oasis of peace" by declaring it a nuclear weapon-free zone and allow the Palestinians and the Israelis to live in peace and not in hostility. A peaceful Middle East is the best guarantee for ensuring international peace and security.

REFERENCES

Arab League. (1992). *The Economic and Social Council, 50th Session, 2–5 February, Report and Resolutions.* Cairo: Arab League Secretariat.

Arab League. (1992). *The Arab Unified Economic Report 1991.* Cairo: Arab League Secretariat.

Cantori, L. (1991, Winter). Democratisation in the Middle East. *American Arab Affairs,* no. 36.

Carnoy, M., Castells, M., Cohen, S., & Cardoso, F. H. (1993). *The new global economy in the age of information.* University Park: Pennsylvania State University Press.

Cordesman, A. H. (2000). *The Gulf and transition: US policy ten years after the Gulf War.* Washington, DC: Center for Strategic and International Studies.

Crystal, J. (1995). Civil society in the Arab gulf states. In J. Schwedler (Ed.), *Toward civil society in the Middle East? A primer.* Boulder, CO: Lynne Rienner.

Dodge, T. (2002, March). Globalization, the Middle East and terrorism. *World Today, 58*(3).

Falk, R. (1997). State of siege: Will globalization win out? *International Affairs, 73*(1).

Fukuyama, F. (1989, Summer). The end of history. *The National Interest, 16.*

Fuller, G. E. (1992, January 14). Let's see how Islamic politicians cope and learn. *International Herald Tribune.*

Giddens, A. (1999). *Runaway world: How globalization is reshaping our lives.* London: Profile Books.

Goldstone, J. A. (1982). The comparative and historical study of revolutions. *Annual Review of Sociology, 8.*

Held, D., & McGrew, A. (2001). The great globalization debate: An introduction. In D. Held & A. McGrew (Eds.), *The global transformation: A reader.* Oxford: Polity Press.

Hitti, N. (1994). The internationalization of the state in the Middle East. In Y. Sakamato (Ed.), *Global transformation: Challenges to the state system.* Tokyo: UN University Press.

Hitti, P. K. (1949). *The Arabs: A short history.* Princeton, NJ: Princeton University Press.

Ibn Khaldun Centre, Files of the Arab Data Unit, Cairo, n.d.

Ibrahim, S. E. (1995). Civil society and prospects for democratization in the Arab world. In A. R. Norton (Ed.), *Civil society in the Middle East.* New York: E. J. Brill.

McGrew, A., & Lewis, P. G. (Eds.). (1992). *Global politics.* Oxford: Polity Press.

Muslih, M. (1995). Palestinian civil society. In J. Schwedler (Ed.), *Toward civil society in the Middle East? A primer.* Boulder, CO: Lynne Rienner.

Norton, A. R. (Ed.). (1995). *Civil society in the Middle East.* New York: E. J. Brill.

O'Brien, R. (1992). *Global financial integration: The end of geography.* New York: Council for Foreign Relations.

Ohmae, K. (1991). *The borderless world.* New York: Harper.

Pauly, L. W., & Reich, S. (1993). National structures and multinational corporate behaviour: enduring differences in the age of globalization. *International Organization, 51*(1).

Pfaff, W. (1989). *Barbarian sentiments: How American century ends?* New York: Hill & Wang.

Russett, B. (1993). *Grasping the democratic peace: Principles for a post–Cold War world.* Princeton, NJ: Princeton University Press.

Shatta, I. D. (1995, 20 July). Hazza a tahil a dimocrati an al Islam was Nazarriuatitihi fi al Siyasa [This democratic disposition of Islam and its theory of politics]. *Al-Hayat.*

Strange, S. (1995). The defective state. *Daedalus, 124*(2), 55–74.

Tomilson, J. (1999). *Globalization and culture.* Cambridge, UK: Polity Press.

Torres, R. (2001). *Towards a socially sustainable world economy.* Geneva: International Labour Organization.

Tyson, L. D'A. (1991, Winter). They are not us. *The American Prospect, 4.*

Part III

CULTURE OF PEACE PERCEPTIONS

CHAPTER 9

THE OSLO PROCESS AND THE ISRAELI-JEWISH PUBLIC

A Paradox?

Ephraim Yuchtman-Ya'ar

A BRIEF HISTORICAL BACKGROUND

The Israeli–Palestinian conflict is over 100 years old, though it has become more intense and widely known since the late 1940s, when on November 29, 1947, the General Assembly of the United Nations adopted Resolution 181, which called for the partition of Palestine into a Jewish state and an Arab state.

The partition plan was accepted by the Jewish community, albeit following a bitter internal controversy, while the Palestinians and the Arab League totally rejected it. Objections within the Jewish community were based on two main arguments, which have some relevance to the present internal political debate: The right camp, which consisted mainly of the Revisionist Movement (later, the Herut Party) and the paramilitary organizations of Etzel (the National Military Organization) and the more extremist Lehi (the Fighters for the Freedom of Israel), insisted that the Partition Plan was unjust because the Arabs had already been granted by Britain the

Educating Toward a Culture of Peace, pages 131–146
Copyright © 2006 by Information Age Publishing

Eastern Bank of Palestine, when in 1923 it created the Emirate of Trans-Jordan, which in 1947 gained independence and became the Hashemite Kingdom of Jordan. The second source of objection came from within the left and center of the political map. Thus, some prominent leaders of Mapai, the General Zionists and the Orthodox parties, were worried that the small Jewish community of about 650,000 would not be able to hold up against the Arab armies that were expected to invade Palestine upon the departure of Britain. However, David Ben-Gurion, the undisputed leader of the then dominant party, Mapai, was able to convince the large majority of the political parties to support the Partition Plan, claiming that the historical opportunity for the establishment of an independent Jewish state should be seized since it may not repeat itself in the future.

The Arabs' objection to the Partition Plan was based mainly on the argument that Palestine as a whole was an inseparable part of the Arab Land, to which the Jews had no historical, legal, or moral rights. In the Arabs' eyes, all prior decisions that acknowledged Jewish rights over Palestine—the Balfour Declaration, the recognition by the League of Nations of these rights, as formulated in the Mandate, and finally, the United Nations Partition Plan—violated the legitimate rights of self-determination of the Arab inhabitants of Palestine. This line of argument was later incorporated into the Palestinian National Charter of the PLO, according to which those resolutions and "everything that has been based upon them" were "null and void." The Charter also explicitly stated that any "historical or religious ties of Jews with Palestine are incompatible with the facts of history and the true conception of what constitutes statehood" (July 1968, Article 20). Put differently, according to the Arab view, any decision that involved the recognition of the entitlement of Jews to Palestine, let alone to establish in it or in parts thereof an independent state, was illegitimate.[1]

The Arab rejection of the Partition Plan led to two stages of warfare. The first stage, which lasted from the end of November 1947 through mid-May 1948, was essentially an internal military struggle between the Arab and Jewish communities inside Palestine—both of which were, during that time, still under the rule of the British Mandate. Subsequently, on May 15, 1948, when the British forces departed and the Mandate was de facto terminated, Palestine was invaded by five Arab states—Egypt, Syria, Jordan, Iraq, and Lebanon—in order to prevent the implementation of the Partition Plan. On the day before, David Ben-Gurion proclaimed the establishment of the State of Israel and became its first prime minister.

The war ended in 1949 with a series of armistice agreements between Israel and its neighboring Arab countries. As an outcome of its victory, these agreements granted Israel a significant territory (nearly 6000 squared kilometers) over the area to which it was entitled according to the Partition Plan.[2] At the same time, Jordan gained the territory of the West

Bank, including East Jerusalem and the Old City, while Egypt seized the Gaza Strip. The 1948 war also witnessed the creation of the refugee problem, as hundreds of thousands of Palestinians left, or were forced to leave, their homes during the war.[3] Consequently, what has become known as the "war of independence" for the Jewish community has been depicted as the "Nakba" (calamity) in the Palestinian narrative.[4]

The territorial arrangements of 1949 remained essentially intact until the 1967 war. During those years, Jordan and Egypt kept under their respective control the West Bank and Gaza Strip, while making no serious attempt to establish in these territories an independent Palestinian state. However, as a result of its sweeping victory in 1967, Israel occupied the West Bank and the Gaza Strip, thus controlling the entire territory west of the Jordan River. In addition, it conquered the entire Sinai Peninsula, which was an integral part of Egypt, and the Golan Heights, which belonged to Syria.

Following the outcomes of the 1967 War, Israel's official policy was that its territorial gains, including the West Bank and Gaza Strip, would be used as bargaining chips in order to reach recognition and peace agreements with the Arab countries.[5] This strategy has subsequently proven itself, at least in part (albeit following another costly military confrontation in October 1973, the Yom Kippur War), when under the auspices of the United States, Israel and Egypt signed a peace agreement in March 1979. In return, Israel withdrew its forces from the Sinai Peninsula back to the internationally recognized border with Egypt. However, the Palestinians and the other Arab states refused to participate in the Camp David negotiations and rejected the Israeli–Egyptian peace accord, accusing Egypt of betraying the Arab cause.

With no significant change in the political stalemate in the aftermath of the 1967 War, Israel has changed in practice its previously declared policy with respect to the occupied territories, gradually allowing and later actually encouraging the establishment of Jewish settlements in those areas. This shift in policy was heavily influenced by internal pressures originating from radical nationalist movements, some of which were motivated by religious fervent and sentiments,[6] others by secular right-wing ideologies. With the passage of time, the spirit of these movements gained wider popular support, though it has been mostly nourished by the religious and secular right. However, it should be borne in mind that the construction of Jewish settlements in the occupied territories—Judea and Samaria in the official Israeli terminology—has begun and progressed under the rule of left-wing coalition governments, including the coalition headed by the late Yitzhak Rabin, during his first term as Israel's Prime Minister between 1974 and 1977. Nevertheless, the policy of expanding Jewish settlement beyond the

"Green Line" has been considerably more rigorous and widespread in the periods when the right-wing parties, led by the Likud, were in power.[7]

It is now almost universally accepted that the facilitation and encouragement of civilian Jewish settlements in the Occupied Territories by the Israeli authorities has been a grave historical error—the detrimental consequences of which can be witnessed these very days. At the same time, it must be acknowledged that the Palestinians and the rest of the Arab world cannot be exonerated, having made significant contributions of their own to these developments. For example, shortly after 1967, eight Arab heads of state attended an Arab summit conference held in Khartoum (August 29–September 1, 1967). Among the resolutions adopted at the conference with respect to Israel was what has become to be known as the "three no's": no peace, no recognition, and no negotiation. This decision weakened the moderate voice in Israel and played into the hands of the hawkish camp. Indeed, it convinced many Israelis that the Arabs would not make peace in the foreseeable future, regardless of Israel's own policy. Moreover, in addition to the religious and nationalist ideological justification for the build-up of settlements, according to which the entire territory of Palestine has historically been the biblical "land of Israel," some Israelis raised the argument that the construction of settlements, at least in certain key areas such as the Jordan Valley and the mountainous vicinity of Jerusalem, was essential for Israel's national security.[8] Still others invoked the original position that the settlements improved Israel's bargaining position, if and when the Arabs would change their attitudes and be ready to enter into peace negotiations with Israel.

Nonetheless, all these arguments could not deny the reality of an Israeli occupation of a land over which it has no legal rights by international law, of controlling a large population against its will, and above all, of allowing a large-scale intrusion into that land by Jewish settlers. It goes without saying that with the passage of time, the settlers' attachment to their new homes, reinforced by the coming of a second, and in some cases even third generation, has turned them into a formidable community that cannot be ignored. In other words, the shortsightedness of Israel's political leadership during the last decades resulted in the creation of a Golem that has acquired a spirit and a power of its own.

THE OSLO ACCORD AND ITS AFTERMATH

With the notable exception of the peace agreement between Egypt and Israel, various attempts made during the 1970s and 1980s to initiate peace negotiations between Israel and the rest of the Arab world have failed. However, at the end of the 1980s and early 1990s, the combined effects of several critical developments at the global (the collapse of the Soviet Union), regional (the Gulf War), and local (the First Palestinian Intifada) levels resulted in the emergence of a new political climate that was conducive to a new international effort to bring peace to the Middle East. It is beyond the scope of this presentation to discuss these historical developments, which led, first, to the Madrid Conference in 1991, and subsequently to the signing of the Oslo Accord in September 1993—an event widely acclaimed as a historical turning point in Israeli–Palestinian relations. For the first time in their long history of hostility and bloodshed, both sides mutually agreed to recognize the legitimate existence of one another and committed themselves to a peaceful resolution of their disagreements via direct negotiations according to the principles and procedures embedded in the Oslo Accord. However, despite widespread optimism that surrounded this event, particularly within the international community, it must be borne in mind that the Israeli society was far less than unanimous in welcoming the Oslo Accord, nor was it accepted by all segments of the Palestinian society and the Arab world.

As for Israel, the main opposition to the Oslo Accord derived primarily from the ideological stance of the right-wing parties, which refused to accept the underlying principle of the Oslo spirit, namely "land for peace," and its implication for the eventual evacuation of the Jewish settlements and the establishment of an independent Palestinian state. For the right, accepting such a compromise would imply giving up the vision of "Eretz Israel Hashlemah" ("Greater Israel") and the right of Jewish citizens of Israel to settle in all parts of that land. On a more pragmatic level, a few observers have pointed to some major deficiencies in the Oslo Accord, particularly its vagueness with respect to the mechanisms of implementation and handling of violations, as well as the postponement of critical issues, such as the future status of Jerusalem and the problem of the Palestinian refugees, to the final stages of negotiations. To be sure, the architects of the Oslo Accord on the Israeli side, as well as some outside experts, believed that this vagueness should be regarded as a classical case of "constructive ambiguity,"[9] allowing both sides a degree of flexibility and adjustment in the subsequent phases of the "Oslo process." However, this view was not universally accepted. For the skeptics, such mechanisms were vital because Israel was expected, according to the Oslo Accord, to provide the Palestinians with tangible achievements, notably territory ("Jericho and Gaza First"), whereas the latter was expected to pay mostly in terms of political and symbolic currency, such as the removal from the Palestinian Charter of clauses that explicitly called for the destruction of Israel. The closest to a concrete action on the Palestinian side was their obligation to fight terror and stop the anti-Israeli incitement and propaganda by the Palestinian leadership and mass media. The observation that from the very beginning of the Oslo process, Palestinian terror and agitation continued on a larger than ever scale,[10] convinced many Israelis that Palestinians could not be trusted and that the Oslo Accord lacked the means to ensure compliance with their responsibility to combat terror.[11]

Be it as it may, the Oslo Accord has been accompanied by a deep divide in Israeli society, which was reflected in the emergence of two distinct camps of supporters and opponents of the Accord since its signature. An examination of the relative size of the two camps over time suggests that they can be distinguished by two periods. During the first period, which lasted until the middle of 1999, the two camps had been of nearly equal size, with but a few and generally small fluctuations, though toward the end of that period, the trend pointed to a small and gradual increase of the pro-Oslo camp. The peak of that camp was reached in May 1999, namely when Ehud Barak was elected as Israel's prime minister. However, the second period began just shortly afterward, when the pro-Oslo camp begun to shrink slowly yet steadily, so that by the end of Barak's government and throughout Sharon's ongoing term, it represented a small minority within the Israeli Jewish community. These two trends, which can clearly be seen in Figure 9.1, are discussed below.[12]

The most salient characteristic of the first period, which lasted for nearly 6 years, was the high level of stability of the collective attitudes of the Israeli-Jewish public toward the Oslo Accord. This stability reflects to a large extent the crystallization within the Israeli-Jewish community of pro- and anti-Oslo camps, which have retained their relative size almost throughout that period. This phenomenon should not be taken lightly, given the prior observation that most of those years were characterized by widespread Palestinian terror, which claimed the lives of hundreds of mostly Israeli-Jewish civilians killed in residential neighborhoods and

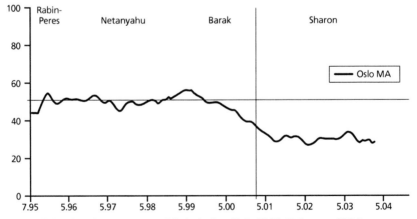

Figure 9.1.   Moving averages of Oslo index (July 1995–February 2004).

public places, such as bases, restaurants, and shopping centers. Further-more, the killings took place both within the Green line and the occupied territories, with the largest number of victims resulting from terror attacks within the borders of the Green Line. Thus in the first year after the sign-ing of the Oslo Accord, during which time the "Jericho and Gaza" agree-ment between Israel and the Palestinian Authority was signed and implemented, over 50 Israeli civilians were assassinated by Palestinian ter-rorists. The list of victims had grown in the next five years—still prior to the beginning of the second Palestinian Intifada—to an overall figure of about 280 persons.[13]

As argued elsewhere (Hermann & Yuchtman-Ya'ar 2002), the relative stability of the pro- and anti-Oslo camps can largely be explained by the divide in the political and ideological convictions underlying the attitudes of the Israeli public toward "Oslo." Accordingly, each camp interpreted Palestinian terror and framed it in a manner that was consistent with its own deeply entrenched predispositions. Thus, the left camp argued that resort to terror by Palestinians was essentially the result of their state of despair due to the continuation of the Israeli occupation and the expan-sion of Jewish settlements. Hence, the intensification of Palestinian terror demonstrated the urgent need for advancing the peace process, even at costly concessions. Some members of the pro-Oslo camp went as far as to suggest that those killed or injured by Palestinian attacks should be per-ceived as "victims of the peace process," namely as a regrettable cost that should be tolerated, however painful, for the sake of the larger goal it serves. The anti-Oslo camp, in contrast, viewed the intensification of terror, and the perceived reluctance of the Palestinian Authority to make a serious effort to fight it, as an indication that the Palestinians were not genuinely ready to make peace with Israel and that their moral standards, as mani-fested in the deliberate and systematic killings of innocent Israeli civilians, including children, women, and the elderly, made them unworthy and unreliable partners for peace.

As noted above, the virtual tie between the two camps was briefly bro-ken during the elections campaign of May 1999, when the then prime minister and leader of the Likud Party, Benjamin Netanyahu, was defeated in his race against Ehud Barak, the Labor's party candidate. As indicated by the breakdown of the elections results according to party affiliation on the basis of the "peace index" polls, it appears that Barak won the race because he was able to obtain the support of some center and right-wing voters, apparently the moderate, more pragmatic members of this camp.[14] Barak's added value to this group of voters as well as to the Israeli-Jewish electorate in general, derived mainly from his much-acclaimed military background ("the most decorated soldier in the history of the Israeli army") and his image as "Mr. Security," namely one who would not compromise Israel's vital national interests and security in his efforts to advance the peace process. This interpretation is supported by the observation that Barak's personal victory against Netanyhu in the direct race between them for the leadership of the government was not accompanied by a similar victory for his Labor party in the general Parliamentary election. In fact, the right-wing camp was able to maintain its power in the Knesset, and it took Barak considerable effort and manipulation before he was able to put together a coalition government that one of its major partners—Shas—was not part of the pro-Oslo camp.[15] As anticipated by several observers, his coalition quickly proved fragile and was finally dissolved 18 months after it was formed.

Indeed, within a few months following his rise to power, it became clear that despite his energetic efforts, Barak's policies had not produced the promised results, with little or no gains in either the Palestinian or Syrian arenas.[16] Furthermore, the public did not appreciate the price that Barak was apparently willing to pay in order to reach an agreement, especially in light of the widespread perception that the Palestinians have not given any sign of reciprocity, particularly with respect to their obligation to eliminate terror and stop the viciously anti-Israeli propaganda conducted by prominent Palestinian leaders, religious figures, school teachers, and the mass media. In fact, findings of the Peace Index polls have consistently shown that the majority of the Israeli Jewish public, including a significant minority on the left, mistrusted Palestinians' intentions to the extent that they did not believe the historical conflict with the Palestinians would be brought to an end even if the two sides were to sign a formal peace agreement.[17]

The trend of growing disaffection of the Israeli Jewish public with the Oslo process was evident during the Camp David Summit of July 2000, when Barak's far-reaching proposals, as reported by the media, were totally rejected and rebuffed by the Palestinians.[18] As for the Israeli public—not only did it disapprove of Barak's concessions but it also widely believed that during the Camp David negotiations, Arafat represented the Palestinian national interests more wisely and shrewdly than Barak did. In short, just over a year after being elected by a comfortable margin, Barak's policy lost the support of the majority of the Israeli Jewish public. From the viewpoint of this public, the subsequent eruption of the Palestinian uprising (Intifada) in the fall of 2000, barely 2 months after the failure of the Camp David Summit, was the final blow to the Oslo process and the leadership responsible for it.[19] To be sure, toward the end of his term and after announcing his resignation, Barak still made a last-minute attempt to salvage the peace process by initiating an Israeli–Palestinian conference in Taba under the sponsorship of Egypt. However, by that time he had already become a "lame duck" head of state, lacking the legitimate authority to conduct further negotiations with the Palestinians. Collective disdain was clearly evident in the outcomes of the February 2001 elections, when Ariel Sharon, Benjamin Netanyau's successor as head of the Likud, defeated Ehud Barak by a landslide, with a margin of over 25% of the total votes.

Turning again to the second half of Figure 9.1, the observation that the decline of the peace index has been gradual rather than abrupt is telling. It suggests that the disaffection with the Oslo process should not be interpreted as whimsical and emotional—two of the characteristics that have often been attributed by political scientists to changes in mass behavior and attitudes.[20] Instead, we suggest that it represents a "learning curve," based on the experience that the Israeli Jewish public has accumulated during the preceding decade of the Oslo process and the frustration with its outcomes. Interestingly, the downward trend of the Oslo Index has cut across all parts of Israeli-Jewish society, regardless of political orientations and religious identities, as reflected in Figures 9.2 and 9.3. In other words, despite the differences between left and right, or secular and religious, in their initial dispositions toward Oslo, practically all the Jewish groups have responded uniformly to the acts and signals sent by the Palestinians and their leaders, while maintaining the differences between them.[21] At the same time, they have apparently become deeply mistrustful of the left wing leadership, which was associated with the Oslo Accord, as reflected in the elections results of 2001 and 2003. Indeed, findings of the "Peace Index" over the last few years reveal that about 40% of the Israel-Jewish public tends to define themselves as right, 30% as center and another 20% as left, with the remaining 10% undecided.

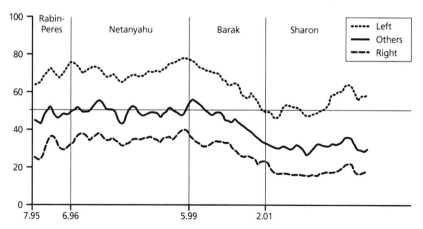

Figure 9.2.   Moving averages of the Oslo index by ideology (Left/Right/Others) (July 1995–December 2003).

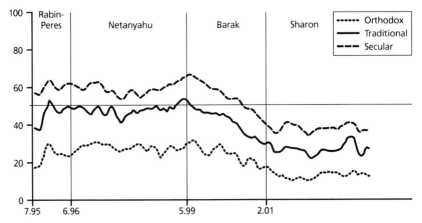

Figure 9.3.   Moving averages of Oslo support and belief by religiosity (July 1995–December 2003).

THE PARADOX

Granted the massive shift to the right of the Israeli-Jewish electorate, along with the decline in the Oslo Index, we would have expected a corresponding change in the public's attitudes toward the future of the Israeli–Palestinian conflict. That is, hardening its position with respect to the conditions for resolving the conflict and adopting the right's traditional hawkish stance on this issue. As it turned out, there has been indeed a change in attitudes—but in the opposite direction. An examination of the findings of the "Peace Index" reveals that the prevailing attitudes of Israeli-Jewish in last few years have become considerably more moderate and conciliatory in comparison with attitudes they held before the signing of the Oslo Accord. In this regard, the entire left–right scale has moved considerably toward the left despite the massive voting for the right. This shift is mainly due to the fact that many members of the moderate right camp, particularly Likud's voters, are today ready to accept some critical concessions that were totally rejected by them a decade ago, when they still adhered to the vision of "Greater Israel." Specifically, according to recent findings of the "Peace Index" polls, it appears that a clear majority within the Israeli-Jewish public currently supports the establishment of an independent Palestinian state and, perhaps most importantly, the evacuation of all the Jewish settlements from the Gaza Strip and most of the settlements in the West Bank.

These prevailing attitudes suggest that the general disappointment with the Oslo process, as reflected in the decline of the "Oslo Index" and the electoral shift to the right, should not be interpreted as an acceptance of the right's ideology. Furthermore, although the left represents to date a small minority within the Israeli-Jewish electorate, it appears that the message of "Oslo," in interaction with the harsh reality of the mounting Palestinian terror with which Israelis had to live since the signing of the Oslo Accord, has left its mark on Israeli society. In other words, while rejecting the "spirit of Oslo," as reflected in Shimon Peres's optimist vision of a "New Middle East," the Israeli-Jewish public has learned to accept, in part grudgingly, the reality of its major parameters. Overall then, we witness in recent years two seemingly countervailing trends in the Israeli-Jewish public as far as peace and security are concerned: preference for the political hegemony of the right and assimilation of the ideas of the left.

Perhaps one of the main clues for understanding what has been going on in the mind of the Israeli-Jewish public is the so-called "demographic factor." Put briefly, Israeli Jews have become increasingly alarmed by the possibility that the continuation of the Israeli occupation of the West Bank and Gaza Strip, combined with the high level of fertility that characterizes Palestinian society, is likely to change the demographic composition of the two peoples so that within a few decades, the Palestinians will become the majority group within the population living west of the Jordan River. This possibility, which has been repeatedly pointed out by prominent Israeli demographers, such as Sergio Dellapergola (2003) and Arnon Soffer (2001), convinced the Israeli-Jewish community that the occupation would eventually lead to a de facto binational state, comprised of a Palestinian majority and Jewish minority.[22] From the perspective of this community, for which the preservation of Israel as a Jewish and Democratic state is its *raison d'etre*, such a possibility is deeply feared and totally rejected. Indeed, this concern has been a major factor, along with the threat of Palestinian terror, behind the widespread support given by the Israeli-Jewish public to the construction of a fence that would separate the Israeli and Palestinian populations both physically and symbolically.[23] The sensitivity of the Israeli-Jewish public to the threat of the "demographic factor" also accounts for the broad consensus within the Israeli-Jewish community against any compromise on the Palestinian demand for the "right of return" of the Palestinian refugees inside Israel.

Since the Palestinian Authority, as distinguished from some individual Palestinian leaders, has so far insisted on this demand, and given the wide gap that separates the two sides with regard to some other critical issues such as the future status of Jerusalem and Temple Mount, it should be of no surprise that the collective state of mind of the Israeli-Jewish community is, to a large extent, very pessimistic with regard to the chances of reaching a genuine peace with the Palestinians, with the latter considered totally untrustworthy and deeply suspected of their intentions with regard to the existence of Israel as a Jewish state. In other words, in contrast to the original idea of the architects of Oslo, who envisioned an end to the historical conflict between Israelis and Palestinians, and a lasting peace which would be based on close ties and economic cooperation between the two states and the two peoples, the Israeli-Jewish community currently accepts the two-state formula as an inevitable solution, but prefers that the two states would keep a distance from each other and be separated as much as possible so that Israel would be able to maintain its identity as a Jewish state.[24] Ehud Barak reflected these sentiments during an interview with an Israeli journalist in September 2003, when he succinctly summarized his view on the preferable relations between Israel and the Palestinians as follows: "We are here and they are there."[25]

This collective state of mind of the Israeli-Jewish public may explain the apparent paradox to which we have pointed, namely the disaffection with the Oslo process, on the one hand, and the adoption of at least some of its major parameters, on the other. Realizing that the end of occupation is both inevitable and desirable for Israel's own sake as a Jewish state, while at the same time deeply mistrusting the left leadership because of its perceived association with the bitter outcomes of the Oslo process, the Israeli-Jewish public clearly prefers that the responsibility for advancing the peace process, while safeguarding Israel's national interests, should be entrusted on the leadership of the right.[26] Ironically, then, the ideas of the left are expected to be delivered by the right. This fits well with the traditional saying according to which "The labors of the righteous are performed by others."

SOME IMPLICATIONS FOR PEACE EDUCATION:

Under the present circumstances of continued mutual bloodshed and deeply rooted mistrust, the challenge for "peace education" appears to be undoubtedly an enormous task. How is it possible, some would ask, to educate ordinary Israeli and Palestinians about the value and possibility of peace with an enemy perceived as a ruthless aggressor whose aims are to prevent the fulfillment of the national aspirations of their own people? Moreover, these perceptions have been constantly nourished by the political elites of both sides and the institutions under their control, including the educational system, with the mass media not lagging far behind. Consequently, ordinary Palestinians and Israelis have developed negative sentiments and stereotypes about each other, thus making the mission of peace education at the level of people-to-people much more difficult.

Under such adverse circumstances and inhospitable climate, the most effective, and perhaps the only, avenue for the implementation of peace education is through the activation of viable organs of the civil society. Both the Israeli and Palestinian societies have witnessed in recent years the development of different kinds of nongovernmental organizations that have dedicated themselves to advancement of peace and education, directly or indirectly. In fact some of the Palestinian and Israeli organizations have created fruitful frameworks of cooperation that were able to function, albeit with great difficulties, even during the Palestinian Intifada. However, at least in the Israeli case, these organizations have not operated in a concerted effort, thus underutilizing their potential impact on the Israeli public. Furthermore, most of these organizations have usually failed to reach large segments of Israeli society, often concentrating on and competing over the same constituency, which typically consists of sympathizers of the left. In other words, they are mobilizing the support of those who are already committed to the cause of peace.

What is needed, therefore, is the emergence of an open-minded leadership that would bring these organizations together in order to find ways for enhancing their effectiveness, including the possibility of merger. This is not a simple task since organizations of all kinds, including NGOs, often tend to protect their own existence and independence, sometimes at the expense of the goals for which they have been created. In sociological research this phenomenon is known as "goal displacement." Nevertheless, for those who believe in the idea of peace education, only sincere reexamination of the functioning of the relevant organizations and readiness for change may bring the idea to the mainstream of Israeli society. Without such a breakthrough, the opportunity for using peace education as a means to achieve peace would be largely missed.

NOTES

1. For different accounts of the Partition Plan and the 1948 War, see Galnoor (1995); Kedourie (1974); Morris (1994); Peretz (1996); Pape (1992); Gilbert (1998); Safran (1978), Shamir (1974).

2. The total territorial size of Palestine under the British Mandate was little over 26,300 square kilometers. According to the Partition Plan, the areas allocated to the future Jewish and Palestinian states were about 14,900 (56.7%) and 11,300 (42.9%) square kilometers, respectively. The borders demarcated by the armistice agreements (the "Green Line" increase the size of Israel's territory to about 20,700 square kilometers).

3. According to the United Nations sources, the number of refugees was about 750,000. Arabs' estimates are typically higher while those of Israeli sources tend to be lower. A detailed account of the various estimates is given in: Haway (2001).

4. For the Palestinian narrative on the 1948 War and its aftermath, see Khalidi (1997); Masdaha (2000); Zureik (1979).

5. On the evolution of the Israeli policies with respect to the future status of the West Bank and the Gaza Strip in the aftermath of the 1967 War, see Naor (2001).

6. The best known and most effective of the religiously driven movements has been Gush Emunim ("The Block of the Faithful"), which still plays an important role in advancing the interests of the Jewish settlements in the occupied Tterritories.

7. For a detailed account of the process of Jewish settlement and the policies that have guided it over time, see Benvenisty (1984).

8. This consideration was critical in the "Alon Plan."

9. Watson (2000). This view doesn't take into consideration the sociological argument that an ambiguous agreement can be constructive only if the various sides share precontractual elements of trust, to borrow from Durkeim's theory. Clearly such elements were absent when the Oslo Accord was signed.

10. See Figures 9.1, 9.2, and 9.3.

11. This is not to say that Israel has complied with all of its own obligations under the Oslo Accord, particularly by its policy of expanding Jewish settlement in the occupied territories. However, this observation reiterates the inherent weakness of the Accord with respect to its dealing with the problem of violations.

12. Our main source of data is an ongoing longitudinal survey of Israeli attitudes toward the peace process, known as the Peace Index. The time frame of the findings we present here extends from June 1994, when the first poll was conducted, to May 2003 when the last survey included in this study was performed. The polls continue at present. The main dependent variable is a monthly index constructed from two questionnaire items pertaining to the Oslo process between Israel and the Palestinians. The first item is a standard attitudinal question in which respondents were asked to indicate the degree to which they support or oppose the Oslo process on a five-point Likert scale, with 1 coded for "strongly oppose" and 5 for "strongly support." The second item probes to what extent the respondents believed that the Oslo process would lead to a peace agreement between the two sides in the coming years. This item also was designed as a five-point Likert scale, ranging from 1 ("do not believe at all") to 5 ("completely believe"). For the sake of clarity we rescored the original scales from a low of zero (originally 1) to a high of 100 (originally 5), by (old score −1) × 25. This linear transformation preserves the original distances between individual scores while presenting the results in a more convenient metric, anchored between zero and 100. Correlations and similar statistics are unaffected.

13. Following the eruption of the Second Palestinian Intifada, the number of terror victims increased dramatically, reaching the figure of about 1,000 by the end of 2003. Note that these are the numbers of deaths. It has been estimated that the average ratio of wounded to deaths is about five to one.

14. Some experts on Israeli elections have suggested that quite a few voters within the Likud were disaffected with Netanyahu's personal style and behavior.

15. On the misperception of Shas as a dovish party, see Yuchtman-Ya'ar and Hermann (2000).

16. It is important to note in this context that Barak's main efforts during the first year of his term were concentrated on the Syrian track, thus reinforcing

the view that the chances to advance the peace process with the Palestinians were not promising. His dramatic initiative to renew direct negotiations with the Palestinians at the Camp David Summit came late (July 2000) and, regardless of who was the guilty party, proved to be a total failure, as discussed below.

17. This pessimism is nourished by the widespread (over 70%) and consistent belief of the Israeli-Jewish public that the Palestinians have not accepted the existence of the State of Israel would destroy it if it could.

18. For a systematic discussion of different explanations given to the failure of the Camp David Summit, see Rabinovich (2004).

19. For a systematic and detailed analysis of the Oslo Accord and its aftermath, see Hirschfeld (2000).

20. See, for example, Caspary (1970); Chittick, Billingsley, and Travis (1990); Holsti (1992).

21. Segmentations of the sample by other criteria such as education, income, age, gender, and ethnicity have yielded similar patterns of uniformity. This remarkable uniformity across the various Israeli-Jewish groups in terms of the response to the Oslo process suggests the existence of an underlying common code on the basis of which they interpret and give meaning to the events and developments associated with the Israeli–Palestinian conflict.

22. According to the "Peace Index" poll of October 2003, over two-thirds of the Israeli-Jewish respondents believed in such an outcome, while only one-quarter didn't believe in it.

23. In the same poll of October 2003, 83% of the Jewish respondents supported the construction of a separation fence, 12% objected, and 5% didn't have an opinion. Moreover, a similar percentage preferred a policy of closed rather than open borders even after the signing of a peace agreement and the establishment of a Palestinian state.

24. For the meaning of Jewish identity for Israeli-Jews, see Yuchtamn-Ya'ar and Oren (2003).

25. From *Tel-Aviv,* a weekly magazine (2003, September 26). In the same interview Barak said that he had held the same view a few years earlier.

26. In the January 2001 "Peace Index" poll, the majority of the Jewish public (53%) felt that Sharon, rather than Barak (27%), was more capable of "advancing the peace process with the Palestinians and safeguarding the vital interests of the State of Israel." The balance was divided between those who felt both men were equally capable (3%), or that neither was capable (11%) or did not know (6%). By no coincidence, the gap between the evaluations of Sharon and Barak was nearly identical to the margin by which Sharon beat Barak in the elections held the following month. A few months earlier, when Netanyahu was still in the race, he also enjoyed a comfortable lead over Barak.

REFERENCES

Benvenisty, M. (1984). *The West Bank data project, A survey of Israeli policies.* American Enterprise Institute for Public Policy Research, Washington DC.

Caspary, W. R. (1970). The mood theory: A study of public opinion and foreign policy. *American Political Science Review, 64*, 536–547.

Chittick, W. O., Billingsley, K. R., & Travis, R. (1990). Persistence and change in elite and mass attitudes toward U. S. foreign policy. *Political Psychology, 11*(2), 385–401.

Dellapergolla, S. (2003). Demographic trends in Israel and Palestine: Prospects and policy. *American Jewish Yearbook, 103*, 3–68.

Galnoor, I. (1995). The partition of Palestine: Decision crossroads in the Zionist movement. New York: State University of New York Press.

Geoffrey, W. (2000). *The Oslo Accords: International law and the Israeli–Palestinian peace agreements.* Oxford: Oxford University Press.

Gilbert, M. (1998). *Israel: A history.* New York: William Morrow.

Haway, M. (2001). Between the right of return and attempts of resettlement. In G. Joseph & E. J. Perkins (Eds.), *The Palestinian refugees: Old problems—new solutions* (pp. 34–45). Brighton, UK: Academic Press.

Hermann, T., & Yuchtman-Ya'ar, E. (2002). Divided yet united: Israeli-Jewish attitudes towards the Oslo process. *Journal of Peace Research, 39*(5), 597–613.

Hirschfeld, Y. (2000). *Oslo, a formula for peace: From negotiations to implementation.* Tel-Aviv: Am Oved.

Holsti, O. R. (1992). Public opinion and foreign policy: Challenges to the Almond-Lippmann Consensus. *International Studies Quarterly, 36*, 439–466.

Khalidi, R. (1997). *Palestinian identity: The construction of modern national consciousness.* New York: Columbia University Press.

Kedourie, E. (1974). The Arab–Israeli conflict In *Arabic political memoirs* (pp. 218–231). London: Cass.

Masdaha, N. (2000). *Imperial Israel and the Palestinians: The politics of expansion.* London: Pluto Press.

Morris, B. (1994). *1948 and after.* Oxford: Oxford University Press.

Naor, A. (2001). *Greater Israel—Theology and policy.* Haifa: Haifa University Press.

Pape, I. (1992). *The making of the Israeli–Arab conflict 1947–1951.* London: Tavris.

Peretz, D. (1996). *The Arab–Israeli dispute.* New York: Facts on File.

Rabinovich, I. (2004). *Waging peace.* Princeton, NJ: Princeton University Press.

Safran, N. (1978). *Israel—The embattled ally.* Cambridge, MA: Belknap Press.

Shamir, S. (1976). The Arab–Israeli conflict. In A. L. Udovich (Ed.), *The Middle-East: Oil, conflict and hope.* Lexington, MA: Lexington Books.

Soffer, A. (2001). *Israel, demography 2000–2020: Risks and possibilities.* Haifa: University of Haifa, National Security Studies Center.

Watson, G. (2000). *The Oslo Accords: International law and the Israeli–Palestinian peace agreements.* Oxford: Oxford University Press.

Yuchtman-Ya'ar, E., & Hermann, T. (2000). Shas—the Haredi-Dovish image in a changing reality. *Israeli Studies, 5*(2), 32–77.

Yuchtamn-Ya'ar, E., & Oren, A. (2003). *Jewish identity, religious beliefs and tradition.* Tel Aviv: B. I. Cohen Institute for Public Opinion Research, Tel Aviv University.

Zureik, E. (1979). *The Palestinians in Israel: A study in internal colonialism.* London: Routledge & Kegan Paul.

CHAPTER 10

HOPE IN TIMES OF THREAT

The Case of Palestinian
and Israeli-Jewish Youth

Shifra Sagy

This chapter discusses and measures "hope" as a "culture of peace" component, examining levels and contents of hope among young people in the
conflicted region of the Middle East.

Hope is a cognitive–affective resource that has long been recognized as
a psychological asset. The emotion of hope arises when a concrete positive
goal is expected (Stotland, 1969), such as situations of yearning for relief
from negative conditions (Lazarus & Folkman, 1984). It consists of cognitive elements of visualization and expectation, and affective elements of
feeling good about the expected pleasant events or outcomes (Staats &
Stassen, 1985).

Current definitions of hope in the psychological domain focus on an
individual-centered hope, in which individuals feel they can enact positive
outcomes in light of a perceived difficulty or a desired goal. Snyder (1994),
for example, defined hope as the perceived capacity to produce pathways

Educating Toward a Culture of Peace, pages 147–160
Copyright © 2006 by Information Age Publishing
147

to desired goals, along with the motivations to initiate and sustain movement toward those goals. According to Snyder (1994, 2000), the affective
components of hope have the form of subjective feelings based on goal-
directed thinking, which combines goal-directed determination with planning to achieve this goal.

Hobfoll, Briggs-Phillips, and Stines (2005) suggest distinguishing between
two types of hope: individual-centered hope assumes that the individual has
the personal or social resources required to meet a goal, or overcome an
obstacle, whereas existential hope is the strength that individuals with few
resources call upon to sustain themselves through difficult times.

Some researchers noted the significance of hope in initiating change, a
willingness to learn, and a sense of well-being (Breznitz, 1986). Corre-
spondingly, lack of hope, or hopelessness, introduces significant risk of
depression, sociopathy, and suicidal behaviors (Magaletta & Oliver, 1999).
However, in spite of these scholarly contributions, considering its role in
the lives of many individuals and collectives, the psychology of hope is an
almost totally neglected area of study.

Most theories dealing with hope have focused on the psychological
aspects, concerning the individual and his or her primary relations (Jacoby,
1993), while the larger social context has usually been ignored. Social environmental variables, as well as cultural factors, may exert a significant
impact that justifies a comprehensive investigation.

The purpose of our study was to examine the impact of living in a continuous national intergroup conflict on hopes among young people. Two questions led our research: the first one concerns the content of hopes among
the students. More specifically, we asked about the differentiation between
personal and collective hopes in each group. Based on the theoretical framework offered by Triandis (1995), as well as on research results on dimensions
of collectivism and individualism in Palestinian and Israeli societies (Sagy,
Orr, Bar-On, & Awwad, 2001), we hypothesized that Palestinian-Arab society
would contribute to a more collectivist orientation among students, as would
be expressed by their hopes for their collective. Their Israeli-Jewish counterparts would represent, according to our hypothesis, a closer tendency toward
individualism, as would be expressed by their personal hopes.

Our second question relates to changes in the level of hopes over time,
in the context of a changing reality. For this purpose, we carried out the
study during a period of 3 years (1999–2002). In this period, the context of
the conflict was dramatically changed, since the first stage took place during the period of Oslo Accords talks, while the second stage was carried out
during the events of the Al-Aksa Intifada and the terror attacks.

According to theories of well-being and conflict resolution (e.g., Fisher,
1997), the extent of fullfillment of basic human needs have impact on
hopes, expectations, and wishes. We hypothesized that hope would

increase in time of threat, conflict, and distress. If hope is considered an asset, its importance becomes even greater in times of threat. Furthermore, one might predict specific increases in specific hopes that are driven by needs arising from specific threats. According to this rationale, hope for peace, for example, should increase in times of war. Some research results of studies that were carried out in the United States showed such a tendency. Hope for peace increased, for example, during the Gulf War in 1991 in comparison to other times (Staats & Partlo, 1992). Thus, we expected hope to increase among adolescents of both national groups in the second stage of the study.

METHOD

Measures

In the longitudinal research we used a questionnaire that was developed by a research group composed of two Palestinians, two Israeli Jews, and one Israeli–Palestinian (for more details, see Sagy, Adwan, & Kaplan, 2002). The questionnaire examined beliefs regarding the Israeli and Palestinian historical narratives, political attitudes, and hopes. In this chapter we present the results regarding the hope measures only.

Hope is defined in this study as the interaction between wishes and positive future expectations (Staats & Stassen, 1985). This definition implies both a *cognitive* aspect, such as expectation of a future event, and an *affective* aspect, as the things that we hope for are pleasant events or good outcomes.

We used the Hope Index of Staats (1989), which is constructed as the interaction of wishes and expectations and includes items of hopes referring to *self* and to *others*, or to broad global concerns. Items comprising the HopeSelf Scale are those that reflect hope for self such as "to be competent" or "to be happy." Items comprising the HopeOther Scale reflect hope for others, or global issues such as "other people to be helpful," "justice in the world," etc. One of the items in the Hope Index (item 15) specifically refers to hope for "peace in the world."

The students were asked to rate independently how much they would wish a particular future occurrence and the extent to which they would expect this to occur. Responses were on a scale of 1 (not at all) to 5 (very much). The multiplication of the Wish value by the Expect value generated the measure of Hope.

The Cronbach Alpha of Hope scale was .91 for the Israeli sample and .93 for the Palestinian sample. The Cronbach Alpha of HopeSelf was .86 for the Israeli sample and .89 for the Palestinian sample. The Cronbach Alpha of HopeOther was .93 for the Israeli sample and .90 for the Palestinian sample.

Sample

The study was carried out in two stages. In the first stage (1999–2000), 2,371 students comprised the random sample of the study (1,188 Israeli Jews and 1,183 Palestinians). The sample in the second stage (2001–2002) was comprised of 1,882 students (996 Israeli Jews and 886 Palestinians). Careful considerations were taken by each research team to provide representation of all types of schools and types of locations. Table 10.1 represents the characteristics of the sample in the first stage.

Table 10.1.   Demographic Characteristics of the Two Study Groups: Israeli Jews and Palestinians

Sociodemographic characteristics	Palestinians N = 1183	Israeli Jews N = 1188
Gender		
Girls	39.1	60.4
Boys	60.9	39.6
Grades		
10th grade	55.8	55.0
12th grade	44.2	45.0
School		
Public secular school	79.7	77.6
Public religious school	—	22.4
Private school	20.3	
Religion		
Muslims	85.9	
Christians	14.1	
Jews	—	96.4
Others		3.6
Dwelling		
Cities	59.5	35.9
Small towns	25.6	32.6
Moshav, Kibbutz, and settlement	—	31.5
Refugee camps	14.6	—
Residence Distribution		
Northern area	23.9	16.4
Central area	17.3	27.0
Jerusalem area	26.9	11.5
Southern area	18.3	32.5
Gaza area	—	—
Other	13.6	7.6

Table 10.1.   Demographic Characteristics of the Two Study Groups: Israeli Jews and Palestinians

Sociodemographic characteristics	Palestinians N = 1183	Israeli Jews N = 1188
Father's Schooling		
No schooling	3.3	1.5
Primary	23.8	5.1
Secondary	30.6	33.2
Professional	13.9	26.7
Academic	28.3	33.5
Mother's Schooling		
No schooling	6.4	1.6
Primary	23.4	2.6
Secondary	42.3	29.9
Professional	14.5	28.9
Academic	13.2	37.1
Place of Birth		
Israel		84.0
West Bank	76.7	—
Gaza	9.9	—
Eastern Europe	—	8.2
Other	13.4	7.8
Economic Status (respondent evaluation)		
Lower class	4.0	2.0
Middle class	83.1	77.3
Upper class	12.9	20.8
Father Working		
Yes	89.7	91.3
No	10.3	8.7
Mother Working		
Yes	17.3	77.8
No	82.7	22.2
Average Number of Children in Family	5.5	3.7
Palestinians		
Nonrefugees	65.7	—
Refugees	31.7	—
Returnees*	2.6	—

* Returnees—returned to the Palestinian National Territories after the signing of the Oslo Accords in 1993

Procedure

Questionnaires were administered to the students in their native languages (Hebrew and Arabic) in their classrooms during a normal class period. The first stage took place in the first semester of the 1999/2000 academic year (during the period of the Oslo Accords talks). The second stage was carried out during the events of the Al-Aksa Intifada (January–March 2002).

RESULTS

Table 10.2 presents the means and standard deviations of HopeSelf and HopeOther of the Israeli and Palestinian groups at two points of time.

Table 10.2.   Means and Standard Deviations of HopeSelf and HopeOther for the Israeli and Palestinian Groups in Time-1 and Time-2

| | Time 1 | | | | Time 2 | | | |
| | Israeli Jews n = 1,055 | | Palestinians n = 1,141 | | Israeli Jews n = 910 | | Palestinians n = 848 | |
Item	M	SD	M	SD	M	SD	M	SD
HopeSelf:								
1. To do well in school	4.81	1.13	4.85	1.41	4.82	1.15	5.00	1.25
2. To have more friends	4.23	1.53	4.33	1.51	4.16	1.53	4.44	1.45
3. To have good health	4.78	1.16	4.50	1.54	4.77	1.21	4.74	1.31
4. To be competent	4.72	1.16	4.87	1.26	4.74	1.15	4.84	1.23
5. To achieve long-range goals	4.66	1.19	4.35	1.41	4.62	1.29	4.16	1.52
6. To be happy	4.98	1.09	4.55	1.39	5.00	1.10	4.37	1.47
7. To have money	3.71	1.45	3.75	1.51	4.20	1.39	3.50	1.66
8. To have leisure time	3.59	1.49	3.75	1.49	3.80	1.57	3.64	1.68
9. Understanding by my family	4.22	1.59	4.43	1.52	4.08	1.67	4.51	1.69
10. Personal freedom	4.36	1.34	4.03	1.67	4.39	1.37	4.07	1.67
Total HopeSelf:	4.45	0.91	4.34	1.02	4.45	0.95	4.33	1.03
HopeOther:								
11. Other people to be helpful	3.59	1.49	3.69	1.60	3.42	1.61	3.71	1.69
12. The crime rate to go down	3.05	1.52	3.76	1.83	3.00	1.63	3.66	1.86
13. The country to be more productive	3.50	1.43	4.13	1.66	3.47	1.51	4.16	1.61
14. Justice in the world	3.10	1.60	3.88	1.73	2.98	1.67	3.86	1.83
15. Peace in the world	3.25	1.57	3.74	1.80	2.97	1.70	3.72	1.88
16. Resources for all	3.39	1.53	4.03	1.67	3.42	1.58	3.97	1.67
Total HopeOther:	3.21	1.31	3.86	1.39	3.21	1.40	3.85	1.43
Total Hope:	4.02	0.95	4.16	1.07	3.99	1.01	4.15	1.07

As evident from the table, there is some similarity between these two groups of adolescents. First, both Israelis and Palestinians gave priority to their personal hopes. In both samples, for example, the items that got the highest rank among the students were "to be competent," "to do well in school," or "to be happy." The Palestinians had higher scores in their hope to do well in school, while the personal hopes of being happy and being rich were higher among the Israelis.

Second, although they gave priority to individual hopes, while they are compared to other samples (see, e.g., Staats & Partlo, 1992), there are still high levels of hopes for the collective in both groups.

Despite the similarities, some differences between the two groups are noteworthy. First, the overall measures show significantly higher levels of hopes for the collective among the Palestinian students than among their Israeli counterparts ($F_{(3970,1)} = 180.84$, $p < .001$). A significant, but smaller difference was also found between the groups in the HopeSelf scores. In this measure, however, the Israelis were higher than the Palestinians ($F_{(3899,1)} = 14.17$, $p < .001$).

Second, the examination of the combinations of hopes by separating *expectations* and *wishes* reveals a more complicated picture. *Wishes* were significantly higher than expectations in both groups ($t = 49.16$, $p = .000$ in the Israeli sample; $t = 21.45$, $p = .000$ in the Palestinian sample). However, while *wishes* were somewhat higher among the Israelis than among their Palestinian counterparts ($F_{(3959,1)} = 153.44$, $p < .001$), the *expectation* components of hope were significantly higher among the Palestinians ($F_{(3964,1)} = 137.08$, $p < .001$).

No significant changes *over time* occurred in the overall measures of hopes for the self and for the collective. This tendency characterized both groups. Table 10.3 presents means and standard deviations and ANOVA

Table 10.3.   Means, Standard Deviations, and ANOVA Results of *HopeSelf* and *HopeOther*, by Group and by Time

Hope		*Israelis-Jews*			*Palestinians*			*Group effect*	*Time effect*	*Time × Group interaction*
		n	*Mean*	*SD*	*n*	*Mean*	*SD*			
Hope Self:	Time 1:	1,054	4.45	.91	1,142	4.34	1.02			
	Time 2:	926	4.45	.94	852	4.33	1.03			
								14.17***	.002	.063
Hope Other:	Time 1:	1,051	3.31	1.31	1,138	3.86	1.39			
	Time 2:	923	3.21	1.40	848	3.84	1.43			
								180.84***	1.85	1.14

*** $p \leq 001$, ** $p \leq .01$, * $p \leq .05$

results of HopeSelf and HopeOther by group and by time. The ANOVA yielded only significant Group effect.

A different pattern of changes over time was found, however, while examining the Wishes scale separately. While the Israeli group showed a small decrease in its collective wishes, the Palestinians expressed a higher level of wishes for the collective over time. The ANOVA analysis yielded no time effect ($F_{(3960,1)} = .11$, n.s.) but a significant two-way interaction of Group x Time ($F_{(3960,1)} = 12.91$, $p < .001$).

The item "hope for peace in the world" was rated relatively low in both groups. Moreover, among the Israelis, hope for peace was not only low, but also decreased over time (from mean of 3.25 in the first stage to 2.97 in the second stage, $F_{(3459,1)} = 7.05$, $p < .01$).

Table 10.4 presents the Pearson correlations of "hope for peace in the world" with other items of hopes among both groups, at times 1 and 2. The correlations of this item with their personal hopes were relatively low.

Table 10.4.   Pearson Correlations between "Hope for peace in the world" and Other Wish Items, at Two Points of Time for Israeli-Jews and Palestinians

	Peace in the World			
	Time 1		Time 2	
	Israeli Jews $n = 1,055$	Palestinians $n = 1,141$	Israeli Jews $n = 910$	Palestinians $n = 848$
1. To do well in school	.13	.17	.19	.10
2. To have more friends	.16	.24	.25	.07
3. To have good health	.15	.20	.18	.14
4. To be competent	.10	.17	.18	.12
5. To achieve long-range goals	.16	.18	.17	.14
6. To be happy	.08	.19	.10	.13
7. To have money	.11	.18	.14	.10
8. To have leisure time	.15	.22	.16	.15
9. Understanding by my family	.19	.27	.21	.22
10. Personal freedom	.11	.29	.14	.29
11. Other people to be helpful	.27	.20	.27	.27
12. The crime rate to go down	.19	.20	.22	.11
13. The country to be more productive	.22	.37	.23	.34
14. Justice in the world	.33	.37	.26	.53
15. Resources for all	.29	.30	.22	.24

DISCUSSION

Our study attempted to examine levels and contents of hope among Palestinian and Israeli young people, living in two societies in conflict. Our first issue concerned the levels of hope for *self* and hope for *others*. The results of the study revealed some similarities between the two groups with regard to this issue. Both groups gave priority to individualistic hopes for themselves. These results are not in accordance with our hypotheses. Research data concerning the question of collectivism and individualism between the two societies (see, e.g., Angvik & Von-Borries, 1997; Sagy et al., 2001) revealed a high level of collectivism among Israelis and Palestinians relative to most of their European counterparts.

However, our findings of higher levels of personal rather than collective hopes, expressed by the two groups, are in congruence with research data about future orientation of adolescents (for a review, see Seginer, 2002), which indicate young people *all over the world* to be focused mainly on their private world. It seems that when the measure of the research concerns the future (and not past or present time) it reveals a more individual-oriented approach.

This pattern of similarities between hopes of the two groups can also be explained by some similarity in the socioeconomic status of the Israeli and Palestinian adolescents. Studying in high school, especially in Palestinian society, could indicate a medium or high socioeconomic level. Studies have shown a high correlation between socioeconomic level and personal-oriented expectations in both Western and non-Western societies (Seginer, 1988). Moreover, this result can be a reflection of the focus on education among the medium and high socioeconomic levels of both Palestinian and Israeli families as a meaningful resource in times of depression and uncertainty.

It has to be noted, however, that although our results showed a clear tendency to individual hopes, comparison of our data to other national groups (e.g., Staats & Portlo, 1992), reveals a picture of a relatively collectivist orientation in both samples. It seems that these are two groups of high school students who reflect a bicultural worldview (Oyserman, 1993), that, on the one hand, is universal and crosses cultural borders of youth (perhaps due to Internet, TV, etc.) and, on the other hand, this worldview is combined with ethnocentric-collective orientation, which is characteristic of their conflicted nations.

Despite the similarity, some differences are noteworthy. First, the Palestinian group expressed a higher level of collective hopes than their Israeli counterparts. This is in congruence with some other studies concerning collectivism, which found similar results in both groups, namely, the orientation toward collectivism among Arab-Palestinian youth was much more prominent than among Israeli-Jewish adolescents (e.g., Sagy et al., 2001).

Another difference between the groups is revealed in the examination of hopes by separating expectations and wishes. Wishes relate to how much one would wish a particular future occurrence, while expectations concern the extent one expects it to really occur. While the wishes component was higher among the Israelis than among the Palestinians, the expectations component was significantly higher among their Palestinian counterparts. These different patterns can be explained on two levels: the real life context in which the young people were living and the cultural codes of their societies.

The first possible explanation concerns the *different context* in which the two groups were living. It seems that the cognitive elements of hope—the expectations—were more biased among the Palestinian group, who lived in a more difficult reality as an occupied nation. Tversky and Kahanman (1974) taught us about the biases or errors of human judgment under conditions of uncertainty. The results of these errors might be expressed as a more positive outcome than realistic estimates of the future, when the situation is threatening or depressing.

Another explanation concerns the *different cultural codes* of the two groups. This explanation may refer to the distinction between individual-centered hope and existential hope (Hobfoll et al., 2005) mentioned earlier. The individual-centered definition of hope (e.g., Snyder, 1994) is based on the Western way of thinking and assumes that the individual has the personal or social resources required to meet a goal. Existential hope seems to reflect a more Eastern way of dealing with hope, and relates to the strength that people with few resources call upon to encourage themselves through difficult times. In other words, this implies that, even against facts saying that there are considerable odds against you, you believe that you will ultimately win. The Palestinian adolescents seemed to refer to this existential hope, and, therefore, kept their expectations relatively high, even in hard times.

Our second question concerned the changes in hopes in times of greater threat. As mentioned, the second stage of the study was carried out in a completely different time with regard to the Israeli–Palestinian conflict. While the first stage took place during the Oslo Accords talks of peace negotiations, the second stage, which was carried out during the Al-Aksa Intifada and terror attacks, reflected a reality of increasing violence among the two nations. Generally, the hopes of both Israelis and Palestinians were relatively high and did not change over time. These findings are not in congruence with our hypothesis that hope would increase in times of greater threat.

However, when separating wishes from expectations, a different pattern is revealed, which indicates differences between the groups. Thus, at the second time, the Israeli group showed a small decrease in their collective wishes, while the Palestinians, indeed, expressed a higher level of this measure.

These findings can be explained by the above-mentioned assumption related to well-being and conflict resolution (Fisher, 1997), namely, that wishes are increased in times of distress. Moreover, the distinction between the individual-oriented versus existential way of hoping (Hobfoll et al., 2003) may be relevant to this differentiation. While the Palestinians indeed raised their wishes in times of greater threat, their Israeli counterparts decreased theirs. The Israelis, it seems, were more individual oriented in their pattern of coping, while the Palestinians expressed a more existential way of hoping.

Another explanation, which relates to the new social context, can also be attributed here: the activity of the young Palestinians in the Al-Aksa Intifada events might have raised their pride and through this their collective wishes. The Israeli adolescents were more passive in their state of living and coping with terror attacks. Thus, the effect of the Intifada on them could increase their disillusionment.

The item "Peace in the World" is of particular interest here. In both groups hope for peace was rated relatively low. Moreover, among the Israelis, hope for peace was not only low, but also decreased over time, as their threat increased.

According to needs theory, it is expected that wishes for good outcomes should *increase* as negative changes occur in reality (Staats & Partlo, 1993): Greater threats lead to greater hopes, or we wish for that which we do not have, but want. As previously mentioned, among the American samples, for example, hopes for peace increased under conditions of the Gulf War. The Gulf War for Americans, however, is a far cry from the situation we are dealing with here.

Nevertheless, it seems that the relatively low expectations in the two groups reflected the sense of reality of those young people: the reality of despair and hopelessness with regard to peace in the context of the intractable conflict. Those feelings seem to have come out of the prolonged period of the continuing conflict, war, occupation, and terror. The meaning of this could be that they did not consider peace as relevant to any improvement in their personal lives.

Another possible explanation is noteworthy. Hope is not only connected with expectations for a positive event, but also strongly reflects our value system: When we hope for something to happen, we consider it worthwhile. We hope for something meaningful even when the probability of its occurrence is low. In this study, as well as in our previous research in 1995 (Orr, Sagy, & Bar-On, 2000; Sagy et al., 2001), we found that both groups attributed lower importance to the value of "peace" (as compared to their European counterparts). Moreover, in both groups, peace had low connections with their personal wishes. Living in a time of continuing conflict, one can assume that peace must have a special meaning in both societies. The history of the region has linked these two peoples and national movements; neither can make the other disappear, and neither can achieve peace without relinquishing some deeply held aspirations. However, the youth in these two societies have not only failed to consider peace as one of the most important parts of their value system, but have also failed to understand the connection between peace and the fulfillment of other personal wishes and hopes that are important to them. It seems that the perception of peace among these youngsters is not of a pleasant event but of a complex and painful process. This perception seems to be even stronger among the Israeli group.

The perceptions of the future of both Israeli and Palestinian adolescents have not changed dramatically over time. After many years of bloody and vicious conflict, the opposing societies, as reflected by their young people, were not fully driven by hope for a peaceful future. Other measures in our longitudinal study (Sagy, Adwan, & Kaplan, 2002) revealed that they were occupied and fixated with feelings of anger and delegitimization of the other group. They lived, it seems, without being able to fulfill their basic needs for identity, security, dignity, and justice (Kelman, 1990). Unfortunately, it is the threat to these basic needs that sustains the intractable conflict.

To sum up, both groups in this study were found to be more individualistic than collectivistic in their hopes for the future. This indicates that the adolescents in our study groups—despite the intractable violent conflict in which they are living—expressed a universal tendency of young people all over the world to be focused mainly on their private world. This, unfortunately, includes their perceptions of peace as not connected to their personal wishes.

Our findings of similarity between the groups express, perhaps, the growing tendency in human society to cross borders. However, the different patterns that were found between them seem to reflect their different real-life context as well as the cultural codes of their societies. Longitudinal research should examine whether these tendencies indeed reflect a common expression of "youth culture," which, in some way, "overcomes" the "conflict culture" of the two investigated societies. Measuring hope levels in societies, however, seems to be a useful and meaningful tool in the larger attempt to educate and promote a culture of peace.

REFERENCES

Angvik, M., & Von-Borries, B. (Eds.). (1997). *Youth and history: A comparative European survey on historical consciousness and political attitudes among adolescents.* Hamburg, Germany: Korber Edition.

Breznitz, S. (1986). The effect of hope on coping with stress. In: M. H. Appley & R. Trumbull (Eds.), *Dynamics of stress: Physiological, psychological and social perspectives* (pp. 295–306). New York: Plenum Press.

Fisher, R. (1997). *Interactive conflict resolution.* Syracuse, NY: Syracuse University Press.

Hobfoll, S. E., Briggs-Phillips, M., & Stines, L. R. (2005). Fact or artefact: The relationship of hope to a caravan of resources. In: R. Jacoby & G. Keinan (Eds.), *Between stress and hope: From a disease-centered to a health-centered perspective.* New York: Greenwood.

Jacoby, R. (1993). "The miserable hath no other medicine, but only hope": Some conceptual considerations on hope and stress. *Stress Medicine, 9,* 61–69.

Kelman, H. C. (1990). Applying a human needs perspective to the practice of conflict resolution: The Israeli–Palestinian case. In J. W. Burton (Ed.), *Conflict: Human needs theory* (pp. 89–112), New York: St. Martin's Press.

Lazarus, R. S., & Folkman, S. (1984). Coping and adaptation. In W. D. Gentry (Ed.), *The handbook of behavioral medicine* (pp. 282–325), New York: Guilford Press.

Magaletta, P. R., & Oliver, J. M. (1999). The hope construct, will, and ways: Their relations with self-efficacy, optimism, and general well being. *Journal of Clinical Psychology, 55*(5), 539–551.

Oyserman, D. (1993). The lens of personhood: Viewing the self and others in a multicultural society. *Journal of Personality and Social Psychology, 65,* 993–1009.

Orr. E., Sagy, S., & Bar-on, D. (2000) Social representations in use: Israeli and Palestinian high-school students' collective coping and defense. *Social Representations: Thread of Discussion, 9,* 2.1–2.20.

Sagy, S., Adwan, S., & Kaplan, A. (2002). Interpretations of the past and expectations for the future of Israeli and Palestinian youth. *American Journal of Orthopsychiatry, 72.*

Sagy, S., Orr, E., Bar-On, D., & Awwad, E. (2001). Individualism and collectivism in two conflicted societies: Comparing Israeli and Palestinian high school students. *Youth and Society, 32,* 3–30.

Seginer, R. (1988). Adolescent orientation toward the future: Sex role differentiation in sociocultural context. *Sex Roles, 18,* 739–757.

Seginer, R. (2002). Adolescent future orientation: An integrated cultural and ecological perspective. In W. J. Lonner, D. L. Dinnel, & S. A. Hayes (Eds.), *Online readings in psychology and culture.* Bellingham, WA: Center Cross Cultural Research.

Snyder, C. R. (1994). *The psychology of hope.* New York: Free Press.

Snyder, C. R. (2000). Hypothesis: There is hope. In C. R. Snyder (Ed.), *Handbook of hope: Theory, measures and applications* (pp. 3–21). San Diego, CA: Academic Press.

Staats, S. R. (1989). Hope: A comparison of two self-report measures. *Journal of Personality Assessment, 53*, 366–375.

Staats, S. R., & Partlo, C. A (1993). Brief report on hope in peace and war, and in good times and bad. *Social Indicators Research, 29*, 229–243.

Staats, S. R., & Stassen, M. A. (1985). Hope: An affective cognition. *Social Indicators Research, 17*, 235–242.

Stotland, E. (1969). *The psychology of hope*. San Francisco: Jossey-Bass.

Triandis, H. C. (1995). *Individualism and Collectivism*. Boulder, CO: Westview Press.

Tversky, A., & Kahaneman, D. (1974) Judgment under uncertainty: Heuristic and biases. *Science, 185*, 1124–1131.

CHAPTER 11

PERCEPTIONS OF PEACE

A Case Study of Visiting Students in Israel

Erik H. Cohen

INTRODUCTION: PEACE EDUCATION AND PERCEPTIONS OF PEACE IN ISRAEL

Conflict has dominated the Israeli political and social landscapes since the founding of the state. The attempted Oslo Peace Accords, their subsequent failure, the outbreak of the "Al-Aqsa *intifada*," and escalated fighting between the Israeli military and Palestinians have increased public awareness and debate over issues related to peace and conflict, both within Israel and in Jewish Diaspora communities (and indeed throughout the world). Perceptions and portrayals of the peace process and the conflict vary widely. The peace process has been portrayed as everything from the salvation of both peoples, to suicide for Israel, to a betrayal of the Palestinians. Reporting and interpretation of events vary widely among different media and education channels: religious versus liberal or secular Jewish institutions, right- and left-wing movements in Israel and their sympathizers in the Jewish Diaspora, Islamic media, Christian media, European media, American media, and so on. Individuals' perceptions of the situation are affected by their education and by the media to which they are exposed. It

Educating Toward a Culture of Peace, pages 161–189

is reasonable to predict that the various subpopulations involved (Jew/Arab; religious/nonreligious; Zionist/non-Zionist; Ashkenazi/Sefardi; left/right; center/periphery; male/female; etc.) have fundamentally different understandings and perceptions of the concept of peace.

Spending time in Israel has become an important part of the education of Jews throughout the Diaspora. The relationship between time spent in Israel and perceptions of peace are complex. The political situation will necessarily affect students' time in Israel in some way. The political attitudes the students bring with them may have some impact on their experience in Israel, influencing activities in which they participate, social groups they join, and so on. And the time in Israel will likely deepen their understanding of the political situation, changing, reinforcing, or perhaps confusing their previous assumptions. Students will almost certainly hear or take part in discussions among other students, Israeli and visiting from other countries. In order to effectively plan and evaluate the study abroad programs, whatever their particular goals and agendas, it is important to first know the attitudes toward Israel, Judaism, and the peace process that visiting students bring with them.

To this end, a pilot survey was designed and administered to Jewish students spending a semester or a year at Israeli universities. Though there have been past surveys of visiting students exploring their attitudes toward Israel and Judaism, the addition of questions related to attitudes about the peace process is groundbreaking. One of the goals of this pilot research project was to establish the validity of the questionnaire. We wanted to determine whether the questionnaire sufficiently took into consideration all of the relevant subissues related to peace. If the questionnaire is proven to be an accurate measure of attitudes toward peace, it will allow assessment of educational programs and may be used in subsequent, larger-scale surveys.

Visiting Students to Israeli Universities: Background and Past Surveys

Jewish youth from the Diaspora who choose to take part in a long-term study program in Israel represent a self-selected group seeking an intense, perhaps life-altering experience and exploration of their ethnic and religious identities. In general, "Education abroad challenges one's basic assumptions, not only about the external world around us, but also about the inner world of one's identity" (Laubscher, 1994, p. 84). The adolescent and young adult years are an important time in identity formation, and a long-term education program in Israel offers Jews from the Diaspora an opportunity to reexamine the assumptions and opinions they held until that point (Chazan, 1992, 1993; Kronish, 1983; Nitzan, 1992).

Study abroad programs include social, cultural, religious, and recreational, as well as educational aspects (Mittelberg, 1994, 2000). The universities plan numerous tours, social activities, and encounters with Israeli peers as part of the offered program. Ninety percent of foreign students at Israeli universities are Jewish (Cohen, 1998), and the extracurricular events offered as part of the visiting students program are generally aimed toward their interests. Some study abroad programs offer extracurricular events that deal directly with politics and the peace process.

The first major studies of visiting students in Israel were conducted by Simon Herman (1962, 1970). He noted two important traits of this population: they are members of a minority in their home country, and they have a prior attachment (emotional, cultural, and/or religious) to the host country. Subsequent studies of visiting students in Israel (Cohen, 1986; Halpern, 1993; Mittelberg, 1994; Nitzan, 1992) confirmed the identity-forming component of the Jewish study abroad experience in Israel. My own comprehensive 3-year survey of over 6,000 visiting students (Cohen, 1998) found that, like participants in short-term educational tours, Jewish youth who study in Israel are more actively involved in their home Jewish communities, have a stronger Jewish educational background, and are more attached to Judaism and to Israel than their Jewish peers as a whole. Their decision to spend a year in Israel is more motivated by a quest for ethnic and religious identity than by academic interests (Cohen, 2003).

In the present study, we expand the survey of visiting students' Jewish identity to explore what is arguably the most pressing issue in Israel today: attitudes related to the conflict and attempted peace process with the Palestinians and neighboring Arab nations.

Given that this is a self-selected population, it should be noted that views related to the peace process described in this chapter might not reflect those of these students' peers who have never visited Israel. Additionally, there may be variations between those for whom this is a first visit to Israel and those who have spent time there previously.

The current analysis directly addresses two of the four "common places of education" identified by Schwab (1973): learner and curriculum (content). The content is mapped using multidimensional analytic techniques, enabling the development of a typology of attitudes toward peace. Various subgroups of students are compared to identify factors impacting attitudes toward peace (i.e., gender, nationality, religious affiliation). Of the remaining two common places (context and teacher), context is indirectly addressed in that the visiting students are studying in Israel as opposed to their home countries. The fourth, attitudes held by teachers and their impact on peace studies, is not addressed here. The applicability of

Schwab's common places to specifically Jewish education has previously been verified (see, e.g., Fox, Scheffler, & Marom, 2003).

Previous Surveys

A survey directed by Dr. Yossi Harel of Bar-Ilan University dealt with the perceptions and behaviors of Israeli youth concerning personal safety since the outbreak of the *intifada*. In 2002, 6,196 Israelis of various religious and ethnic backgrounds between the ages of 11 and 15 were surveyed. A quarter of the students said they fear for their lives. A third reported fearing for family members, said they knew someone who had been wounded in an attack, and that an attack had occurred near where they live. Thirteen percent had themselves been at the scene of an attack; 46% said they now avoid certain types of transportation; and 35% go out less due to security concerns. Forty percent worry that the State of Israel faces the threat of destruction (Krieger, 2004).

Peace Now commissioned surveys in 2002 and 2003 of Israelis concerning their attitudes toward various possible political outcomes of the conflict and the peace process. While the respondents of this survey were not adolescents, the results provide a comparison and context for the analysis of the "painful consequences" section in this report. In June 2003, Dr. Micha Hopp directed the survey of 644 households in the West Bank and Gaza and a control group of 400 households within the Green Line. The survey found that while 71% of those living in the West Bank and Gaza would prefer to be able to stay where they are and 54% would oppose dismantling of settlements, only 9% said they would violate the law in their protests and 74% think the State should offer evacuees compensation and allow them to choose where to resettle. Forty-six percent support continued building only in existing settlements, 36% support building new settlements, and 18% think building should be frozen. Seventy-one percent think a peace agreement should be reached with the Palestinians. Forty-four percent think the Palestinians deserve their own state (borders were not defined in the survey) and 47% believe a Palestinian state will eventually be established in the West Bank and Gaza (Peace Now, 2003).

The Women's Commission for Refugee Women and Children has organized surveys of youth and adolescents in various regions of conflict around the world, including Kosovo (1999), northern Uganda (2001), and Sierra Leone (2002). An interesting feature of these surveys is the training of teams of adolescent researchers who work along with adult researchers in interviewing their peers. These studies identify key concerns of adolescents and suggestions for resolution and improving their futures. The organization issued a report entitled *Untapped Potential: Adolescents Affected by*

Armed Conflict (WCRWC, 2000), which emphasizes the need to address the unique but largely overlooked effects of conflict on adolescents (sexual violence, responsibility for caring for family members, lack of education, manipulation into participating in violence, loss of potentially productive members to society, etc.).

METHODOLOGY

The Survey

In October–November 2003, a questionnaire was given to 550 Jewish students spending a semester or a year studying in Israel in various settings. Surveys were available in English, French, and Spanish. A number of organizations and movements agreed to allow us to distribute these questionnaires to their students: Young Judaea; Hebrew University of Jerusalem, School of Overseas Students; UJIA Israel; Department of Education, JAZO; Bnai Akiva; Hebrew Union College; and Ulpan Etzion. Due to the participation of students from many countries learning at many different educational settings in Israel, the survey population includes students from various religious, ideological, national, and cultural backgrounds. We received 420 completed questionnaires, which represent a very high answer ratio (more than 76%). Students were asked to respond to a variety of questions related to Jewish identity, Israel, and the peace process, in an attempt to better understand these students' perceptions of these issues. The questionnaire is shown in Appendix A. In order to allow for comparability with previous research on this population, we included items from earlier questionnaires on items related to Jewish identity and Israel (Cohen, 2004). The items dealing specifically with the peace process are new, and form the core of this pilot research.

Demographic Makeup of the Study Population

Table 11.1 shows some basic demographic data on the study population. Certain countries are far more represented than others, particularly Argentina, Brazil, England, France, Uruguay, and the United States. The vast majority of the students are between the ages of 18 and 20, at the end of their high school or beginning of their college education. The "gap year" between graduating from high school and starting as an undergraduate seems to be a popular time to study in Israel. Over half the respondents are in this category. Less than 10% are still in high school. The rest have already begun college or university studies. Female students outnumber

Table 11.1.   Demographics of the Study Abroad Population

	Number	Percent
Total of valid questionnaires[a]	420	
Gender		
Male	176	42.00
Female	243	58.00
Country of origin		
Argentina	44	10.50
Australia	27	6.44
Brazil	18	4.30
Chile	1	0.24
England	63	15.04
France	42	10.02
Guatemala	1	0.24
Holland	5	1.19
Hungary	1	0.24
Israel[b]	13	3.10
México	4	0.95
Morocco	4	0.95
New Zealand	5	1.19
Norway	2	0.48
Paraguay	1	0.24
Peru	1	0.24
Scotland	2	0.48
South Africa	10	2.39
Sweden	4	0.95
Uruguay	41	9.79
United States	124	29.59
Venezuela	1	0.24
Nonspecified	5	1.19
Ethnicity		
Ashkenazi	282	68.12
Sefardi	75	18.12
Both	43	10.39
Other	4	0.97
Do not know	10	2.42

Table 11.1.   Demographics of the Study Abroad Population

	Number	Percent
Status in Israel		
Tourist	133	32.68
New immigrant	83	20.39
Other	19	46.93
Religious denomination		
Orthodox	136	37.16
Conservative	131	35.79
Reform	37	10.11
Just Jewish	62	16.94
Year of birth		
1952 (51 years old)	1	0.25
1968 (35 years old)	2	0.50
1974 (29 years old)	1	0.25
1977 (26 years old)	1	0.25
1979 (24 years old)	3	0.76
1980 (23 years old)	2	0.50
1981 (22 years old)	4	1.01
1982 (21 years old)	9	2.27
1983 (20 years old)	21	5.29
1984 (19 years old)	130	32.75
1985 (18 years old)	203	51.13
1986 (17 years old)	14	3.53
1987 (16 years old)	5	1.26
Educational status		
High school	38	9.60
Post high school	226	57.07
College/university	132	33.33

[a] in some cases, totals do not equal 420, since individual questions may have been left blank or unreadable on some questionnaires
[b] Nationality is determined by the response of the students to a questionnaire item that simply read country. Some students who have become Israeli citizens wrote Israel. It is impossible to determine the country of their birth from this data.

the males by about 15%. Females have also been found to be overrepresented in short-term educational tours (Cohen & Cohen, 2000; Goldberg, 2002; Heilman, 2002). The reasons for this are not fully understood, but it has been found consistently over a number of years and therefore must be considered a real trend, and not a fluke. Ashkenazi Jews (European origin) make up nearly 70% of the population. Sefardi Jews (Eastern/Mediterranean origin) make up about 18%. Another 10% are of mixed background. Less than 5% described themselves as "other" (e.g., Indian or Ethiopian Jews) or said they do not know their families' ethnic background. Since some countries have large Sefardi populations (such as France) while other countries have predominantly Ashkenazi populations (such as England and the United States), this data reflects the breakdown by country of origin. Twenty percent of these visiting students are new citizens of Israel. The rest are tourists or other types of noncitizen visitors.

This population has a large representation of religious students. Thirty-seven percent call themselves Orthodox and 36% call themselves Conservative or Traditional. Another sixth of the students opt not to affiliate with a certain denomination, and call themselves "just Jewish." Only 10% belong to the Reform movement. While these terms have different connotations in the various countries and represent a range of religiosity, these students are strongly connected to their religious heritage. Attitudes toward Israel and the peace process will necessarily be affected by the religious upbringing and education they received and the media to which they are exposed.

Verifying the findings of earlier studies, the population surveyed here is motivated by a combination of academic, ideological, and social reasons for deciding to study in Israel (Table 11.2). Socializing with Israelis and other Diaspora Jews, seeing the country, learning the language, and experiencing the Holy Land are all part of the Jewish adolescents' search for identity in Israel. Tables 11.3 and 11.4 show the students' level of connection to and involvement with Israel and the Jewish community. These visiting students are coming to Israel with a strong Jewish educational background, active involvement in their home communities, and a sense of connection to Israel. Two-thirds have visited Israel previously, almost half multiple times.

Multidimensional Analysis

Survey results were analyzed using a number of techniques. Traditional cross-tabulations generally produce a fruitful first look at the results. The multidimensional scaling technique known as Smallest Space Analysis (SSA) makes it possible to graphically portray the underlying structure of a

Table 11.2.   Motivations for Studying in Israel

	Very important	Important	Not so important
Language studies	69.30	26.62	4.08
Ideological factors	56.87	35.42	7.71
Social	51.57	44.10	4.34
Fun	53.96	41.25	4.80
Studies	38.50	41.40	20.10
Religious factors	37.26	44.23	18.51
Touring	43.37	40.72	15.90

Table 11.3.   Relationship with Israel

	Number	Percent
Relationship with Israel		
Very close	234	56.66
Close	154	37.29
Distant	25	6.05
Previous visits to Israel		
Never been before this trip	131	33.76
Been once before this trip	69	17.78
Been twice or more before this trip	188	48.45
Consider him/herself as Zionist		
Definitely	201	49.26
Yes	179	43.87
No	28	6.86

Table 11.4.   Connection to Jewish Community

	Number	Percent
Involved once a week or more	287	68.50
Attended Jewish day school	296	71.84
Attended Jewish afternoon school	97	23.54
Attended Sunday school	135	32.77
Involved in Jewish youth organization	357	86.65
Attended a Jewish camp	301	73.06

large number of variables (Canter, 1985; Guttman, 1968; Levy, 1994; Shye, 1978). This methodology has proven successful in a number of studies analyzing attitudes (Ben-Sira & Guttman, 1971; Cohen, 2003, 2004; Canter, 1985; Schwartz & Bilsky, 1987, 1990; Levy, 1994; Cohen & Cohen, 2000; Cohen, Clifton, & Roberts, 2001; Cohen, Ifergan, & Cohen 2002).

In the SSA technique, first a matrix of the correlation between the variables is calculated. The Monotonicity Coefficient (MONCO) procedure, a regression-free coefficient of correlation (Guttman, 1986, pp. 80–87), was used. A computer program (HUDAP) plots the information from the correlation matrix as points on a cognitive map called the "smallest space." The points are plotted so that the higher the correlation between two items, the closer they are on the map and, conversely, the lower the correlation, the further apart they are (Guttman, 1968; Levy, 1985, 1994). The map allows the researcher to recognize distinct semantic regions (Canter, 1985; Guttman, 1968, 1982; Levy, 1994; Shye, 1978).

External variables, such as subpopulations, can be plotted on the map (Cohen & Amar, 1993, 1999, 2002). This is done in such a way that the structure of the original map is not affected. An algorithm has been conceived to "fix" the map so that only the relationships between the original variables are considered in the structure into which the external variables will be introduced. The computer program takes into account the correlation between a single external variable and the matrix of all of the primary variables, placing the external variables on the map one by one. The correlations between the external variables are not considered.

In this study, the SSA technique is used to analyze the response to a questionnaire item in which students were given a list of 57 terms (names, places, concepts, etc.) related to peace, the peace process, and the Arab–Israeli conflict and asked to indicate all the items that they felt express their perception of peace in the Middle East. The 57 items were selected after a long process of sending various drafts of preliminary lists to colleagues and others involved personally or professionally with issues related to Israel, Judaism, and/or the peace process. The goal was to arrive at a list that portrayed a wide spectrum of possible attitudes toward peace, without making the list so long as to be cumbersome in the questionnaire.

Into the basic map of the 57 primary items (perceptions of peace), subpopulations of students divided by nationality were introduced as external variables. This allows us to examine differences in perception among various groups.

I also used the more widely known factor analysis technique on the data, and compared the resulting factors to the regions found in the SSA, further verifying the results.

RESULTS

Perceptions of Peace

Table 11.5 shows the responses to a list of 57 names, places, and concepts related to the issue of peace in Israel. Students were asked to select all the items that express their perception of peace, and then to indicate their first and second choices. The most commonly selected, and the most popular first choice is "Jewish State." For these students, a peaceful solution would have to include Israel as a Jewish State. Education and tolerance are widely believed to be aspects of peace. So are borders and the Israeli Defense Forces. These indicate a balance of idealism and self-defense. Over half the respondents selected "democracy," although it was not the most important item for many. In fact, there was no single item that received even 20% of the vote as most important. Only five items were selected as first choice by more than 5% of the respondents: Jewish State, Tolerance, Education, Coexistence, and Two People/Two States. These students express a wide range of opinion about the issue of peace. The least chosen items were Christianity, the Palestinian Right of Return, and Ecology. Christianity and ecology may seem irrelevant to the issue of peace for many students. It should be noted that the *perception* that these issues are irrelevant does not necessarily mean that they *are* irrelevant. The students' responses reflect media coverage, education, and popular discourse about the issue. Although environmental problems cross borders and many ecological issues, particularly those related to water, are relevant to the Middle East peace process (Hillel, 1994; Schnell, 2001), they have gotten relatively little attention in the press and are considered marginal to the conflict by many. Despite the facts that the Holy Land is also holy to Christians, a portion of the Palestinian population are Christian, in the past Christians have played a major role in the region's politics, and today fundamentalist Christians have some influence on U.S. policy concerning Israel, Christians have been marginalized in what is largely seen as a conflict between Jews and Muslims. The Palestinian right of return, a central point of contention in the peace process, is not likely to be seen as irrelevant, but rather incompatible with their perception of peace, which includes a Jewish State.

The Peace Process

Several questionnaire items presented students with specific preconditions and policies related to the peace process. Table 11.6 shows the responses to these questions. One question asked what policy regarding

Table 11.5.   Perceptions of Peace

Item	Number	Percentage	First choice	Second choice
In the following list of names, places, and concepts please indicate all those that express your perception of the Peace, its foundations and its consequences, in the Middle East. (Circle as many possibilities as relevant)				
Jewish State	307	73.62	69 (19.27%)	13 (3.67%)
Tolerance	266	63.79	36 (10.06%)	27 (7.63%)
Progress	255	61.15	10 (2.79%)	15 (4.24%)
Education	239	57.31	27 (7.54%)	26 (7.34%)
Zahal (Israeli Defense Forces)	228	54.68	8 (2.23%)	11 (3.11%)
Democracy	223	53.48	5 (1.40%)	12 (3.39%)
Borders	223	53.48	0	0
Freedom	213	51.08	12 (3.35%)	14 (3.95%)
Stability	213	51.08	7 (1.96%)	13 (3.67%)
Co-existence	206	49.40	20 (5.59%)	27 (7.63%)
Jerusalem	206	49.40	1 (0.28%)	5 (1.41%)
National identity	205	49.16	6 (1.68%)	9 (2.54%)
Judaism	200	47.96	4 (1.12%)	8 (2.26%)
Solidarity	193	46.28	4 (1.12%)	8 (2.26%)
Aliyah	191	45.80	7 (1.96%)	5 (1.41%)
God	184	44.12	15 (4.19%)	6 (1.69%)
Holy sites	178	42.69	1 (0.28%)	4 (1.13%)
Ideology	177	42.45	4 (1.12%)	2 (0.56%)
Welfare	176	42.21	8 (2.23%)	8 (2.26%)
Calmness	175	41.97	8 (2.23%)	3 (0.85%)
Dream	170	40.77	7 (1.96%)	10 (2.82%)
Two people/two states	167	40.05	21 (5.87%)	20 (5.65%)
Development	167	40.05	1 (0.28%)	4 (1.13%)
Separation	160	38.37	7 (1.96%)	3 (0.85%)
Friendship between nations	158	37.89	6 (1.68%)	9 (2.54%)
Equality	155	37.17	3 (0.84%)	13 (3.67%)
Terror	150	35.97	1 (0.28%)	6 (1.69%)
Sharing values	147	35.25	0	3 (0.85%)
Day to day life	147	35.25	4 (1.12%)	6 (1.69%)
Diplomacy	139	33.33	2 (0.56%)	8 (2.26%)
Nationalism	137	32.85	2 (0.56%)	2 (0.56%)
Initifada	135	32.37	4 (1.12%)	2 (0.56%)

Table 11.5. Perceptions of Peace

Item	Number	Percentage	First choice	Second choice
Victims	131	31.41	3 (0.84%)	4 (1.13%)
Fear	127	30.46	2 (0.56%)	2 (0.56%)
Pluralistic society	122	29.26	2 (0.56%)	6 (1.69%)
Painful concessions	116	27.82	9 (2.51%)	3 (0.85%)
More resources for education	109	26.14	1 (0.28%)	5 (1.41%)
Prayer	105	25.18	2 (0.56%)	2 (0.56%)
Oslo accords 22.49	98	23.50	1 (0.28%)	3 (0.85%)
Tourism	98	23.50	0	0
Islam	93	22.30	1 (0.28%)	1 (0.28%)
Realistic	91	21.82	5 (1.40%)	2 (0.56%)
Health	91	21.82	2 (0.56%)	1 (0.28%)
Blessing	90	21.58	2 (0.56%)	0
Healing	86	20.62	1 (0.28%)	3 (0.85%)
American intervention	82	19.66	0	3 (0.85%)
United Nations	81	19.42	0	0
Wealth	77	18.47	1 (0.28%)	1 (0.28%)
Unrealistic	74	17.75	7 (1.96%)	2 (0.56%)
Shoah	72	17.27	4 (1.12%)	0
Citizens of the world	71	17.03	0	0
Camps of refugees	68	16.31	0	0
Utopia	66	15.83	2 (0.56%)	5 (1.41%)
Impossible	60	14.39	2 (0.28%)	6 (1.69%)
Palestinian right of return	44	10.55	0	0
Ecology	42	10.07	1 (0.28%)	1 (0.28%)
Christianity	25	6.00	0	0

Israeli settlements in the West Bank and Gaza they felt Israel should adopt in the case of a real, lasting peace agreement on the part of the Palestinians.

Students were given several possible "preconditions" for peace and asked to what extent they felt each was essential for peace to be achieved. An understanding of the shared and unique values of different people and cultures was considered absolutely essential or essential by a vast majority of the students. The vast majority of the students also said that democracy is essential for achieving peace. The students were more reluctant to state that establishing a pluralistic society is an essential condition for peace. This contrast seems to indicate that for these students, mutual understand-

Table 11.6.   Questions Related to the Peace Process

In a lasting peace agreement with the Palestinians, Israel should:	
Hand over all settlements	11.14%
Hand over some settlements	33.91%
No change in settlement policy	24.50%
Don't know	30.45%
Understanding values of different cultures is essential to peace (yes/yes, absolutely)	88.86%
Pluralistic society is essential to peace (yes/yes, absolutely)	62.44%
Democracy is essential to peace (yes/yes, absolutely)	86.31%
Should Israel make effort toward peace, including painful concessions? (yes/yes, absolutely)	55.08%
Is peace possible without a Palestinian state? (yes/yes, absolutely)	36.18%
Would a Palestinian state guarantee peace? (yes/yes, absolutely)	10.33%

ing between neighboring political entities (preferably democratic political entities) is necessary, but Israel itself should remain a Jewish state, and not a pluralistic society. Israel's struggle to remain simultaneously a Jewish state and a democracy with a growing non-Jewish citizenship is one of the core challenges facing the country today. Opinion was split as to whether they thought Israel should make painful concessions in order to get a peace agreement with the Palestinians. The most common "painful concessions" discussed in the peace process relate to the settlements in the West Bank and Gaza, the "right of return" for Palestinian refugees and their offspring to their previous homes throughout Israel, the status of Jerusalem and her holy sites, and the establishment of an independent Palestinian state. Since the "painful concessions" were not specified, the students' responses may represent a variety of political attitudes.

Two additional questions were asked regarding the establishment of a Palestinian state. Thirty-six percent said they think peace would be possible without a Palestinian state, while 64% think it would not. However, only about 10% think that the establishment of a Palestinian state would guarantee peace in the Middle East, and only a single respondent thinks that it would be an absolute guarantee of peace. Ninety percent think the conflict may, or likely would, continue even if Israel allowed the Palestinians to establish an independent state in part or all of the West Bank and Gaza. This means that there is a significant group of students who think that peace will not be possible without a Palestinian state, but would not be guaranteed with it.

Structure of Attitudes toward Peace

Figure 11.1 shows the results of the SSA analysis, using the 57 perceptions of peace concepts as primary variables. The clear structure found in only two dimensions attests to the appropriateness of the methodology used. Six regions may be recognized, emanating from a common center. The central item, the core concept in the structure of these students' perception of peace, is National Identity. Starting in the upper left hand corner, a region labeled Democracy and Dialogue contains items such as pluralism, education, and sharing values. It represents a grassroots, person-to-person perspective on peacemaking. Continuing clockwise, the next region is labeled International Diplomacy and contains items related to international peacemaking efforts such as the Oslo Accords or a two-state solution. The next region, Violence and Fear, contains items such as the *intifada*, painful concessions, Palestinian right of return, and refugee camps. It represents a fearful and perhaps cynical or distrustful attitude toward the peace process. Next is a region labeled Judaism, Israeliness, and Jewish religion, or more concisely, Judaism and Israeli Identity. It represents a particularly Jewish attitude, mixing religion and Zionism, as seen by the inclusion of both God and Zahal.

Next is a region labeled Dream, with items that put peace in the realm of an unreachable, utopian dream. The final region, Personal and Social

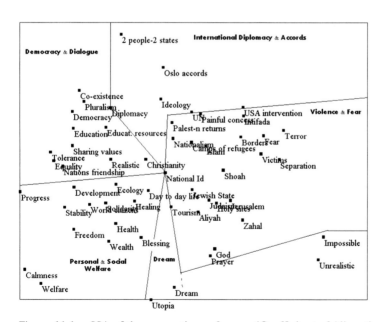

Figure 11.1.   SSA of the perceptions of peace (Coefficient of Alienation .23)

Welfare, contains items related to a positive daily life, such as freedom, health, wealth, and ecology. These represent the expected benefits of an end to the conflict.

The item Tourism, significantly, is found close to the items Judaism and *aliyah*. The relationship between peace and tourism in Israel goes beyond its most obvious economic impacts. As noted by anthropologist Rebecca Stein in her essay on peace and tourism in the Middle East, "In Israeli newspapers, stories about tourism were simultaneously stories about the nation-state, about the meaning and boundaries of Israeli identity, citizenship, and culture during the peacetime era" (2002, p. 518). Jewish tourists coming to pray at the Western Wall and visit Israeli family members are viewed quite differently than Palestinians with tourist visas from Jordan coming to pray at the al-Aqsa mosque and visit Arab-Israeli family members. Christian pilgrims, too, who comprise a large segment of the tourists visiting Israel, do not seem to be included in this view of tourism to Israel. Had the item Tourism been placed in the Personal and Social Welfare region or the Democracy and Dialogue region, it would have shown very different attitudes about tourism to Israel among these students, for example freedom to travel, economic benefits to the country, and increased contact between people from different countries. For these Jewish tourist-students, tourism is related to peace in the context of Judaism, the Jewish state, and potential *aliyah* (immigration).

This type of arrangement of regions around a central item, known as a *polar* structure, is typically found among such issues in which several domains of equal importance are concerned. In other words, the regions do not follow a sequence of least to greatest or central to peripheral. The polar configuration seems to stem from three pairs of opposed concepts:

1. **Negative versus positive aspects of peace**. The Fear and Violence region and the Dream region, representing negative aspects of the peace process, lies opposite the Personal and Social Welfare region.

2. **Unique characteristics of a Jewish state versus coexistence and shared values.** The Judaism, Israeliness, and Jewish religion lies opposite the Democracy and Dialogue region.

3. **Optimism versus pessimism.** The International Diplomacy and Accords region, representing efforts to reach a peace agreement, lies opposite the Dream region, representing disbelief in the possibility of achieving such an agreement.

Factor Analysis and the SSA

In addition to the SSA, we calculated the reliability coefficient of the alpha Crombach: its very high (.923) figure seems to prove that the new scale is reliable.

In the factor analysis, 13 factors were found. Table 11.7 shows the first five factors. Here we will consider those items with a communality index of at least .50. Eight items have a communality index of greater than .5 for factor 1. Each of these is related to Judaism and a Jewish state. In factor 2, we find universal values related to tolerance and democracy. Factor 3 includes items related to fear and violence. Factor 4 includes items related to equality. Factor 5 includes three items that do not seem directly related to each other: Christianity, Islam, and ecology. These may have been pushed together due to their differences from the other concepts. Factor 8 (not shown in the table), contains the four items that assign peace to the realm of an impossible utopian dream.

Nine of the factors correspond to regions found in the SSA. Figure 11.2 shows the SSA map with borders drawn around the items included in nine of the factors as found by the factor analysis. The congruence between these two methodologies is encouraging, the results of each verifying the findings of the other, even though the factor analysis tends to divide the items into more regions.

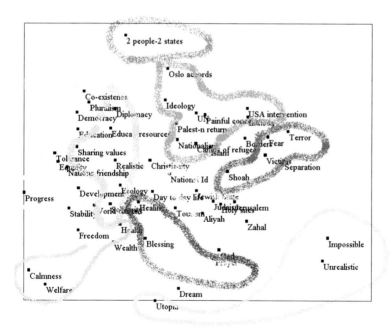

Figure 11.2.   Results of factor analysis (9 factors) as projected into the SSA.

Table 11.7. Results of Factor Analysis (First Five Factors)

Factor 1		Factor 2		Factor 3		Factor 4		Factor 5	
Jerusalem	.72949	Progress	.66650	Victims	.69903	Sharing values	.74400	Christianity	.66451
Aliyah	.68530	Democracy	.62450	Terror	.69440	Equality	.66429	Ecology	.56229
Holy sites	.63404	Education	.61313	Intifada	.66243	Friendship between nations	.64388	Islam	.52748
Judaism	.62920	Stability	.55921	Fear	.59902				
Jewish State	.61434	Tolerance	.53564	Shoah	.52121				
Zahal	.60173								
God	.59327								
National identity	.55756								

Subpopulations' Perceptions of Peace

As stated earlier, we can expect that various subgroups will have different attitudes toward the concept of peace in general as well as toward specific issues related to the peace process. These subpopulations are introduced into the SSA map as external variables.

Gender and Perceptions of Peace

Table 11.8 (first two columns) shows responses to the peace perceptions of male and female students. The similarity between the responses of male and female students to most items is in itself interesting. The female students seem somewhat more responsive to dialogue and democracy as responses to the conflict. We see significantly stronger response difference (10% or greater) between male and female students in relation to quite a few items, but only in the cases of fear and tolerance does the difference exceed 15%. The males had stronger responses to a few items, but the differences in these cases were very small. It should be noted that the students' responses might differ from their internal beliefs. For example, males may find it harder to admit feeling fear. However, though female students expressed more fear, we saw earlier that they are more likely to join the program in the first place.

Perceptions of Peace and Religious Denomination

Similarly, the differences between the denominations between students of varying degrees of religiosity are smaller than may be expected, given the involvement of religion in the conflict, as seen in the last four columns of Table 11.8. Even where differences are seen, they do not necessarily reflect stereotypes such as an inverse relationship between religiosity and liberal attitudes. For example, the conservative students, not the orthodox, had the lowest response rate to the item "Tolerance" and the reform students had the lowest rate of choosing "Democracy."

On critical items such as "painful concessions," responses were very similar along denominational lines. Only on specifically religiously oriented items such as "God" do we see large differences between the denominational groups. It will be interesting to compare these results to the proposed survey among Israeli and Palestinian populations, where the connection between national–religious ideologies and political positions is much stronger (Khashan, 1996, 2000; Yuchtman-Ya'ar & Peres, 2000).

Table 11.8. Gender, Nationality, and Denomination in Relation to the Perceptions of Peace

	Male	Female	USA	UK	AU/NZ	FR	ARG	BRA	URU	OTH	Orth.	Conser.	Reform	Just Jewish
Jewish State	71	75	76	75	75	78	57	88	59	85	78	76	65	67
Tolerance	54	71	63	68	69	46	75	53	71	58	63	58	73	70
Progress	59	62	59	66	50	49	77	59	68	57	55	62	59	66
Education	54	59	54	55	72	34	66	71	68	57	54	58	62	61
Zahal	57	53	55	48	84	73	34	41	37	64	65	62	41	36
Democracy	53	54	52	58	44	51	73	53	51	43	51	53	49	59
Borders	50	56	67	57	50	46	39	29	29	62	60	52	57	46
Freedom	43	56	45	65	47	51	52	47	49	53	51	52	57	48
Stability	50	51	50	58	53	56	39	59	49	49	49	57	46	57
Co-existence	47	51	54	66	44	29	45	47	46	43	46	48	57	61
Jerusalem	46	51	56	54	56	71	11	29	27	62	56	60	46	30
National identity	45	52	54	58	56	41	30	47	34	58	55	46	68	41
Judaism	46	49	56	43	66	46	30	35	27	62	58	49	46	41
Solidarity	41	50	46	49	56	41	36	41	49	51	50	45	43	52
Aliyah	46	46	44	52	63	54	25	35	32	57	54	51	35	31
God	45	44	44	43	66	56	18	29	17	72	59	49	35	23
Holy sites	39	45	50	48	53	41	14	24	32	53	54	45	46	25
Ideology	38	45	40	45	56	22	48	41	44	49	48	37	41	38

Welfare	37	46	20	32	28	68	68	53	63	55	30	55	32	43
Calmness	42	42	25	34	16	73	64	59	56	47	28	55	35	44
Dream	34	46	53	37	38	39	34	6	34	43	46	46	30	31
Two People/Two States	34	45	36	35	22	54	55	53	46	34	28	44	43	39
Development	34	45	42	51	31	39	39	24	44	32	40	40	49	44
Separation	35	41	49	31	34	37	18	12	32	57	40	43	43	34
Friendship between nations	29	44	44	48	25	24	43	29	32	32	33	34	57	46
Equality	31	41	35	42	25	20	59	47	41	32	32	32	41	49
Terror	32	39	55	29	41	12	25	24	22	38	43	34	38	33
Sharing values	27	41	37	42	25	24	45	29	37	30	30	32	43	41
Day to day life	30	39	40	42	41	24	30	12	29	40	41	35	35	36
Diplomacy	37	31	44	34	28	37	25	18	17	32	32	38	38	30
Nationalism	29	36	46	25	25	20	30	41	20	38	33	33	43	25
Intifada	29	35	41	35	38	7	34	29	12	38	41	26	27	30
Victims	27	34	44	31	41	15	18	6	15	43	45	28	24	25
Fear	21	37	40	28	34	15	25	29	24	32	36	28	24	26
Pluralistic society	25	32	32	34	16	5	32	29	54	25	24	25	43	31
Painful concessions	29	27	38	37	31	17	16	6	5	32	30	29	27	28
More resources for education	25	27	31	28	34	17	20	12	22	28	27	25	35	25
Prayer	23	27	28	29	41	32	2	6	2	42	38	26	30	10
Oslo accords	23	24	26	15	22	12	34	24	32	21	21	22	16	18

Table 11.8. Gender, Nationality, and Denomination in Relation to the Perceptions of Peace (Continued)

	Male	Female	USA	UK	AU/NZ	FR	ARG	BRA	URU	OTH	Orth.	Conser.	Reform	Just Jewish
Tourism	26	22	25	18	25	17	16	24	20	40	26	21	24	23
Islam	20	24	34	25	16	5	14	18	5	32	28	17	32	20
Realistic	21	23	32	26	28	15	7	12	10	21	24	22	35	20
Health	21	22	20	22	9	20	27	18	27	30	21	24	19	23
Blessing	19	23	27	26	19	29	5	12	5	30	28	23	30	15
Healing	20	21	35	17	22	15	7	6	5	25	24	22	30	11
American intervention	21	19	25	11	25	17	18	12	10	28	21	21	24	16
United Nations	18	20	28	12	13	10	18	18	27	17	18	17	24	21
Wealth	18	19	19	20	13	39	9	12	7	23	14	24	24	20
Unrealistic	21	15	24	15	28	12	5	0	12	26	26	18	5	10
Shoah	14	20	23	14	31	5	2	12	12	28	23	19	11	10
Citizens of the world	14	19	21	12	9	15	7	12	27	23	15	22	11	18
Camps of refugees	11	20	24	9	9	2	25	6	7	25	17	13	22	20
Utopia	13	18	15	12	6	15	30	12	17	17	11	22	19	13
Impossible	15	14	17	12	19	10	9	6	10	23	18	15	8	11
Palestinian right of return	10	11	15	11	16	0	18	0	7	4	10	6	24	11
Ecology	9	11	17	3	9	5	7	6	10	11	9	9	16	13
Christianity	6	6	11	8	3	2	7	0	0	4	4	7	11	10

Perceptions of Peace and National Origin

Differences between the students from the various countries are far more dramatic, as seen in the eight central columns of Table 11.8. In previous studies of youth Diaspora Jews' perceptions of Israel and Judaism, I found that the country of origin has a profound effect (Cohen, 2001, 2004; Cohen & Cohen, 2000). Other researchers of Jewish identity have noted the extent to which Jews internalize the values of the larger society in which they are raised and educated. This appears to be the case in relation to perceptions of peace as well. For example, only 11% of students from Argentina selected the item "Jerusalem" compared to 71% of the students from France. Repeatedly, we see the students from the South American countries were far less likely to select items related to religion than those from France, the United Kingdom, and the Pacific Rim. The Jewish communities in these Catholic countries are not strongly religious and have been found to take a cultural or ethnic view of Jewish identity, with a strong attachment to Israel.

Figure 11.3 shows the SSA with the national subgroups plotted as external variables. Each of the nations occupies a distinctive space in the map. Argentina and Brazil are closest to each other and in the same region as Uruguay, reflecting their geographical proximity and relative cultural similarity. They are in the far upper lefthand corner of the map, in the Democ-

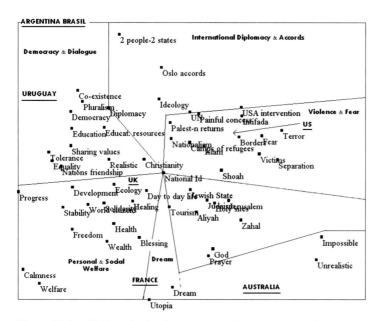

Figure 11.3.   Nationality in the structure of peace perceptions.

racy and Dialogue region. They were "pushed" away from the items related to the Jewish religion. They express a relatively liberal approach to the conflict, perhaps influenced by conflicts in their own countries and the media presentation of Middle Eastern politics.

At the far side of the map, in the Dream region, we find the students from the Pacific Rim and from France. France is on the border with the Personal and Social Welfare region. These students are removed from the "hard" issues of the conflict or attempts to negotiate a solution. For the students from Australia and New Zealand, this may be a result of their geographical isolation. For the French students, it is harder to interpret. Currently in France, debate about the Israeli–Palestinian conflict is intense and the local Jewish community has found itself under attack both physically and in the press. Perhaps the French Jews' strong commitment to Israel and the vocal support of the Palestinians in their country has led these students to believe peace is impossible there. French students are likely to have family in Israel and may think of peace in the region in terms of a better daily life for them, thus their proximity to the welfare region.

Closer to the center of the map we see the students from the United Kingdom and the United States. The British students are on the border between the Social and Personal Welfare region and the Democracy and Dialogue region. The American students are in the Fear and Violence region. The British students take a relatively more liberal and positive stance. Media in the United States focuses on the violent aspects of the conflict (and other conflicts in the region). American culture in general has been described as one of fear, particularly in the wake of the September 11 attacks. In addition, the American right wing's staunch support of Israel and the left wing's criticism of Israel has pushed the traditionally liberal U.S. Jewish population further to the right.

It must be emphasized that my interpretations of the responses by students from the various countries are very preliminary. Further research and investigation are needed to fully understand the complex relationship between the home country and attitudes towards peace.

CONCLUSION

This pilot study was a first exploration of attitudes about peace and the Middle East peace process. The typology presented here may serve as a theoretical basis for future studies among other populations. The high reliability coefficient of the alpha Crombach, the clear structure found in the SSA, and the high communality index of most of the items found through the factor analysis are strong indicators of the accuracy of this questionnaire as an instrument in measuring attitudes toward peace.

For these young, strongly affiliated Jewish Diaspora students, peace in Israel and the Middle East centers around national identity and a Jewish State. Democracy and dialogue as well as international diplomacy are seen as playing roles in negotiating a solution. Improved personal and social welfare are the benefits expected from a peaceful solution. Fear and cynicism prevent unreserved support of peace-making efforts. Peace in the Middle East, for these students, is not a John Lennon-esque "Imagine there's no countries and no religion too," but rather is a vision that includes borders, the army and painful concessions, but also tolerance, education, and progress toward a situation in which a Jewish state exists at peace with her neighbors.

The preliminary analysis of the differences between students from the various Diaspora countries was particularly fruitful, and I hope to have the opportunity to further explore this and better understand the reasons behind the differences seen and their relationship to ways in which the peace process is discussed in various educational settings in Israel. As mentioned earlier, two of Schwab's four common places of education remain to be investigated in terms of peace studies: context and teacher. Comparing attitudes prior to, during, and after the study abroad experience could shed light on the impact of physically being close to the conflict as compared to viewing it from afar through the filter of media. The impact of teachers' perceptions of peace would be a fruitful direction for future research. The structure of peace from the viewpoint of the teachers could be compared to that of the students, and various subgroups of teachers (religious, secular, age, gender) could be compared.

I would like to note that these students express a surprisingly mature and sophisticated understanding of the issues involved, considering their relatively young ages. They consider democracy a precondition; they recognize that Israel has to make an effort to reach a peace agreement with the Palestinians; moreover, they consider that without a Palestinian state, peace is not possible in the Middle East, and nevertheless, that the creation of a Palestinian state will not be a guarantee for peace in the Middle East. These results show clearly how complex the conflict is, as perceived by the Jewish visiting students in Israel. Overall, they have neither a dogmatically right-wing nor left-wing attitude. While they approve of concessions and dialogue, they are not naive about the ease with which a peaceful solution will be reached.

A public opinion poll conducted among Jewish Israeli citizens found a similar complexity of attitude toward these difficult issues (Shamir & Arian, 1994). In interpreting the results, the researchers differentiated between discrete values, and a cohesive, consistent ideology, concluding that Israelis tended to have the former rather than the latter. "These values serve as shortcuts or heuristics to guide people's interpretation of a complex and changing world, but they may or may not be connected, integrated or coherent" (Shamir & Arian, 1994, p. 250).

As stated earlier, one of the goals of this pilot survey was to verify the questionnaire for use in larger surveys of Israeli and Palestinian populations. The finding that nationality has such a major impact on perceptions of the peace process, even among the relatively homogenous population of Jewish Diaspora students, has relevance for the anticipated future surveys. Palestinians and Israelis will certainly have views different from each other and from the Diaspora Jewish populations surveyed here. The methodology used in this first stage of the research has been shown capable of measuring and presenting for interpretation the data related to external factors that impact peace. It will also be possible to examine gender, age, education, and other demographics that may affect attitudes toward peace.

ACKNOWLEDGMENTS

I would like to thank Prof. Yaacov Iram (Chair) and Mr. Shimon Ohayon (Coordinator) for allowing a special grant to this pilot research, under the auspices of the UNESCO/Burg Chair in Education for Human Values Tolerance and Peace, School of Education, Bar Ilan University.

Many people helped me to design the questionnaire: Reuven Amar, Dr Mordekhai Bar-On, Yoni Bedine, Adam Cohen, Avner Cohen, Eynath Cohen, Itamar Cohen, Noemie Grynberg, Maurice Ifergan, Prof. Yaacov Iram, Dr. Shlomit Levy Allison Ofanansky, and Shimon Ohayon.

I would like to thank Dan Krakow and Sarah Lazarus, Young Judaea; Andrée Hini, Hebrew University of Jerusalem; Dani Newman, UJIA Israel; Dr. Ilan Ezrahi, Oshrit Weldman, Department of Education, JAZO; Gael Grunwald, Ilan Ozean, and Anton Gudman, Bnai Akiva Olami; Baruh Kraus, Hebrew Union College; Arie Garcia, Ulpan Etzion, for their understanding and support in distributing the questionnaires.

Dr. Nava Maslovety, and Prof. Shlomo Kaniel, Bar Ilan University, spent time with me reading the first results of the survey. Dr Itzhak Weiss spent time with me preparing and reading the factor analysis of the data. Allison Ofanansky helped me in the preparation and editing of the report. Thanks to the anonymous reviewers whose comments and suggestions improved the quality of this chapter.

REFERENCES

Ben-Sira, Z., & Guttman, L. (1971). *A facet theoretical approach to research on the use of media and on attitudes among elite groups.* Jerusalem: Israel Institute of Applied Social Research.

Canter, D. (1985). *Facet theory: Approaches to social theory.* New York: Springer-Verlag.

Chazan, B. (1993). The metamorphosis of Jewish education. In B. Reisman (Ed.), *Adult education trips to Israel: A transforming experience.* Jerusalem: JCC, Melitz, Melton Center for Jewish-Zionist Education in the Diaspora.

Chazan, B. (1992). The Israel trip as Jewish education. *Agenda, 1,* 30–34.

Cohen, E. H. (1998). *The Israel university experience: A comprehensive study of visiting students in Israel 1994–1997.* Jerusalem: Jewish Agency for Israel.

Cohen, E. H. (2001). Images of Israel: Diaspora Jewish youth's preconceived notions about the Jewish state. In D. Elizur (Ed.), *Facet theory: Integrating theory construction with data analysis* (pp. 197–209). Prague, Czech Republic: Mafytz Press.

Cohen, E. H. (2003). Tourism and religion: A case study. Visiting students in Israeli universities. *Journal of Travel Research, 42,* 36–47.

Cohen, E. H. (2004). Components and symbols of ethnic identity: A case study in informal education and identity formation in diaspora. *Applied Psychology, 53,* 87–112.

Cohen, E. H., & Amar, R. (1993). *External variables in WSSA1 (including external profiles and POSAC regions): A contribution.* Prague: The 4th International Facet Theory Conference.

Cohen, E. H., & Amar, R. (1999). *External variables as points in SSA: Comparison with unfolding techniques.* Berne: The 7th International Facet Theory Conference.

Cohen, E. H., & Amar, R. (2002). External variables as points in smallest space analysis: A theoretical, mathematical and computer-based contribution. *Bulletin de Méthodologie Sociologique, 75,* 40–56.

Cohen, E. H., Clifton, R. A., & Roberts, L. W. (2001). The cognitive domain of the quality of life of university students: A re-analysis of an instrument. *Social Indicators Research, 53,* 63–77.

Cohen, E. H., & Cohen, E. (2000). *The Israel experience: An educational research and policy analysis.* Jerusalem: Jerusalem Institute for Israel Studies.

Cohen, E. H., Ifergan, M., & Cohen E. (2002). A new paradigm in guiding: The "Madrich" as a role model. *Annals of Tourism Research, 29,* 919–932.

Cohen, S. M. (1986). *Jewish travel to Israel: Incentives and inhibitions among US and Canadian teenagers and young adults.* Jerusalem: Jewish Education Committee, Jewish Agency for Israel.

Fox, S., Scheffler I., & Marom D. (Ed.). (2003). *Visions of Jewish education.* Cambridge, UK: Cambridge University Press.

Goldberg, H (2002). A summer on a NFTY Safari 1994: An ethnographic perspective. In B. Chazan (Ed.), *Studies in Jewish identity and youth culture* (pp. 23–142). Jerusalem: Keren Karev.

Guttman, L. (1968). A general nonmetric technique for finding the smallest coordinate space for a configuration of points. *Psychometrika, 33,* 469–506.

Guttman, L. (1982). Facet Ttheory, smallest space analysis and factor analysis. *Perceptual and Motor Skills, 54,* 491–493.

Guttman, L. (1986). Coefficients of polytonicity and monotonicity. In S. Katz & N. L. Johnson (Eds.), *Encyclopedia of statistical science* (Vol. 7, pp. 80–86). New York: Wiley.

Halpern, J. (1993). A comparative study of adjustment difficulties of American male and female students in Israeli institutions of higher learning. *Ten Da'at, 7*, 45–48.

Heilman, S C. (2002). A young Judea Israel discovery tour: The view from inside. In B. Chazan (Ed.), *Studies in Jewish identity and youth culture* (pp. 143–268). Jerusalem: Keren Karev.

Herman, S. (1962), American Jewish students in Israel: A social psychological study in cross-cultural education. *Jewish Social Studies, 34*, 3–29.

Herman, S. (1970). *American students in Israel.* Ithaca, NY: Cornell University Press.

Hillel, D. (1994). *Rivers of Eden: The struggle for water and the quest for peace in the Middle East.* New York: Oxford University Press.

Khashan, H. (1996). *Partner or pariah? Attitudes toward Israel in Syria, Lebanon and Jordan.* Washington, DC: Washington Institute for Near East Policy, Policy Paper #41.

Khashan, H. (2000). Arab attitudes toward Israel on the eve of the new millenium. *Journal of Social, Political and Economic Studies, 25*, 131–230.

Krieger, H. L. (2004, June 3). Survey: One in four teens live in fear of terror. *Jerusalem Post*, Online edition.

Kronish, R. (1983). Israel as a resource. In A. F. Marcus & R. Zwerin (Eds.), *Jewish principal's handbook.* Denver, CO: Alternatives in Religious Education.

Laubscher, M. R. (1994) *Encounters with difference: Student perceptions of the role of out-of-class experiences in education abroad.* Westport, CT: Greenwood Press.

Levy, S. (1985). Lawful roles of facets in social theories. In D. Canter (Ed.), *Facet theory: Approaches to social theory* (pp. 73–74). New York: Springer-Verlag.

Levy, S. (1994). *Louis Guttman on theory and methodology: Selected writings.* Aldershot, UK: Dartmouth.

Mittelberg, D. (1994). *The Israel visit and Jewish identification.* New York: American Jewish Committee.

Mittelberg, D. (2000). *The Israel connection and American Jews.* Westport, CT: Praeger.

Nitzan, M. (1992). *The effect of long-term Israel sojourns on identity formation in late adolescent diaspora teens.* MA thesis, Hebrew University of Jerusalem.

Peace Now. (2003). *Israeli Peace Now survey of settlers: Most reject extremists, would accept compensation to leave.* Washington, DC: Author.

Schnell, I. (2001). Transformation in territorial concepts: From nation building to concessions. *GeoJournal, 53*, 221–234.

Schwab, J. (1973). The Practical 3: Translation into curriculum. *School Review, 81*, 501–522.

Schwartz, S. H., & Bilsky W. (1987). Toward a universal psychological structure of human values. *Journal of Personality and Social Psychology, 53*, 550–562.

Schwartz, S. H., & Bilsky W. (1990). Toward a theory of the universal content and structure of values: Extensions and cross-cultural replications. *Journal of Personality and Social Psychology, 58*, 878–891.

Shamir, M., & Arian, A. (1994). Competing values and policy choices: Israeli public opinion on foreign and security affairs. *British Journal of Political Science, 24,* 249–272.

Shye, S. (1978). *Theory construction and data analysis in behavioral sciences.* San Francisco: Jossey-Bass.

Stein, R. L. (2002). First contact' and other Israeli fictions: Tourism, globalization, and the Middle East peace process. *Public Culture,* 14, 515–543.

WCRWC. (2000). *Untapped potential: Adolescents affected by armed conflict: A review of programs and policies.* New York: Women's Commission for Refugee Women & Children.

Yuchtman-Ya'ar, E., & Peres, Y. (2000). *Between consent and dissent: Democracy and peace in the Israeli mind.* New York: Rowman & Littlefield.

CHAPTER 12

CONTEXT AND AGE-RELATED DIFFERENCES IN JUDGMENTS ABOUT REFLECTIVE RACIAL TOLERANCE

The Case of Israel

Rivka T. Witenberg
Rachel Gali Cinamon

INTRODUCTION

The elimination of all forms of discrimination and intolerance including those based on race and color is one of the main aims of the United Nations Culture of Peace Declaration. Considering current events in the world and the global increase of racial and cultural diversity, better understanding about tolerance has never been more important (Thomas, 1998). Tolerance focuses on the positive aspects of social perceptions and behaviors and is arguably prosocial in nature. Yet, little research to date has investigated the development and nature of tolerance in its own right and even less research has focused on racial tolerance from a psychological per-

Educating Toward a Culture of Peace, pages 191–206

191

spective (Robinson, Witenberg, & Sanson, 2001; Vogt, 1997). In contrast, an important and large body of research has examined prejudice, using social cognitive and social identity theories (Aboud & Doyle, 1996; Aboud & Levy, 2000; Ashmore & DelBocka, 1981), and from a developmental perspective, primarily exploring the development of prejudice in young children (Nesdale, 2001). This research often defines prejudice as the reflection of an unfavorable judgment toward a particular group (Augoustinos & Reynolds, 2001) with the corollary that absence of prejudice reflects tolerance. However, Vogt (1997) has suggested that conceptually, prejudice and tolerance are different processes that are often investigated as if they were the opposite of each other, confounding much of the psychological research into tolerance. Other researchers have suggested that a fuller, separate understanding of each process may offer unique implications for educational and social policy (Robinson et al., 2001; Witenberg, 2000, 2002b).

Moreover, only limited research has adopted a cognitive developmental approach and methodology to investigate racial tolerance (Vogt, 1997). In contrast, in the moral and prosocial domains, researchers often adopt such an approach (e.g., Piaget, 1932/1965, 1955). Typically, such a methodology maps children's, adolescents', and young adults' reasoning and judgments using stories or dilemmas that present a character with conflicting events requiring resolution (e.g., Kohlberg, 1981, 1984; Nucci, Camino, & Milnitsky-Sapiro, 1996). In the case of moral and prosocial reasoning, general consensus upholds an age-related progression from less to more maturity, even if the progression is not as invariant as first believed (Eisenberg, 1998). To expand the limited available knowledge concerning the age-related progression of racial tolerance, the current study used a cognitive developmental methodology. We asked children, adolescents, and young adults to reason and make judgments about dilemma-like stories based on real-life incidents that could be resolved using either tolerant or intolerant judgments. At the same time, cognitive development is no longer viewed as an all-or-nothing process and the influence of contextual information on development has been acknowledged in recent times in studies examining moral judgments (Navarez, 2001), judgments about freedom of speech (Helwig, 1995, 1998), as well as judgments about dissenting beliefs and political tolerance (Sigelman & Toebben, 1992; Wainryb, Shaw, & Maianu, 1998). These findings suggest that contextual information may influence judgments and mediate age-related differences.

Accordingly, in the current study we assessed racial tolerance in its own right using a cognitive developmental approach and methodology informed by domain-specific theories (Case, 1992). We also asked a different set of questions about tolerance from those proposed by the research about prejudice. That is, when tolerance manifests itself, what is the pattern of responses for racially tolerant judgments and what is the effect of context and age on the pattern of judgments? Possible gender differences were also explored. Context in this research involved two aspects. First the studies examined situational context or to whom and under what circumstance the participants were willing to extend their tolerance. The second context was behavioral and involved making judgments about three different aspects of behavior (beliefs, speech, acts).

How tolerance is defined was also considered. The next section addresses the complexity of definitional issues of tolerance (Mendus, 1989; Newey, 1999; Oberdiek, 2001).

DEFINING TOLERANCE

Walzer (1997) argues that tolerance can be traced across a continuum from forbearance to full acceptance. Alternatively, tolerance can be perceived in at least four distinct ways, and the way it is viewed has implications for research.

Forbearance or endurance is the most commonly regarded definition of tolerance. Specifically, this form of tolerance is viewed as "putting up with" without interference something that is found to be threatening, disgusting, unacceptable, or even morally wrong. On the basis of this definition a person can endure, and refrain from acting intolerantly but remain biased, disapproving, or judgemental. Restraint, rather than acceptance of diversity, guides this type of tolerance, which likely leads to prejudiced thoughts and beliefs but not to discriminatory actions (as in LaPiere's classic 1934 study). For example, a shopkeeper may dislike people with dark skin but will continue serving them politely to avoid losing their business or because of legal ramifications. This possibility is rarely acknowledged in the literature, which tends "to assume that tolerance and prejudice are mutually exclusive of each other" (Robinson et al., 2001, p. 74). Embedded in the idea of tolerance as endurance is also the notion that what is endured is socially or morally less valuable or even wrong in comparison to culturally specific practices.

Conversely, tolerance can be defined as full acceptance, which recognizes, values, and even celebrates differences (Oberdiek, 2001; Robinson et al., 2001; Vogt, 1997). Although seemingly an ideal form of tolerance, indiscriminate acceptance in its most extreme form could also lead to acceptance of questionable practices and human rights violations; for instance, if freedom of speech is extended to all forms of intolerant views including neo-Nazi propaganda (Oberdiek, 2001; Vogt, 1997).

Between endurance and acceptance, tolerance can be defined as the absence of prejudice of what is disliked, resented, and possibly even abhorred (Robinson et al., 2001; Walzer, 1997). This definition focuses on absence of prejudice and goes beyond simply enduring or refraining from interfering, and can even manifest itself in "benign indifference to difference" (Walzer, 1997, p. 11). This sort of conceptualization of tolerance has been adopted by much of the psychological research into prejudice, particularly with children (Robinson et al., 2001; Vogt, 1997). However, the absence of prejudice both in children and adults does not necessarily entail the presence of tolerance (Witenberg, 2000). In fact, Aboud (1988) pointed out that we cannot always know why children choose playmates from diverse cultural backgrounds, which much of the research about prejudice with children focuses on. She argued that the choice could be simply that children will play with anyone for the sake of playing and this choice has nothing to do with tolerance.

Therefore, another view of tolerance involves not only the absence of prejudice but also a conscious rejection of prejudiced attitudes, beliefs, and responses and a recognition that others have rights (Robinson et al., 2001; Walzer, 1997). Recognizing and rejecting intolerant views moves a person from simply being "a narrow-minded bigot who shows restraint" (Burwood & Wyeth, 1998, p. 469) to a reflective individual. We adopted "reflective tolerance" for the purpose of this research because this definition involves an active, conscious, reflective agent. Reflection allows for consideration of both the endorsement of tolerance and the rejection of intolerance.

PAST DEVELOPMENTAL RESEARCH ABOUT TOLERANCE

In a series of studies using a cognitive developmental approach, Enright and Lapsley (1981) asked children from grade 1 through to college students to judge people who held dissenting beliefs from them on a range of social, moral, and political dilemmas. They concluded that tolerance involved an age-related progression from less to more tolerance toward those holding dissenting beliefs consistent with Piagetian development. However, no consideration was given to the influence of context, as more recent studies have done. For example, Sigelman and Toebben (1992) examined the development of both political and dissenting beliefs tolerance in grades 2, 5, and 8. They found that tolerance increased with age, but was mediated by context for both political and dissenting beliefs tolerance.

Research about dissenting beliefs also found age-related differences that were mediated by contextual cues. Wainryb and colleagues (1998) examined under what circumstances and what behaviors students from grade 1 through to college undergraduates would extend their tolerance to those holding dissenting beliefs from the respondents in the study. Wainryb and her colleagues found that irrespective of age, holding dissenting beliefs was the most sanctioned behavior, while engaging in acts based on these beliefs was least sanctioned. Clearly, tolerance was influenced by the kind of behaviors participants were asked to make judgments about.

Recent Australian research using a similar approach reported that racial tolerance has its own unique developmental trajectory, which is mediated by context. Contrary to research on belief-discrepancy and political tolerance, where tolerance level increased with age, the shift in racial tolerance with age occurred in the opposite direction than anticipated (Witenberg, 2002b). Children age 6–7 years tended to respond globally, always endorsing racial tolerance (Hogan, 2002) followed by 11- to 12-year-olds who rarely disaffirmed tolerance. However, racial intolerance was sometimes supported in the responses of the 15- to 16-year-olds and peaked in the responses of 19- to 24-year-olds (Witenberg, 2002b).

Beyond the age-related shifts, important contextual influences also emerged in the Australian studies, corroborating findings about political and dissenting belief tolerance. Within-subject manipulation showed variability in response patterns to the three stories used in the research. Respondents rejected other people holding intolerant beliefs and acting on such beliefs considerably more often than they rejected others speaking about such beliefs (Neale, 2002; Witenberg, 2002b). Witenberg argued that the older respondents' more organized and abstract schemata allowed them to better distinguish within- and between-story contexts. Younger respondents' more global responses may have stemmed from their less developed knowledge structures and experience, which may have led them to overlook many of the contextual cues, whereas older students could observe and consider these contextual cues when making judgments (Bjorklund, 2000; Schneider, 2000; Siegler, 1996). Gender differences also emerged, particularly an overall tendency for females to be more tolerant than males. Interestingly, the findings showed that when gender was considered, young adolescent males between 15 and 16 years of age tended to be more intolerant than females of that age and also more intolerant than both older and younger males and females.

Broadly then, racial tolerance research to date has substantiated the research about both political and dissenting-belief tolerance, suggesting that human judgments are contingent upon contextual cues and indicating that people are generally neither globally tolerant nor intolerant. Thus, tolerance and intolerance do indeed appear to coexist (Wainryb et al., 1998). However, age-related patterns of responses for racial tolerance seemed to differ from those evidenced for political and belief-discrepancy tolerance. The question becomes whether the findings about racial tolerance can be generalized and point to a universal pattern not only within but also between societies and cultures.

THE CULTURAL STRUCTURE OF TOLERANCE
AND INTOLERANCE

Apart from definitional issues, an important consideration when investigating tolerance in any given population is the specific cultural and social backdrop against which the investigation takes place and creates possibilities for bringing tolerance and intolerance into play (Gaasholt & Togeby, 1995). Inasmuch as the present study addressed the specific issues of tolerance in Israeli society, understanding about the cultural makeup of this society sets the background for the study. Disregarding the highly publicised Arab–Israeli conflict, Israel is a multicultural society that has absorbed many new immigrants since its establishment in 1948 and continues to remain a migrant society in the new millennium. Over the past six decades, waves of Jewish immigrants from diverse Arab countries, western and eastern Europe, Ethiopia, and other nations around the world have repeatedly changed the ethnic composition of Israeli society (Iram, 2001). For example, according to the Israeli Ministry of Immigrant Absorption, between 1989 and 2000, Israel absorbed 1,154,980 new migrants. The most recent large waves of immigration in the early 1990s arrived mainly from Russia and Ethiopia, resulting in a further cultural and social diversification of Israeli society (Iram, 2001). Recent statistics indicate that between 2001 and 2003, 115,303 immigrants arrived in Israel from the former Soviet Union. During the same period, Israel absorbed 11,060 Ethiopians.

To assess racial tolerance relevant to the Israeli experience, the current study examined the influence of context- and age-related differences on tolerance judgments of children, adolescents, and young adults living in Israel. We employed real-life media-reported incidents commenting on different forms of intolerant behaviors toward people from Russian, Ethiopian, and Israeli backgrounds. In line with previous findings, we anticipated that racial tolerance would be influenced by context and would decrease with age. We also anticipated that females would be more tolerant than males.

METHOD

Participants

The participants comprised 129 students from three different age groups: n = 40 (21 male, 19 female) aged 9 to 11 years (M = 10.4), n = 47 (19 male, 28 female) aged 14 to 16 years (M = 14.8), and n = 42 (17 male, 25 female) aged 18 to 24 years (M = 21.5).

Instruments and Procedure

The stimuli to assess tolerance consisted of three short dilemma-like stories. Each dealt with an event depicting a form of intolerance relevant to the Israeli context and based on real-life events. The content of the stories was gathered from reports in the Israeli media. The key figures in each story originated from three different backgrounds: Ethiopian, Russian, and Israeli.

Story 1 concerned a swimming pool manager who refused entry to people of Ethiopian background, claiming that "these people with black skin were dirty." Story 2 dealt with a dance club manager who refused entry to people of Russian background, claiming that they were "violent and drunk." Story 3 involved a restaurant manager who refused entry to Israelis, claiming that they were "rude and difficult."

To explore the behavioral context of racial tolerance, each story was presented three times and each presentation dealt with a different aspect of the behavioral context: holding prejudicial beliefs, expressing these beliefs, and acting on these beliefs. In the first instance the protagonist of the story holds prejudicial beliefs, in the second the protagonist tells others about these beliefs and in the final presentation acts on these beliefs (Wainryb et al., 1998).

The issues in the stories could be viewed from either a tolerant or intolerant perspective. Participants were asked to make judgments about the events in the stories and then asked to explain and justify their judgments. Students from the two older age groups responded in writing while a trained interviewer read the stories aloud to the youngest age group, asked the questions, and wrote down the children's responses. We adopted this procedure in light of difficulties the youngest age group encountered in writing down their responses during a pilot study. (A more detailed account of procedures is available from the authors.)

DATA CODING AND RELIABILITY ASSESSMENT

Responses were assessed using a four-point rating scale that was developed across a series of pilot studies and used in previous research (Witenberg, 2002a, 2002b). The four-point rating scale was devised to capture levels of tolerance within stories and across the behavioral dimensions rather than to simply score responses as tolerant/intolerant as in survey research. In the first instance a response was categorized as either tolerant or intolerant on the basis of each participant's affirmation or disaffirmation of tolerance when responding to question 1 for each behavioral dimension (of belief, speech, and act) for each story. For example, affirmation of tolerance included responses such as "It's not okay to believe such a thing" or "What the manager did was not right at all." Disaffirmation included such comments as "It's OK, I have no problem with it" or "It's fine with me. He can believe what he wants."

Tolerant responses were coded as representing reflective tolerance when students' rejected prejudicial beliefs, speech, and actions and supported their tolerant judgments by appealing to one or more of fairness/ equality, empathy, and reasonableness, established in previous research (Witenberg, 2002a; Witenberg & McDowall, 2001). Fundamental beliefs about equality and fairness were reflected in such responses as "It is wrong," "It's not fair," "We are all equal," and "We are all alike." This category was represented by statements such as, "I would explain that we are all equal," "We should all be treated fairly and equally," "We should be treated the same." Empathy was reflected in responses such as "I would ask you, how would you feel if you were a Russian person and not allowed to go to a dance club?" Reasoned thinking was reflected in such responses as "How could you possibly think that way? A person cannot help their color." Inter-rater reliability for the classification of these beliefs was established through agreement with a second rater who coded 25% of the responses from the total set. There was an 82% inter-coder agreement between the two raters.

Level of tolerance for each situational/story context and each behavioral context depended on the number of responses that were coded as tolerant or intolerant. Six scores were calculated for each participant using the four-point rating scale: a separate score for each situational/story context (Ethiopian, Russian, Israeli) and a separate score for each behavioral context (belief, speech, acts). (Scoring directions are available from the authors.)

RESULTS

Effects of age, gender, and situational context on racial tolerance. To assess the effect of situational context (story content) on tolerance level, a $3 \times 3 \times 2$ within-subject analysis of variance (ANOVA) was performed, with the three contexts entered as the repeated-measures within-subject variables. Age and gender were entered as between-subject variables. Table 12.1 presents the mean tolerance levels and their standard deviations for situational context by age and gender.

The analysis showed a significant main effect for situational context $F(2, 246) = 11.15$, $p < 0.00$, $\eta^2 = .083$. Students were most tolerant toward the Ethiopian person in the swimming pool situation and least tolerant toward the Israeli person in the restaurant situation. The between-subjects analysis

Table 12.1.   Mean Scores and Standard Deviations of Level of Racial Tolerance by Racial Context, Age Group, and Gender (N =129)

Situational context	Age group (in years)	Total sample		Females		Males	
		M	SD	M	SD	M	SD
Ethiopian	9–11	3.75[a]	.49	3.89[d]	.46	3.62[g]	.50
	14–16	3.26[b]	.79	3.34[c]	.73	3.11[h]	.88
	18–24	2.81[c]	.89	2.80[f]	.87	2.82[i]	.95
	Total	3.26	.83	3.31	.83	3.21	.84
Russian	9–11	3.50[a]	.75	3.68[d]	.75	3.33[g]	.73
	14–16	2.96[b]	.75	3.19[c]	.72	2.63[h]	.68
	18–24	2.76[c]	.91	2.76[f]	.83	2.76[i]	1.03
	Total	3.12	.85	3.67	.84	2.92	.86
Israeli	9–11	3.50[a]	.68	3.79[d]	.54	3.24[g]	.70
	14–16	2.98[b]	.79	3.18[c]	.77	2.68[h]	.75
	18–24	2.64[c]	.93	2.60[f]	.87	2.71[i]	1.05
	Total	3.03	.87	3.14	.87	2.89	.86

[a] $n = 40$, [b] $n = 47$, [c] $n = 42$, [d] $n = 19$, [e] $n = 28$, [f] $n = 25$, [g] $n = 21$, [h] $n = 19$, [i] $n = 17$

indicated a significant effect for age, $F(2, 123) = 15.72$, $p < 0.00$, $\eta^2 = .204$, and a significant effect for gender on tolerance judgment, $F(1, 123) = 4.39$, $p < 0.05$, $\eta^2 = .034$.

Post hoc tests using Bonferroni showed significant differences in tolerance judgments between participants in the 9–11 and the 14–16 age groups ($p = 0.002$), and between participants in the 9–11 and the 18–24 age groups ($p = 0.000$). The youngest group expressed significantly more tolerant judgments than did participants in both other age groups. No significant differences emerged between participants in the two older age groups; however, a tendency did emerge for the 14–16 age group to extend more tolerance to others than did the 18- to 24-year-olds ($p = 0.08$). Examination of the means showed that, overall, female participants were more tolerant than male participants. A tendency also emerged for 14- to16-year-old males to show less tolerance than their same-age female peers, particularly regarding the Russian and the Israeli contexts.

Effects of age, gender, and behavioral context on racial tolerance. A within-subject analysis of variance was also used to examine the effect of the three behavioral contexts (scored on the four-point rating scale across the three stories), with the three behaviors of belief, speech, and acts as repeated measures. Age and gender were entered as between-subject variables. Table 12.2 presents the mean tolerance levels and standard deviations for the behavioral contexts by age group and gender.

Table 12.2.   Mean Scores and Standard Deviations for Level of Racial Tolerance by Behavioral Context, Age Group, and Gender (N =129)

Situational context	Age group (in years)	Total sample M	Total sample SD	Females M	Females SD	Males M	Males SD
Belief	9–11	3.63[a]	.70	3.84[d]	.69	3.43[g]	.68
	14–16	2.57[b]	1.31	2.64[e]	1.39	2.47[h]	1.22
	18–24	2.16[c]	1.36	2.04[f]	1.27	2.35[i]	1.50
	Total	2.77	1.31	2.75	1.38	2.78	1.24
Speech	9–11	3.53[a]	.85	3.63[d]	.83	3.43[g]	.87
	14–16	3.17[b]	1.17	3.54[e]	.96	2.63[h]	1.26
	18–24	2.33[c]	1.46	2.40[f]	1.44	2.24[i]	1.52
	Total	3.01	1.28	3.17	1.24	2.81	1.30
Acts	9–11	3.60[a]	.84	3.89[d]	.32	3.33[g]	1.06
	14–16	3.45[b]	.97	3.54[e]	.84	3.32[h]	1.16
	18–24	3.71[c]	.74	3.72[f]	.68	3.71[i]	.85
	Total	3.58	.86	3.69	.68	3.43	1.04

[a] $n = 40$, [b] $n = 47$, [c] $n = 42$, [d] $n = 19$, [e] $n = 28$, [f] $n = 25$, [g] $n = 21$, [h] $n = 19$, [i] $n = 17$

The analysis revealed a significant main effect for behavioral context, $F(2, 246) = 20.80$, $p < 0.01$, $\eta^2 = .145$, and a significant interaction between behavioral context and age, $F(4, 246) = 7.80$, $p < 0.01$, $\eta^2 = .113$. With respect to the main effect, students rejected discriminatory acts most often, with 89% of the sample regarding such actions as intolerable. In contrast, holding prejudicial beliefs was only rejected by 60% of the sample and speaking to others about such beliefs was considered intolerable by 66% of the sample. With respect to the interaction, tolerance level decreased with age for both beliefs and speech behavioral contexts, but this pattern was not evident for the acts behavioral context. As expected, the between-subject analysis indicated a significant effect on tolerance judgments both for age group, $F(2, 123) = 15.72$, $p < 0.01$, $\eta^2 = .204$, and for gender, $F(1, 123) = 4.39$, $p < 0.05$, $\eta^2 = .034$. Again the youngest age group endorsed tolerance more often than the other two groups. Females expressed more tolerance than males for both the speech and acts behavioral contexts.

DISCUSSION

This study investigated contextual and age-related differences in racial tolerance judgments using a developmental approach and methodology.

Although the majority of students supported racial tolerance, judgments were influenced by both within- and between-subject variations. As anticipated, both situational context (content of the stories) and behavioral context (belief, speech, and acts) were found to influence tolerance judgments. Between-subject differences were also evident, where tolerance level decreased with age but was mediated by context. Gender differences emerged, with females demonstrating more tolerance than males. The current data suggest with some degree of confidence that findings from the Australian studies can be generalized and do point to a universal pattern for racial tolerance judgments.

In this study, students' different responses to the content of the three stories, extending the greatest tolerance to a person from Ethiopian background in the swimming pool situation and the least tolerance to an Israeli in the restaurant situation, supported the hypothesis that contextual cues influence tolerance judgements. Clearly, participants considered to whom and under what circumstances they would express tolerance, corroborating Witenberg's (2002b) study, but these findings did not provide detailed data on the reasons underlying these judgments. However, anecdotal evidence suggests that young people living in Israel viewed skin color to be beyond the person's control ("You cannot wash away the color of your skin"), while there seems to be indications that rudeness was regarded as an individual choice. Further analysis is required to determine the underlying reasons for the variation in response patterns for the three stories. However, what we can be sure of with some degree of confidence is that different situational contexts influence variability in response patterns supporting domain-specific theories. The effect of contextual cues on racial tolerance judgments also provides more general support for the influence of contextual information on belief discrepancy (Wainryb et al., 1998) and political tolerance (Sigelman & Toebben, 1992).

Likewise, the students' different responses to the three aspects of the behavioral context confirmed the assumption that tolerance is influenced by contextual cues. Students rejected acting on prejudicial beliefs considerably more often than speaking about such beliefs, and they rejected speaking about intolerant beliefs more often than merely holding such beliefs. The current findings resembled Wainryb and colleagues' (1998) outcomes on belief-discrepancy tolerance and differed somewhat from Witenberg's (2002b) study in regards to the behavioral context. Witenberg's students rejected holding intolerant beliefs and acting on them considerably more often than speaking about them. On the positive side, it appears that acting intolerantly is rarely sanctioned whether for dissenting belief or racial tolerance. On the negative side, holding prejudicial beliefs and talking about them seems in each case more admissible. Wainryb and colleagues hypothesized that their participants had considered the possible harm each behavior could cause. In contrast, Witenberg found that students in her study appealed spontaneously to freedom of speech and argued that it was admissible to openly express intolerant beliefs and at times also to hold such views. The subordination of tolerance to freedom of speech was least evident in 11- to 12-year-olds and most pronounced in the 18- to 22-year-olds (Witenberg, 2004). At least anecdotally, it appears that students in Israel also appealed to freedom of speech and freedom of opinion arguments to justify their judgments in the current study. One could wonder whether such findings are an outcome of civic education in democratic societies, which tend to emphasize freedom of speech without a great deal of consideration of its relationship to other basic human rights such as tolerance. In Helwig's (1995, 1998) studies about freedom of speech, he also found that older adolescents and young adults subordinated equality of opportunity to freedom of speech. How rights are coordinated and why some rights are subordinated to others when in conflict with each other comprises an important further step for future research investigating the developing comprehension of basic human rights.

Overall, the present findings confirm that racial tolerance does not form a global construct. Judgments were clearly influenced by the contextual cues, whether situational or behavioral, which students were asked to consider. From a developmental perspective, the emerging variations in response patterns supported cognitive schema theories and social cognition, where prior knowledge about a situation provides the basis by which the information is interpreted and decisions or judgments are made (Nishida, 1999; Schneider, 2000). According to Schneider (2000), increased domain knowledge improves the proficiency by which we process information and use meta-cognitive knowledge.

Age also influenced tolerance judgments. Racial tolerance decreased with age in this study, as found in previous work (Witenberg, 2002a, 2002b). This finding can be seen as controversial. The literature on child development elicits the general expectation that cognitive maturity will lead to more or better outcomes. Yet, a decrease in racial tolerance is likely to reflect cognitive maturity, which entails the ability to think more abstractly and consider different aspects of the same problem. It is now well recognized that younger children encode a situation more narrowly and tend to focus on the most salient issue, often disregarding the complexity of the problem, in contrast to older people whose processing capacities allow them to consider several aspects of a problem simultaneously (Schneider, 2000; Siegler, 1996). The stories used in the current research presented competing considerations, which older respondents were able to regard. However, an understanding of the possible moral limits to extending tolerance to intolerable beliefs and behaviors may emerge as a next step in their development.

Finally, females tended to show more tolerance overall. The least tolerant of the four groups were boys aged 14–16, particularly noticeable in the

Russian and Israeli situational context. The finding that females tend to be more tolerant and that young adolescent boys have a tendency to be least tolerant was also evident in previous studies (Witenberg, 2002b). Prejudices need to be understood within the context and culture of the developing adolescent. Do young adolescent males focus on different aspects of their sociocultural environment compared to their female counterparts? This question deserves future research scrutiny. It is also worth noting that Helwig (1997) too found gender differences related to freedom of speech as applied to three nonconflictual contexts (society, school, and family) among young people between the ages of 6 and 22. Helwig reported that females were generally more accepting of rule violations that restricted freedom of speech; males were more likely to subordinate freedom of speech across all contexts. He attributed some of these differences to the kind of stimulus material used in the study. Findings about both tolerance and freedom of speech do not necessarily point to global differences between males and females; however, variations in response patterns based on gender require further exploration.

Implications for curriculum design and education programs to promote tolerance and peace can be drawn from our findings. Traditionally, civic education programs begin in early adolescence. However, findings from the current study and those conducted in Australia uphold that preadolescents are able to understand tolerance and intolerance and that they reject intolerance vigorously. Harnessing preadolescents' strong rejection of intolerance and support for tolerance should not be underestimated in designing curricula for elementary students. The contextual nature of racial tolerance poses a particular set of challenges for curriculum developers and educators who are interested in promoting tolerance and peace. The finding that young people do not think of tolerance as a global and inclusive concept, as shown by the current study and those in Australia, must be considered during educational planning. Different story contents were treated differently as were holding prejudicial beliefs, speaking about them, and acting on them. Educational programs advocating the promotion and protection of racial tolerance would do well to account for the multifaceted relationship between tolerance and its situational and behavioral contexts. Furthermore, the finding that young adolescent males are least tolerant indicates the need for targeted, innovative educational programs to challenge this group into reflecting about their thinking toward others.

NOTE

The collection and the analysis of the data were supported by a grant from the UNESCO/Burg Chair in Education for Human Values, Tolerance, and

Peace. We would like to thank Limor Segev, who helped to collect the data and Dee B. Ankonina for her valuable comments.

REFERENCES

Aboud, F. E. (1988). *Children and prejudice.* Oxford: Basil Blackwell.

Aboud, F. E., & Doyle A. B. (1996). Does talk of race foster prejudice or tolerance in children? *Canadian Journal of Behavioural Science, 28,* 161–170.

Aboud, F. E., & Levy, S. R. (2000). Intervention to reduce prejudice and discrimination in children and adolescents. In S. Oskamp (Ed.), *Reducing prejudice and discrimination* (pp. 269–293). Mahwah, NJ: Erlbaum.

Ashmore, R., & DelBocka, F. (1981). Conceptual approaches to stereotypes and stereotyping. In D. L. Hamilton (Ed.), *Cognitive processes in stereotyping and intergroup behavior* (pp.1–36). Hillsdale, NJ: Erlbaum.

Augoustinos, M., & Reynolds, K. (Eds.). (2001). *Understanding prejudice, racism and social conflict.* Thousand Oaks, CA: Sage.

Bjorklund, D. F. (2000). *Children's thinking—Developmental function and individual differences* (3rd ed.). Belmont, CA: Wadsworth.

Burwood, L., & Wyeth, R. (1998). Should schools promote toleration? *Journal of Moral Education, 27,* 465–473.

Case, R. (1992). *The mind's staircase: Exploring the conceptual underpinnings of children's thought and knowledge.* Hillsdale, NJ: Erlbaum.

Eisenberg, N. (Ed.). (1998). *Handbook of child psychology: Socialization, personality, and social development.* New York: Wiley.

Enright, R. D., & Lapsley, D. K. (1981). Judging others who hold opposite beliefs: The development of belief-discrepancy reasoning. *Child Development, 52,* 1053–1063.

Gaasholt, Y., & Togeby, L. (1995). Interethnic tolerance, education and political orientation: Evidence from Denmark. *Political Behavior, 3,* 265–285.

Helwig, C. C. (1995). Adolescents' and young adults' conception of civil liberties: Freedom of speech and religion. *Child Development, 66,* 152–166.

Helwig, C. C. (1997). The role of agent and social context in judgments of freedom of speech and religion. *Child Development, 68,* 484–495.

Helwig, C. C. (1998). Children's conception of fair government and freedom of speech. *Child Development, 69,* 518–531.

Hogan, L. (2002). *An examination of racial tolerance in 6–7 year old children: The influence of young children's thinking patterns and underlying beliefs.* Unpublished honor's thesis, University of Melbourne, Australia.

Iram, Y. (2001). Education for democracy in pluralistic societies: The case of Israel. In L. Limage (Ed.), *Democratizing education and educating democratic citizens: International and historical perspective* (pp. 213–226). New York: Falmer Press.

Kohlberg, L. (1981). *The philosophy of moral development: Essays on moral development* (Vol. 1). San Francisco: Harper & Row.

Kohlberg, L. (1984). *The philosophy of moral development: Essays on moral development* (Vol. 2). San Francisco: Harper & Row.

LaPiere. R. T. (1934). Attitudes vs. action. *Social Forces, 13,* 230–237.

Mendus, S. (1989). *Toleration and the limits of liberalism.* London: Macmillan.

Ministry of Immigrant Absorption (Israel). (2004). Available at http://www.moia.gov.il

Navarez, D. (2001). Moral text comprehension: Implication for education and research. *Journal of Moral Education, 20,* 43–54.

Neale, C. (2002). *The role of reflective judgments and empathy in reflective racial tolerance among young adults.* Unpublished honor's thesis, University of Melbourne, Australia.

Nesdale, D. (2001). The development of prejudice in children. In M. Augoustinos & K. Reynolds (Eds.), *Understanding prejudice, racism and social conflict* (pp. 57–72). Thousand Oaks, CA: Sage.

Newey, G. (1999). *Virtue, reason and toleration: The place of toleration in ethical and political philosophy.* Edinburgh, UK: Edinburgh University Press.

Nishida, H. (1999). A cognitive approach to intercultural communication based on schema theory. *International Journal of Intercultural Relations, 23,* 753–777.

Nucci, L. P., Camino, C., & Milnitsky-Sapiro, C. (1996). Social class effects on Northeastern Brazilian children's conceptions of personal choice and societal regulation. *Child Development, 67,* 1224–1242.

Oberdiek, H. (2001). *Tolerance: Between forbearance and acceptance.* Oxford: Rowman & Littlefield.

Piaget, J. (1955). *The child's construction of reality.* London: Routledge and Kegan Paul.

Piaget, J. (1932/1965). *The moral judgment of the child.* New York: Free Press.

Robinson, J., Witenberg, R. T., & Sanson, A. (2001). The socialisation of tolerance. In M. Augoustinos & K. Reynolds (Eds.), *Understanding prejudice, racism and social conflict* (pp. 73–88). Thousand Oaks, CA: Sage.

Schneider, W. (2000). Research on memory: Historical trends and current themes. *International Journal of Behavioral Development, 24,* 407–420.

Siegler, R. S. (1996). Unidimensional thinking, multidimensional thinking and, characteristic tendencies of thoughts. In A. J. Sameroff & M. M. Haith (Eds.), *The five to seven year shift: The age of reason and responsibility* (pp. 63–84). Chicago: University of Chicago Press.

Sigelman, C. K., & Toebben J. L. (1992). Tolerant reactions to advocates of disagreeable ideas in childhood and adolescence. *Merrill-Palmer Quarterly, 38,* 542–557.

Thomas, T. (1998). The great wall of racial divide. *Australian Quarterly Journal of Contemporary Analysis, 5,* 38–41.

Vogt, W. P. (1997). *Tolerance and education: Learning to live with diversity and difference.* Thousand Oaks, CA: Sage.

Wainryb, C., Shaw, L. A., & Maianu, C. (1998). Tolerance and intolerance: Children's and adolescents' judgments of dissenting beliefs, speech, persons, and conduct. *Child Development, 69,* 1541–1555.

Walzer, M. (1997). *On toleration.* New Haven, CT: Yale University Press.

Witenberg, R. T. (2000). Do unto others: Towards understanding racial tolerance and acceptance. *Journal of College and Character* [Online], *1.* Available at http://www.collegevalues.org

Witenberg, R. T. (2002a). *Profiles of reflective racial tolerance and their relationship with justifications.* Paper presented at the 32nd annual meeting of the Jean Piaget Society, Philadelphia.

Witenberg, R. T. (2002b). Reflective racial tolerance and its development in children, adolescents and young adults: Age related difference and context effects. *Journal of Research in Education, 12,* 67–79.

Witenberg, R. T. (2004). The subordination of racial tolerance to freedom of speech: Some consideration for education. *Australian Psychologist, 39,* 114–117.

Witenberg, R. T., & McDowall, J. (2001). *In favour of tolerance: How young adolescents justify their stance about racial tolerance.* Paper presented at the 36th Annual Conference, Australian Psychological Society, Adelaide, South Australia.

CHAPTER 13

THE ROLE OF EMOTIONS IN PEACE-BUILDING ACTIVITIES

Yaacov B. Yablon

Contact between social groups is one of the most popular strategies to enhance tolerance and understanding between groups in conflict. The underlying principle of this approach is based on the contact hypothesis (Allport, 1954; Williams, 1947), which holds the idea that constructive and guided face-to-face meetings between members of conflict groups can reduce intergroup tensions and promote understanding between the members of the conflict groups. Sherif's summer camp study (Sherif, 1966; Sherif, Harvey, White, Hood, & Sherif, 1961) is one of the first and most well-known intervention programs, which was designed based on the contact hypothesis. In this study the contact hypothesis principles were put into practice in order to create an opportunity for members of conflict groups to work together on joint tasks for enhancing tolerance and understanding between them. Following Sherif's study a great number of similar programs were established all over the world and today more students than ever participate in peace intervention programs. Nonetheless, the contri-

Educating Toward a Culture of Peace, pages 207–222
Copyright © 2006 by Information Age Publishing
All rights of reproduction in any form reserved.

bution of contact and other peace intervention programs to the establishment of peace between conflict groups is still a riddle.

PEACE INTERVENTION PROGRAMS

In addition to the contact hypothesis there are many other approaches used in what we today call "peace education programs" that became an essential part of many school curriculum all over the world. It is since its inception of peace education during the 19th century (Stomfy-Stitz, 1993) through UNESCO's (United Nations Educational, Scientific and Cultural Organization) declaration of the year 2000 as the "International Year of the Culture of Peace" (UNESCO, 2000) that both governmental and non-governmental organizations promoted the establishment of school-based peace intervention programs and students all over the world participate in these programs. This development may be seen as a result of both the notion that negotiation between groups is more productive than any violent way to end a conflict (Kelman, 1990), and of the sociodemographic changes in recent years including large emigration waves, new independent countries, and the expansion of the European union.

During the years peace education had deferent meanings and has altered in response to changes in social, educational, and political developments. Salomon (2002) even addresses the need not only for the distinction between the great variety of peace programs, but also for better definitions and research on peace programs. However, the multiple identities of peace programs can all be related to John Dewey's work and his concepts about society, democracy, communication, and experience, as well as on his emphasis on the role of education (Dewey, 1916/1985). Thus, all peace education related programs including conflict resolution, cultural studies, democratic education, violence prevention, and many others at both micro and macro levels are all included in the peace education pedagogy, which emphasizes personal responsibility in the peace-building process.

In addition, Salomon (2002) classifies peace education programs into three distinctive categories based on the nature of the peace program and the characteristics of the involved societies. In the first category of peace education programs, the involved groups are in a situation that can be titled as intractable conflicts and the programs are designed to change group members' misperceptions about the "other," as well as to develop a sense of responsibility toward the other. The second category of peace education programs strives to enhance understanding and collaboration among groups of a single multicultural society. Within this category we can find, for example, programs designed to reduce tension between majority and minority groups of a single nation, programs to enhance equality between ethnic groups, and programs to increase coexistence among religious groups (e.g., Maoz, 2000; Staub, Pearlman, & Miller, 2003). The third category of peace education programs takes place in regions of experienced tranquility in which the main concern is education *about* peace rather than education *for* peace. Although it has not been directly suggested by Salomon, this third category can also be expanded to include programs that promote positive self-oriented behavior, nonviolent behavior, moral values, citizenship, and environmental education.

Other ways to distinguish between different types of peace education programs is by identifying the underlying philosophy and the core meaning of "peace" that evolve to create each of the peace interventions. Groff (2002) reviewed the definitions of "peace" that have developed since the end of World War II and pointed to seven different perceptions. According to Groff the initial definition of peace was the absence of war. This perspective is still widely held by the general population (Harris, 2002), and even seen as part of many other related definitions of peace. However, by this definition, peace is nothing further than the absence of war. The second view of peace is that peace describes a balance between forces. This view is related to the former definition through the underlying thinking of peace with a stress on war prevention. However, in this later definition, peace involves social, cultural, political, and other forces. Any significant change in one of the above forces requires corresponding changes in the others in order to restore balance and maintain peace.

As the second view of peace involves dynamic changes in its definition, the next two views add social-structural dimensions to the peace definition. The third view of peace distinguishes between negative and positive peace and is related to Galtung's (1973) pioneering work in the field of peace education. While "negative peace" is defined as the absence of war or any direct violence between groups, "positive peace" is the absence of any structural violence. Structural violence is harm caused as a result of the society's structure, and especially as a result of existing inequalities and injustices within that structure. For example, if people starve from sickness even though there is food available for them somewhere in the world, then structural violence exists. According to this view, peace is defined not only by the absence of violence but also as the existence of collaboration and integration between groups and nations.

The fourth perspective of peace adds a meaningful emphasis to the elimination of physical and structural violence at micro levels. This perspective was established during the 1970s and 1980s, and was evoked by feminist scholars through their extension of both positive and negative peace to the individual level (Groff, 2002). According to this perspective, the definition of peace includes not only the existence of positive and negative peace at macro levels, such as countries and nations, but also in the abolishing of any violence, harm, or discrimination in micro levels, such as ethnic groups, religious sects, families, and individuals.

The following three perspectives of peace are moving toward a definition of peace as a more holistic structure that exists within complex systems that view diversity as a source of strength. The core of the fifth perspective is the perception of the need for coexistence and harmony between different cultural, ethnic, racial, and religious groups. As argued in other perspectives, this view of peace as "intercultural peace" stresses not only the need to eliminate the global phenomena of cultural violence but also stresses the need for positive co-evaluation among cultures and the acceptance of the notion that a multicultural society and a diversity of groups and species are a source of strength for humanity.

The sixth perspective of peace goes beyond the notion of peace relationships between humankind and includes environmental and ecological life forms in the peace definition. According to this perspective, Earth is seen as a complex living system of which humans are only one part. Therefore, peace is not associated only to relationships between people, but also at the environment level. It is argued that the fate of our planet is an important goal, and peace is a holistic definition that includes responsible relationships of humans to bioenvironmental systems. Finally, the seventh perspective of peace derives from ancient eastern and western cultures, and emphasizes the need for "inner peace" in order to establish all of the other peace relationships described above. This spiritual approach for holistic inner and outer peace sees inner peace as an essential component for living, and as the necessary condition for a peaceful world.

THE CONTRIBUTION OF PEACE PROGRAMS

Although the development in the meaning of peace can be seen during the years and in a time that more students than ever are involved in peace education programs there is only a moderate amount of evidence-based studies for the positive contribution of such peace interventions (Cairns & Hewstone, 2002; Harris, 1992; Nevo & Brem, 2002; Salomon, 2002). There have been even fewer research studies where participants demonstrated higher levels of hostility after their participation in such intervention programs than before (Bargal, 1990; Brewer, 1996; Hewstone & Brown, 1986; Maoz, 2002a; Tal-Or, Boninger, & Gleicher, 2002).

Different studies were conducted in order to explain why peace intervention programs and especially contact interventions do not fulfill their promise. One result of these studies was the explanation that "just contact" between groups is not enough in order to enhance understanding between groups, and that there are required conditions for constructive contact that would enhance positive change. Amir (1969), Pettigrew (1998), and Tal-Or and colleagues (2002) summarized the most important conditions that were found to be necessary in order to create the desired positive change. In their research, they suggested that contact between groups should take place in a supportive environment that can enrich the experience, and provide a fruitful base for the development and foundation of positive relationships. Equal status between the groups was also found to be a fundamental condition for an effective contact since it helps to create an environment where similarities are reinforced and stereotypes or prejudices are challenged and possibly condemned. Another component for positive contact was found to be related to the frequency and intensity of the contact. It is argued that only close and sustained interaction between group members can afford the opportunity for self-disclosure and for the deconstruction of false conceptions. Finally, it was found that it is important that the interaction between the counterparts will be based on an environment of cooperation that allows the development of close friendships.

Other attempts to study the failure of contact activities focus on the cognitive aspects of the meetings, and suggest that participants do not really confront their misconceptions about their counterparts, but, instead, use any new information to reinforce their preliminary false perceptions (Koehler, 1990). Maoz (2000) suggests that the designed contacts are ineffective because they do not necessarily address each of the countergroups' desires regarding the meeting's agenda and the revocation of topics that are important to any of the participants' groups such as national identities and the demand for recognition. In a later study, Maoz (2002b) even challenges the core idea of the contact activities by showing that to a certain degree there is a lack of intergroup interaction within the contact activities themselves.

THE ROLE OF EMOTIONS IN PEACE PROGRAMS

As the cognitive aspects of the conflict are directly addressed and seem deeply imbedded in the structure of the peace programs, the emotional aspects are often overlooked as consequences of the conflict. They are usually neither seen as the core of the peace education programs nor directly addressed as cause for the success or failure of the peace programs. In addition, a review of available peace education programs indicates that most of the programs were designed around cognitive theories (Harris, 1999), and that the main strategy for enhancing understanding and tolerance between conflict groups is to create forums where participants can learn about each other, make friends, and thereby reduce stereotypes and prejudices.

Nevertheless, many studies do stress the relationship between emotions and behavior, and there is no doubt that negative emotional reactions have implications on behavior (Murphy & Eisenberg, 2002). Studies suggest that emotions serve to organize and enhance behaviors and decrease or increase the occurrence of behavioral patterns (Frijda, 1986; Lemerise & Arsenio, 2000; Magai & McFadden, 1995; Moore & Ison, 1990). Both cognition and emotions are seen as types of information processing, there is growing evidence of their distinct functioning, and that emotions play a meaningful role in providing direction for cognitive processes and behavior (Izard, 1994; Lemerise & Arsenio, 2000).

In addition to studies on the contribution of emotions to behavior in general, there are few studies that directly address the contribution of emotions to intergroup relationships. The main focus of these studies is the mutual attitudes of conflict group members and the way that emotions can affect these attitudes. The basis of some of those studies is the general notion that attitudes are a reflection of cognitive, affective, and behavioral components (e.g., Zanna & Rempe, 1994) and it was suggested that when it comes to intergroup relations emotions rather than cognition are the underlying process of intergroup attitudes (Eagly, Mladinic, & Otto, 1994; Esses, Haddock, & Zanna, 1993; Jussim, Nelson, Manis, & Soffin, 1995; Stangor, Sullivan, & Ford, 1991). Furthermore, the intergroup emotion theory (Mackie, Devos, & Smith, 2000; Smith, 1993) is a theory that explicitly points to the emotions as the basis for the development of intergroup attitudes. According to the theory the identification of any individual with a social group makes the group part of his or her self-identity and therefore group belonging gets an emotional significance. Emotions are generated when either the individual or the social part of his or her self appraisal are threatened and lead to the development of prejudice toward another group or individual.

Although the intergroup emotion theory was supported in a few studies (Devos, Silver, Mackie, & Smith, 2002; Mackie, Silver, & Smith, 2002), other studies suggested that the emotions contribution to intergroup attitudes depend on the nature of intergroup relations (Haddock, Zanna, & Esses, 1994) or the specific issue of concern. For example, Dovidio, Esses, Beach, and Gaertner (2002) found in their study on attitudes of white participants toward blacks and Asians that attitudes were based on affect when it concerned further contact with members of the other group and on cognition when it comes to the endorsement of social policies.

While in many studies affect is seen as either a moderator of attitudes or as an intervention outcome, there is not enough evidence to conclude the mutual influence of emotions and cognition as a result of encounters between conflict groups. The aim of this study was to reveal the relationships between emotions and cognition as results of participation in contact intervention programs. This was done in the context of planned encounters between 11th-grade Israeli Jewish and Arab students that were conducted in Israel.

METHOD

Sample

The research sample consisted of a group of Israeli Arab students who participated in a peace education encounter program between Israeli Arab and Jewish students. The sample comprised of two 17-year-old 11th-grade classrooms that participated in the encounters as part of their school curriculum. Nonetheless, students had the free choice to decide whether to attend the program or not. Fifty-one students (13 male, 38 female) fulfill the research questioner at the onset of the program and 46 (11 male, 35 female) at the end of the program.

Measures

Four different questionnaires were used to measure different aspects of the social relationships between the Jewish and Arab participants. The four aspects were: (1) feelings toward the members of the "other group"; (2) prejudice regarding personal traits of the members of the "other group"; (3) willingness to engage in intergroup contact; (4) motivation regarding participation in planned encounters between Israeli Jewish and Arab social groups. The four questionnaires were used in many other studies in Israel in order to measure the relationships between different social groups of Israeli society (Saporta, 1993). In order to deliver the questionnaires to the Arab participants of this study a Hebrew version of the questionnaire was translated into Arabic by a professional translator, proficient in social science research. The four questionnaires used to measure the four aspects of the social relationships were:

1. *Feeling Checklist.* A 21-item "Feeling Checklist," based on a valid and reliable established checklist (Stephan, Ybarra, & Bachman, 1999), was translated and fitted to the needs of the Israeli population by TurKaspa-Shimoni (2001). The checklist included 21 emotions such as "anger," "warmth," and "shame," and the respondent is requested to indicate on a seven-point Lickert scale the degree of each emotion toward members of the other group. Face validity as judged by four experts was set as the validity criterion for the 21 items. Items were summed to yield a single index of

emotions and high mean score of the 21 items related to positive and favor-able emotions toward the other. Internal consistency for the feeling check-list was measured by alpha Cronbach and yielded a correlation of .82.

2. *Trait Rating.* Prejudice regarding the other traits were measured by a 21-item semantic differential scale used to measure the participants' per-ception regarding the traits of the "typical other." The questionnaire was used by Ben-Ari and Amir (1987) and revised by Saporta (1993) for use in Israeli society. Respondents were asked to characterize their perception of the "other" triads with bipolar adjectives such as honest–dishonest, open-minded–close-minded, and gentle–rough on a seven-point scale. High mean score in the 21 items related to positive perception of the other traits. Internal consistency for the trait rating was measured by alpha Cron-bach and yielded a correlation of .81.

3. *Social Distance Scale.* A 13-item questionnaire was used to measure the participants' willingness to interact with someone from the "other group." The scale developed by Saporta (1993) was based on the Social Distance Scale (SDS), which originally was developed by Bogardus (1928). The questionnaire samples verbal reports about how much the participants are willing to interact with persons from the "other group." Thirteen state-ments such as "study with him/her for exam," "live with him/her in the same building," and "be his/her partner for a trip" were introduced to the participants, and they were asked to rate their willingness on a one- to seven-point willingness scale. Participants were instructed to "rate the fol-lowing statements on the following scale about a same-sex person from the other group." Items were summed to yield a single index of social distance. Internal consistency for the questionnaire was measured by alpha Cron-bach and yielded a correlation of .83.

4. *Motivation.* Motivation regarding future participation in peace educa-tion programs was measured by an eight-item questionnaire based on a questionnaire developed by Saporta (1993). The eight items included statements such as "It is important to organize common programs for Jew-ish and Arab students" and "I would like to participate in future encoun-ters between Israeli Jews and Arabs." The items were compiled in conformity with a Likert scale structure in which responses were provided on a five-point scale varying from a very low level of support (1) to a very high level of support (7). Items were summed to yield a single index of atti-tudes. Internal consistency for the questionnaire was measured by alpha Cronbach and yielded a correlation of .77.

Procedure

A research assistant who explained the aims of the study and the ques-tionnaires administered the research questionnaires twice to the participants in their school classroom. The first administration was a week before the onset of the encounters and the second administration was a week after the end of the last session of the encounters. The intervention included three meeting days (six hours each), which included small group discussions, lectures, and social activities. There was a month interval between each of the meeting days so the elapsed time between the first and the second administration of the research questionnaire was 3 months. In accordance with the Israeli educational system, anonymity of the questionnaire respondents was ensured.

RESULTS

In the first stage of the study, and in order to examine the influence of participation in the contact intervention on feelings, prejudice, motivation, and willingness to engage in intergroup contact, participants' responses were compared in a series of "before–after" t-test design. Results indicated (see Table 13.1) a significant difference in feelings and prejudice while no differences were found in motivation and willingness to engage in intergroup contact. Thus, after their participation in the peace intervention program participants showed more positive feelings and less prejudice toward their Jewish counterparts but no differences were presented in their motivation to meet with members of the other group or in their willingness to engage in intergroup contact.

Table 13.1.   Means, Standard Deviation, and t-test values of Feelings, Prejudice, Motivation, and Social Distance of Arab Students Before and After Participation in Peace Contact Intervention

| | Time | | | | |
| | Before | | After | | |
Factor	M	SD	M	SD	T
Feelings	2.98	0.36	3.22	0.53	−2.59**
Prejudice	3.68	0.59	3.94	0.57	−2.27*
Motivation	3.59	0.41	3.43	0.55	1.61
Willingness to meet with the Other	3.00	0.63	2.94	0.67	0.34

$* p < .05 ** p < .01$

In the second phase of the study the main question of the research regarding the role of emotions in the peace-building process was examined. A structural equation modeling (SEM) was used to test the role of emotions by using the Analysis of Moment Structure (AMOS) program (Arbuckle & Wothke, 1999). SEM serves purposes similar to multiple regression and is an extension of the general linear model (GLM) that enables testing a set of regression equations simultaneously and permits examination of more complex relationships. In using the SEM the researcher first specifies a model based on theory, and then inputs the data into the SEM software. By using this statistical analysis he or she compares the data to the specified model in order to find the results, which include overall model fit statistics and parameter estimates. In this study the AMOS program utilizes that the preferred maximum likelihood method was used in order to estimate parameters in the data by calculating a log function of the model parameters from the raw data (Bollen, 1989).

The SEM developed for this study focused on the relationship of the four variables (Feelings, Prejudice, Motivation, and Social Distance) as were measured at the end of intervention, and estimated the path from emotion to both prejudice and motivation and of those two on the willingness to interact with members of the other group (social distance). Results of the SEM analysis revealed that the overall fit of the model was good [$X^2 (1) = 0.72$; P = .39] as the relationships between variables as proposed in the model are not significantly different from the overall sample correlations. Interpretation of fit and modification of indexes was also based on goodness-of-fit indexes. It is mostly recommended to examine several goodness-of-fit indexes and although there are continuing debates as to the "best" measures and the "best" index values there are four indexes that are most commonly recommended and used. The four indexes are the Normed Fit Index (NFI), the Non-Normed Fit Index (NNFI), the Incremental Fit Index (IFI), and the root mean square error of approximation (RMSEA) (Arbuckle & Wothke, 1999; Ulman, 2001). A value near 1.0 in the first three indexes and less than 0.10 in the RMSEA indicates a good fit (Bollen, 1989). Fit indexes in our model had values of 0.98 or above (NFI = .987; NNFI = 1.05; IFI = 1.0; RMSEA = .01)

Individual path parameter estimates are reported in Figure 13.1. The label that appears on each box describes the measured variable, the errors indicate the predicted relationships between the variables, and standardized path coefficients are shown next to arrows. It should be noticed that residual error terms appear only in relation to the dependent variables (Motivation, Prejudice, and Social Distance) but not to the independent variable (Feelings). This reflects the unexplained variance in the dependent variables (also called *endogenous*) due to all unmeasured causes. Feelings were positively related to motivation ($\beta = 0.41$; $p < .01$) and to willingness to meet with the other ($\beta = 0.12$; $p < .05$) while negatively related to prejudice ($\beta = -0.44$; $p < .01$). Motivation was positively related to willing-

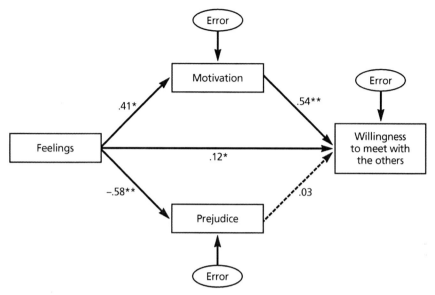

Figure 13.1.   Structural equation model with observed and path coefficients. Solid lines indicate significant paths (*p < .01; **p < .05) and dashed lines show nonsignificant paths.

ness to meet with the other ($\beta = -0.55$; $p < .001$), while prejudice was not significantly related to willingness to meet with the other ($\beta = 0.09$; $p > .05$).

DISCUSSION

The pattern of significant relationships within the model (see Figure 13.1) provides insights into the complex influence of emotional and cognitive underlying processes in peace intervention programs. This study suggests that emotions have more important roles than cognition in enhancing participants' willingness to interact with members of a conflict group. Findings that support both the intergroup emotion theory (Mackie, Devos, & Smith, 2000; Smith, 1993), which suggests emotions as the basis for the development of intergroup attitudes, and other studies suggesting that negative emotional reactions have implications on behavior and social relationships (Murphy & Eisenberg, 2002).

The findings of this study suggest not only that emotions have positive effects on the willingness to interact with members of a conflict group but also that they have a positive contribution to the decrease in prejudice (or development of positive attitudes), which by themselves do not contribute to the enhancement of positive social relationships. Thus, although in many other studies the cognitive aspects are seen as the mediating factor that can enhance understanding between conflict groups (Harris, 1999), and while many studies are conducted in order to reveal the ideal intervention characteristic for such change (e.g., Amir, 1969; Pettigrew, 1998; Tal-Or et al., 2002), the current study suggests that negative attitudes should be moderated by positive emotions and that emotions themselves have a more significant role than cognition in the enhancement of positive social relationships between conflict groups.

Additional findings of this study were that the contribution of the peace intervention program toward the participants' positive modification was only moderate and did not achieve any change in the participants' willingness to interact with members of their conflict group. This finding joins many other studies suggesting only a moderate amount of evidence for the positive contribution of peace intervention programs in general and particularly of contact intervention programs (Cairns & Hewstone, 2002; Harris, 1992; Nevo & Brem, 2002; Salomon, 2002). Nevertheless the results of this study indicate some improvement in both emotions and attitudes. These findings suggest that both emotional and cognitive changes are prior to any behavioral modification and can be achieved more easily than the behavioral change itself. Based on the previous discussion in this study it is also suggested that more meaningful changes of the participants' emotions could result also in the desired behavioral change.

Following the study results it is suggested that emotions should be seen as a core component and a main strategy of peace intervention programs. Educators and other practitioners should pay more attention to the design of peace programs rather than planning intervention programs that emphasize the reconstruction of thoughts about members of a conflict group, it is the emotions that should be referred to. In one line with those recommendations it is important that the assessment of any intervention program should not be limited to cognitive or behavioral changes but also to measure any emotional change.

It should be mentioned that the present findings are not without limitations. The SEM approach does not determine casual inferences and although the suggested model was supported, the generalization of this study should be limited to similar samples. Nevertheless, given the importance of peace intervention programs a description of the complex set of relationships between emotional and cognitive aspects to the enhancement of collaboration between conflict groups is an incremental step toward the understanding of the potential contribution of emotions to peace prevention programs, and providing a framework that can help to assess peace intervention programs and their outcomes.

ACKNOWLEDGMENT

This study was supported by the Institute for Community Education and Research, School of Education, Bar-Ilan University.

REFERENCES

Allport, G. W. (1954). *The nature of prejudice*. Cambridge, MA: Addison-Wesley.

Amir, Y. (1969). Contact hypothesis in ethnic relations. *Psychological Bulletin, 71,* 319–342.

Arbuckle, J. L., & Wothke, W. (1999). *Amos 4.0 user's guide*. Chicago: Smallwaters.

Bargal, D. (1990). Contact is not enough—The contribution of Lewinian theory to inter-group workshops involving Palestinian and Jewish youth in Israel. *International Journal of Group Tensions, 20,* 179–192.

Ben-Ari, R., & Amir, Y. (1987). Tayarim yisraelim bemitzraim: mifgash veshinuy amadot [Israeli tourists in Egypt: Meetings and attitude change]. *Megamot, 30*(2), 21–30.

Bogardus E. S. (1928, 1933, 1959). Social distance scale. In J. P. Robinson, P. R. Shaver, & L. S. Wrightsman (Eds.), *Measures of political attitudes. Measures of social psychological attitudes* (pp. 335–339). New York: Academic Press.

Bollen, K. A. (1989). *Structural equations with latent variables*. New York: Wiley.

Brewer, M. (1996). When contact is not enough: Social identity and intergroup cooperation. *International Journal of Intercultural Relations, 20,* 291–303.

Cairns, E., & Hewstone, M. (2002). Northern Ireland: The impact of peacemaking in Northern Ireland on intergroup behavior. In G. Salomon & B. Nevo (Eds.), *Peace education: The concept, principles and practices around the world* (pp. 217–228). Mahwah, NJ: Erlbaum.

Devos, T., Silver, L. A., Mackie, D. M., & Smith, E. R. (2002). Experiencing intergroup emotions. In D. M. Mackie & E. R. Smith (Eds.), *Beyond prejudice: From outgroup hostility to intergroup emotions* (pp. 111–134). Philadelphia: Psychology Press.

Dewey, J. (1916/1985). *Democracy and education: The middle works of John Dewey 1899–1924* (Vol. 9). Carbondale: Southern Illinois University Press.

Dovidio, J. F., Esses, V. M., Beach, K. R., & Gaertner, S. L. (2002). The role of affect in determining intergroup behavior: The case of willingness to engage in intergroup contact. In D. M. Mackie & E. R. Smith (Eds.), *Beyond prejudice: From outgroup hostility to intergroup emotions* (pp. 153–171). Philadelphia: Psychology Press.

Eagly, A. H., Mladinic, A., & Otto, S. (1994). Cognitive and affective bases of attitudes toward social groups and social policies. *Journal of Experimental Social Psychology, 30,* 113–137.

Esses, V. M., Haddock, G., & Zanna, M. P. (1993). Values, stereotypes, and emotions as determinants of intergroup attitudes. In D. M. Mackie & D. L. Hamilton (Eds.), *Affect, cognition, and stereotyping: Interactive processes in group perception* (pp.137–166). New York: Academic Press.

Frijda, N. H. (1986). *The emotions.* Cambridge, UK: Cambridge University Press.

Galtung, J. (1973). *Peace: Research, education, action.* Copenhagen: Christian Ejlers.

Groff, L. (2002). A holistic view of peace education. *Social Alternatives, 21*(1), 7–10.

Haddock, G., Zanna, M. P., & Esses,V. M. (1994). Mood and the expression of intergroup attitudes: The moderating role of affect intensity. *European Journal of Social Psychology, 24,* 189–205.

Harris, I. (1992). The challenge of peace education: Do our efforts make a difference? *Educational Foundations, 6*(4), 75–98.

Harris, I. (1999). Types of peace education. In L. Oppenheimer, D. Bar-Tal, & A. Raviv (Eds.), *How children understand war and peace.* San Francisco: Jossey-Bass.

Harris, I. (2002). Conceptual underpinnings of peace education. In G. Salomon & B. Nevo (Eds.), *Peace education: The concept, principles, and practices around the world.* Mahwah, NJ: Erlbaum.

Hewstone, M., & Brown, B. (1986).Contact is not enough: An intergroup perspective on the "contact hypothesis." In M. Hewstone & R. Brown (Eds.), *Contact and conflict in intergroup encounters.* New York: Basil Blackwell.

Izard, C. E. (1994). Cognition is one of four types of emotion activating systems. In P. Ekman & R.J. Davidson (Eds.), *The nature of emotions: Fundamental questions* (pp. 203–207). New York: Oxford University Press.

Jussim, L., Nelson, T. E., Manis, M., & Soffin, S. (1995). Prejudice, stereotypes, and labeling effects: Sources of bias in person perception. *Journal of Personality and Social Psychology, 68,* 228–246.

Kelman, H. (1990). Interactive problem solving: A social psychology approach to conflict resolution. In J. Burton & F. Dukes (Eds.), *Conflict: Reading in management and resolution* (pp. 199–216). New York: St. Martin's Press.

Koehler, D. J. (1990). *Persistence of conflicting views* (Working Paper No. 10). Stanford Center for Conflict and Negotiation.

Lemerise, E. A., & Williams, F. A. (2000). An integrated model of emotion processes and cognition in social information processing. *Child Development, 71*(1), 107–118.

Mackie, D. M., Devos, T., & Smith, E. R. (2000). Intergroup emotions: Explaining offensive action tendencies in an intergroup context. *Journal of Personality and Social Psychology, 79,* 602–616.

Mackie, D. M., Silver, L. A., & Smith, E. R. (2002). *The nature of intergroup emotions.* Unpublished manuscript, University of California, Santa Barbara.

Magai, C., & McFadden, S. (1995). *The role of emotions in social and personality development.* New York: Plenum Press.

Maoz, I. (2002a). Conceptual mapping and evaluation of peace education programs: the case of education for coexistence through intergroup encounters between Jews and Arabs in Israel. In G. Salomon & B. Nevo (Eds.), *Peace education, the concept, principles, and practices around the world* (pp. 259–269). Mahwah, NJ: Erlbaum.

Maoz, I. (2002b). Is there contact at all? Intergroup interaction in planned contact interventions between Jews and Arabs in Israel. *International Journal of Intercultural Relations, 26,* 85–197.

Moore, B. S., & Ison, A. M. (1990). Affect and social behavior. In B.S. Moore & A.M Ison (Eds.), *Affect and social behavior* (pp 1–21). New York: Cambridge University Press.

Murphy, B. C., & Eisenberg, N. (2002). An integrative examination of peer conflict: Children's reported goals, emotions and behaviors. *Social Development, 11*(4), 534–557.

Nevo, B., & Brem, I. (2002). Peace education programs and the evaluation of their effectiveness. In G. Salomon & B. Nevo (Eds.), *Peace education, the concept, principles, and practices around the world* (pp. 271–282). Mahwah, NJ: Erlbaum.

Pettigrew, T. F. (1998). Intergroup contact theory. *Annual Review of Psychology, 49*, 65–85.

Salomon, G. (2002). The nature of peace education: Not all programs are equal. In G. Salomon & B. Nevo (Eds.), *Peace education, the concept, principles, and Practices around the world* (pp. 271–282). Mahwah, NJ: Erlbaum.

Saporta, N. (1993). *The change of attitudes resulting from meetings between religious and non-religious, and the effect of trait anxiety on the change process.* MA dissertation, Bar-Ilan University.

Sherif, M. (1966). *Group conflict and cooperation.* London: Routledge & Kegan Paul.

Sherif, M., Harvey, O. J., White, J., Hood, W., & Sherif, C. (1961). *Intergroup conflict and cooperation: The Robber's Cave experiment.* Norman: University of Oklahoma Institute of Intergroup Relations.

Smith, E. R. (1993). Social identity and social emotions: Toward new conceptualizations of prejudice. In D. M. Mackie & D. L. Hamilton (Eds.), *Affect, cognition, and stereotyping: Interactive processes in group perception* (pp. 297–315). San Diego, CA: Academic Press.

Stangor, C., Sullivan, L. A., & Ford, T. E. (1991). Affective and cognitive determinants of prejudice. *Social Cognition, 9*, 359–380.

Staub, E., Pearlman, L. A., & Miller, V. (2003). Healing the roots of genocide in Rwanda. *Peace Review, 15*(3), 287–294.

Stephan, W. G., Ybarra, O., & Bachman, G. (1999). Prejudice toward immigrants: An intergrated threat theory. *Journal of Applied Social Psychology, 29*, 221–237.

Stomfay-Stitz, A. M. (1993). *Peace education in America, 1828–1990: Sourcebook for education and research.* Metuchen, NJ: Scarecrow Press.

Tal-Or, N., Boninger, D., & Gleicher, F. (2002). Understanding the conditions and processes necessary for intergroup contact to reduce prejudice. In G. Salomon & B. Nevo (Eds.), *Peace education, the concept, principles, and practices around the world* (pp. 89–108). Mahwah, NJ: Erlbaum.

Tur-Kaspa-Shimoni, M. (2001). *Evaluation of the integrated threat theory of prejudice in three domains of intergroup rivalry in Israeli society.* Doctoral dissertation, Department of Psychology, Bar-Ilan University.

Ulman, J. B. (2001). Structural equation modeling. In B. Tabachnick & L. Fidell (Eds.), *Using multivariate statistics* (4th ed.). New York: Allyn & Bacon.

UNESCO. (2000). Culture of peace: A declaration on a culture of peace. UN General Assembly, Fifty-third Session Res. 53/243. Available at http://www.unesco.org/cpp/uk/ declarations /2000.htm

Williams, R. M. (1947). The reduction of intergroup tensions: A survey of research on problems of ethnic, racial, and religious group relations. *Social Science Research Council Bulletin, 57,* 1–153.

Zanna, M. P., & Rempel, J. K. (1988). Attitudes: A new look at an old concept. In D. Bar-Tal & A.W. Kruglanski (Eds.), *The social psychology of knowledge* (pp. 315–334). Cambridge, UK: Cambridge University Press.

Part IV

RELIGIOSITY AND CULTURE OF PEACE

CHAPTER 14

EDUCATION FOR MUTUAL UNDERSTANDING

The Cases of Northern Ireland and Israel

F. Michael Perko

INTRODUCTION

Education for peace, tolerance, and pluralism is one of the most critical pedagogical needs in the contemporary world. Though post-Enlightenment thought tends to minimize the importance of religion, one has only to open the newspaper to see how dominant religion remains as a force in intercommunity conflict. To a significant degree, the growth of fundamentalist movements has contributed to this tendency (Perko, 2003, pp. 289–295).

The ways in which religion either promotes or retards education for tolerance and pluralism thus become a critical factor both in the creation of social conflict and its amelioration. Especially in traditional and developing societies in which there is little or no dichotomy between secular and sacred, religion serves a key role in determining both present issues and the future direction of civil society.

Educating Toward a Culture of Peace, pages 225–246

In much of the world, organized religion remains a major sponsor of educational institutions and activities. In Islamic countries like Pakistan, *madrasah*'s offer the only education many children receive, while Catholic schools in Northern Ireland and Israeli institutions sponsored by *Agudat Israel* and *Shas* are major features on the educational landscape of those countries.

Additionally, religion remains an important curricular element even in schools directly sponsored by civil government. Thus, in Northern Ireland's "controlled" educational sector, serving a largely Protestant population, religious instruction and practice are significant parts of the school culture.[1] The same can be said for what are termed the "state religious" schools in Israel.[2]

For these reasons, examination of the role of religion and especially of the religious factor within education in both civic strife and development is important in order to gain an understanding of how religion contributes to social tension and its potential for helping to ameliorate civil strife and contribute to social cohesion.

Here, two communities exhibiting significant social tension will be the focus of attention. These are the State of Israel and Northern Ireland. In numerous respects, these two societies invite comparison despite their divergences in geographical locale and culture. Roughly analogous historical situations brought the conflict in each into being. In the case of Northern Ireland, this involved the establishment of the "plantation" by which the English crown promoted the settlement of Scottish Presbyterians in heretofore universally Catholic Ireland in order to graft the island more firmly to Britain. In fact, it had the opposite effect, fomenting civil unrest and deepening the Irish commitment to Catholicism (Mulholland, 2002). Similarly, the population dynamics of Israel/Palestine began to change in the late 19th century with the First *Aliyah*, an initial in-migration of Jews. This reached a peak in the years following World War II as the Jewish population, 650,000 in 1948, grew to over 4 million by the late 1980s (Sachar, 1996).

In both societies, recent years have witnessed struggles by the indigenous population to achieve political equality. In Ireland, this took the form of a national liberation movement that resulted in the creation of the Republic of Ireland in 1922, and led to the partition of the country along religious lines. Subsequently, in the six counties that comprise Northern Ireland, a struggle for political and economic equality by Catholics has created a high level of tension that continues to the present day.

Similarly, in Israel, the period since the declaration of the state in 1948 has been characterized by intense conflict between the Jewish state and the Arabs.[3] This was exacerbated after the 1967 War that brought the West Bank and Gaza under Israeli control.

Within the State of Israel proper, the situation of Arabs has also been problematic. Most of their territory was designated as "defense areas" in the state's early years and was ruled by military governors operating under army rather than civilian norms (Sachar, 1996, pp. 383–386). While Israel's Compulsory Education Law resulted in a significant increase in Arab primary education (Sachar, 1996, pp. 389–390), both the numbers and quality of institutions lagged far behind the Jewish sector of the population. Most recently, the report of the Or Commission investigating the shooting of Arab Israeli citizens by police in October 2000 commented that discrimination within the Arab sector is the most important contemporary domestic issue, and insisted that "the state must initiate, develop, and operate programs emphasizing budgets that will close the gaps in education, housing, industrial development, employment, and services."[4]

Finally, in both communities, religion plays a key role in self-definition and, as a result, in the ensuing social and political conflicts. In the case of Northern Ireland, whether one is Catholic or Protestant defines, to a significant degree, the individual's politics and status. Within the State of Israel, two of five intersecting social rifts—orthodox/secular and Arab/Jewish—have significant religious components (Barzel, 1995, p. 456). Additionally, Israel defines itself as the "Jewish state," with concomitant attention to the religious and ethnic components of identity.

Both societies, too, have elements of fundamentalist religion that complicate attempts at tolerance and pluralism. In Northern Ireland, the most obvious example is the leadership role in the most hardline of the Unionist parties, the Democratic Unionists, played by the Rev. Ian Paisley.

In Israel, manifestations of such tendencies are seen in the religious fundamentalism of some in the settler movement, as well as the growing power of Hamas and Islamic Jihad both within the Palestinian territories and, more recently, Israel proper (Perko, 2003, pp. 289–293). Increasingly, political controversies are viewed from the perspectives of their transcendent dimensions.

For all of these reasons, Northern Ireland and Israel invite comparison on a variety of topics including education. It is not by accident that one of the most prominent scholars involved with attempts to use educational programs to bridge the divide between communities in Northern Ireland, Seamus Dunn, has also been involved with a joint schools project in northern Israel (Dunn, 1990, p. 24). Less benevolently, graffiti in cities such as Belfast indicate the identification of both major factions in the Northern Ireland political struggle with parties in the contemporary Middle East. Thus, the portrayal of the Israeli flag is a common theme in Protestant neighborhoods, while Catholic iconography exhibits a similar support of the Palestinian cause, shown in the depiction of the Palestinian flag and figures in military fatigues and *kaffiyeh*'s.

The comparative approach taken here will be that of transnational history. As Ilan Troen and others have shown, such analysis helps illuminate the situations of the geographical entities studied through the lenses of comparison and contrast that sharpen observers' perspectives of both.[5] Specifically, an examination will be made first of the history and state of education for tolerance and pluralism within Israeli schools, followed by a comparable analysis of Northern Ireland education. Finally, suggestions will be made about the policy implications suggested by this comparison and contrast.

ISRAEL

For the most part, Israeli education has avoided attempts to provide for schooling aimed at integrating the Arab and Jewish sectors of the population, or indeed, any serious attempt on a large scale to use schooling as a vehicle for ameliorating conflict across the religious and cultural divide. Since the founding of the state in 1948, Israeli education, with a few notable exceptions, has perpetuated and fostered the divisions present in pre-state Palestine, implicitly endorsing state-sponsored education in which Jewish and Arab children are educated in separate schools operating with their own curricula.

Israeli Education: The Context

Israel's first legislation regarding education came shortly after the establishment of the state. The Compulsory Education Act (1949) introduced free primary education for children between the ages of 5–13. This was extended in 1968 to include grades 9 and 10, and, in 1979, free education was extended to grade 12, though not made compulsory.

In the very first years, education was controlled directly by political parties, reflecting the intense ideological orientations of the State's founders. In 1953, however, the State Education Law abolished these "trend" schools, and made the government directly responsible for education.

Two main forms of primary education are recognized: state education and recognized non-state education. The former sector is divided into three categories. State schools are largely secular, with a strong emphasis on the Zionist tradition. State religious schools also have this emphasis, but their curriculum includes a larger amount of religious instruction and activity. In addition, there are Arab state schools teaching a somewhat distinct curriculum and having Arabic as the language of instruction.[6]

There is also recognized non-state education. These institutions are privately controlled, but subsidized and supervised by the state. In the Jewish sector, most of these schools are ultra-orthodox in character, sponsored by *Agudat Israel* or *Shas*. The remaining recognized non-state schools, enrolling some 10% of all children, are mainly sponsored by Christian groups, and serve Muslim and Christian students from the Arab sector, although private Jewish schools in West Bank settlements and institutions catering to immigrants from the former Soviet Union are also to be found (Benporath, n.d., p. 30).

Arab Education

Arab schooling in Palestine prior to Israeli independence was meager. In 1948, there were only 45 elementary schools and one high school. Numbers of Arab schools and students grew significantly over the next 50 years, so that by 1995, there were 369 Arab elementary schools and 149 secondary ones (Iram & Schmida, 1998, p. 92, Table 7.1). Especially notable was the gender shift. In the early 1950s, 18.6% of Arab students were women; by 1996, this had increased to 47% (Iram & Schmida, 1998, p. 92).

Despite these advances there are significant discrepancies between the Arab and Jewish educational sectors. The dropout rate among Arabs is notably higher. From children who attended first grade in 1978, only 13.7% of Arab students received a matriculation certificate (*bagrut*), compared to 42.3% of Jewish students, and the most successful Arab group, the Christians, still did only as well as the weakest Jewish group, those from Middle Eastern backgrounds (Iram & Schmida, 1998, p. 93).

Arab schools generally have fewer resources than Jewish ones. The student/teacher ratio is higher in Arab schools, and teachers tend not to be as well educated. While the appointment of teachers at the elementary level is done by the Ministry of Education and Culture, at the secondary level the local authority has a major say in their hiring and firing. This has damaged teacher standing in the eyes of students who view them as compliant civil servants (Iram & Schmida, 1998, pp. 96–97).

The result is an inferior and highly conservative educational system. It has been estimated that, even were affirmative action to provide more funding for Arab schools and teacher education, it would take ten 10 to 15 years to bring them to parity with the Jewish sector.

The Curricular Divide

From a historical perspective, curricular development for Arab schools has taken a different course from their Jewish counterparts. Prior to the mid-1970s, Jewish schools focused on Zionism, Jewish culture and religion, and national identity. Arab schools, however, emphasized a curriculum that focused on Arab–Jewish coexistence, and deemphasized elements having to do with Arab religion, culture, and identity. In language studies, the requirements for Arabic studies by Arab students were largely technical, with little attention to Arab literature and culture. These same students, however, utilized a Hebrew curriculum in which not only language but Jewish culture and heritage were taught, as well as a sense of Israeli citizenship. Jewish and biblical studies had a privileged place within the curriculum of the Arab schools. Indeed, more time was spent on them than on Islamic studies.

While considerable change has taken place since the mid-1970s, attempts at education for tolerance, pluralism, and national unity still are asymmetrical. Even after the Peled Committee in 1975 had suggested that state education for the Arab sector should be based on Arab culture as well as love of and loyalty to the State of Israel, curricular disparities remain. At the secondary level, the revised history curriculum emphasizes Jewish–Arab coexistence, along with Judaism's contribution to world culture. However, there is not comparable attention to coexistence or Arab history and culture in Jewish schools (Benporath, n.d., p. 9). Most dramatic is the difference in teaching objectives regarding the Arab–Israeli conflict. In Arab schools, the conflict is presented so that students understand both national movements. In Jewish schools, however, the main effort is to strengthen the students' identification with the Zionist movement "to deepen the student's belief in the just struggle of the Jewish people to a national renewal in their homeland" (Iram & Schmida, 1998, pp. 98–103).

These differences are unremarkable given the divergences between the two communities. The War of Independence concretized the disparities between the state's major communities, and contributed significantly to solidifying the cultural, political, and ideological divergences.[7]

For Arabs, including Israeli citizens, the 1948 War was traumatic in a different sense. In the interests of security, some were forcibly removed from their homes in Galilee villages. It is hardly a wonder that what Jewish Israelis see as the War of Independence is referred to by Arabs as the *Nakbah* (disaster).

Subsequently, the two societies have continued to diverge in many ways. As a result of the two *intifadah*'s and terrorist bombings in which Israeli Arabs have been implicated, many Jewish Israelis regard their fellow citizens with suspicion, as a kind of "fifth column." Israeli Arabs, for their part, have chafed under years of discrimination in the economic, educational, and political sectors and have grown increasingly resentful and restive about Jewish hegemony.[8]

Education for Tolerance and Pluralism in Israel

What activities have been undertaken to establish integrated education or programs focused on education for tolerance and pluralism have largely come from private interest groups or academic institutions. Though comparatively few in number, they are important in demonstrating that such efforts are viable.

Integrated Education

Genuinely integrated education is hard to find. In some schools, faculty include both Jews and Arabs, but the student body does not. Here, the schools established in Ibillin by Archimandrite Elias Chacour (2001) are illustrative. One of the few examples of genuinely integrated education is found in the village of Neve Shalom/Wahat al-Salam. This community, founded in 1972, is devoted to the principle of egalitarian coexistence. Schooling in the village began with the establishment of a preschool and kindergarten in 1981, and an elementary school 3 years later. Jewish and Arab children learn together on a daily basis, within a context that is bilingual, bicultural, and binational. The school has two directors, one Arabic and the other Jewish. The teachers, both Arabs and Jews, come from the village itself and surrounding communities (Feuververger, 1998, p. 695).

While the negotiation of competing identities, cultures, and loyalties requires significant effort, research suggests that the school is characterized by high morale and a strong sense of purpose. The children work and play together as well as examine their respective cultures, histories, religions and languages within a safe context.

Even though problems such as asymmetry in children's use of language (Hebrew predominates for both groups) and a relative difficulty in attracting Jewish children continue, the experience seems fundamentally positive. In 1994, the Ministry of Education agreed to fund 50% of the cost for each child up to Grade 5. More recently, the school's directors have been invited to attend monthly meetings of school directors in the Jerusalem region.[9]

Neve Shalom/Wahat Al-Salam represents a bold attempt to provide for integrated education. It is to be noted, however, that it and a few similar ventures represent only a minuscule portion of education in Israel.

Cross-Community Programming

Besides the small number of genuinely integrated schools, some attempt has been made at providing for cross-community student contact across the Jewish–Arab divide. Typically, these efforts have been the product of interested individuals and institutions, rather than of the state school structures, although the Ministry of Education, and especially its Unit for Education for Democracy and Coexistence, has been instrumental in providing funding and other resources.

One notable example is the program created under the auspices of the Yosef Burg Chair at Bar Ilan University, under the direction of Yaacov Iram. The goal has been "to train prospective teachers to be aware of stereotypes and to cope with prejudice toward individuals and groups by modifying conceptual and attitudinal bases." The program also foresees the development of curricular materials for Israeli and Palestinian schools.[10]

Without denigrating this effort, it is nonetheless worth noting that this program is designed to deal with university-age students and adult faculty, rather than directly with children. Also noteworthy is that these are the only university-sponsored workshops of their kind.[11]

An example of direct school-to-school contact emanating from the Arab side is the project created by the Greek Catholic priest Emile Shoufani. Shoufani, who achieved international recognition for his organization of a pilgrimage to Auschwitz by Israeli Arabs and Jews,[12] has long been recognized as a leader in Arab–Jewish dialog. In 1989, he instituted a 3-year exchange program with a school associated with the Hebrew University in order to help Jewish and Arab students "to meet each other, to erase prejudice, to learn to discuss their rights democratically and work together for peace," while giving Arab children "the tools for a full integration in the State of Israel while retaining their identities."[13]

The 2001 winner of the UNESCO prize, Givat Haviva, remains one of the most important contributors to cross-community efforts. Perhaps its most innovative activity is the "Children Teaching Children" program, which, since 1987, has brought together junior high school students as equals for encounters designed to promote learning about themselves and others. Student participation is equally divided between Jews and Arabs and to date, some 1,700 students in 42 classes have been taught by around 100 teachers. Measures of success include demands by students in several locations to continue the program for a third year and the emergence of dialog programs for teachers who voluntarily take part.

Beyond this flagship program, Givat Havivah also has programs to promote dialog among student leaders as well as among Jewish and Arab teachers via a series of workshops. Additionally, it sponsors programs in which Jewish and Arab students in mixed groups study Israeli history and geography, and engage in painting and photography projects. For Jewish students there are one- or two-day seminars on Arabic language and culture and for Arab teachers, workshops on the *Shoah*.[14]

This multiplicity of projects is not without its difficulties. Some observant Jews are opposed because they fear assimilation while some Arab parents believe that they encourage their children to become involved in the conflict and to question authority and traditional Palestinian social structure. Identity issues among the Arab students also present problems. Because the program is relatively expensive, and requires outside fundraising as well as grants from the Ministry of Education and local schools, and because of its high organizational demands, it is unlikely that it will ever be mandatory in the state school system.[15]

The Van Leer Institute in Jerusalem, also in cooperation with the Ministry of Education, has also developed a "Values and Citizens" program for secondary schools. Utilizing an active learning model, students examine current social issues as well as connection with their own cultural heritage. In academic year 2002–2003, 186 schools participated in the program, of which 69 were state Arabic, 18 state religious, and 99 state secular.[16] Additionally, the institute has established the "Coexistence as Curriculum" project, a 2-year effort in which Jewish and Arab teachers from 10 Israeli schools met every second week with facilitators. The results currently are being modified and piloted with over 300 students at 10 Israeli Arab and Jewish schools.[17]

A final agency worthy of mention is the Unit for Education for Democracy and Coexistence of the Ministry of Education. This unit works with voluntary organizations and institutions in creating in-service program for teachers and principals including traveling seminars for Jewish and Arab principals in the same district and workshops (in conjunction with Givat Haviva) for Arab teachers on education for life in a democracy. It also publishes curricula such as *We and Our Neighbors* for grades 3 and 4 to teach children in mixed neighborhoods about each other, *Jews and Arabs in Israel* for grades 5 and 6 (within the unit on northern Israel), and *Arab Citizens of Israel*, the textbook required for the *bagrut* citizenship curriculum.[18]

Summary

Within Israel there are modest programs attempting to deal with inter-community issues as they relate to tolerance and pluralism. As important as the example of integrated settings like the school at Neve Shalom/Wahat Al-Salam are, they represent a minuscule portion of the total Israeli educational ecology. More widespread are programs such as those of Fr. Shoufani, the Burg/UNESCO chair at Bar Ilan, and especially, those of the Van Leer Institute and Givat Haviva that bring administrators, teachers and children together for organized encounters and dialog. The absence of overarching state educational structures to require such activities and provide funding for them inevitably means that they will continue to be sporadic and reach only a small sector of Arab and Jewish Israeli children and teachers.

NORTHERN IRELAND

"I do not know any measures which would prepare the way for a better feeling in Ireland than uniting children at an early age, and bringing them up in the same school, leading them to commune with one another and to form those little intimacies and friendships which often subsist through life" (Richardson, 1992, p. 2). So spoke Roman Catholic Bishop Doyle of Kildare and Leighlin in 1826, arguing against the religiously segregated Irish schools. Despite the passage of over 170 years, his comment is nearly as applicable in Northern Ireland today as when first made. Only a few recent initiatives such as the formation of integrated schools and the creation of the governmentally sponsored Education for Mutual Understanding (EMU) and Cultural Heritage curricula offer much in the way of educational support for the creation of a unified society.

Northern Ireland Education: Historical Contexts

Prior to the establishment of Northern Ireland in 1921, the six counties were part of the National School System. While the original intent had been the formation of free elementary schools catering to both Catholic and Protestant children in jointly organized schools, by the end of the 19th century the various churches had successfully fought for educational control (Morgan, Dunn, Cairns, & Frasier, 1992, pp. 6–7).

Given that a substantial minority of the population questioned the legitimacy of the state, it is unsurprising that attempts to create structures to serve the whole community met with near universal failure. The Catholic Church, which had lost significant school funding as a result of opposition to state-controlled schooling, complained bitterly of discrimination. Protestants were unhappy because of perceived secularization of schools under direct state control. By the 1930s, bitter controversies over education had left Northern Ireland with an almost completely segregated school system.[19]

Various attempts at revision and reform had limited success. On the one hand, the Education Act of 1968 raised funding for voluntary schools, virtually all of which were Catholic. On the other, attempts by the Minister of Education in a power-sharing government in 1974 to promote "shared education" came to nought when a loyalist strike brought the government down.

Three traditional categories of schooling, based on management structures, remain dominant. Controlled Schools, under the direct governance of the local Area Education and Library Boards, serve an almost exclusively Protestant population. Maintained Schools are church controlled but linked to the Area Education and Library Boards. These are virtually all Roman Catholic. Voluntary Schools, which are under the direct control of the Department of Education of Northern Ireland (DENI) may or may not have a close church tie, but are usually entirely Catholic or Protestant.[20]

The Education Reform Order of 1989, however, formalized two initiatives that represent major ways in which the educational divide can be bridged. Under it, the small number of integrated schools that had begun to appear were allowed to receive full grants, and Education for Mutual Understanding and Cultural Heritage were established as mandatory themes in all schools.[21]

Integrated Education

While integrated schools might appear to be a logical alternative to Northern Ireland's sectarian segregated schools, they were a long time in arriving. From the early 1970s, there were a series of social analyses raising the question of the impact of traditional educational structures on an already divided society, and researchers had begun to study interaction among young people.

Out of these beginnings, groups of parents who felt that separation damaged their children came together in informal groups that resulted in the 1974 foundation of the All Children Together (ACT) movement. While ACT initially lobbied for change in the existing schools, they quickly ran into opposition from religious groups. This was unremarkable, given the escalation of sectarian violence, imposition of direct rule by Westminster, and collapse of the power-sharing executive that had come into existence as a result of the Sunningdale Agreement (Morgan et al., 1992, pp. 10–12).

What was most remarkable about ACT was its staying power. Members continued to meet and plan, and, when it had become obvious by the late 1970s that it was extremely unlikely that any existing school would opt to become integrated, they decided to found such a school themselves.

Finally, in 1981, Lagan College was opened with 28 pupils and two full-time teachers in a rented scout hall to a blaze of mixed publicity. For 3 years this first integrated school in Northern Ireland received no government funding, relying instead on parent contributions, donations by European friends, and gifts by charitable trusts and donors in the United Kingdom.

In January 1982 it moved to its first permanent quarters in a redundant primary school. In 1986, Lagan College leased a new site from the National Trust and began to build a permanent home in stages. Finally, in September 1991, the first part of this new facility was opened, 10 years after the College's original formation. One measure of Lagan's success is that its student population numbered around 1,000 in Fall 2003.[22]

Lagan was followed by two primary schools and another secondary one, all in the Belfast area. At the same time, new "umbrella" organizations were established to promote integrated education and, in one case, to provide a coherent structure through which the schools could deal with government departments, founding bodies, and the churches. By 2003, there were 46 integrated schools in Northern Ireland, 17 secondary and 29 primary, as well as an additional 13 nursery schools. In academic year 2000–01, some 1,140 applicants for places in integrated schools were turned away for lack of space.[23] Especially encouraging is the fact that recent years have witnessed schools changing their status from Controlled to Integrated, something unheard of in the movement's earlier days. However, the pupils enrolled represent only about 4% of Northern Ireland's total school population.[24]

The conventional wisdom that integrated schools serve a predominantly middle-class constituency is somewhat inaccurate. Across Northern Ireland, around 27% of students receive free school meals, an index of economic deprivation. In integrated institutions, the number is around 25%, only slightly lower (Tell, 1999, p. 60). While such schools serve a diverse population, however, studies show that they tend to have large middle-class constituencies. Among the teaching staff, especially older members have more experience in living outside Northern Ireland than do their peers in other types of schools (Morgan et al., 1992, pp. 54–60).

It would be hard to assess the effect of integrated schooling on children simply because the integrated schools differ in other significant respects from the general run of Northern Ireland education. Because most of them were directly created by their constituencies, there tends to be a high level of parent involvement. Most also were created around "child-centered" models of education, a marked contrast to the highly traditional educational culture that predominates in Northern Ireland.[25]

From student interviews and surveys, it seems clear that the goal of bringing children of different communities into contact with each other is being met. Also, and contrary to fears expressed by critics of integrated education, the children seem secure in their own community identity despite mixing with members of the other group.[26]

Many of the problems of integrated education appear to have to do with broader societal issues. Ultra-conservative Protestants have opposed them as agents of thinly disguised ecumenism. Roman Catholic bishops have remained opposed, arguing that it jeopardizes children's religious education, especially as a preparation for receiving the sacraments. This opposition has made it difficult for some parents to supported integrated schools, and for the schools to find Catholic priests as chaplains. At the same time, and somewhat ironically, some parents find difficulties with the schools because of their stated Christian character.[27]

Education for Mutual Understanding

More broadly based than integrated education has been the move to utilize the regular curriculum to teach children about the other community, and about common elements in their histories. This is subsumed under the cross-curricular themes of "Education for Mutual Understanding" (EMU) and "Cultural Heritage." In addition, various cross-community contact schemes have developed.

The concept of EMU began in the mid-1970s when DENI was charged with responsibility for improving community relations. Eventually, the Education Reform Order of 1989 that began funding of integrated schools also introduced EMU as a statutory part of the common curriculum for all Northern Ireland pupils.

EMU and Cultural Heritage are themes that are mandated for instruction across all curricular areas.[28] The goals of EMU are to encourage pupils to respect themselves and others, to appreciate interdependence within society, to know what is shared and what is different in cultural traditions, and to see how conflict can be handled in nonviolent ways. The related area of Cultural Heritage is also concerned with interaction, interdependence, continuity and change, shared, diverse and distinctive cultural features of both communities, and international and transnational influences. Each goal is conjoined with an EMU one.[29]

Various regular curricular areas have concrete objectives for each of these EMU goals. For example, at Key Stage 1 (ages 4–8), historical studies must include treatments of "similarities and differences between themselves and other children in the class and beyond" and in geography of "the roles and responsibilities of the adults they know and how people cooperate and depend on each other for help, goods, and services, at home, in the school, and in the local community." Key Stage 4 (ages 15–16) Political Studies "must require the study of contemporary political issues, including a Northern Ireland dimension."[30]

Good examples of this are found in texts designed to introduce students to church buildings and to the way baptisms, weddings, funerals, and communion are celebrated in Protestant and Catholic contexts. In the former unit, students are asked to consider why people were forced to worship outdoors at various times, visit and compare the several churches at the Ulster Folk and Transport Museum (an historic village), and do historical studies of the churches in their community.[31] In the latter, pupils are divided into groups to note similarities and differences among the religious rituals of the major Christian communities as well as to understand changes over time (e.g., the restoration of communion under both bread and wine to Roman Catholics).[32]

Besides formal academic study, EMU also makes use of a variety of activities designed to bring children from different communities into contact with each other. These may involve common service projects or field trips. Among the most significant are the residential programs developed by the ecumenical Corrymeela community, which bring adolescents from different groups together for structured activities (Department of Education Northern Ireland, 2000, pp. 22–23). While such cross-community contacts are not required by law, they appear to be fairly numerous, and generally positively received (Department of Education Northern Ireland, 1990, p. 25).

Still, Education for Mutual Understanding/Cultural Heritage faces formidable problems. Definition of the term EMU is vague, and so, there is lack of clarity about what precisely is contained in this area. School commitment varies widely from place to place. Like curricular innovations everywhere, it seems to be regarded as marginal by many teachers and school administrators despite the mandate for its inclusion. In those schools where it is successful, a major factor is commitment by school administrators and school governors to the process.[33]

Finally, there is some religious opposition to it. This emanates mostly from conservative Protestant quarters, who see it as an attempt to expose their children to false religion.

Summary

Integrated Education and Education for Mutual Understanding have the potential to be major factors in the creation of a new Northern Ireland. By providing children from their earliest years with experience of those in the other community, and by creating an academic context in which similarities and differences can be understood, these programs offer the possibility of lessening blind prejudice.

While the integrated school sector is steadily growing, and exercises an influence disproportionate to its size, the small numbers of students is an indication of its relative marginality. Education for Mutual Understanding and Cultural Heritage have more potential to exert an influence precisely because they do not call for the dramatic changes in attitudes and educational structures that integrated education demands. However, because they have not been, until recently, mandated, there is continual risk that they will be viewed as mostly irrelevant. Moreover, the political sensibilities that disallow the possibility of mandatory cross-community contact as part of EMU also severely limit its potential impact.

In both of these programs lies an inherent difficulty. Without the legal ability to compel participation in integrated schools or cross-community contact in Education for Mutual Understanding, it is almost inevitable that these movements will remain limited in terms of far-reaching influence.

ISRAEL AND NORTHERN IRELAND: CONTRASTING SITUATIONS

While similarities between Northern Ireland and Israel encourage comparison, differences are also worthy of note. These have had significant contextual effect not only upon schooling but also the general sociocultural situation.

Politically, Israel and Northern Ireland are significantly different. Israel is a sovereign state. It has, for all practical purposes, complete freedom to order its social agencies, including education, in the manner it wishes as long as the results conform with the state's Basic Laws. Northern Ireland, on the other hand, is part of a larger political entity, the United Kingdom. As such, its local governmental autonomy is circumscribed. What this means is that Northern Ireland does not have complete authority to chart its own course, educationally or in any other way. What this also has meant is that the British government has been able to promote activities aimed at easing cross-community tension in ways that would have been unlikely to emerge from any more local governmental structures. Educationally, this has included support for both Integrated Education and EMU from both Parliament and the Northern Ireland Office.

In several respects, the sociocultural divide in Northern Ireland seems less complex than that of Israel. The inhabitants of the province are divided along Protestant and Catholic lines, though these serve more as cultural identifiers than as explicitly religious ones. Within the communities there are differences, many of which have to do with the desirability of specific political outcomes. However, each is relatively coherent and within-group cultural differences are fairly minimal. Each group has its own unique narrative in light of which most of the members identify themselves and others.

Within Israel, the situation is considerably more complex. The Arab–Jewish rift is only one of five intersecting divisions within Israeli society. At least two of the others, the orthodox-secular and ethnic rifts, are intra-Jewish and cause their own sets of tensions within Israel, demanding educational attention as well (Barzel, 1995, p. 456). Furthermore, Israeli Arab society is hardly a cultural monolith.

From an educational perspective, these complexities create additional difficulties in attempts to deal with tolerance and pluralism. Structurally, a wider range of cultural groups in Israel have responsibility for, and control of, education than in Northern Ireland. Political debates over schooling cover a wide range of issues besides cross-community ones. It is hardly surprising, then, that projects such as those of the Burg/UNESCO chair are also concerned about within-group relations, or that even relatively ambitious proposals to create programs for cross-community civic education like those of Benporath admit that this likely must be done in the context of the present separate educational frameworks.[34]

Of great importance are the differences in the religious sector's stance toward the necessity and even desirability of education for tolerance and pluralism. One of the most important factors in Northern Ireland's recent attempts to deal with cross-community divisions has been the commitment of the vast majority of the province's religious leadership to ending violence and creating a greater degree of social cohesion. Cardinal Cahal Daly, the major Catholic leader in Northern Ireland from 1990 to 1996, was a relentless opponent of sectarian violence. While he resisted integrated education because of his commitment to Catholic schooling, he was a supporter of EMU. On the Protestant side, a comparable figure has been Dr. John Dunlop. A strong advocate for cultural diversity in Northern Ireland, he was Moderator of the General Assembly of the Presbyterian Church in Ireland in 1992–93. His election to this position is especially significant, since it had been the conventional wisdom that a supporter of cross-community activities would be unable to garner the support to be elected. The Dunlop election was a testimony to the support of this religious body for cultural pluralism.

More broadly, innovative educational work has been carried on by a wide variety of religious groups including the Corrymeela Community, which sponsors cross-community student encounters and the Columbanus Community of Reconciliation, a Protestant and Catholic living community that for years supported a schools worker for tolerance and pluralism in Belfast. Numerous other groups could be named as well.

Within the religious sector in Israel, it is hard to find analogs. To approximate the role of leaders like Daly and Dunlop in Northern Ireland in the Israeli context, for example, would necessitate support by the Chief Rabbis, Grand Mufti of the al-Aqsa Mosque, and Latin Catholic Patriarch of Jerusalem. While at least the last of these has spoken of the necessity for peaceful coexistence, none has made efforts to develop or support concrete programs to promote this, and, in fact, several have consistently supported positions that undercut efforts at developing meaningful strategies for

Arab–Jewish coexistence. The absence of efforts among prominent religious institutions is also striking. The Shalom Hartman Institute's Charles E. Smith High School, for example, numbers religious tolerance among its key values, but appears to concentrate almost exclusively on doing this within the Jewish sector.[35] It is noteworthy that institutions like the Van Leer Institute, Givat Haviva, and the Abraham Fund that are heavily involved in coexistence activities, especially in the educational sector, are essentially secular. It appears that the Israeli religious sector, Christian, Jewish, and Muslim alike, is not only uncommitted to the creation and support of educational activities for tolerance and pluralism, but too often opposed to them.

This contrast in the attitudes and actions between the two societies is one of the most striking differences. Given the high value placed within all three Abrahamic religious communities on formal religion as both an expression of piety and as a major element of cultural identity, the absence of institutional religious support for coexistence activities inevitably consigns them to the secular sector of education in both Arab and Jewish communities. Because, especially in the Jewish and Muslim cases, religious conservatism is highly associated with political conservatism and, all too frequently, right-wing radicalism, those segments of Israel's Arab and Jewish schools most likely to benefit from basic programs in peace education are the very ones least likely to be exposed to such activities. Thus, Islamic schools and *yeshivot* likely will continue to produce graduates rooted in stereotypes that can only confirm and strengthen their already intransigent ideological positions.

CONCLUSION

What do the similarities and differences between these two societies tell us about the dynamics affecting peace education in each? What do they suggest about future directions for such programs?

The generally similar contours of the ethnoreligious conflicts argue forcefully for attention to be devoted to the development and support of religiously based strategies for education for tolerance and pluralism. Given the close proximity in each instance of two communities that have long regarded each other with suspicion and hatred, it is unlikely that there will be any long-term reduction in tension and violence, or positive movement in the direction of cross-community understanding and involvement absent significant intervention by the educational establishment supported by religious and civil leaders.

At the same time, differences in the political and religious climates have already led to different strategies for approaching these issues, and, apparently, different levels of commitment. In Northern Ireland, the presence of a powerful nonlocal force, the national government in Westminster, has assisted in the creation and promotion of Integrated Education, and has been instrumental in mandating Education for Mutual Understanding and Cultural Heritage. This exercise of control by a party not immediately involved in the conflict has provided support for cross-community efforts that might otherwise not have been developed, and allowed more distant governmental entities to shoulder criticism for these efforts that would otherwise have fallen on local political and educational leaders.

The religious divide in Northern Ireland is not as great as that in Israel. Virtually all of the significant actors in Northern Ireland come from within a European Christian context. While intra-Christian religious and political controversies have played out since the Reformation, there is at least a common text and some shared symbols. Moreover, both mainstream Protestantism and Roman Catholicism there have been influenced by broader ecumenical movements that seek to develop common understandings and programs of action. The result has been the gradual marginalization of the most extreme elements within Protestant society, and a softening of Catholic attitudes. Thus, mainstream religion in Northern Ireland has been a significant force in attempts to develop education for tolerance and pluralism.

In Northern Ireland, then, both mainstream religious and political forces have exhibited considerable commitment to education for tolerance and pluralism. The success of their efforts is shown in the Integrated Schools movement and especially in the seriousness with which EMU is regarded. This latter can be seen in the political mandate requiring such education, the development of an impressive array of curricular materials, and the willingness of the Department of Education for Northern Ireland to assist, evaluate, and expand such efforts.

The Israeli situation is more complex, and education for tolerance and pluralism faces greater challenges. Because Israel is a sovereign state, it is the sponsor, funding agent, and regulator of most education. Thus, one of the major protagonists controls the educational structures. It is hardly surprising, then, that different emphases are given in the curricula of Arab and Jewish schools to issues related to the conflict. It is easy to understand why the national political will is ambivalent about the need to develop and mandate such programs, since these might be viewed as a threat to Jewish hegemony.

The absence of a robust religious center tends to thwart efforts to establish education for tolerance and pluralism in at least two respects. Because of their highly conservative character, both Judaism and Islam in Israel understand their truth claims to be univocal. Given this stance, it is easy to see why such educational activities can be seen as a betrayal of one's religious identity. Among those with the strongest convictions, the response is one of unconditional opposition. Even among the more irenic, it is highly unlikely that there will be meaningful support for these kinds of education, since these latter groups tend to be of the opinion that the two communities ought simply to go their own ways. Because of its largely Western orientation, and ongoing relations with broader Church structures, the Christian community tends to be somewhat less ultra-conservative. However, its marginal status limits its ability to shape larger policy and discourages it from becoming too visible in any kind of political process. The absence of substantial centerist religious groups is thus a significant one.

Israel, then, lags somewhat behind Northern Ireland in efforts to promote education for tolerance and peace. There seems to be less of a societal commitment to mandate or even provide for such programs. The nearly total absence of any analog to Northern Ireland's integrated schools is also a signal of the less developed status of efforts within Israel.

Still, both Northern Ireland and Israel remain challenged in creating and sustaining such educational programs. Within Northern Ireland, expanded support for Integrated Education ought to be a key civic goal. One intermediate objective might be to increase governmental assistance until 10% of the student population matriculates in integrated institutions. While Education for Mutual Understanding and Cultural Heritage have become significant elements, within institutional support might be greater.[36] Efforts need to be made to provide incentives for institutions to devote more attention and expertise to these programs. Teachers and teacher educators ought to be more directly targeted. While Northern Ireland has made significant progress over the last 15 years, much work still remains to be done.

With respect to Israel, anything analogous to Integrated Education remains an unrealistic goal. The lack of even rudimentary contact between Arabs and Jews, together with the magnitude of social, cultural, and religious divergences, makes it an impractical strategy.

While the infusion of education for tolerance and pluralism into all elements of the required curricula would be ideal, this, too, does not appear to be a viable option. Factors such as the separate educational streams within the state sector make this immediately unrealistic.

Probably the most workable option is that advocated by Benporath, the creation of a compulsory core curriculum in civics. At times, this would require significant curricular changes. The relatively uncritical approach taken in historical studies, for example, aimed at promoting a Zionist/nationalist spirit among the Jewish population, and an ethic of coexistence among Arabs, might be replaced by a more critical examination of the historical record utilizing multiple perspectives, among them the work of "new historians" like Benny Morris or Baruch Kimmerling.[37]

Genuine commitment to such a common civics core would require a high level of support by religious and political leaders, as well as the educational establishment. This would necessarily mean that both communities' authorities would need to exert a high level of authentic leadership in the face of what likely would be a groundswell of popular opposition. Without such efforts, activities would remain marginal to mainstream educational institutions and vulnerable to continuing political shifts.

In both instances, questions centering on democratic values will need continuing examination and reflection. How can one justify, for example, using non-democratic compulsory tactics to establish the means for promoting democratic values? Northern Ireland and Israel both exhibit a similar paradox within the schools themselves. Evaluations of Education for Mutual Understanding, for example, point to the intimate connection between successful programs and the utilization of pedagogical techniques that emphasize more horizontal styles of teaching.[38] In all likelihood, Israeli schools would have to orient themselves in a similar direction. Such major pedagogical shifts would require, in each case, major changes, especially in the process of teacher education.

The cases of Israel and Northern Ireland illustrate the continuing power of religion both as a spiritual and political factor. Tradition and desecularization remain dominant forces (Perko, 2003, pp. 286–289). As such, religion has the capability either of advancing values such as coexistence, tolerance, peace, and pluralism or retarding them. In societies characterized by their traditional religious character and unwillingness to dichotomize between secular and sacred, this capability is especially pronounced. Thus, it remains incumbent upon religious leaders and their secular allies to help create educational structures to ameliorate cross-community conflict and promote mutual understanding and peace. Abdication of such leadership by religious authorities would inevitably doom such efforts to marginality at best, and total failure at worst.

NOTES

1. www.deni.gov.uk/about/d_ed_system.htm, pp. 2–3.
2. Cf. the definition of the *Memlachti Dati* in Iram and Schmida, 1998, p. 149.
3. Khalidi (1997) argued that the Palestinian national movement took shape simultaneously to the rise of political Zionism, bringing the two communities into a virtually inevitable conflict.
4. An English translation of the Or Report's summary is to be found at www.haaretz.com. See especially nos. 25–26.
5. The December 1999 issue of the *Journal of American History* is entirely devoted to this topic. Cf. especially Ilan Troen (pp. 1209–1230). A similar case is made in Perko (2002, pp. 101–119).
6. A useful summary of the historical and contemporary structures of Israel education is found in Iram and Schmida (1998, pp. 9–10).
7. Benporath, "From Belligerence to Peace: The Role of Civic Education," p. 9.
8. The Orr Report is the most recent of many governmental studies demarcating these inequities and their consequences.

9. For an insightful description, see Feuververger (1995, pp. 123–149).

10. Yaacov Iram, "Culture of Peace: The Israeli Palestinian Case" (ERIC Document Reproduction Service No. ED 453 138), pp. 8–9.

11. Ibid., p. 8.

12. The widest report of this was given on the program, "Reconciling Histories," on BBC 4 on June 5, 2003.

13. www.hagia-maria-sophia.net/engl/awardengl.htm, p. 4.

14. Cf.www.inter.net.il/~givat_h/givat/arabcent.htm

15. www.inter.net.il/~givat_h/givat/ctcfaqs.htm

16. www.vanleer.org.il/english/2civil/2c_programs_values.htm

17. www.vanleer.org.il/english/2civil/2c_programs_coexistence.htm

18. www.us-israel.org/jsource/bridges/one.html

19. A good general history of Catholic attitudes and response is to be found in McGrath (2000).

20. www.deni.gov.uk/about/d_ed_system.htm, pp. 2–3.

21. *The Education Reform (Northern Ireland) Order 1989* is to be found in full at www.hmso.gov.uk/si/si1989/Uksi_19892406_en_1.htm. Especially important are no. 8, "Educational Themes," which deals with the cross-curricular themes including Education for Mutual Understanding and Cultural Heritage, and Part VI, which treats Integrated Education.

22. *Lagan College: A Brief History* (Belfast: Lagan College, n.d.).

23. "Planned Integrated Education" at www.nicie.org/files/rightside.htm.

24. Ibid.

25. *Integrated Education: The Views of Parents* (Queens University, n.d.), pp. 10–22.

26. Interviews conducted by author, February 1990 and May 1993.

27. *Integrated Education*, pp. 26–33.

28. Cf. *The Education Reform (Northern Ireland) Order 1989*, no. 8, "Educational Themes," which mandates these cross-curricular themes.

29. "Education for Mutual Understanding and Cultural Heritage: A Summary of Objectives" (Belfast: Northern Ireland Curriculum Council, 1990), pp. 1–2.

30. Cf. www.ccea.uk/curriculum.htm for these specifics of goals for all required areas of study and cross-curricular themes.

31. Lambkin (n.d.).

32. Lambkin (n.d.).

33. See p. 27 of *Report of a Survey of Provision for Education for Mutual Understanding in Post-Primary Schools* for a summary of these conclusions.

34. Benporath, "From Belligerence to Peace: The Role of Civic Education," p. 24.

35. www.hartmaninstitute.com.

36. Cf. *Report of a Survey of Provision for Education for Mutual Understanding in Post-Primary Schools.*

37. Benporath, "From Belligerence to Peace: The Role of Civic Education," pp. 24–27.

38. For example, *Report of a Survey of Provision for Education for Mutual Understanding in Post-Primary Schools*, pp. 14–16.

REFERENCES

Barzel, N. (1995). Between fanaticism and tolerance: education for tolerance in the israeli society. In Y. Iram (Ed.), *The role and place of the humanities in education* (p. 456). Tel Aviv: Bar-Ilan University.

Benporath, S. (2002) *From belligerence to peace: The role of civic education.* ERIC Document Reproduction Service No. ED 471 587.

Chacour, E. (2001). *We belong to the land.* Notre Dame, IN: Notre Dame University.

Department of Education Northern Ireland. (1990). *The cross community contact scheme.* Bangor: DENI.

Department of Education Northern Ireland. (2000). *Report of a Survey of Provision for Education for Mutual Understanding in Post-Primary Schools.* Bangor: DENI.

Dunn, S. (1990). EMU–Policy into practice. In *Education for mutual understanding* (p. 24). Bangor: DENI.

Feuerverger, G. (1995). Oasis of peace: A community of moral education in Israel. *Journal of Moral Education, 24,* 123–149.

Feuerverger, G. (1998). Neve Shalom/Wahat Al-Salam: A Jewish-Arab school for peace. *Teachers College Record, 99,* 695.

Ilan, T. (1999, December). Frontier myths and their application in America and Israel: a transnational perspective. *Journal of American History,* pp. 1209–1230.

Iram, Y., & Schmida, M. (1998). *The educational system of Israel.* Westport, CT: Greenwood Press.

Khalidi, R. (1997). *Palestinian identity: The construction of modern national consciousness.* New York: Columbia University Press.

Lambkin, B. (n.d.). *Comparing Protestants and Roman Catholic churches.* Bangor: DENI.

McGrath, M. (2000). *The Catholic Church and Catholic schools in Northern Ireland.* Dublin: Irish Academic Press.

Morgan, V., Dunn, S., Cairns, & Frasier, G. (1992). *Breaking the mould.* Coleraine: University of Ulster.

Mulholland, M. (2002). *The longest war: Northern Ireland's troubled history.* New York: Oxford University Press.

Northern Ireland Curriculum Council. (1990). *Education for mutual understanding and cultural heritage: A summary of objectives.* Belfast: Northern Ireland Curriculum Council.

Perko, F. M. (2002). Education, socialization, and development of national identity: the American common school and Israel defense forces in transnational perspective. *Shofar, 21,* 101–119.

Perko, F. M. (2003). Recent trends in religion. In H K. Bond, S. D. Kunin, & F. A. Murphy (Eds.), *A companion to religious studies and theology* (pp. 289–295). Edinburgh, UK: Edinburgh University Press.

Richardson, N. (1992). *Roots if not wings.* Coleraine: University of Ulster.

Sachar, H. M. (1996). *A History of Israel.* New York: Knopf.

Tell, C. (1999). Understanding race, class, and culture, *Educational Leadership, 56,* 60.

CHAPTER 15

ARAB AND JEWISH WOMEN'S INTERRELIGIOUS DIALOGUE EVALUATED

Ben Mollov
Chaim Lavie

This chapter[1] explores a number of issues connected to the efficacy of interreligious dialogue as a tool for perception change and attitudinal moderation between Israelis and Palestinians and Arabs and Jews within the State of Israel, along with control data with relevance to the impact of dialogue. Particular emphasis here is placed on the impact of gender concerning mutual perceptions among Arabs and Jews. Methodology is based on both qualitative and quantitative data.

INTERRELIGIOUS DIALOGUE AS A BASIS FOR PERCEPTION MODERATION BETWEEN ISRAELIS AND PALESTINIANS

Popular wisdom assumes that injection of religion into the dynamics of conflict between groups locked into acute strife can only serve to exacerbate the tensions existing between them. However, more recent research has indicated that religion can indeed be a "two-edged" sword and under certain circumstances can also serve as a factor for moderating conflict (Appleby, 2000; Gopin, 2000) and not merely exacerbating it.

Educating Toward a Culture of Peace, pages 247–258
Copyright © 2006 by Information Age Publishing
247

Previous research of these authors (Mollov & Lavie, 2001) has documented the positive impact that interreligious encounters had on dialogue between Israelis and Palestinians in the period between 1994 to late 2000. Their work in part utilized the theoretical framework of social psychologist Yehuda Amir (1969), who emphasized that for inter-group encounters to be successful, four elements needed to be present, they being: "equal status contacts"; "intimate" as opposed to merely "casual encounters"; "cooperative" as opposed to "competitive" relationships; and "institutional" supports for such efforts. They further cited the insights of various social psychologists concerning the contribution that the discovery of commonalties in another group can have on improved mutual perceptions (Byrne, 1969; Hewstone, 1990; Newcomb, 1961; Rokeach, 1960). Pettigrew (1998) has amplified on Amir's work and cited the importance of "friendship potential" emerging out of intergroup encounters, which parallel Saunders's (1999) emphasis on relationship building.

Field Work Described

In 1994, Mollov was able to co-initiate with a group of Palestinian students from the Hebron area, a series of dialogues between those students and Israeli students from Bar-Ilan University. These meetings and activities continued in various forms until virtually the start of acute Israeli–Palestinian violence in the fall of 2000, and focused on commonalties between Islam and Judaism. They eventually led to a variety of spin-off cooperative efforts, facilitated by the leading partners of the dialogue themselves. Participants reported on a warm atmosphere in these face-to-face meetings and attributed that achievement to the discovery of commonalties in the other's religious culture (Mollov & Barhoum, 1998).

Specifically it should be noted that approximately 100 students on each side had at some point been directly involved in the process. The activity led to the participation and graduation of a Palestinian student from the Beit Ommar village, in proximity to northern Hebron, in Bar-Ilan University's International Program in Business Administration. Similarly it facilitated the participation and graduation of another Palestinian student in the Peace Studies Program at Notre Dame University.

Family visitations and strong friendships developed during the process between the principle organizers, as they responded to each other during illness and joy and expressed condemnation and condolences to each other in the wake of violent events on either side, even during the period of acute Israeli–Palestinian hostilities.

The "Bar-Ilan–Hebron dialogue" underwent a number of phases. Face-to-face dialogues continued regularly from the period of January 1995 until mid-1997. Important spin-offs also occurred, which laid the groundwork for a "virtual" dialogue to later take place that was the primary framework in which the dialogue continued until virtually September 2000, with this activity described elsewhere (Mollov, Schwartz, Steinberg, & Lavie, 2001).

As the Bar-Ilan–"Hebron" dialogue began as an ad hoc effort under difficult circumstances, no hard quantitative data was collected to measure perception changes among the participants, although a more thorough description of the face-to-face process and interactions has appeared elsewhere (Mollov, 1999).

Lavie, a social psychologist who had originally undertaken a graduate research project under the direction of Yehuda Amir, in the 1970s focusing on perception change among Jewish/Israeli workers toward Arab/Palestinian employees, later joined Mollov to further assess the impact of such dialogue efforts. Lavie's earlier work had taken place within the context of Israel's initiation of the "open bridges" policy, which was meant to facilitate face-to-face contact between Israelis and Palestinians in the wake of the Six-Day War, following geopolitical changes, as well as meeting joint economic needs (Steinberg, in prep).

It was hoped, particularly by then defense minister Dayan, that direct contact between the two populations might contribute to ameliorating tensions by reducing negative stereotypes and promoting coexistence. Lavie examined attitudes among Jewish workers in two factories employing Arab workers, against attitudes in two "control" firms in which there were no Arabs employed. Lavie's questionnaire-based data essentially confirmed Amir's hypotheses that positive changes in perceptions among the Jewish workers could come about only under circumstances in which Jewish workers came into contact with Arab workers of an equal status (Lavie, 1975).

Mollov and Lavie (2001) together reported on the impact of an Israeli–Palestinian interreligious dialogue held in Gaza in February 1999, which afforded the opportunity to collect quantitative data on the impact of Israeli–Palestinian interreligious dialogue. In this Friday–Saturday (Sabbath) encounter in which approximately 80 participants on each side participated, Jewish and Moslem prayer rituals were discussed, the services of both religions were conducted, and the religious dietary requirements of the Jewish guests were respected. Israelis and Palestinians were asked to fill out questionnaires reflecting their mutual perceptions, both before and after the encounter.

According to this research, there is a potential for the interreligious encounter to change mutual perceptions towards a more positive direction, despite intuitive expectations to the contrary. This result is sharpened particularly as sample control data collected among both Israeli Jewish students at Bar-Ilan University, and Palestinian Arab students at several Palestinian universities, prior to the Gaza meeting, indicated that religious students on both sides held the most negative preconceptions of each other (Mollov & Lavie, 2001).

Most notably the data collected from the participants at the Gaza encounter (admittedly a small sample based on a single encounter) indicated that perceptions among Palestinian Moslem participants shifted to a more favorable position than any other subgroup among the Palestinian participants.[2]

These quantitative findings added further credence to the anecdotal evidence offered by Mollov and Barhoum (1998) and Mollov (1999) in regard to the dialogue co-initiated by them, which involved students from both Bar-Ilan University and Palestinian students from the Hebron area. In that dialogue, religion, and in particular, similarities in structure and practices between Islam and Judaism, became a constructive basis for interactions and relationship building as students began to perceive something important and familiar in the other side. This further corroborated the impact that the discovery of commonalties can have on improving mutual perceptions (Byrne, 1969; Hewstone, 1990; Newcomb, 1961; Rokeach, 1960), between groups in conflict.

The requirements that Yehuda Amir identified as being necessary for successful intergroup encounters also seemed to find expression in these dialogue experiences. Amir (1969) particularly emphasized the importance of equal status contacts as being essential for such encounters, and from our experience, a religious focus can offer greater possibilities for equal status contacts than those of another source. For in Israeli–Palestinian dialogues with a more secular/political focus the complaint is frequently voiced by Palestinian participants that they cannot meet their Israeli counterparts as equals as they lack an equal status political framework such as a state of their own. However, in a dialogue with an interreligious dimension and framework, Israeli Jews and Palestinian Arabs could meet as equals, with each side appearing as representatives of their respective religious traditions and heritages, rather than as members of political entities, which may or may not be equal.

Amir also emphasized the importance of "intimate" as opposed to formal or merely casual contact and cooperative versus competitive relations. In the two dialogues, an emphasis was placed on providing ample opportunities for informal interactions over refreshments or during meals so that informal bonds could be developed. Furthermore, the sense of sharing some larger commitment to religious ideals and practices also seemed to have the effect of bringing the sides together and helping to create an environment favorable to constructive relationship building.

In this connection we also believe it relevant to refer to Kelman's (1979) extensive work in Israeli–Palestinian dialogue. Although he has made a strong case for encouraging the parties to reflect on the key elements of their identity and to ultimately develop a "transcendent identity" (Kelman, 1999), he was less clear as to how that process could be facilitated. We believe that the intercultural dialogue with roots in religious heritage can provide an approach toward accomplishing that goal. For key elements of identity rooted in religious culture provide both a foundation for expressing the essence of one's collective identity while providing points of transcendent spiritual contact. Indeed suggestions for utilizing religious symbolism to build links of reconciliation were made during the course of Egyptian–Israeli peacemaking (Cohen, 1987).

The Problem of Institutional Support

Amir's fourth element for successful intergroup encounters—the need for institutional support—was also demonstrated both positively and negatively in various ways in the two dialogues. The various ways in which the dialogues have been facilitated or inhibited by this element has been presented elsewhere (Mollov & Lavie, 2001).

WOMEN AND PEACE IN THE MIDDLE EAST?

A collateral observation culled from the data collected from the Gaza dialogue indicated that the attitudes of Arab (Palestinian) women were more extreme toward Israeli Jews than those of their male counterparts. This observation by Mollov and Lavie (2001) runs parallel to the conclusion of other researchers (e.g., Tessler, Nachtwey, & Grant, 1999) who suggested that the "women and peace hypothesis does not appear to be operative in the Middle East."

To further test the efficacy of the "women and peace" hypothesis in the Middle East, along with the impact of the interreligious dialogue within the State of Israel, the researchers were able to gather both quantitative and qualitative data at an interreligious dialogue held between Arab and Jewish women in Nazareth in July 2003. An Arab–Jewish follow-up dialogue held in Acre in December 2003 involving both men as well as women served as the opportunity to gather control data and additional qualitative impressions concerning the impact of the interreligious dialogue. Both meetings were organized by the Interfaith Encounter organization, and each lasted for 2 days.

The first dialogue held in Nazareth had as its theme, "Tolerance and Social Justice," and the second held in Acre focused on the theme of "Love thy neighbor as thyself." At the start of both dialogues, questionnaires concerning the perception of the "other" along with willingness to have contact with either Arabs or Jews was distributed to the participants. These questionnaires were essentially the same used in the Gaza encounter reported on by Mollov and Lavie (2001), but were slightly adapted for the subject group of Arabs and Jews, all citizens of the State of Israel. Questionnaires were both in Hebrew and Arabic. At the close of both encounters, participants were once again asked to fill out the identical questionnaires.

In addition to smaller discussion groups, participants first gathered in large plenaries. Ample time was also set aside for informal interactions, and some formal cultural activities.

QUANTITATIVE RESULTS

Participants responded to 30 questions concerning perceptions of the other, including willingness to have contact, and could be answered on a scale from one to five, with one representing the most favorable attitude. While we analyzed the results according to several population subgroupings we are presenting here the most salient results.

Table 15.1.   All

Before and after	N	Mean	Std. Deviation
Before	33	2.0317	.56367
After	18	2.1050	.54920

Table 15.1 provides a composite view of all responding participants before and after participation in both dialogues. We note that the average score of about two represented a favorable view of the other, and remained at that level both before and after the dialogue.

Table 15.2.   Females

Before and after	N	Mean	Std. Deviation
Before	19	2.0733	.57722
After	12	2.0955	.45193

Table 15.2 provides a composite view of the questionnaire responses of all females (Arab and Jewish) who attended and responded to the questionnaires, both before and after the encounters. Again, here we also report on positive perceptions (around two), which remained stable both before and after the dialogues.

Table 15.3. Males

Before and after	N	Mean	Std. Deviation
Before	14	1.9752	.56106
After	6	2.1239	.75864

Table 15.3 offers a composite view of the perceptions of the men (Arab and Jewish) who participated only in the second encounter, in Acre. Once again their before and after perceptions are consistent with the favorable findings of the previous two sets, and likewise were not altered by participation in the activity.

While we are not presenting here subgroup breakdowns of Arab and Jewish women separately, nor parallel breakdowns of men, the results we have on hand indicate no appreciable difference between either of the groups (Arab or Jewish, women or men by ethnic affiliation). Furthermore, we also note that in general fewer Jewish women responded to the questionnaires than Arab women, and in the Acre encounter, a number of Jewish women expressed criticism of surveys of this type, although the Arab women expressed no such opposition.

QUALITATIVE DATA

Anecdotal impressions were gathered in both encounters to complement the quantitative data. It was reported that the meetings began with a degree of tension, expressed in physical distance between many of the participants, with some disagreement over the language of discussion (Hebrew or Arabic) (Al-Haj, 2002). Eventually modus vivendis were worked out—with translation made into both languages.

In both cases, the atmosphere improved during the course of the meetings—both in the formal discussions and informal activities. The experience of an interreligious dimension was judged by some of the participants to be a gateway into entering into other issues including painful political ones. Joint cultural activities and prayers further contributed to the emergence of a warmer atmosphere. In both cases a larger degree of physical contact between the women participants (both Arabs and Jews) than between the men was observed to be especially pronounced.

INTERRELIGIOUS DIALOGUE WITHIN THE STATE
OF ISRAEL AND THE ATTITUDES OF WOMEN

Our analysis of two dialogue activities focusing on interreligious themes, involving both Israeli Arabs and Jews, with a particular focus on women, afforded an opportunity to test the impact of the interreligious dialogue within Israel and women's attitudes toward the other. In this context it should be noted that while there has been previous dialogue and corroborating research conducted on dialogue between Israelis and Palestinians (Adwan & Bar-On, 2000; Maoz, 2000a) and on dialogue between Arabs and Jews within the State of Israel (Abu-Nimer, 1999; Bar, 1995; Maoz, 2000b), the approach to dialogue has generally focused on political issues and/or purely psychological models (Bar-Tal, 2000; Kelman, 1998, 1999). With the exception of one researcher (Bekerman, 2002) who hinted at the potential importance of the intercultural religiously based dialogue between Arabs and Jews within the State of Israel the religious component of the conflict has not been addressed.

As noted, the researchers' earlier findings (Mollov & Lavie, 2001) offered quantitative and qualitative support for the efficacy of the religiously based intercultural dialogue in moderating attitudes between Israelis and Palestinians. We also noted, however, the tendency for women to be more extreme in their attitude toward the other, and earlier juxtaposed this finding with other literature, which suggested that the "women and peace hypothesis does not appear to be operative in the Middle East" (Tessler, Nachtwey, & Grant, 1999).

In the two dialogues under study, we noted the fact that attitudes (both of women and men) did not change following the encounters, however began and remained favorable. Thus at a minimum we can suggest that the interreligious dialogue certainly has the potential to be effective as a basis of dialogue between Israeli Arabs and Jews, particularly based on the qualitative impressions gathered that indicated an evolution in atmosphere from more tense relations to more positive relations. The dynamics engendered by the interreligious dialogue was deemed by the participants to be a factor in engendering those favorable changes. However, the fact that attitudes (based on the quantitative data) began and remained favorable suggests that the pool of participants involved in both activities were probably a self-selected group who have been involved with dialogue before, and/or already predisposed positively toward the other. Thus for dialogues of this sort to have a wider impact, ways will need to be found to expand the population base for those involved with such encounters.

CONTACT CONTROL DATA

Despite the apparent self-selection of the two groups referred to above, we may well ask the question, Does dialogue and contact with the "other" matter? In late November 2003, 62 Israeli-Jewish students at Bar-Ilan University were surveyed for their perceptions toward Arabs. Responding to the same questionnaires utilized in the Nazareth and Akko meetings, the respondents were predominately women (49) with the remainder of valid respondents (12) men. These students constituted a control group as they were not as a whole involved previously in dialogue or contact with Israeli Arabs or Palestinians.

Although these questionnaires were distributed after approximately 3 years of bitter strife between Israelis and Palestinians, which has in general led to a more polarized atmosphere between Arabs and Jews within Israel, student attitudes were relatively moderate with a mean score of slightly less than three, as indicated in Table 15.4.

Table 15.4.   Combine Means Chac. and Attitudes (Group Statistics)

Gender	N	Mean	Std. Deviation	Std. Error Mean
Male	12	2.64	.698	.202
Female	49	2.83	.713	.102

As indicated, the respondent attitudes were divided between women and men, thus allowing for the opportunity to compare attitudes of Israeli-Jewish women who had not been involved with dialogue with the women surveyed in the Nazareth and Akko dialogues. In Table 15.5, we are able to discern that the women (both Arabs and Jews, who had similar mean scores) participating in the two dialogues clearly held more favorable perceptions of the "other" than the Bar-Ilan control group of women who had not participated in dialogue.

Table 15.5.   Previous Survey Female Mean (Group Statistics)

Female Survey 1 & 2	N	Mean	Std. Deviation	Std. Error Mean
New Survey	49	2.83	.713	.102
Old Survey	31	2.08	.524	.094

While as we noted, the perception of those women who had participated in the dialogues began and remained favorable, we cannot conclusively attribute an improved change in measurable perception to the dialogue itself, as the group may have been self-selected. However, qualitative impressions gathered from the two encounters definitely pointed to a process that began with a degree of tension between the two groups and later evolved into improved relationships. And the difference between those groups of women who had participated in the dialogue against those who did not again points to the possible impact and contribution of interreligious dialogue in improving mutual perceptions between Arabs and Jews within the State of Israel.

DISCUSSION AND CONCLUSIONS

The purpose of this chapter has been to further develop a new paradigm concerning the efficacy of Arab–Jewish intercultural dialogue rooted in religion as a means of peace building and dialogue between Israelis and Palestinians and Arabs and Jews—citizens of the State of Israel. Previously the authors (Mollov & Lavie, 2001) have argued that contrary to intuitive assumptions, a religiously based Israeli–Palestinian intercultural dialogue has the potential of moving perceptions to more positive levels between those religiously committed populations that have been assumed to be the most resistant to attitudinal moderation. Research presented here, despite the small sample of participants who were admittedly self-selected with a favorable predisposition to dialogue, points to the contribution that the interreligious encounter can have in moderating Arab–Jewish tensions. These research efforts, which ought to be expanded, contradict assumptions that religion can only serve to escalate interethnic tensions in societies seeking modes of conflict resolution.

Concerning, however, the issue of women attitudes within the framework of the Arab–Israeli conflict, our findings in the current study do not confirm our earlier results (Mollov & Lavie, 2001) regarding the more negative attitudes of women as opposed to men. The strong emphasis on relationship building exhibited between women in our current research also suggests the possibility that there may indeed be a specific repertoire of skills possessed by women in connection to peacemaking (d'Estree & Babbit, 1998). However, the fact that women's attitudes toward the other were not more positive than those of men might also suggest that in terms of gender and conflict management, there may be "less than meets the eye" (Ruble & Schneer, 1994).

Finally, we conclude with some additional reflections on the potential importance of the interreligious dialogue between Arabs and Jews in the Middle East. While this chapter has focused on dialogue between Arabs and Jews within the State of Israel, such processes cannot be separated from larger regional dynamics. Indeed, it has been suggested that the State of Israel as the Jewish state meets the Arab world on three levels—its own

Arab community, the Palestinians, and the larger Arab world. Improvement in interactions on any of those levels can strengthen the larger whole. Thus evidence of the efficacy of the interreligious dialogue on both the Palestianian and Arab Israeli tracks ought to serve as incentive to further explore this approach for the larger context of Arab–Israeli peacemaking. Indeed, when civilizations today potentially confront each other in intercultural tension (Huntington,1996) we note the parallel suggestion that civilizations need to find important commonalties with each other to moderate their clashes (Huntington,1996).

NOTES

1. An earlier version of this paper was presented by the authors at the UNESCO scientific conference held in Jyvaskyla, Finland, June 15–18, 2003.
2. In this particular case perceptions of the Israeli Jewish participants, both religious and nonreligious, began and remained favorable.

REFERENCES

Abu-Nimer, M. (1999). *Dialogue, conflict resolution and change: Arab–Jewish encounters in Israel.* Albany: State University of New York Press.

Adwan, S., & Bar-On, D. (2000). *The role of non-governmental organizations in peace building between Palestinians and Israelis.* Jerusalem: PRIME (Peace Research in the Middle East), with the support of the World Bank.

Al-Haj, M. (2002). Multiculturalism in deeply divided societies: the Israeli case. *International Journal of Intercultural Relations, 26,* 169–183.

Amir, Y. (1969). Contact hypothesis in ethnic relations. *Psychological Bulletin, 71,* 319–342.

Appleby, S. (2000). *The ambivalence of the sacred: Religion, violence, and reconciliation.* Lanham, MD: Rowman & Littlefield.

Bar, H. (1995). *Living with the conflict.* Jerusalem: Jerusalem Institute for Israel Studies.

Bar-Tal, D. (2000). From intractable conflict through conflict resolution to reconciliation: Psychological Analysis. *Political Psychology, 21,* 351–365.

Bekerman, Z. (2002). The discourse of nation and culture: Its impact on Palestinian–Jewish encounters in Israel. *International Journal of Intercultural Relations, 26*(4), 409–427.

Byrne, D. (1969). Attitude and attraction. In L. Berkowitz (Ed.), *Advances in experimental and social psychology* (Vol. 4, pp. 36–89). New York: Academic Press.

Cohen, R. (1987). *Theatre of power: The art of diplomatic signaling.* London: Longman.

D'Estree, T. P., & Babbit, E. F. (1998). Women and the art of peacemaking: Data from Israeli–Palestinian interactive problem-solving workshops. *Political Psychology, 19*(1), 185–209.

Gopin, M. (2000). *Between Eden and Armageddon: The future of world religions, violence, and peacemaking.* New York: Oxford University Press.

Hewstone, M. (1990). The ultimate attribution error? A review of literature on intergroup casual attribution. *European Journal of Social Psychology, 20,* 311–335.

Huntington, S. P. (1996). *The clash of civilizations and the remaking of world order.* New York: Simon & Schuster.

Kelman, H. C. (1979). An interactional approach to conflict resolution and its application to Israeli–Palestinian relations. *International Interactions, 6,* 99–122.

Kelman, H. (1998). Social-psychological contributions to peacemaking and peace-building in the Middle East. *Applied Psychology, 47*(1), 5–29.

Kelman, H. (1999). Transforming the relationship between former enemies: A social-psychological analysis. In R. Rothstein (Ed.), *After the peace: Resistance and Reconciliation* (pp. 193–205). London: Lynne Rienner.

Lavie, C. (1975). *Influence of contact between Jews and Arabs at work on the views of Jews as a function of their status in the enterprise.* Master's thesis, Bar-Ilan University, Ramat Gan, Israel.

Maoz, I. (2000a). An experiment in peace: Reconciliation-aimed workshops of Jewish-Israeli and Palestinian youth. *Journal of Peace Research, 37*(6), 721–726.

Maoz, I. (2000b). Power relations in intergroup encounters: A case study of Jewish–Arab encounters in Israel. *International Journal of Intercultural Relations, 24*(4), 259–277.

Mollov, B., & Barhoum, M. (1998). *Building cultural/religious bridges between Arab and Jewish university students.*

Mollov, B. (1999). *The role of religion in conflict resolution: An Israeli–Palestinian student dialogue.* Jerusalem: Jerusalem Center for Public Affairs.

Mollov, B., & Lavie, C. (2001). Culture, dialogue and perception change in the Israeli–Palestinian conflict. *The International Journal of Conflict Management. 12*(1), 69–87.

Mollov. B., Schwartz, D., Steinberg, G., & Lavie, H. (2001, June). *The impact of Israeli–Palestinian intercultural dialogue: "Virtual" and face to face.* Paper presented at the annual conference of the International Association for Conflict Management, Cergy, France.

Newcomb, T. M. (1961). *The acquaintance process.* New York: Holt, Rinehart & Winston.

Pettigrew, T. F. (1998). Intergroup contact theory. *Annual Review Psychology, 49,* 65–83.

Rokeach, M. (Ed.). (1960). *The open and closed mind.* New York: Basic Books.

Ruble, T. L., & Schneer, J. A. (1994). Gender differences in conflict-handling styles: Less than meets the eye? In A. Taylor & J. B. Miller (Eds.), *Conflict and gender* (pp. 155–166). Cresskill, NJ: Hampton.

Saunders, H. (1999). *A public peace process.* New York: St. Martin's Press.

Steinberg, G. (in prep). *Dayan's indirect functionalist approach.* Unpublished manuscript.

Tessler, M., Nachtwey, J. & Grant, A. (1999). Further tests of the women and jpeace hypothesis: Evidence from cross-national survey research in the Middle East. *International Studies Quarterly, 43,* 519–531.

CHAPTER 16

VOICES FROM AMONG THE ZIONIST RELIGIOUS COMMUNITY REGARDING THE PEACE PROCESS AND THE DISENGAGEMENT PLAN

Zehavit Gross

INTRODUCTION

Religious Zionists are a very active segment of the Jewish Israeli population. They make up the absolute majority of the population on the West Bank, called "Judea and Samaria" by Israelis. Having their own unique separate school system, they, like no other segment of Israeli society, are able to mobilize thousands of their members for right-wing-oriented political activism.

Despite the fact that religious Zionists have substantial influence on Israel's society and future, there seems to be very little literature on their ideology regarding the current peace process and the plan of disengagement from the Gaza Strip, a religious Zionist stronghold called "Gush Katif." Individual opinions are voiced, but they have not been systematically analyzed. This points to a theoretical gap whereby many do not recognize the unique religious Zionist ways of thinking, especially concerning

Educating Toward a Culture of Peace, pages 259–279
Copyright © 2006 by Information Age Publishing
All rights of reproduction in any form reserved.

the deeply controversial peace process issues at hand. Conceptually, these are still uncharted waters. Exploring the gap and understanding at least some of the voices from among the Zionist religious community may enhance communications with this community and help initiate peace education projects within the religious Zionist schools.

The aim of this chapter is to investigate the conceptions that some graduates of the State Religious Educational (SRE) System employ when they express themselves on the peace process in general and the Disengagement Plan in particular.

Official policy statements on religious education tend to avoid a discussion of philosophical or practical treatment of the peace process in its current political context (Gross, 2003b). The term "peace process" was first mentioned in a circular of the State Religious Educational Authority issued in 1978:

> As this circular was being printed, a great event occurred in Israel. For the first time in many years, the State's leaders were able to speak face to face with the ruler of an Arab state about possible peace arrangements. Moreover, this took place in the Knesset, in Israel's eternal capital. We cannot fathom all the mysteries of the universe and consequently cannot determine whether the peace for which we yearn is already on the horizon. There is one thing that we do know, however: prayer is effective. Let us beseech our Heavenly Father to instill wisdom in the hearts of the leaders of nations: "The Lord will give strength unto His people; the Lord will bless His people with peace." [Psalms 29:11]

The text of this circular reflects opacity and skepticism, which were characteristic of the early days of the peace process. It speaks of the peace process with an amorphous hope for a redemptive, divine peace.

The state religious educational literature, which includes policy statements and a special collection of articles published at the time of Prime Minister Yitzhak Rabin's assassination, does not render a thorough treatment of the peace process in any context whatsoever. Moreover, it avoids taking a stand on Religious Zionism. A letter circulated by the State Religious Authority after Rabin's assassination (Israel's Ministry of Education, "For my Brethren's and Companions' sake" [Psalms 122:9], 1999) did not refer to the subject of peace. This is puzzling because Rabin was assassinated for his views and his desire to advance the peace process. Is it possible that State Religious Education officials would ignore a process so central to the formation of our generation? Does an approach that ignores the peace process prepare Religious Zionist students practically and authentically for life outside the hothouse atmosphere of school?

In this chapter, we attempt to understand what the official educational premises and purposes of the state religious educational system are and how they affect the way its graduates cope with the peace process in general and with disengagement policy in particular.

In the theoretical introduction, we describe the purposes of State Religious Education, its achievements, and the main criticism against this educational system. The description is followed by the presentation of a case study on the attitude of Religious Zionist graduates toward the peace process. We will try to show the impact of their socialization on their attitude toward this specific matter.

STATE RELIGIOUS EDUCATION

The Jewish population in Israel consists of three basic groups: Secular, Religious Zionist, and Ultra-Orthodox. Accordingly, there are three types of state-supported school systems within the Jewish Israeli educational system: the secular State Educational System, the Religious Zionist Educational System, and the Ultra- Orthodox Educational System. The latter is subdivided into Sephardic (Oriental) and Ashkenazi (Western).

From its establishment in 1948 onward the State of Israel, unlike the United States or Europe, has no separation of state and religion. This stems from the fact that the Jewish Nation has for long considered nationhood and religiosity to be one historical entity (Horowitz & Lissak, 1990; Waxman, 2003). The phenomenon of nonseparation of state and religion affects the public sphere. For example, the national symbols of the state are religious in essence and the State is governed according to the Jewish calendar. Also, it has a strong impact on the educational system. State Religious Education is an integral part of the State Educational System in Israel, and its role is to provide educational services to a population interested in both secular and religious education.

In 1953, the State Religious Educational System (SRE) was defined by law. On the one hand, it was granted administrative and ideological autonomy; on the other, it was subject to the procedures of the State Educational System (Goldschmidt, 1984). According to this law, "state education amounts to education provided by law, according to a curriculum, without any connection to any political or ethnic institution except the government and under the supervision of the Ministry of Education…. State Religious Education means state education, but its institutions are religious according to their (i.e., the religious Zionist) way of life, curriculum, teachers, and inspectors. Within this framework, students are educated to follow the Jewish law according to the Jewish religious tradition and the religious Zionist spirit" (Law Book, 131, September 1953). SRE has been given a great deal of independence in shaping the lifestyle and atmosphere in its schools, constructing curricula, and selecting staff and students who are required to meet specific criteria of religious behavior.

POLICY AND PURPOSES OF THE SRE

The SRE policy is not organized as a systematic philosophy and has no mandatory practical applications (Goldschmidt, 1984). This is both the strength and weakness of this dynamic system. Its principles are continuously forged and developed in accordance with changing circumstances and practical needs (Gross, 2003, p. 150). We can learn a lot about the guidelines underlying this policy from the circulars for religious principals. These are regularly published by the SRE Administration. We can also learn about the guidelines from a document called *Guidelines for Shaping the SRE Philosophy* (1992). This document was written by previous SRE directors, but it may be changed and shaped by SRE directors yet to come.

The theoretical and practical principles behind SRE are based on a combination (Katz, 2004) of the values of traditional, religious yeshiva education, which has always been part of the Jewish people, and modern Jewish education, which was developed primarily in Germany under the influence of the 19th-century Jewish Enlightenment (Haskalah) movement (Feiner, 2002; Schweid, 2002). Rabbi Samson Raphael Hirsch was one of the main proponents of integration of traditional Judaism with secular education (Ayalon & Yogev, 1998; Rosenak, 2003).

In light of this philosophy the State Religious Educational system is based on three main tenets (Gross, 2003, pp.150–151; Kiel, 1977):

1. **Religious education**. A traditional, Jewish religious education that includes teaching belief in God and the observance of precepts; the advanced study of sacred texts (i.e., the Bible, Oral Law, Jewish law, Talmud) and the writings of the rabbis and Jewish thinkers who have shaped the spiritual heritage of the Jewish people for generations.

2. **Modern education.** Teaching the basic skills that students need to acquire in order to function properly as future citizens in a secular, democratic state. Therefore, the SRE system has created a mandatory curriculum that incorporates secular subject matter such as math, physics, and English. These subjects will enable the students to pass the national matriculation examinations and, upon completion of their education, to either continue with their studies or find a job and to contribute to society.

3. **Nationalist education**. Zionist education is required in order to preserve the unity of the Jewish people, may they be secular or religious, living in Israel or in the Diaspora; to strengthen their feeling of iden-

tification with and contribution to the Land of Israel, which is perceived as having religious significance; and to reinforce their sense of loyalty and belonging to the State of Israel and its laws. According to Rabbi Kook, the revival of Jewish nationalism had a religious meaning. He considered the establishment of the Jewish state as the first step toward Jewish redemption. In accordance with his philosophy SRE promotes the founding of settlements throughout the country and encourages Jews to contribute to the homeland through army service in elite military units (Gross, 2003, p. 150). Furthermore, the SRE system requires identification with the state on national holidays, such as Independence Day and Jerusalem Day—in contrast with the ultra-Orthodox sector, which does not celebrate these holidays.

The ideal graduate of the SRE school system acts in the private and public spheres in accordance with Jewish law on the one hand and integrates in modern society by applying the general secular knowledge acquired during schooling, on the other (Dagan, 1999). This integration of tradition and modernity becomes even stronger in the context of the civic responsibility required of an SRE graduate. He or she is taught that the founding of the State of Israel is the beginning of the Jewish redemption. Thus, his religious and civic obligations are clear. The fact that there is no separation between state and religion enables teachers to refer to religious and civil issues simultaneously in the course of the years. The success of SRE can be gauged by the accomplishments of its graduates.

ACCOMPLISHMENTS OF THE SRE

The accomplishments of the Religious-Zionist educational system can be found in the following three spheres:

1. **In the social sphere**. SRE graduates have played key roles in all spheres of endeavor in Israel, while they publicly preserve their religious way of life. Similarly, SRE has become one of Israel's important official institutions for absorbing new immigrants. Because of its policy of "being open to everyone," it absorbed many new immigrants who came from deprived socioeconomic backgrounds. Jewish immigrants from Muslim countries were absorbed into the schools in the 1950s, and Jewish immigrants from Ethiopia and the former Soviet Union were absorbed in the 1980s and 1990s. Their successful integration into Israeli society can serve as an example of a minority coping with the needs of other minorities.

2. **In the academic field.** State religious education can be proud of the fact that a high percentage (66%) of its graduates turn out eligible for matriculation. Success in matriculation exams can be shown with regard to general subjects such as math and English, as well as Judaic studies. State religious education is particularly noteworthy for its high success rate among students defined as disadvantaged youth. In 1995, the former director of the State Religious educational division, Mr. Mati Dagan, decided to cancel vocational studies in religious schools as these studies did not prepare the students for their matriculation examinations. By doing so, he converted the SRE schools into academic institutions where students would be able to finish their studies with a full matriculation certificate. As a result of this, the academic and educational status of high schools in the peripheries has improved, and the low-income population has become more successful in finishing high school with a certificate.

3. **In the religious sphere.** Most of the SRE graduates (approximately 70%) remain religious with varying degrees of observance, even after completing the school socialization process (Leslau & Rich, 1999). Moreover, Israeli yeshiva high schools and advanced academic yeshivas, which accommodate graduates of the SRE schools, contributed to the revival of Jewish religious centers in Israel following the destruction of the centers of Jewish religious life in Europe during the Holocaust (Gross, 2003a). The Jewish religious revival in Israel, a secular, liberal, democratic state, constituted a new pattern of religiosity that integrated Jewish tradition with aspects of modernity and sovereignty. The accomplishments of the SRE graduates in the three domains attest to the possibility of a combination between religiosity and modernity. This special synthesis is not only a theoretical issue but it also has practical manifestations (Gross, 2003, pp. 160–161).

Notwithstanding the meaningful contribution of SRE graduates to the community in the State of Israel, their educational system is criticized for its ideological characteristics (Lamm, 1991; Schwartzwald, 1990; Silverman-Keller, 2000). What are the characteristics of ideological education and what are its possible implications for the graduates of SRE in general and for peace education in particular?

CHARACTERISTICS OF POLITICAL AND IDEOLOGICAL EDUCATION

Lamm (1991) distinguishes between ideological and political education. He claims that ideological education amounts to the use of political contents and curricular contents for enhancing the support of a student for a specific political approach preferred by his or her teachers or institution of learning. Political education is education aimed at the development of the intellectual skills and moral sensitivity of the student, enabling him or her to function in political situations.

According to Lamm, the contents of ideological education serve as an aim, whereas political education, or "political mode," serves as a means. The basic educational approach of ideological education is heteronomous, whereas the political approach is autonomous. From the viewpoint of ideological education, the school is perceived as a means of indoctrination; according to the political mode it is a place where students are exposed to different points of view and are able to choose whatever they want. Students that study according to the political approach become aware of the alternatives, whereas students that study according to the ideological approach have only one Truth. According to the ideological approach, the teacher chooses his or her ideology and the students are expected to obey and imitate the teacher; according to the political approach, critical thinking is perceived as the foundation of education.

In the ideological system, the educational role of teachers is identical to their political role, whereas in the political approach these roles are considered to be separated. The focus of ideological education is the content and subject matter, whereas the core of political education is the student and his holistic needs. The ideological attitude is rooted in emotion, whereas the political attitude is rooted in rationality. In conclusion, ideological education is narrow, closed, and focused, whereas political education is more open and flexible.

Lamm claims that both the Israeli SRE system and the educational system of the Kibbutzim provide ideological education. The question is: how do graduates of such schools cope with the peace process and peace education? Both have to do with negotiation and compromises and require a priori openness, flexibility, and a rational approach (Salomon, 2002).

Here we present a case study on the attitude of SRE graduates toward the Disengagement Plan of the Israeli government (2004–2005) in particular and toward the peace process and peace education in general.

THE DISENGAGEMENT PLAN

For 15 years several Israeli governments have aspired to a resolution of the Palestinian–Israeli conflict and the advancement of the peace process. In 2004, when Prime Minister Sharon understood that there is no reliable Palestinian partner for achieving progress in a bilateral peace process, he developed a new peace program called the Disengagement Plan. The first stage was to evacuate Jews from the Gaza Strip and Northern Samaria and to dismantle the Israeli settlements there. Prime Minister Sharon hoped that the Palestinians would take advantage of the opportunity to break out of the cycle of violence and to reengage in a process of dialogue and peace negotiations.

Although the plan was backed by the government, it caused great disagreement and led to protests by Israeli citizens, especially by the settlers and their supporters, the religious Zionist sector. Hence, it is important to understand the ideological basis of the objections. This chapter analyzes the positions of two authentic Religious Zionists who are SRE graduates. The analysis of their thoughts will help us determine how the premises and purposes of the SRE system were internalized and how they affected its graduates discourse and way of thinking.

METHODOLOGY

The central research question is: What are the conceptual categories that emerge from examining attitudes of SRE graduates toward the peace process in general and peace education in particular?

Since there is very little literature on religious Zionist ideas about the peace process today, these categories have not yet been made explicit. An in-depth analysis is best served by a case study of a small sample. The methodology to be employed in this situation is therefore qualitative. Its aim is to expose tacit categories (Phillion & Connelly, 2005; Sabar- Ben-Yehoshua, 1990) in the individual's mindset. The prerequisite for doing this is open-ended research with a constructivist epistemological orientation (Connelly & Phillion, 2003; Sabar-Ben-Yehoshua, 2001).

A case study can be used to investigate complex phenomena not yet theoretically described. It contributes to our knowledge of individuals, groups, and uncharted phenomena (Yin, 2003, p. 1). The goal is to produce an integrated, holistic description of real-life events and to establish a framework for discussion and debate (Lovat, 2003).

Yin argues that the case study method is appropriate when the goal is to uncover contextual conditions of a contemporary phenomenon and "when the boundaries between phenomenon and context are not evident." Case study research can include both single and multiple case studies (Yin, 2003, 2004). It's difficult to conduct research on the issue at hand by quantitative questionnaires.

An unintentional merit of the qualitative approach to investigating religious Zionist settlers in the Gaza Strip was their uncooperativeness with any other research attempts. When I visited settlers in the Gaza Strip, I received at least 5–6 different quantitative questionnaires. These had been distributed to them by researchers from different research institutions. Some of the settlers regarded the questionnaires as part of a government conspiracy against them, despite the fact that the institutions that designed them had no official ties with the Establishment. Almost all told me that they don't plan to answer or return the questionnaires. Those who said they will fill out the questionnaires may give biased or unserious responses.

In this case, one cannot rely on clear-cut questions from the traditional quantitative questionnaire methodology, because the phenomenon under investigation is complex, vague, and unclear. In addition, one cannot rely on questionnaires considered a threat by the target population. This experience also convinced me of the merit of a face-to-face dialogue between researcher and research participants from the researched community, as a way of establishing contact with the participants and obtaining information.

A case study is a technique for organizing information and social findings in a way that preserves the uniqueness of the objects that are investigated (Sabar-Ben Yehushua, 1990, p. 115).

Two interviews were conducted during a tour to the Gaza Strip. Notes were taken immediately after the tour and rewritten by the researcher and one of the participants (David). Subsequently, the two participants (Moshe and David) added to the notes what they thought was missing. Two short interviews were held with the main participant (David) 3 days after the tour, in order to clarify points not understood.

First, I present the case. Stake (2004) claims that there are two ways to present a case study: as a fragment or as a whole. Because of the complexity of the phenomenon discussed, one can get the picture only by reading the interviews in their entirety. Editing and summarizing the interviews could turn them into reports biased by the researcher's preconceptions. Then I suggest an axis of analysis and finally, I discuss its theoretical and educational implications.

THE ENCOUNTER: A THICK DESCRIPTION

The following account is a contextual, detailed and narrative description, a so-called "thick description" (Geertz, 1973), of an encounter with two interviewees during a visit to the Gaza Strip in April 2005.

My family had decided to go to Gush Katif in the Gaza Strip and stay with relatives for Passover. Initially, I thought it was a bad idea because I regard the location as dangerous. However, my husband and my children urged me to go with them. Prime Minister Ariel Sharon recently declared: "We will allow our people to bid farewell to the Gaza Strip during Passover, before the evacuation." I had not been there for almost 5 years. One hundred thousand people participated in the tour. We gathered at the entrance to Neve Dekalim, one of the biggest settlements in Gush Katif.

Five minutes after we started the tour, a Qasam missile landed across the street, 10 meters from where I stood. I froze in horror, I couldn't believe my eyes: a missile had just flown over the heads of 100,000 people.

We saw two helicopters in the sky, a few tanks on land, a combat boat in the sea, and some armed soldiers who were supposed to guard us. However, the army didn't respond to the attack. Somebody shouted: "Why doesn't the army do anything?" The answer was: "Officially, there is a Hudna [ceasefire] now, and the soldiers are not allowed to react." One of the settlers who had been living in the settlement for 20 years said to me: "Now you can feel what we have been going through for a long time." I honestly did not know what to do: to return to the home of my relatives or to continue the tour with everybody else.

I decided to continue the tour and thought to myself: "Here I go with 100,000 other stupid people." They were stupid in *my* eyes because they continued marching despite the missile attack. Nobody asked a question. I was angry. I went into the crowd, asking people: "Why do you continue walking? Aren't you afraid? You are not normal!" Of course, they, in turn, considered *me* abnormal. We had a long discussion about normality. What made me furious was the thought that nobody around me had a different voice. I was not prepared to assume the heroic role. I see things from a practical point of view and not from an idealistic or ideological one. After a few minutes, I met a security guard, who told me that a second missile had fallen in close proximity of the people a few minutes before. I started shivering; I thought of my parents, my children; I couldn't breathe; however, I continued walking with the other 100,000 "idiots."

I went to a group of soldiers and asked them what they thought of the situation. They said that they are not allowed to talk about politics. A young man who stood behind me accused me of discouraging the soldiers. I had a long conversation with him. I told him: "I can see that ideology is more important to you than human life." He said: "The halachic rules [Jewish religious law] have specific answers to these questions. We are fighting for our existence here and therefore the land of Israel is more important than human life. And besides, this is not a dangerous place." I looked at him in astonishment and said: "How dare you say that it is not a dangerous place; a missile flew over my head only a few minutes ago." He said that it is more dangerous to drive a car; careless drivers kill more people than missiles. In addition, he said that it is more dangerous to go abroad and attend professional conferences than to come to Gush Katif.

I was angry and continued: "I don't understand how all these people think the same way and nobody returns home." He said: "If you were driven by real love for God and by real faith, you would not be afraid. You are the only coward here!" When a family member noted that I spoil the happiness of the holiday, I told him that it is my obligation to keep talking.

Somebody has to assume the role of saying something different. "Yes," somebody said, "only those who don't trust God can talk this way." I got upset and said: "You are going against the Jewish law. In Judaism, life is valued above all else. You are playing roulette with your life. You risk your life and say that this is done out of faith, you are crazy." The young man next to me whose name was David explained that the government is crazy for allowing such a situation to happen. "We are like sitting ducks," he added.

The young man continued: "This is the safest place in the world, look how many soldiers are around us… it is really safe." Again, I said: "You are not normal." They responded that I am abnormal. Then somebody (Moshe) interrupted and said: "We should do something…" I asked: "What can we do?" He said, "Do you see those Arabs sitting in the corner?" He pointed to some Arab villagers who sat on the shoulders of the road. "Let's go and hit them." I looked at this man—he had three little children with him—and asked him: "What do you mean?" He said: "Let's go and hit them," I asked him:" Why? Are you serious?" He said: "Yes. Arabs understand only the language of force; they broke the ceasefire. We should answer them with force. Look how they are laughing at us." I said: "But these Arabs are innocent. They didn't do anything." He looked at me and said: "There are no innocent Arabs, all of them are killers and potential suicide bombers. If we don't kill them—they will kill us."

I asked him: "But can you imagine what would happen if you go and hit the Arabs sitting there? You have three little children, so you should be responsible. Be rational, people may get killed, be rational!" He answered: "Rational people led the world to hell. Look at the Germans, they were rational. They argued that the final solution of the Jewish question is *the* solution for an unpolluted, modern, civilized world. All the rational people who don't react when Jews are attacked are continuing this concept." David, who was still standing next to me, took over: "You have to understand—we are not a bunch of individuals, we are part of a unique whole, which is called 'Klal Israel' [all of Israel]. We should not think about the present because it is not a question of here and now. It is part of the question of whole: How we, as part of a greater whole, are supposed to act, while fulfilling our responsibility to this whole in order to preserve it as such."

At the time of the Exodus from Egypt, the people who were afraid probably stayed in Egypt and said: Why should we do this to Pharaoh? We should negotiate with him. How will we cross the Red Sea? How will we defeat the Egyptians? They are strong, it is irrational. And you see, because we followed God we were able to leave, we were a free people." Moshe added: "Passover is the celebration of this freedom, we have our sovereignty, and we are not supposed to act like slaves…. I see those tanks and aircraft in the sky and the soldiers. The Palestinians shoot missiles at us, but we, like in the Holocaust, do not react, although we are free people. This government is a secular government. When you do not believe in God, the Arabs will overcome you. If you do not have faith, you lose your strength. We are the sons of God and we have to complete our religious mission."

I told Moshe: "Listen, you are a teacher; you are not supposed to talk that way." Moshe answered: "You have to be neutral…of course, only the leftist are neutral. We, the rightist, are dogmatic. My civic obligation is to teach my students to protest. This is the best education I can give them… you, at the university, are talking about peace education. I once saw that there was a big conference about peace education at the university. Those who are connected to peace education use the subject as a cover so as to bring their leftist opinions to the classroom and to the radio. Interestingly enough, there are no normal rightists, but only radical extreme rightists. The leftists are normal, balanced, and neutral, of course. Listen, the Jews of Israel will survive thanks to the simple people who will conquer the land with their simple faith. The sophisticated scholars who sit in their ivory towers and speak about peace will bring war and disaster upon the land of Israel."

I asked David, the young man who walked beside me, what he thinks of this conversation. He thought for 2 minutes and then said: "The problem with you is that you are thinking in short-term goals. We in Judaism speak about long-term goals. In education, if you think about short-term goals, you achieve nothing. It is very easy to talk about the present, but we need to be responsible for eternity. Jewish history can be judged only from this perspective. Educators, especially religious educators, should consider long-term goals. We are talking about eternity. To be trapped in the present is to misunderstand Jewish national history."

I asked him: "What is eternity? All the slogans on stickers written by the organizers of the protest refer to eternity: 'Gush Katif will remain forever'; 'Eternal Israel will conquer'; 'The eternal nation isn't afraid.' Did you pay attention to this? What is eternity?"

David answered: "Eternity is not the future. It incorporates past, present, and future. When we analyze something concerning our life, we should discuss it in terms of eternity. The eternal parameters are those of the Torah (Bible). What does the Torah say in this situation? The way the Torah looks at it, we who have faith look at it. According to the Torah there is no long or short term, but only the correct way: not only what is right concerning a certain issue but also what is right for the whole cosmos, for the flowers in the garden, for the animals, and for human beings. What is right for us? Of course, there is one absolute truth. We own the land of Israel. This land is part of the organism, which is called the people of Israel. As a person doesn't give part of his body to somebody else for anything, so we cannot give parts of the land to others. This is your body and you need it for your existence. You cannot compromise on parts of your body. The idea of the body implies depth; we are not talking about it in its simplistic meaning. It implies personality, the personality of the whole, the holistic nation. There are no short-term aims. The question is: How can we do our best to influence eternity?

The chances of success regarding the Disengagement Plan are 50/50. Nobody can assure us that it will work and that the Arabs will stop slaughtering us. In terms of security, there is no clear-cut answer. So you cannot think about the immediate present, only about the long and distant future. You are asking if it is dangerous, if we should leave because of *Pikuach Nefesh* [life saving]. According to Jewish law, you have to guard the periphery more than the center; you have to build and maintain cities in the periphery so that you have control over the center. To drive a car is dangerous too; to travel abroad for research is dangerous. How can we determine what is dangerous and what is not? You are asking: "When can a place be considered a dangerous place? Jewish law gives us valid parameters: it's 1:1,000. The proportion for danger is that one person out of 1,000 people may die. However, we don't have this proportion yet. So according to Halachic parameters there is no *Pikuach Nefesh* ("no need to risk your life").

In Judaism, there is a religious war and there is an optional war. There are all sorts of rules and the Jewish law gives us clear criteria. Therefore, when rabbis claim that it is not dangerous, they know the Halachic rules. I will give you an example: there are people who claim that living in Israel is dangerous. I heard that an Ultra-Orthodox rabbi who lives in America doesn't allow his community to visit Israel at all because he considers it a dangerous place, surrounded by five hostile Arab countries. He claims that his community is forbidden to visit Israel according to Jewish law. Do you think it is dangerous to live in Israel? No. So it depends on your perspective.

From the religious perspective one perceives things differently. The Gaza Strip is a religious issue. Therefore, we don't see it in terms of danger. We fulfill God's commandments. We are commanded to settle in all of Eretz Israel [Land of Israel]."

I said: "It is absurd. Missiles fly over our heads and you are saying it is not dangerous. You are not living in reality." David said that I consider one specific point only. However, if one wants to understand Jewish history, one has to look at the whole picture. One should take three steps backward. (Like in a good picture if you want to see well you should take three steps backwards.)

Then I blamed his educational system. It had made him think and act like a robot. His education was not neutral. He tried to tease me and asked me if I thought that my research was neutral and that there is such a thing as neutral education. I told him that his teachers are biased. Therefore, he had gotten a biased education.

David asked me: "Can peace education be neutral?" He added: "The educational role of the teacher is to teach about Eretz Israel. This is also the role of a responsible citizen. As educators, we should not think about the present. We should think about the future or the past. You are deluded by the present. Your inability to see anything beyond the here and now characterizes all the peaceniks. Therefore, we had this movement Peace Now. The peaceniks cannot see anything; their horizon is deluded by the *realistic future.* You see, we now have a ceasefire with the new ruler Abu Maazen ("Mahmoud Abbas"), yet they are shooting. I feel like a sitting duck, waiting for the next missile. Nothing has changed: Jews remain cowards. (Like in the Holocaust, Jews don't react.) You don't understand, you should walk proudly. If they think you are afraid they will ruin you. It's a world of power—those who don't react are considered to be cowards. According to their theory they are supposed to kick you out of this country. It's a matter of survival; it's either them or us in this world; a survival of the fittest for those who adjust themselves to the rules of war and power."

A few minutes later, we met a member of the security staff. I asked him what was going on. He said that five missiles had landed that day. He regarded it as a miracle that they didn't hit anybody in the crowd of 100,000 people." I asked David if he was afraid and he said: "No."

I asked: "Don't you think that there are also short-term goals in education?"

David: "Yes, there are. However, they are dependent on long-term goals. The long term is the landmark; it gives us orientation. The short-term goals are part of the big end. We need means to achieve our end and the short-term purposes are an instrument for achieving our end. The problem with the secular population in Israel is that it has departed from the long-term goals and chooses short-term purposes. This is the problem of Western civilization in general. Eat and drink today because we will die tomorrow.

Democracy is an instrument and not a value. It is an important instrument because it expresses the will of the people of Israel. The people of Israel are the end. It is difficult to differentiate between the means and the end, because they seem to be one and the same. The instrument is the State. It was established so that religious aspects could be materialized. If it so happens that the State opposes the people of Israel and the divine plan, something should be done. For example, if you sell Jewish land to Arabs, something should be done because it means that democracy endangers your existence. The teachers think that they, as citizens, must teach you to rebel in order to rescue the country. "A teacher should set an example to his students, especially in religious education. There is no separation between secular and religious life; religion concerns everybody and everything. This is the main premise of Rabbi Kook, so you cannot separate between your educational role and your civic obligation. They are one and the same thing and come from one source: God. Peace education is an education that erases your identity. Everything becomes imagination. Our Torah teaches us to love the stranger. We must supply the Arabs with their basic humanitarian needs, but they should remember that they are guests in this country. We host them, but they should know and we should know that we are the owners of this land. That is an objective fact."

I commented that he had been brainwashed by his educational system. I wished he had studied peace education as part of his socialization in school.

David: "Peace education is education for withdrawal. There is no moral lesson or positive message, but a message of retreat and destruction."

"Living in Eretz Israel is a precept like keeping the Sabbath, putting on phylacteries during the morning service, and having faith in God. There are no priorities. The question of Eretz Israel does not have to do with politics. The commandment to conquer the land is a commandment that we have to obey. Part of my socialization is to believe that I am commanded to settle the whole country. I cannot separate myself from the people or split my personality. As students, we expect our teachers to lead us and tell us how we should behave as citizens. The question of citizenship is an educational question and it must follow Jewish Law. The teachers used to say: we are not allowed to talk about politics but..."

He thought for few minutes and then continued: "I'd like to explain. The connection between the land of Israel and us is not a political matter; we are talking about fundamental principles. It is part of our religious education. If the rabbi wants me to pray, he also wants me to live in the Land of Israel. We are religious Zionist people. The fact that we are Zionists and citizens in Israel is an integral part of our religiosity. Therefore, the teachers cannot be neutral."

ANALYSIS

The account incorporates two units of analysis: the first unit is an interview with David, the main participant, and the second unit is an interview with Moshe, the man with three children. The two units will be analyzed in relation to the general setting, namely, the settlement and its surroundings.

The greater part of the interviews dealt with ideology and education. The ideology was right wing and loaded with emotional connotations. Rationality was rejected openly and purposely. Both participants thought that the rational dimension is irrelevant for analysis in this context.

As for education, we spoke about three issues: (1) the purpose of education and of the peace process; (2) the nature of education neutrality versus indoctrination; (3) the role of the teacher. These three topics are analyzed in general and in relation to peace education in particular. The participants claim that education should be analyzed in relation to long-term goals. Even a short-term goal derives from the long-term one. Both participants claim that there is no neutral education and that all education is biased. They perceive peace education as a means for convincing students of leftist ideas.

Four main categories could be elicited from this account:

The *first* category is time, a fundamental issue in this context. It gives a perspective on the whole context. The participants live in an unrealistic time orientation (eternity). From a psychological point of view, this might endanger the coherence of their ego identity, because the dilemma between stable and vague time is a key issue in the construction of the healthy "self" (Erikson, 1950; Tzuriel, 1990). From the participants' theological point of view, the vague time is the traditional redemption that, according to Jewish Theology, will come about in a time "that is not a day and not a night."

The fact that the only meaningful time perspective to the main participant is the future implies that he is committed to long-term goals rather than to short-term purposes. Hence the rejection of the peace process and peace education is regarded as part of his rejection of the immediate here and now in favor of the stable and the perpetual future. In his opinion, the peace process implies the withdrawal from perpetual values in favor of temporal ends. The peace process is connected to hedonism and secular considerations rather than to altruistic, religious, eternal values.

This argumentation has historical roots. Jews lived in a nonhistoric time perspective until the Renaissance. The establishment of the Zionist Movement meant that the Jews became part of normative human history. The Jewish nation started to function like all other "normal" nations of the Western civilization. Lamm (1991) distinguishes between goals that can be achieved and goals that will never be achieved. Goals that can be achieved are rational goals. Lamm says that politicians use political manipulation when they claim that they attained the impossible. When Theodor Herzl, the founder of the Zionist Movement, said: "If you will it [the establishment of a Jewish State], it is not a dream," he took into account the political circumstances and the revival of nationalism in Europe. Because of this realistic political analysis, he was able to talk about rational, attainable dreams rather than utopian, imaginative, and delusive goals.

According to Lamm, one of the main differences between political and ideological education is that political education deals with rational, attainable goals, whereas ideological education deals with utopian, unreachable goals. The aim of political education is to provide students with means that enable them to expose the interests that lie behind the goals. In this case study, both participants reject rationalistic goals and prefer to stick to Messianic goals, whereby they have different time perspectives and irrational horizons.

The *second* category is place. Is it a real or a visionary-mystical place? Schwartz (1997) claims that throughout Jewish history, Jews walked the fine line between fact and fiction concerning the land of Israel as an integral part of their existentiality. The conquest of the sacred historical places Jerusalem, Hebron, and Bet Lehem during the Six Day War in 1967 was considered a theological change rather than a political one (see also Gross, 2003; Schwartz, 1999). Actually, the political outcome of the war was regarded as compatible with the original messianic worldview. The victory was a sign from God for ushering in the messianic age. The beginning of the peace process in 1978 was seen as a retreat from this messianic vision and led to a split between the dream and reality, and consequently, religious confusion. The participants do not see the Gaza Strip as a dangerous place because of its religious significance. In their eyes, the peace process is not part of an international agreement between nations but rather a theological war against God and his commandments.

Keller (2000), following Lamm (1991) and Sholem (1988), writes that one of the ways to combine eternity and history is mystification. According to Sholem, mysticism is "the will to experience God here and now" (Keller, 2000, p. 141). In this case study, the two participants tend to use mystification in order to cope with the gap between ideology and reality.

The *third* category deals with the nature of the contents: positivistic versus constructivistic nature. Positivistic argumentation is objective and based on conclusions, the bottom line, rather than on a gradual process of reflection where sequential facts lead to the coherent construction of meaning within a constructivistic argumentation the context is taken into account. The contents are based on absolute truth, *the* truth. There is no attention to relative, subjective considerations. They base their truth on the Holy Scriptures. They are not aware of the fact that their argumentation is only one interpretation of the scriptures. Their inability to combine religion and reality makes them use mysticism. The use of conclusions rather than facts is part of their mystification. It should be noted that argumentation based on conclusions rather than facts is typical of ideological settings. Mystification is cultivated in religious education through a consistent system of ideological education (Lamm, 1991).

The *fourth* category deals with the methodology used to create educational messages: dogmatism. The teachers code their religious messages in a dogmatic fashion. The national and civic message is a religious message. Students are apt to accept it without doubt or exploration. The rigorous process of indoctrination is part and parcel of the religious repertoire into which they have been socialized. Keller (2004) writes that traditional societies justify and legitimize actions by religious convictions. In modern times, ideology substitutes the role of religion and is supposed to answer fundamental questions concerning general worldviews and education. The combination of religious and national ideology makes the religious Zionist issue more complex and multidimensional. The indoctrination procedure has to be subtle so that it will be accepted as legitimate by the students and their parents.

DISCUSSION

The aim of this research is to bring to light the categorical conceptions of graduates of the SRE system concerning the peace process in general and the Disengagement Plan in particular. The four categories found are: (1) An unrealistic time perspective; (2) a mystic attitude to the place; (3) messages of positivistic nature; and (4) the use of dogmatic methodology.

As this research consists of a small and limited sample, only the potential tendencies are discussed in this case study. Further research should take on a larger sample for which the categories developed here can serve as a point of departure. As these categories were elicited out of SRE graduates, it is assumed that the interviewees did not only communicate their personal worldview but also the messages that they internalized during their socialization and ideological upbringing in SRE schools.

The four categories hint at the fact that the religious Zionist educational system can be considered an ideological educational system (Lamm, 1991; Silverman-Keller, 2000). The participants in this research regard the teachers as representatives of the religious Zionist society whose role is to convey their ideological message as part of their civic obligation.

Lamm (1985) says that one of the main differences between ideological and political education is that the ideological system unifies the role of the teacher and the roles of the citizen, whereas the political educational system separates those roles.

Lamm holds that there are three basic modes of pedagogy: the normative, the formative, and the professional. The first two pedagogies can serve the ideological approach. The normative pedagogy deals with the curriculum to be determined by cultural foundations. The formative pedagogy deals with socialization providing the students with skills and enabling them to function in society according to its unique ethos. The professional pedagogy attempts to develop an autonomous and individualistic teacher who is not motivated by culture or by socializing, but by his individual professional agenda. During his training, the teacher learns about different philosophical approaches. Eventually, he will construct his own pedagogy based on the theories that he studies. This is an independent, open, and secular approach. Thus, the teacher is free to distinguish between his convictions as a citizen and his role as an educator. When the professional pedagogy becomes the domain of the teacher, rational reasoning will enable this separation (Lovat, 2001; Oser, Andreas Dick, & Patry, 1992).

Lamm (1985) regards political education not as education about political parties or political participation but as education about the distribution of power and interests, negotiation between social pressure groups, and so on. This is a logical, rational process and refers to a tangible reality and not to an imaginative mystic reality. The last two categories, positivism and dogmatism, can be understood only within the framework of a certain teaching style (the normative and the formative, which are part of a more traditional teaching style). However, peace education is valid only within a rational context and can be enhanced within the so-called professional teaching mode. Peace negotiations are a rational outcome of the understanding that violence and war lead to loss and destruction, whereas peace dialogue is a reasonable alternative for a better and promising future.

Modernity is characterized by rationalism (Berger, 1979, pp. 3–11) and peace education is perceived as a product of modernity and a logical pedagogical need in modern times. An educational framework that is based on unrealistic premises will find it difficult to cope with a rational culture of peace. The idea that violence leads to nowhere and causes loss and destruction to all produces peace negotiations. Therefore, peace education can only be employed in a modern context.

In the theoretical introduction it was noted that the SRE system is based on three tenets. However, it concentrates on the religious and national aims while neglecting the goal of providing modern education and being part of modernity. The fact that its graduates function in an unrealistic time and mystified place and regard this as a positive achievement of their socialization shows that peace education should be rooted in modernity and rationalism. Overmystification can lead to violence toward the innocent.

Israeli society is largely a traditional society that undergoes modernization. The peace process is part of the modernization process and should be examined in this context. If the SRE system wants to take part in the modernization process, it should challenge its students with modern, rational issues such as the enhancement of democracy and the question of the peace process.

Four categories were elicited from the case study in this research that may become barriers to peace education: (1) an eternal time perception (long-term purposes); (2) a mystical approach of place; (3) positivistic educational messages; and (4) a dogmatic teaching mode. These four main conceptual categories might portray possible difficulties in trying to enhance peace education programs in a religious Zionist population. Examining the questions of time, place, the nature of education, and the role of the teacher in other areas of conflict in the world may help enhance strategies for peace education and create a new peace-building agenda.

REFERENCES

Ayalon, H., & Yogev, A. (1998). Torah with secular studies (Torah im derekh Eretz): The alternative perspective for state-religious high school education. In H. Ayalon (Ed.), *Curricula as social reconstruction* (pp. 33–54). Tel Aviv: Ramot Publishers, Tel Aviv University.

Berger, P. (1979). *The heretical imperative.* New-York: Anchor Press.

Connelly, F. M., Phillion, J., & He, M. F. (2003). An exploration of narrative inquiry in multiculturalism in education: Reflecting on two decades of research in an inner-city Canadian community school. *Curriculum Inquiry, 33*(4), 363–384.

Dagan, M. (1999). State-religious education. In A. Peled (Ed.), *50th anniversary of the education system in Israel* (pp. 1011–1024). Jerusalem: Ministry of Education, Culture and Sport.

Dagan, M., Laval, M., & Greenbaum, N. (1992). *Guidelines for the state-religious education policy.* Jerusalem: Ministry of Education and Culture.(Hebrew).

Feiner, S. (2002). *The enlightenment revolution: The Jewish Haskalah Movement in the 18th century.* Jerusalem: Zalman Shazar Center.

Geertz, C. (1973). Thick description: Toward interpretive theory of culture. In C. Geertz (Ed.), *The interpretation of culture.* New York: Basic Books

Goldschmidt, Y. (1984). State-religious education in Israel. In A. Waserteil (Ed.), *Philosophy and education: Letters of Joseph Goldschmidt.* Jerusalem: Ministry of Education and Culture.

Gross, Z. (2003a). The social roles of state-religious education. In A. Sagi & D. Schwartz (Eds.), *One hundred years of Zionism* (pp. 129–186). Ramat-Gan: Bar-Ilan University.

Gross, Z. (2003b). State-religious education in Israel: Between tradition and modernity. *Prospects, 33*(2), 149–164.

He, M. F., Phillion, J., & Connelly, F. M. (2005). Narrative and experiential approaches to multiculturalism in education: Democracy and education. In J. Phillion, M. Fang He, & M. Connelly (Eds.), *Narrative and experience in multicultural education* (pp. 291–301). Thousand Oaks, CA: Sage.

Horowitz, D., & Lissak, M. (1990). *Trouble in Utopia.* Tel Aviv: Am Oved.

Katz, Y. (2004). State-religious education in Israel: Development trends in the Zionist era. In Z. Gross & Y. Dror (Eds.), *Education as a social challenge.* Tel Aviv: Ramot Publishers, Tel Aviv University.

Kiel, Y. (1977). *State-religious education: Its roots, history and problems.* Jerusalem: Ministry of Education and Culture, Religious Education Division.

Lamm, Z. (1985). The Israeli teacher: Routinization of mission. In W. Ackerman, A. Carmon, & D. Zucker (Eds.), *Education in an evolving society* (pp. 563–598). Tel-Aviv and Jerusalem: HaKibbutz HaMeuchad and van Leer.

Lamm, Z. (1991). Types of ideological education in the Israeli school. In D. Bar-Tal & A. Kelogman (Eds.), *Special issues in psychology and counseling in education* (pp. 7–17). Jerusalem: Ministry of Education.

Lamm, Z. (2002). *In the whirlpool of ideologies. Education in the twentieth century.* Jerusalem: Magnes.

Leslau, A., & Rich, Y. (1999). *Survey of 12th grade pupil on state-religious examinations.* Ramat-Gan: Bar-Ilan University, the Eliezer Stern Center for the Study and Advancement of Religious Education.

Lovat, T. (2001). What we learn about yesterday, today and tomorrow. Tracking social movements through curriculum analysis. In J. Allen (Ed.), *Sociology of education: Possibilities and practices* (2nd ed., pp. 88–106). Sydney: Social Science Press.

Lovat, T. (2003). The relationships between research and decision-making in education: An empirical investigation. *The Australian Educational Researcher, 30,* 43–56.

Oser, F., Andreas Dick, A., & Patry, JL (Eds.). (1992). *Effective and responsible teaching: The new synthesis.* San Francisco: Jossey-Bass.

Rosenak, M. (2003). *On second thought. tradition and modernity in Jewish contemporary education.* Jerusalem: Magnes.

Sabar-Ben-Yehoshua, N. (1990). *The qualitative research.* Givatayim: Massada.

Sabar-Ben-Yehoshua, N. (2001). Ethnography in education. In N. Sabar-Ben-Yehoshua (Ed.), *Genres and tradition in qualitative research* (pp. 101–140). Ganei-Aviv: Dvir.

Sagi, A. (2000). Religious Zionism: Between acceptance and reticence. In A. Sagi, D. Schwartz, & Y. Stern (Eds.), *Internal and external Judaism: A dialogue between two worlds* (pp. 124–168). Jerusalem: Magnes Press.

Salomon, G. (2002). The nature of peace education: Not all programs are created equal. In G. Salomon & B. Nevo (Eds.), *Peace education. the concept, principles and practices around the world* (pp. 3–14). Mahwah, NJ: Erlbaum.

Schwartz, D. (1996). *Belief at the crossroads: Between theory and practice in religious Zionism.* Tel Aviv: Am Oved.

Schwartz, D. (1997). *The Land of Israel in religious Zionist thought.* Tel-Aviv: Am Oved.

Schwartz, D. (1999). *Religious Zionism: Between logic and Messianism.* Tel Aviv: Am Oved.

Schwartzwald, Y. (1990). *State-religious education: Reality and research.* Ramat Gan: Bar-Ilan University Press.

Schweid, A. (2002). *History of the philosophy of the Jewish religion in modern times. Part I: The Haskalah period—A new agenda for philosophically coping with religion.* Jerusalem: Am Oved Publishers and the Shechter Institute for Judaic Studies.

Sholem, G. (1988). Mysticism and society. *Haaretz.*

Silverman-Keller, D. (2000). Education in a multi-cultural society: The case of state-religious education. In M. Bar-Lev (Ed.), *Teaching culture in a multi-cultural society: Issues for teacher in-service training* (pp. 139–158). Jerusalem: Hebrew University.

Silverman-Keller, D. (2004). Three plots, six characters and infinite possible educational narratives. *Educational Philosophy and Theory, 4.*

Stake, R. B. (2000). Case studies. In N. K. Denzin & Y. S. Lincoln (Eds.), *Handbook of qualitative research* (2nd ed., pp. 435–454). Thousand Oaks, CA: Sage.

Stake, R.B.(2004). *Standards-based and responsive evaluation.* London: Sage.

Waxman, C. (2003). Religion in Israeli public square. In U. Rebhun & C. Waxman (Eds.), *Jews in Israel.* New York: Brandeis University Press.

Yin, R. K. (2003). *Case study research design and method* (3rd ed.). New York: Sage.

Yin, R. K. (2004). *The case study anthology.* London: Sage.

Part V

PEACE EDUCATION INITIATIVES

CHAPTER 17

SEARCHING FOR HOME

A Personal and Professional Quest for Peace

Grace Feuerverger

INTRODUCTION

Neve Shalom/Wahat Al-Salam (the Hebrew and Arabic words for "oasis of peace") is a village in Israel that began as an intercultural experiment in the mid-1970s. There, Jews and Palestinians founded a community aimed at demonstrating the possibilities for living in peace—while maintaining their respective cultural heritages and languages.[1] My research work, which spanned a period of 9 years, focused on the two bilingual, bicultural educational institutions in this place of peace—an elementary school where Jewish and Arab children study together in the same classrooms, and the "school for peace," which is a conflict resolution outreach program for Israeli and Palestinian adolescents and their teachers. Both of these educational institutions exemplify a genuine attempt at partnership between two peoples whose entangled story of trauma, loss, displacement, and strangerhood has created an arid terrain of deep enmity. In this chapter I discuss several meta-themes: the commitment of the participants to confront the central question of Jewish–Palestinian coexistence on a grassroots level within the village and school; the two schools as a micro society and as a

Educating Toward a Culture of Peace, pages 283–296
Copyright © 2006 by Information Age Publishing

moral community that can be used as a role model for conflict resolution and peacemaking; the village as a symbol for creating a dialogue between Arabs and Jews in Israeli society and in the larger Middle East arena; negotiation and compromise in an atmosphere of moral complexity.

My personal and professional life has led me to believe that it is essential to critically examine educational initiatives that promote peacemaking and conflict resolution within international settings in order to investigate the broader issues of war and violence, social justice, and human rights, as well as their implications for the culturally diverse classroom. Conflict resolution and peacemaking are clearly intertwined. In fact, peace results not from the absence of conflict but from the ability to cope with it. Thus peacemaking can be regarded as the long, arduous process striving toward conflict resolution, which in itself is a prodigious and continual effort toward intercultural harmony. Many schools in North America, for example, are now committing to the principles of peace education due to deepening crises of violence in their schools. One of the most widely accepted peace education initiatives in the United States and Canada is the school conflict education strategy based on "peer mediation" training. This program teaches students how to manage conflicts constructively using negotiation procedures and peacemaking skills. Developing models of nonviolent leadership, conflict mediation, and respect for difference are key features of these innovations. My commitment to these issues found its expression in this longitudinal research investigation spanning a period of 9 years. One educational endeavor particularly captured my attention. I was very fortunate to have discovered this extraordinary village in Israel where Jews and Palestinians are living together in peace.

I focus on meaning-making as grounded in personal life history and experience—that is, on the social, linguistic, and cultural texts of my participants (and of my own), in order to provide a more nuanced view of peacemaking in education. I explore the woundings and the sense of victimhood that both peoples—both Jews and Palestinians — feel in their different ways. I also share narrative portraits of some of the most remarkable educators I have ever met who are working together on an everyday journey toward reconciliation and who invite us to become fellow dreamers of peace. My purpose here is to engage the discourse of peaceful coexistence in a Jewish-Palestinian village, as it relates to difference, sense of "otherness," and conflict between two peoples yearning for home and safety. I seek to explore several participants' distinctive stories and to construct, along with and through my own personal story, a narrative journey of my/ their desires, dreams, fears, works—past, present, future. I follow the poet Theodore Roethke's words, that "I learn by going where I have to go." Not so hidden within my participants' imaginings of peace for two national homelands is my own desire for a unified self—the "more inclusive and fundamental aim of building and rebuilding a coherent and rewarding sense of identity" (Giddens, 1991, p. 75). Michel Foucault (1984, pp. 37–38) commented that putting your own reason to use (instead of working according to what others want of you) is essential for becoming conscious of your own inner thoughts and desires and in so doing becoming the person you would like to be. For the poet Baudelaire the task of modernity was in fact the challenge of attempting to invent ourselves, all the while understanding that we are limited by our life experiences.

THEORETICAL AND METHODOLOGICAL CONSIDERATIONS

My personal and professional life has been profoundly informed by the "revolutionary" landscape of *Neve Shalom/Wahat-Al-Salam*. Indeed, the fieldwork experience has affected me in myriad ways and has allowed me to reflect on my life story more deeply. In contrast to the classical ethnographic approach where the researcher is expunged from the text, the method of inquiry I offer here is more in concert with postmodern ethnographers who, in spite of having their qualms about the "authorial voice," make themselves more visible and sometimes even central to their research enterprise as a means of better understanding and interpreting the interaction of their past life experiences with the life experiences of their participants during their fieldwork, their data analysis, and in the discussion of their findings (Behar, 1996; Britzman, 1998; Grimshaw, 1992; Marcus, 1998; Oakley, 1992; Rosaldo, 1993). For example, Davies (1999) explains that this interest in *reflexivity* (i.e., the use of autobiography in ethnography) is a positive feature of ethnographic research and indeed it is now gaining status as a legitimate methodological approach. Undertaking the study of the pursuit of peaceful coexistence in this Jewish-Arab village, one must remind oneself that the investigation brings this lived experience into the core of one's own lived experiences. When I first arrived in *Neve Shalom/Wahat Al-Salam* in 1991, I began to reflect on my own reasons for becoming a bilingual education (French Immersion) teacher in Canada almost two decades earlier and later in my university career focusing on immigrant/refugee/peace education. What were the unconscious myths or metaphors that motivated me? Witherell and Noddings (1991) believe that "to take seriously the quest for life's meaning and the meaning of individual lives, is to understand the primacy of the caring relation and of dialogue in educational practice" (p. 5). The narratives that I wrote about the participants and the stories that I shared with them about my own life history began to explain why I had chosen *Neve Shalom/Wahat Al-Salam* for my fieldwork. Or had it chosen me?

Due to my professional history as teacher/educational researcher, I decided to inquire into this study as a social scientist rather than as a story-teller and therefore I struggle with my own subjectivity in interpreting my findings. I am in good company, however, when I say that the two approaches need not be mutually exclusive; in fact, Hammersly and Atkinson (1995) point out that they are both intrinsic aspects of social research. Indeed, one can (and must) be both at the same time in order to do justice to the complex reality of human endeavors. Theorists have suggested that even the most objective of social research methods are clearly subjective (see Davies, 1999). Furthermore, the interview process convinced me that my relationship with the participants in the village formed the basis of my reflective theorizing. This social interaction as well as my reflective field notes turned out to be central in the construction of my participant-observations, which became my data. This methodology corroborates Powder-maker's (1966) classic stance that participant-observation requires both involvement and detachment achieved by developing the ethnographer's "role of stepping in and out of society."

SOCIAL AND EDUCATIONAL SIGNIFICANCE

Using reflexive ethnography as the methodological research approach, my research explores the interaction between the students and their teachers in their everyday classroom activities in the bilingual, bicultural elementary school, as well as in the "School for Peace" conflict resolution program.[2] The theoretical and conceptual underpinnings of this study reside in the innovative educational attempt to deconstruct the traditional school discourses in Israel, which generally perpetuate the dominant/subordinate status of Hebrew and Arabic, respectively, within the curriculum. The use of both languages has become a symbol for inclusiveness and mutual understanding in formal and informal school activities. Such an atmosphere allows teachers and students to rethink the space where dominant and subordinate groups are situated, and thus to transform their own relationships. *Neve Shalom/Wahat Al-Salam* can thus be envisioned as a new "borderland" where emancipatory discourses of national, cultural and linguistic equality are being created. Some research questions that guided this inquiry were:

- What perceptions of the conflict and more generally of the world do these teacher/educators bring to the classroom and how do these perceptions interact with those of the students in the class?
- How do they envision themselves and their respective identities as Jews and Arabs caught in a very complex human struggle?

- How are these views enacted in their school curriculum choices and communication within the classroom?
- Does the school in fact incorporate an egalitarian bilingual and bicultural philosophy into its curriculum?

I cannot help but think that Robert Coles (1997) was discussing my own reflexive ethnographic "gaze" when he wrote: "To some extent we see the world we are looking for. We select for ourselves visually what our minds and hearts crave to notice.... How differently each of us sees even the same scene, selecting from it what we want to emphasize out of our personal needs and nature" (pp. 224–225). Perhaps I, as a child of Holocaust survivors, a "border-dweller," have been searching for *Neve Shalom/Wahat Al-Salam* all my life and finally found it. As a child, I longed to live in a world of harmony and joy and peace. I agree with Britzman (1998) that my own telling is fragmented and dominated by the "discourses of my time and place" and especially by my sense of being a border-dweller, someone still searching for "home." I confess openly to this guilty desire. Perhaps we must indeed acknowledge ethnography as a "regulating fiction, as a particular narrative practice that produces textual identities and regimes of truth" (Britzman, 1998, p. 236).

Craig Kridel (1998) underscores the "power of autobiography and biography—the construction of landscapes and the act of making history personal" (p. 122). Indeed, Denzin and Lincoln (1994) suggest that

> the means for interpretive, ethnographic practices are still not clear, but it is certain that things will never be the same. We are in a new age where messy, uncertain, multi-voiced texts, cultural criticism, and new experimental works will become more common, as will more reflexive forms of fieldwork, analysis, and intertextual representation. (p. 15, as cited in Kridel, 1998)

Renato Rosaldo (1989) contends that there are no "innocent" ethnographers. There is always an interior voice crying to be heard; to be acknowledged; to be recognized within the exterior professional world. We are all moved by deep unconscious forces, and that is nothing if not human. The multiple layerings that become the foundation upon which we do our "formal" ethnographic work emerge from personal, private experiences and ways of knowing (Belenky, Clinchy, Goldberger, & Tarule, 1986)—which are not incongruent with theoretical, epistemological frames of reference. In fact, the fragments have in themselves a certain coherence, a raw clarity of purpose: they represent the emotional chaos—the landscapes of loss, of pain, of fear, of trauma that create the underpinnings of this struggle toward peace with which I became intimately involved. The stuff of ethnography, indeed perhaps of all human endeavor, is in the endless retellings and thus in illuminating the enormous questions located in the vicissitudes and incredible contradictions of human relationships, the "us" versus "them" dichotomies.

I firmly believe that one of the most important contributions we can make as academics is to use the vehicle of our research work as a means of forwarding the cause of peace and equality within an antiracist/multicultural, multilingual, educational context for all societes and to unequivocally support an inclusive curriculum wherein all forms of oppression can be addressed with compassion. Ultimately, educational and all forms of human reform are dependent on the importance and power of love: I cite here Freire's universalist message:

> Dialogue cannot exist, however, in the absence of a profound love for the world and for people.... Because love is an act of courage, not of fear, love is commitment to others. No matter where the oppressed are found, the act of love is commitment to their cause—the cause of liberation.... As an act of bravery, love cannot be sentimental: as an act of freedom it must not serve as a pretext for manipulation. It must generate other acts of freedom; otherwise, it is not love. (1970, pp. 70–71)

I am comforted and empowered by the philosophy of Freire and in the knowledge/belief systems of mindful, compassionate scholars everywhere who stress that "cultural workers must create alliances across national borders... and that, in Freirian terms, revolutionary love is always pointed in the direction of commitment and fidelity to a *global* project of emancipation" (in McLaren, 1999, pp. 53–54). This research study is also an exploration into the desolate psychological landscape that Jews and Palestinians must navigate, and into their highly emotional journey toward breaking down the barriers of fear and mistrust that have saturated their daily existence. I explore the social and psychological dimensions of their educational odyssey, and discuss the sites of struggle, ambiguities, moral dilemmas, and negotiation in the "border dialogues" that these participants have created for themselves in their search to give equal expression to their national identities. I document how these two national groups have been able to create new cultural spaces, new realms of discourse, and new modes of thought in spite of the profound difficulties that envelop them on a daily basis.

The innovative educational initiatives at the two schools of *Neve Shalom/ Wahat Al-Salam* are exemplars for reshaping the pedagogical processes in classrooms and in school policies throughout the world. They have freed the participants to become "border crossers" and so challenge and redefine the limitations of hegemonic domination. Included in the book is my own personal narrative showing how I became a "border crosser" early in my childhood as a way to connect with other cultures and languages and as a vehicle to escape my own family life history. For the participants in this village, language and cultural awareness also is connected to "border cross-ing," and are metaphors for the need to create an egalitarian Hebrew-Ara-bic curriculum for all students, thereby inviting them to cross over into the territory that will allow them to become familiar with the "other." "Border crossing" thus becomes the enterprise of reconciliation with "otherness"— which, at bottom, is the enterprise of peacemaking.

Israelis and Palestinians each continue to search for mutual affirmation of their legitimate place in the Middle East, and the tragedy of their unre-solved histories remains a moral dilemma within a larger quest for global harmony. "Oasis of Dreams" documents both the imagination and the courage of those involved with *Neve Shalom/Wahat Al-Salam* and documents their success in creating a new outlook on the world. Through this research, I came to recognize that knowing the existence of the "foreigner" is a central aspect of language awareness in general, which in turn can be viewed as a sensitivity and a conscious understanding of the languages and cultures in our world and of their role for all of humanity. This study also helped me to understand more fully the dialectical relationship between language and thought in practical educational settings. This kind of thoughtful teaching and learning is a transformative process that appreci-ates the complexities of bilingual and bicultural education within the back-drop of conflict and war. As an investigation of the social, linguistic, and psychological complexities inherent in this pedagogical experiment toward peace, this research work is being widely recognized as a global role model for the 21st century in terms of an exemplary society working to respect differences and to inspire a moral vision of compassion and social justice. The book *Oasis of Dreams* is already being used in university courses as a pedagogical resource. This book's major contribution is the develop-ment of an original emancipatory pedagogy of peace applicable not only for Israel and the Palestinian Authority but also within the wider interna-tional arena.

EDUCATIONAL NARRATIVES OF PEACEFUL COEXISTENCE

One of the greatest challenges in Israeli society is to overcome the fear and enmity that has evolved through the years of war between Jew and Arab. One of the Jewish parents very eloquently expressed her hope, which is shared by all those connected with the school: "We want our children to learn in friendship and joy, not in conflict and sorrow." In order to make friends with "the other," as the residents in this village are doing, we must confront the "other" in the deepest part of our souls, in the psychological no-man's land where the "foreigner" lurks—"he is the hidden face of our identity, the space that wrecks our abode, the time in which understanding and affinity founder" (Kristeva, 1991). In this qualitative study, I examine how the pariticipants acknowledge that a "foreigner" speaks a different language and has a different culture and different values and traditions and competes for the same geopolitical space. This is an excruciating task but when it is embarked upon, it opens up the possibility of collaboration instead of competition and hostility, and in so doing it surmounts the hegemonic discourses and institutions and thereby creates transformative intergroup and interpersonal dialogues. Van Manen (1990) explains that "we gather other people's experiences because they allow us to become more experienced ourselves." Connelly and Clandinin (1990, 1995) support this view and claim that narrative refers to the process of making meaning of experience by telling stories of personal and social relevance.

This research indeed is devoted to the complexity and aesthetic of peace education taking place in the classrooms of the schools in this village. I provide a reflective analysis of the interviews carried out with the teachers and students in the elementary school in the village. My aim is to focus on meaning-making as grounded in personal life history—that is, on the social, linguistic, and cultural stories of my participants (and of myself) in an attempt at a more nuanced view of peacemaking in education. Their philosophy of a Jewish-Arab village in Israel, living and teaching peace and equality, is rooted in the democratic ideals of dialogue and cooperative problem solving. But it is not as simple and utopian as that. It is a "flesh-and-blood" place within a very difficult human circumstance where intergroup conflict in the wider society and the moral problems and dilemmas that ensue are constantly being played out and negotiated. The village is not an island unto itself by any means. Many of the villagers work in towns nearby, and are subject to the social and political turmoil that envelops all of Israel (see Feuerverger, 2001). Effective schools should be sites of political and cultural negotiation that encourage teachers to situate and scrutinize the borders of their own ideological discourses. "Borders elicit a recognition of those epistemological, political, cultural and social margins that define 'the places that are safe and unsafe, [that] distinguish *us* from *them*'" (Anzaldua, 1987). Teachers need to become cognizant of the "unconscious myths" that have shaped the mental and physical landscape of their lives and that now motivate them in the planning of curriculum and in their choice of interpersonal classroom strategies (Clandinin & Connelly, 1995; Richardson, 1994). The conversations I had with the teachers and students in this school were very illuminating in terms of language, culture, and identity formation.

For example, I would like to share the story of a Palestinian teacher in the school who discussed the surprise that his father showed when he first came to visit his son in this village and met some of the children in the school. Here is an excerpt to whet your appetite:

My father grew up in a little Arab village in the north of the country and was at first uncertain about why I should teach in a school where Jewish and Arab kids were together. He just wasn't sure how this would work. Then on the first afternoon that he was here a little 9-year-old girl came up to him and spoke to him in Arabic. They had a lovely conversation and afterward I told him this young student of mine was Jewish. He had assumed she was an Arab because her Arabic was so fluent. When he heard she was Jewish, his eyes filled with tears and he said he thought he would never see this. He was amazed at how all the children were getting along, jumping back and forth into Hebrew and Arabic. They were friends, and that was a revelation to him. That is the beauty of this place.

One of the greatest events that I have ever witnessed in my life was the end-of-term holiday party that took place in the elementary school one cold, late December evening. All three monotheistic religions are respected and honored in the school. I will never forget two women sitting side by side in the audience watching their older children on stage. My eyes fell on an Arab woman in her veil sitting with a lovely little baby on her lap. Right next to her was a Jewish woman also sitting with a little child on her lap. It was the first time they met as human beings, not as "the enemy." "This is what peace is all about," I remember saying to myself with tears streaming down my face as I snapped a photo. I felt disgusted with the world's media for only focusing on the negative and on distortions and sensationalist manipulations.

This village is a sacred space and it has nourished me in ways I could never have expected. I feel truly honored to have been among these extraordinary people. What lies at the heart of this village may seem like only a dream on the larger world stage, but without it we are lost. In fact their moral enterprise may be the only way toward compassion and redemption for us all. Perhaps this little village offers the hope that the biblical Tower of Babel may not necessarily have to be regarded as a punishment for humankind. Perhaps we can discover its meaning in terms of the challenge that has been placed before us—that is, to learn to live in peace with ourselves and our neighbors in a multilingual, multicultural, multiracial, multifaith global society.

When I asked some of the children in the school what they would like me to tell others about their way of life, they responded with these words:

"It is very easy to call people names and to hate them. But when you begin to live with them and go to school with them and play with them, then you realize that, even though they may have different customs and beliefs, they are really very similar in many ways. You have to find a bridge and meet them halfway."

And here is what two teenagers, one Israeli, one Palestinian, shared with me after a grueling 3-day conflict resolution workshop in the "School for Peace." I had asked them whether they thought this workshop would make a difference. Here is what they said:

An Israeli girl:

We're both drowning in quicksand next to each other but can we stretch out our hands to one another or will we sink in the mud with our raised fists?

A Palestinian girl:

It has already made a difference. Something in me has changed. We may not have solved the problem, but I come away with a real treasure—my heart is now filled with less hatred and instead there's a greater understanding of how complicated this conflict is. I saw what's behind the mask of my enemy—and it's a human being just like me.

IMPLICATIONS FOR BILINGUAL EDUCATION

One of the aims of this study was to discuss the need for rethinking and reshaping an understanding of language as a social phenomenon that must be fundamentally linked to teachers' and learners' sense of identity and self-worth within their communities (see, e.g., Corson, 1999; Cummins, 1994). In this school, the use of the two languages has become a symbol for inclusiveness and mutual understanding in formal and informal school activities. This school is innovative in its attempt to deconstruct the traditional school discourses in Israel, which usually perpetuate the dominant/subordinate status of Hebrew and Arabic, respectively, within the curriculum. For Arab students in Israel (and, in fact, for all students who perceive themselves to be in a subordinate position in their societies), it is important that their values and culture be represented within the mainstream curriculum, especially within the texts that they read and write. The author investigated how this elementary school distinguishes itself in that that the dominant/subordinate status of Arab students is contested within the structures and discourses of the school. Various qualitative methods of research were used to focus on how the curriculum and pedagogical strategies in the school have been reconstituted in such a way that they can offer "cognitive empowerment" (see Torrez-Gusman, 1992, pp. 477–490), allowing students to become critical thinkers in dialogue with their teachers. "Teachers need to be reflective practitioners who first examine themselves—their knowledge base, their attitudes, beliefs, values and practices—and then develop approaches to teaching and learning which challenge and empower" (Jackson, 1995). Effective schools should be sites of political and cultural struggle, which force teachers to situate and scrutinize their own ideological discourses.

Giroux (1991) states that by reshaping the pedagogical processes in the classrooms and in the school policies, all the participants become free to be "border crossers" and thus challenge and redefine the borders created by hegemonic domination. And in terms of this specific study, "border crossing" became a metaphor for the realization of the need to create a fully egalitarian Hebrew–Arabic curriculum for all students, thereby inviting them to cross over into uncharted territory in order to become familiar with the "other." Indeed, what was continually witnessed in the classrooms was the contextualization and integration of language activities through the encouragement of real dialogue, inclusion and fairness, and the sharing of stories as a means for better understanding "otherness" and "difference." *Neve Shalom/Wahat Al-Salam* can thus be envisioned as a new "borderland" where emancipatory discourses of cultural and linguistic equality are being created. Stated another way, "border crossing" becomes the enterprise of reconciliation with "otherness" (Anzaldua, 1987; Kristeva, 1991; Shabatay, 1991)—which is, at bottom, the enterprise of peacemaking. This little school offers the hope that the biblical Tower of Babel may not necessarily have to be regarded as a punishment for humankind. Perhaps we can reconfigure its meaning in terms of the challenge that has been placed before us—that is, to learn to live in peace with ourselves and our neighbors in a multilingual, multicultural, multiracial, multifaith global society.

CONCLUDING REMARKS

Conducting this research and writing *Oasis of Dreams* has reinforced for me what I have always believed: that education has the power to create a collective "home"—a vision of the future through the reflective narratives and stories of all the players involved—that is, the teachers, the students, the parents, the researchers, the policymakers, and others too—so that they might clarify and interconnect their dreams for transformative pedagogies of an inclusive social consciousness. The hope is for the creation of a communicative space in which dislocation, marginality, suspicion, and fear can be transcended through authentic dialogue. My book offers a participant-observer's sense of the realms of discourse and modes of thought that make this unique Jewish–Palestinian cooperative village what one grade 5 child had called it: an "*oasis of peace in a desert of war.*" At the core of this reflexive ethnography lies the search for a safe place in the world—for a site of refuge, reconciliation, peace building, and hope for humanity. These villagers provide us with a unique role model where one can discover new ways of seeing reality, new ways of confronting difference, and new ways of understanding ourselves and others. They are my heroes.

My research journey in *Neve Shalom/Wahat Al-Salam* has certainly changed me forever. In the ethnographic research process, I walked through a landscape of spiritual reflection, of pedagogical reveries, of social and political tensions. I listened to painful stories as well as healing ones, and shared narrative portraits of these remarkable individuals who, in their attempt at peaceful coexistence, invite us all to become fellow dreamers of peace. This village is a profoundly sacred space and it nourishes me in ways I could never have expected. It comforts me profoundly in this grim time of terrible violence in Israel and the occupied territories and it brings me closer to the reason I came to it in the first place: to bear witness to the power of what these villagers are trying to accomplish against all odds. At the core of this research study—indeed at the core of all my academic work—will always be that child of the Holocaust searching for a safe place in the world—for a site of refuge, peace building, and hope for humanity. That child will never have the luxury of taking life for granted.[3] She will always feel "homeless"—a psychological orphan. It turns out that the deeper meaning of this Jewish-Palestinian village for me is its call for reconciliation in spite of the deep woundedness that surrounds both the Israelis and the Palestinians.

But do we all not need to be rescued by the message that *Neve Shalom/ Wahat Al-Salam* offers us—that "peace on earth" is possible? I used the book in last year's course and I am gratified by the response of my students. It opened a whole new space for building a discourse of international understanding. We focused on how these courageous individuals have chosen to engage in true dialogue and thus to become architects in their destinies rather than pawns. We discussed how they may be on the threshold of a liberating narrative that urges us to reflect on its global potential for peace building and social justice—in spite of our present despair, or perhaps because of it. Perhaps what lies at the heart of this village is only a dream on the larger world stage, but without it we are lost. In fact, their moral enterprise may be the only way toward compassion and redemption for us all. Our global community has become a much more dangerous place and therefore I believe that now more than ever we as teachers, as educators, as human beings are called to provide for our students, our colleagues a more hopeful view of what the world has the potential to be. This was one of the reasons that I originally decided to write *Oasis of Dreams*—to share this message that individuals do make a difference and that teaching was and always will be what William Ayers so eloquently describes as "an act of hope for a better future."

NOTES

1. This chapter is based on my book *Oasis of Dreams: Teaching and Learning Peace in a Jewish-Palestinian Village in Israel* (RoutledgeFalmer, 2001).

2. The elementary school opened its doors in 1984, the preschool and kindergarten 3 years earlier. What is unique about this village school is that it provides the possibility for Jewish and Arab children to learn *together* on a daily basis in a full Hebrew-Arabic bilingual, bicultural setting. It is coordinated by a teaching team of Jewish- and Arab-Israeli educators, some of whom are residents of the village and others who commute from nearby towns and villages. The "School for Peace" is an outreach conflict resolution program geared toward bringing Jewish and Palestinian adolescents from all over Israel and the West Bank together for workshops conducted by well-trained facilitators in the village, and it has been operating since 1979. To date more than 20,000 Palestinian and Jewish adolescents have had the opportunity to attend the "School for Peace" workshops.

3. This search for a "safe place" is very connected to my own personal life history of trauma resulting from being a child of Holocaust survivors.

REFERENCES

Anzaldua, G. (1987). *Borderlands/La Frontera: The new mestiza.* San Francisco: San Francisco/Aunt Lute.

Ayers, W. (1993). *To teach: The journey of a teacher.* New York: Teachers College Press.

Behar, R. (1996). *The vulnerable observer.* Boston: Beacon Press.

Belenky, M. F., Clinchy, B., Goldberger, N., & Tarule. J.M. (1986). *Women's ways of knowing: The development of self, voice and mind.* New York: Basic Books.

Britzman, D. (1998). On doing something more. In Ayers & Millers (Eds.), *Maxine Greene: A light in dark times* (pp. 97–107). New York: Teachers College Press.

Coles, R. (1997). *Doing documentary work.* New York: Oxford University Press

Connelly, F. M., & Clandinin, D. J. (1990). Stories of experience and narrative inquiry. *Educational Researcher, 19*(5), 2–14.

Corson, D. (1999). *Language policy in schools: A resource for teachers and administrators.* Mahwah, NJ: Erlbaum.

Cummins, J. (1994). From coercive to collaborative relations of power in the teaching of literacy. In B. M. Ferdman, R-M. Weber, & A. G. Ramirez (Eds.), *Literacy across languages and cultures* (pp. 295–331). Albany: State University of New York Press.

Davies, C. A. (1999). *Reflexive ethnography: A guide to researching selves and others.* London: Routledge.

Feuerverger, G. (2001). *Oasis of dreams: Teaching and learning peace in a Jewish-Palestinian village in Israel.* London: RoutledgeFalmer.

Foucault, M. (1984). What is enlightenment? In P. Rabinow, *The Foucault reader* (pp. 32–50). New York: Random House.

Freire, P. (1970). *Pedagogy of the oppressed.* New York: Seabury Press.

Giroux, H. A. (1991). Democracy and the discourse of cultural difference: Towards a politics of border pedagogy. *British Journal of Sociology of Education, 12*(4), 501–519.

Kridel , C. (1998). Landscapes, biography, and the preservation of the present. In Ayers & Millers (Eds.), *Maxine Greene: A light in the dark times.* New York: Teachers College Press.

Kristeva, J. (1991). *Strangers to ourselves.* (L. S. Roudiez, Trans.). New York: Columbia University Press.

Marcus, G. E. (1998). *Ethnography through thick and thin.* Princeton, NJ: Princeton University Press.

McLaren, P. (1999). *Educational Researcher, 28*(2), 49.

Powdermaker, H. (1966). *Stranger and friend: The way of an anthropologist.* New York: W.W. Norton.

Richardson, V. (1994). Conducting research on practice. *Educational Researcher, 23*(5), 5–10.

Rosaldo, R. (1989/1993). *Culture and truth: The remaking of social analysis.* London: Routledge.

Shabatay, V. (1991). The stranger's story: Who calls and who answers? In C. Witherell & N. Noddings (Eds.), *Stories lives tell: Narrative and dialogue in education.* New York: Teachers College Press.

Torres-Guzman, M. (1992). Stories of hope in the midst of despair: Culturally responsive education for Latino students in an alternative high school in New York City. In M. Saravia-Shore & S. F. Arvizu (Eds.), *Cross-cultural literacy: Ethnographies of communication in multiethnic classrooms* (pp. 477–490). New York: Garland.

Van Manen, M. (1990). *Researching lived experience: Human science for an action sensitive pedagogy.* London: University of Western Ontario.

Witherell, C., & Noddings, N. (Eds.). (1991). *Stories lives tell: Narrative and dialogue in education.* New York: Teachers College Press.

CHAPTER 18

TOLERANCE EDUCATION AND HUMAN RIGHTS EDUCATION IN TIMES OF FEAR

A Comparative Perspective

K. Peter Fritzsche

INTRODUCTION: TOLERANCE MATTERS

This chapter presents some findings of a comparative case study carried out within the framework of the International Network "Education for Democracy, Human Rights and Tolerance" of the Bertelsmann Foundation. The network consists of several NGOs, scientists, and experts from different countries in West and East Europe, Israel, Philippines, South America, and the United States. The aim of bringing together this international group was to provide an infrastructure and build a platform for intercultural exchange, projects, and research on issues of tolerance education. Organizations from 10 countries, although working in very different situations, found that they were linked by a common concern to explore the potential of education to foster nonviolence. Especially in times of conflict, the question arises: Is it possible to promote tolerance,

Educating Toward a Culture of Peace, pages 297–307
Copyright © 2006 by Information Age Publishing
All rights of reproduction in any form reserved.

democracy, and human rights through education? The project, "Tolerance Matters" (1998–2003), identifies fundamental issues in the field of education for democracy, human rights, and tolerance. The case studies examine educational responses in a wide range of cultural, social, and economic contexts. Set against an analytical framework that allows for comparison, the case studies explore the complexities, challenges, and opportunities inherent in attempting to use education as a mechanism for fostering understanding and tolerance. This unique collection of case studies offers a cross and intercultural approach to the issue of education for democracy. The hope was that this process would help to uncover some of the questions and concerns that are common to groups working on education for tolerance in different contexts or cultures. In the longer term this might contribute to progress on the identification of fundamental questions about the role of education in situations of cultural, political, or religious division (Dunn, Fritzsche, & Morgan, 2003a, 2003b).

TEN ORGANIZATIONS AND FRAMEWORK OF THE COMPARISON

The organizations of the network that are all involved in education or in research on education are as follows:

- The Adam Institute for Democracy and Peace (Jerusalem)
- The Anti-Defamation League (ADL) (New York)
- The Benigno S. Aquino, Jr. Foundation (Philippines)
- The Bertelsmann Group for Policy Research at the Center for Applied Policy
- Research (CAP), the University of Munich
- The Centre for the Study of Conflict (Coleraine, Northern Ireland)
- The Foundation for Education for Democracy (FED) (Warsaw)
- The International Fellowship of Reconciliation (IFOR) (Alkmaar, The Netherlands)
- Managing Conflict (UMAC) (South Africa)
- Novamerica (Rio de Janeiro)
- PARTICIPA (Chile)

As a first step each of the organizations represented agreed to produce a case study, describing the context in which they operate and the nature of the educational work that they are involved in or support. Through a number of group meetings, agreement was reached about the core issues that would be addressed and the format of each report. At the same time the diversity of the situations in which network members work was recognized and the agreed framework provided sufficient flexibility to allow writers to reflect on the particular characteristics of their situation. In order to try to ensure a degree of structural uniformity in the reports, a very general organizational matrix was produced. This had two dimensions. The first was designed to try to ensure that the specific work under consideration in each study was presented in such a way that the reader unfamiliar with the project would be able to understand its context, background, scope, activities, resources, and so on. The second objective of adopting, as far as possible, a common structure was to make it possible to examine the case studies from a comparative perspective.

In order to make the comparison possible, a structure was developed that would give the case studies a common framework.

- The social and historical context within which they work and the impact of contextual changes such as economic or social crises
- The educational responses
- The resource input
- The strategies developed to ensure that projects become established, promoted, and disseminated.
- The social responses: support or obstacles within their societies.

The first and most obvious differences are to be found in the extent to which intolerance manifests itself and becomes prevalent within each society, and the social and institutional forms that this takes. On the one hand, there are contexts, for example the United States or Germany, with a relatively small number of incidents of discrimination and prejudice and these are mainly of a nonviolent kind (in proportional terms). On the other hand, there are societies that are experiencing, or have recently experienced, major episodes of violent community conflict with large numbers of deaths, as in Northern Ireland and Israel.

The length of time during which the various problems have been developing, and the overall historical backgrounds, are similarly varied. Some examples include the convoluted history of British involvement in Ireland, which provides a direct line between the present problems in Northern Ireland and the invasions of the Anglo-Norman kings almost , years ago; the long history of Spanish and U.S. involvement in the Philippines; the Israeli–Palestinian conflict, which, in its present form, dates from the immediate postwar period; and the difficulties over immigrant workers in Germany that have surfaced mainly during the last 30 years.

Some of the countries involved are, in economic terms, highly developed and prosperous, and the majority of their populations are relatively affluent. In these cases the fear of the loss of economic status or privilege is often an important element in the emergence and growth of prejudice. Other cases involve societies where there are serious problems linked to economic underdevelopment or mismanagement and the accompanying problems of poverty and deprivation. The frustration and anger generated in such situations appears to make the emergence of intolerance possible.

The main convictions the network members had in common are:

- There is a need to overcome intolerance.
- Nonviolence and tolerance matters for the individual as well as for the society.
- Education matters in order to overcome intolerance and to foster tolerance.

CONCEPTS AND DEGREES OF TOLERANCE

What does tolerance mean? Apparently, it has different meanings. A defininition given by UNESCO describes tolerance as the basic, minimum quality of social relationship refraining from violence and force. But who tolerates whom and why? Here, we can see differences in terms of history and conception. A closer look at the diversity of tolerance concepts reveals different degrees of progressing tolerance (Fritzsche, 2001, pp. 1–7): (1) the pragmatic calculating one, (2) the endured passive one, and (3) the active interfering one.

1. Derived from Latin "tolerare," tolerance originally means "to endure a burden or to let something happen you don´t like really." This meaning of endurance is what today most people understand by tolerance. A starting point for the development of tolerance was the relation between a strong and a weak party, between a ruler granting tolerance, and a—usually religious—minority asking for tolerance. Here, the reason for tolerance was of a pragmatic kind, since social and economic advantages gained out of practicing tolerance seemed to be higher than the price of suppression. Such pragmatic calculation could also be decisive at the end of a war led between two almost equally strong enemies, who were aware that they had rather endure the enemy's rights, since the price of intolerance would have been too high.

2. It was during the Enlightenment that a new interpretation of tolerance gained acceptance—without replacing the old pragmatic one: All people must be tolerated because everybody has a right to freedom and to be different. This second concept of tolerance thus also considers the acceptance of others with their right to be different. Acceptance does of course not mean to take over, but to respect the other religion, way of life, and cultural phenomena while keeping in mind that a different lifestyle has the same rights as one's own.

3. UNESCO's interpretation of tolerance goes even beyond this concept: Tolerance is more than the mere absence of intolerance. It implies our involvement in creating an environment in which tolerance is possible.

We can learn from this overview that the central question is not only whether somebody is tolerant, but also how tolerant he or she is. We can also conclude from this that teaching tolerance and human rights education should go hand in hand, because human rights and tolerance belong together. The goal is *to connect the recognition of equal rights with tolerance for differences.* Every person must be granted the freedom of being different, for it is a human right. And it is people's task to tolerate the outcome of the others' freedom. We should demonstrate mutual tolerance specifically because we have a human right to freedom and the right to be different. Tolerance of differences stems from this acceptance of equality. It is precisely when we are not pleased with the way others use their right to freedom in concrete terms and how they live their lives that we must recognize their right to freedom and tolerate the consequences (as long as the freedom is not misused for intolerance). Tolerance that is not based on human rights, but only on the decision of those who are willing to be tolerant, is seen as "weak tolerance." Such tolerance might be rejected as a value to promote by education.

WORLD OF DIFFERENCE—A WORLD OF DIFFERENT APPROACHES

We discovered soon that within our network, we live in a world of different challenges and of different responses. But it was only when the network acquired new members—especially from the Philippines and from Brazil and after the outbreak of new violence in the Israel–Palestine conflict—that it became evident that the notion of human rights was a necessary second focal point of our network. This view is underlined in the report on the work of the International Fellowship of Reconciliation where an important point is made about the effects of particular contexts on how ideas (such as tolerance and human rights) are linked: "In a situation of conflict, the work on education for human rights and democracy may well be at odds with the work on education for tolerance and even more so with work for coexistence; while all are important, they are also all linked inextricably with the prevailing political situation, and if that disintegrates, the emphasis falls increasingly on the human rights/democracy education and away from tolerance" (Dunn et al., 2003a, pp. 287–288).

It became clear that, in many situations where there are serious economic and/or political inequalities, and where the cleavages are very deep, it may, initially, be impossible to develop tolerance. When people within a society suffer under conditions of inequality, then their first demands are not for tolerance, but for human rights and democracy. Tolerance may then follow. In many situations social and political change is necessary in order to establish the preconditions for tolerance.

Some of the case studies make clear that tolerance in itself has little impact or importance in attempts to remedy the difficulties and minimize dangers of lives. When people within a society live and suffer under conditions of inequality, their first demands are not for tolerance, but for human rights and democracy. The power of tolerance may then follow. This was stated in the IFOR paper on the Middle East. "In an imbalanced power situation, the weaker party has no choice other than to „tolerate" the stronger. The only way for them not to tolerate the stronger party is actively to rebel... to talk of teaching human rights is much more clear..." (Dunn et al., 2003a, p. 286).

Similarly, in the case of Brazil, it is stated: "[You have] to be a rebel, becoming outraged with human rights violations" (Dunn et al., 2003a, p. 287). It is therefore clear that in those countries or regions where there are unacceptable human inequalities, and where the cleavages are too deep, it may be impossible to build bridges and to promote a culture of tolerance. This conclusion is not intended as a rejection of tolerance, but it is a recognition of the need for social change in order to establish the preconditions for tolerance.

As a result of our examinations of, and reflections upon, the case studies describing a wide range of places and contexts, we have become aware of a number of often fundamental differences of the educational challenges and approaches that have to be considered. These include:

- In many contexts, there is a need to relate educational activities to two different target groups: the possible victims and the possible perpetrators. For example, in the Philippines the experience has included working with both the people and the police, even though they are sometimes placed in the opposing roles of the victims and the perpetrators.
- Supporting different imperatives (i.e., do not discriminate) and stand up for your rights.
- Fostering different competencies (i.e., the competence to control power and empowerment).
- Working within a framework made up of both civil society and the State.

- Different approaches and key concepts: tolerance, mutual understanding, justice, respect, reconciliation, and human rights.
- Diversity, which demands the promotion of tolerance education and of human rights education.

Even though there was no "official" and binding definition of human rights education within the network, there was consensus on the following understanding:

> Human rights education means the effort to develop in citizens an awareness of human rights: the knowledge of your own rights, the willingness to accept the equal rights of others and to support the defence of the rights of all people according to one's own possibilities. (Fritzsche 2004, pp. 162–167)

There is more than one approach to human rights education. With regard to the content we can distinguish between approaches that focus mainly on legal aspects and "on the documents" and those approaches that focus more on the dimension of principles and values. There are different concepts for different learning environments and for different target groups. Finally, the context of human rights education makes a big difference: How do we practice human rights educations in older democracies, in post-totalitarian or authoritarian countries, in developing countries, or in post-conflict societies? Even though we argue for the indivisibility of human rights, we find different priorities of human rights and human rights education in these societies (Tibbitts, 2002).

THE CHALLENGE OF INSECURITY AFTER SEPTEMBER 11

After September 11, 2001, the world is facing new kinds of risks and threats: global insecurity produced by international terrorism and by the "war on terrorism." Our tasks are becoming more difficult now: to cope with a climate of fear and hate where human rights and tolerance are being sacrificed for a feeling of security. The dilemma was phrased by the World Peace Center as follows: "It is a Herculean task to sensitise people at a time when life is becoming extremly difficult and fraught with dangers" (2000, p. 32). Faced by the present conflicts, two outsets in the fostering of tolerance should be avoided in equal measure: On the one hand, it's important to avoid "overstretched tolerance" (Tibi, 2002)—this would be tolerance of a type that ignores the fact that the intolerant often only complain of their own toleration so as to instrumentalize tolerance for extremely intolerant aims. On the other hand, it is also important to avoid any temptations of a generalized suspicion and of an "end of tolerance" in times of conflicts.

The terrorist attacks of September 11 had an immense impact on human rights and tolerance: on the one side, it was an attack on the culture of human rights, and on the other side the worldwide reactions to the terrorism led to remarkable pressures on human rights and tolerance.

The main challenge arising from terrorism is the reemergence of a feeling of insecurity among citizens. Under the pressure of deciding how to deal with the threat of the new terrorism, priorities have changed. Now security is seen as more important than liberties and human rights. Civil and human rights are being sacrificed in the name of reestablishing and reinforcing security. Amnesty International stated: "In the name of fighting ‚international terrorism,‘ governments have rushed to introduce draconian new measures that threaten the human rights of their own citizens, immigrants and refugees" (Fritzsche, 2003, p. 253).

In many democratic systems we can see the increased empowerment of the state supported by the majority of its citizens. However, we have to take into account that in the past human rights developed out of a similar feeling of insecurity and the need for protection. But today what was the "old threatening state" from which citizens needed protection is perceived as a power to be trusted. Indeed, it is often seen as the only power able to fight terrorism. For those citizens who feel panic even the strong state is acceptable. Thus, for example, an editor of a leading Canadian newspaper stated: "I have a much greater fear of my government's enemies than of my government itself. Desperate times call for desperate measures" (in Fritzsche, 2003, p. 254).

The threat of terrorism leads not only to a change in relations between citizens and the state but also to a change within the society. We have experienced an increase in prejudices, enemy negative images, intolerance, and even hate. Especially significant has been the link, which some politicians and commentators have constructed between migration and terrorism, that has further reduced support for tolerance. According to Human Rights Watch, an increased number of hate crimes has occurred since September 11.

> violent assaults, harassment and threats against Muslims, Sikhs and people of Middle Eastern and South Asian descent. These shameful acts against men, women and children targeted because of their religious beliefs, ethnicity or national origin violate basic principles of human rights and justice.... [People must learn] to reject national or religious stereotyping that would blame whole communities for the appalling deeds of a few—deeds, in fact, whose victims included members of some of the same religious, ethnic and national minorities now being injured by retaliation. (Fritzsche, 2003, p. 255)

Finally, the debate on the torture of (suspected) terrorists has shown how the threat of terrorism even leads to—or is instrumentalized in—a regression in moral and human rights standards. Human rights has lost a lot of its influence in setting standards for the treatment of minorities, immigrants, and human beings in general.

HUMAN RIGHTS AND TOLERANCE EDUCATION AFTER SEPTEMBER 11

After September 11, we are challenged to path the way for a sustainable human rights awareness; we are facing new kinds of risks and threats. We are confronted with a new "wave" of global insecurity produced by international terrorism and by the "war on terrorism." The tasks of human rights education (including tolerance education) are becoming more difficult now: The dilemma is to cope with a climate of fear and hate where human rights and tolerance are no more guidelines of life. Human rights education after September 11 means awareness building under conditions of extreme insecurity and fear. This feeling of insecurity causes a deep reluctance toward humans rights issues and even fosters processes of denying or „unlearning" of human rights and human rights–related standards among many citizens. Even citizens who had learned to support the principles of unalienable and equal rights before September 11 seemed to become willing to restrict human rights and to legitimize discrimination and to permit torture under the stress of extreme insecurity. What is needed is a new empowerment of the learners in order to enable them to cope better with the challenges of insecurity and to counter the feelings of powerlessness.

Therefore the human rights and tolerance educators have to rethink their approaches on how to overcome ignorance, incompetence, and intolerance in times of terrorism. Educators should address questions such as:

- Which kind of critical knowledge is needed to understand the root causes of terrorism, the options of political decisions, and the possibilities to defend human rights?
- How can skeptical learners be convinced that human rights are part of the solution of the fight against terrorism (no human security without human rights) rather than being an obstacle fighting terrorism?
- How can learners be convinced that a suspected terrorist has human rights and that the acceptance of torture leads to a breakdown of the values of our civilization?
- How can the willingness to accept the rights of other people be developed when he or she is suspected to be an enemy or a potential terrorist?
- How is personal empowerment possible so that powerless people (or people that feel powerless) do not take over the powerful temptations of enemy images and intolerance?

- Who can provide those resources and experiences, which enable the learner to accept equal rights of others even under the conditions of social inequality and insecurity.
- How can we educate for a sustainable acceptance of equal rights under conditions of fear, stress, and insecurity?

CONCLUSION

Is there any chance to answer the above questions in a positive way and to fulfill our tasks under conditions of deep insecurity and in times of violent conflicts? We knew really very little about the impact of education until now. There is a strong need for evaluation in this field. Even though there are some indications that education can also matter in situations of conflict and insecurity, the main function of education is a preventive function (Salomon, 2004).

Education also has to realize that its possibilities of influence are limited. Education cannot solve such basic social problems as insufficient resources or their unjust distribution. The threat of terrorism cannot be "educated away," however, it should be possible to influence the perception of terrorism and insecurity through information and education. It is possible to prepare people very early through education to cope with the feelings that terrorism can provoke in a rational way and to develop those competencies that the citizens themselves can participate in the debates on strategies against terrorism and the protection of human rights.

The ability to learn human rights and tolerance cannot be made the responsibility of the learners and the teachers alone. It must still be borne in mind that the process of education is embedded in the political and cultural context of a society. The way in which learning proecesses take place is always also influenced by and open to the influence of understandings and interpretations on offer in public communication. In many cases social stress is produced by opinion leaders, and fears of excessive insecurity thrive only in a climate of public reinforcement. The perceptions of threats depend on interpretations that are brought into the public and amplified by the mass media. Tolerance and human rights are not only a consequence of individual competencies, but also a result of social and political moulding of the political, social, and religious culture of a society.

REFERENCES

Dunn, S., Fritzsche, K. P., & Morgan, V. (Eds.). (2003). *Tolerance matters—International educational approaches.* Güterlsloh: Bertelsmann Foundation.

Dunn, S., Fritzsche, K. P., & , V. (2003). Overview of the case studies: Learning from each other. In S. Dunn, K. P. Fritzsche, & V. Morgan (Eds.), *Tolerance matters—International educational approaches* (pp. 268–289). Gûterlsloh: Bertelsmann Foundation.

Fritzsche, K. P. (2001). Unable to be tolerant? In R. Farnen, K. P. Fritzsche, K. Ivan, & R. Meyenberg (Eds.), *Tolerance in transition.* Oldenburg: Bis

Fritzsche, K. P. (2003). Bad times for tolerance and human tights: The aftermath of September 11. In S. Dunn, K. P. Fritzsche, & V. Morgan (Eds.), *Tolerance matters—International educational approaches* (pp. 252–267). Gûterlsloh: Bertelsmann Foundation.

Fritzsche, K. P. (2004). Human rights education—What is it all about. In V. Georgi & M. Seberich (Eds.), *International perspectives on human rights education.* Gûterlsloh: Bertelmann Foundation.

Salomon, G (2004, February). *Does peace education make a difference in the context of an intractable conflict?* Paper presented at the "Peace Education Around the World" conference, Feldafing, Germany. Available at http://www.peaceeducation.net/index.php?category=topics&subcategory=Peace+Education&id=6

Tibi, B. (2002). Die deutsche verordnete Fremdenliebe. In A. Schwarzer (Ed.), *Die Gotteskrieger und die falsche.* Toleranz, Köln.

Tibbitts, F. (2002). *Emerging models for human rights education.* Available at http:// usinfo. state.gov/journals/itdhr/0302/ijde/tibbitts.htm

World Peace Center. (Ed.). (2000). Human rights education, social change and human values. Pune: Balwant.

CHAPTER 19

THE PRIME SHARED HISTORY PROJECT

Peace-Building Under Fire[1]

Dan Bar-On
Sami Adwan

Peace building is a planned activity, based on bottom-up processes, while peacemaking is a political agreement based on top-down processes. We usually believe that a peace process can become sustainable only when the two are synchronized. For example, the Truth and Reconciliation Commission (TRC) in South Africa was a political agreement, compromising the interests of both sides, which took into account also the bottom-up needs of acknowledgment of past atrocities and taking personal responsibility for them, letting 22,000 victims of the Apartheid give testimonies. Along this analysis, the Oslo Accord gave a political opportunity (and hope) to synchronize the top-down and bottom-up processes in the Israeli and Palestinian conflict. Many bottom-up projects were initiated as a result of such a hope, alas these hopes were shattered by the outbreak of the bloody conflict in October 2000, after the failure of the Camp David talks.

Educating Toward a Culture of Peace, pages 309–323
Copyright © 2006 by Information Age Publishing
All rights of reproduction in any form reserved.

It is quite clear, that when there is no ongoing, top-down peacemaking initiative, the peace-building activities cannot bring about peace all by themselves (Maoz, 2000a). Therefore, they should become more modest in their goals: They have to focus on maintaining the ability of mutual positive interactions of the peace builders (the idea of "islands of sanity") and/or prepare the ground by initiating small projects that could become widespread once a future synchronization with top-down initiatives takes place. Again, to take the example of South Africa, the agreement of the TRC in the 1990s did not take place in a vacuum. Black and white cadres were prepared for more than 30 years, in isolated, mostly Christian refuges, which served as such "islands of sanity" under the most severe external conditions.

This perspective is based on a more mature conclusion that peace processes of intractable conflicts are not linear, have ups and downs, and need a long-term commitment of the peace builders rather than momentary, conjectural optimism or opportunism. We present here a project of a joint school textbook that we developed with Palestinian and Israeli teachers at PRIME during one of the most violent periods of the conflict in 2001, and that helped us maintain our "island of sanity" while developing a project that could become widespread in times of future peace agreements. At the present stage we did not try to advertise it or bring it to the attention of the ministries of education, because the public and the ministries were paralyzed and haunted by the conflict, not the peace process, and we estimated that such attempts would hamper the possibility of future dissemination, rather than accommodate them. Our project was based on a more realistic approach, that at the present stage of hostility and violence, the Israeli Jews and the Palestinians are not able to develop a joint narrative of their history (and we do not expect them to do so under the current conditions). Nevertheless, in the meantime they could learn to acknowledge and live with the fact that there are at least two competing narratives to account for their past, present, and future. We assumed that this is an essential intermediate phase, in the process of learning about the other, legitimizing the other's valid reasoning.

In periods of war and conflict, societies and nations tend to develop their own narratives, which from their perspective become the only true and morally superior narrative. These narratives devaluate and even dehumanize their enemy's right for a narrative. If the enemy's narrative is described at all, it is presented as being morally inferior and the enemy is depicted as a faceless immoral with irrational or manipulative views. These narratives become embedded into everyday culture, into the national and religious festivals, into the media and into children's school textbooks. Textbooks are the formal representations of the society's ideology and its ethos. They impart the values, goals, and myths that the society wants to instill into the new generation (Apple, 1979; Bourdieu, 1973; Luke, 1988).

Children growing up during times of war and conflict know only the narrative of their people. This narrative is supposed to convince them, overtly and covertly, of the need to dehumanize the enemy. It usually indoctrinates children to a rationale that justifies the use of power to subjugate the enemy. This not only causes the development of narrow and biased understandings among children, but also leads to the development of negative attitudes and values toward the other (Levinas, 1990).

This state of affairs is true also for the Palestinian/Israeli situation. First of all some facts: Since the early 1950s, Palestinians have been using Jordanian and Egyptian schoolbooks in their schools in West Bank and Gaza Strip, respectively. The use of these schoolbooks continued after Israel occupied the West Bank and Gaza Strip in the 1967 war but they went through censorship. Palestinians have started preparing their own schoolbooks right after the establishment of the PNA in 1994. In the 2000–01 school year, the first Palestinian-produced textbooks were introduced for grades 1 and 6. Each year the Palestinian curriculum, centered under the supervision of the Palestinian Ministry of , produced textbooks for two grades only. They gradually substituted the Jordanian and Egyptian ones. The Palestinian education system is described as a centralized one. This means the Ministry of Education is the sole producer of the school textbooks and all schools use the same textbooks. Israelis have a longer history of producing their textbooks. It goes back to before the State of Israel was established. The Israeli system of education is described to be a more decentralized system. This means that schools and teachers have some freedom to choose the textbooks they want to use from a list of textbooks that the Ministry of Education has approved. To a limited extent, teachers also may choose the text they want to use from the open market.

Research on textbooks shows how each side, Palestinian as well as Israeli, presents its own narratives. In an analysis of 1948 Palestinian refugees' problem (Adwan & Firer, 1997, 1999) in Palestinian and Israeli textbooks since 1995, both sides failed to talk about the complexity of the refugees' problems. The Israeli texts put most of the blame on the Palestinians and the Arabs for the refugees' plight, while the Palestinian texts mainly blamed the Israelis and the British. The texts even fail to agree on the facts (e.g., the numbers of 1948 Palestinian refugees). Israelis write that there were between 600–700,000 Palestinians who became refugees as a result of the 1948 war, while Palestinians wrote that there were more than 1 million Palestinians who became refugees as a result of the 1948 fighting.

Another comprehensive analysis of narratives of the conflict/relation in Palestinian and Israeli history and civic education (Firer & Adwan, 1999; Maoz, 2000a, 2000b) shows that the texts reflect a culture of enmity. The terminology used in the texts had different meanings. What was positive on one side was negative on the other side. For example, the 1948 War in the

Israeli texts is called the "War of Independence," while in the Palestinian text it is called "Al-Naqbah (the Catastrophe)." While Israeli texts refer to the first Jewish immigrants to Palestine as "the pioneers," the Palestinian texts refer to them as "gangs" and "terrorists." The heroes of one side are the monsters of the other. Also, most of the maps in the texts eliminate the cities and towns of the other side. The texts show the delegitimization of each other's rights, history, and culture. There is also no recognition of each other's sufferings. The Holocaust is barely mentioned in Palestinian texts,[2] and likewise the trauma of Palestinians is ignored in the Israeli texts. The findings show also that both sides' textbooks fail to include the peaceful periods of coexistence between Jews and Palestinians.

Daniel Bar-Tal (1995) analyzed the content of 124 Israeli schoolbooks from 1975–1995. According to Bar-Tal, in times of intractable conflict each side develops beliefs about the justness of its own goals, beliefs about security, beliefs about delegitimizing the opponents, beliefs of positive self-image, beliefs about patriotism, beliefs about unity, and beliefs about peace. These beliefs constitute a kind of ethos that supports the continuation of the conflict. The study showed that beliefs about security were emphasized in the Israeli textbooks. There was rarely delegitimization of Arabs but most of the text stereotype Arabs negatively.

Based on these studies, we concluded that the Israeli–Palestinian conflict is not yet ready, perhaps will never be ready, for one joint narrative; neither are we ready to erase all expressions of hostility toward each other in our textbooks at the current stage of the conflict. We therefore decided to develop an innovative school booklet that contains two narratives, the Israeli narrative and the Palestinian narrative, around certain dates or milestones in the history of the conflict. This would mean that each student will learn also the narrative of the other, in addition to the familiar own narrative, as a first step toward acknowledging and respecting the other. We assumed that a joint narrative would emerge only after the clear change from war culture to peace culture took place. This requires time and the ability to mourn and work through the painful results of the past. We could not expect this to take place while the conflict was still going on. In addition, we had to consider the roles of teachers. Studies have shown that teachers have more power than the mere written texts in forming children's understandings and value systems (Angvik & von Borries, 1997; Nave & Yogev, 2002). As a result, this project focuses on the central role of the teachers in the process of using shared history texts in the classroom. The teachers should therefore develop these narratives and try them out with their 9th- and 10th-grade classrooms, after the booklet has been translated into Arabic and Hebrew. There will be an empty space between the narratives for the pupils and teachers to add their own responses.

THE PARTICIPANTS

The co-founders of Peace Research in the Middle East (PRIME), Sami Adwan and Dan Bar-On, and two history professors, Adnan Massallam (Bethlehem University) and Eyal Nave (Tel Aviv University and the Kibbutzim Teachers Seminar in Tel Aviv), chose the team to work on this project. The team includes six Palestinian history and geography teachers, six Jewish-Israeli history teachers, and six international delegates, as well as one Jewish-Israeli observer. The Palestinian teachers, who are from Hebron, Bethlehem, and East Jerusalem, had never before participated in dialogue encounters with Israelis. Several of the Israeli teachers, who teach in high schools in the center and north of Israel, had participated in previous encounters with Palestinians.

THE PROCESS

All the participants convened four times for three days of workshops at the New Imperial Hotel in the Old City (Eastern, Palestinian part) of Jerusalem in March, June, and August 2002 and in January 2003. As the political and the military situations were very fragile, it was unclear until the last minute whether the Palestinian teachers would get permits to enter Jerusalem, or if they would be able to reach the places where the permits were issued. The workshops were called off several times, but each time we found ways and the energy to call them on again and finally we succeeded to make them happen, mostly with full participation.

As the project operated within the reality of the conflict, it is critical to note the contexts from which the participants came. First, while the situation on both sides was bleak, difference and asymmetry existed with respect to the intensity of the general realities on the ground. For Palestinians, the reality has an unrelenting effect on day-to-day life with experiences of occupation and living under the thumb of the Israeli army (Maoz, 2000a). This translates into restricted freedom of movement, curfews, border checkpoints, and a lot of fear of shootings, killings, and house demolitions. Most have suffered serious losses and have had their own homes or those of relatives damaged. Meanwhile, for Israelis, because of Palestinian suicide attacks, the everyday reality reflects itself mostly in fear. This involves fear of riding buses and of going downtown or anywhere with crowds. Many on both sides even fear sending their kids to school. Rather unsurprisingly, given the situation, faith and hope are commodities that have been difficult for both sides to hold on to—hence our sheer amazement at the fact that the seminars had such high participation and commitment. One of the Israeli teachers mentioned during the fourth seminar: "This work over the last year was my only source of hope in the current desperate situation." A Palestinian teacher commented, "We should look into other ways of resolving our conflict and this project is an example for such a way."

In the first (March 2002) workshop, teachers got acquainted with each other by sharing personal details ("the story behind my name") as well as other biographical stories. That was not an easy process to listen to stories that contained painful moments, which were related to the other's violence or oppression. But it was an important process because it enabled the teachers later to work together on their joint tasks more openly.

During this first workshop we formed three mixed task groups. Each task group created a list of all the events that were relevant to the Palestinian–Israeli conflict and chose one event they would like to work on. In the plenary we followed this process and agreed on the three events: one group worked on the Balfour Declaration of 1917, another on the 1948 war, and the third on the First Palestinian Intifada of 1987. A program was set up for how the groups could communicate and develop their relevant narratives to be reviewed at the second workshop. Professors Naveh and Mussalam provided their professional view of how such narratives should be developed and what should they be composed of. It was the role of the international participants to do some of the translations, when necessary, to summarize the task groups' work and to write an evaluation at the end of each seminar. An additional flavor to our seminars were our evening strolls in the Old City of Jerusalem, which members of both groups did not do lately because of the severe security conditions. In a way we felt like we were in a self-created bubble, disconnected from the hostile surroundings in which we usually lived.

In the second (June 2002) workshop, teachers actually developed their narratives, partially by working in the original task groups and partially by working in uninational groups. We also devoted time to continue our personal acquaintance and joint walks as this became an important ingredient of this kind of work, especially in the current hostile atmosphere outside the group. Between the second and the third workshops the respective narratives were translated into Hebrew and Arabic, as the workshop's language was English.

During the third (August 2002) seminar the teachers had their first opportunity to read both narratives in their own native language, the way they will have to present these narratives to their pupils in the following year. This time, most of the work was done in the plenary and it was interesting to follow jointly how the teachers accepted these narratives. Most of the questions posed during these sessions were informative. Was the translation precise? Who was the person you mentioned in 1908? Why did you try to describe this event so briefly, while the others are described at length? Interestingly, there were almost no attempts of delegitimization of the other's narrative. According to our interpretation, the fact that each side could feel safe with their own narrative made it easier to accept the other's narrative, being so different from one's own. At this workshop we learned about the sudden death of one of Palestinian teacher from Hebron of cancer, while we were convening. There was some deliberation if we should stop the workshop, but the Palestinian teachers felt that he would have liked them to continue and they decided to stay and continue our work. The whole group later decided that his picture and a dedication would be in the opening page of the forthcoming joint booklet. The groups departed with the task to introduce corrections in their narratives as a result of the discussion and to develop a glossary for the teachers and the pupils, concerning definitions that the other side may not be familiar with.

In November 2002 the booklet was to come out in Hebrew, Arabic, and English. The teachers were then supposed to try it out in their classrooms, which meant that in this experimental phase already hundreds of Israeli and Palestinian pupils would be exposed to this new booklet (see a sample in Appendix A). The following teachers' workshops would then be dedicated to get the pupils' responses, make corrections, support the teachers in their work, and develop more such narratives around additional dates. However, the continued and renewed curfews of the Palestinian towns and the additional necessary proofreadings did not enable us to follow this timetable. Therefore, when we convened for our fourth workshop in January 2003, the booklet was not yet ready, but the texts were on paper and most of the teachers have at least tried them out in one classroom. We devoted the first day to listen to their evaluations of the initial testing and then devoted the second day to decide about three additional dates around which more narratives will be developed.

The teachers' reports of their classrooms were very interesting and diverse. For example, one Israeli teacher taught these texts in a classroom comprised predominantly by children of foreign workers, children of new immigrants (partially not Jewish), and Arab children. She had first to make them acquainted with the Israeli narratives (that many of them never learned about before) and only then introduce the Palestinian narrative. She was very creative in visualizing for her pupils what these texts actually represented. Her students could quite easily accept the two narratives as legitimate as they lacked the emotional involvement and identification with "their" narrative. Another Israeli teacher reported that his students were suspicious ("Are these texts really translated into Arabic and taught there?"). Some students showed great interest and asked to take them home to study them further.

One of the Palestinian teachers had to ask the permission of his principal (who actually came to our workshop and showed great interest in our work). He gave his students the texts and invited them to his house to discuss them (as the school was closed because of the curfew). Another Palestinian teacher brought written reactions of her pupils. Some of them expressed an interest to meet Israeli pupils to discuss these texts together. Others wanted to know more about this date or that person, mentioned briefly in the texts. There were reports of students who right away started to deconstruct the other's narrative. In general there was a surprise effect by presenting the two narratives, a surprise that created interest and curiosity. We could feel a general feeling of ownership and accomplishment of the teachers from both sides, in spite of the deteriorating external situation. They felt that they are creating something new for the future, which no one tried to do before.

During the second day the plenary discussed the general concept of the final book. Will we continue to focus on the historical aspects, or will we turn now to specific topics (like women, religions), or even to our contemporary situation? The plenary decided in favor of the historical continuity of the book and chose three additional dates: the 1920s, 1936–1948, and the Six Days 1967 war. These additional dates will fill in the gaps among the initial dates (1917; 1948, the first Palestinian Intifada) and create a continuity of dates. The teachers divided the dates between them and committed themselves to prepare a draft for the following workshop. We decided to convene again in March 2003 to review these new narratives, in addition to further explore the testing of the initial narratives in more classrooms.

In the third year we plan to run a formal evaluation by comparing the binarrative classes with single narrative classes. In June 2004 we would like to have a conference at PRIME, where we will summarize the first experimental phase. We hope by then to have a more positive political climate into which this work will fit in better. In the second phase we will recruit more teachers and use the first group of teachers as assistants to accommodate the new ones.

SUMMARY

The violence that took place around us often also affected our interactions. Yet we continued to do the work, and we were rewarded with glimmers of hope and enthusiasm about the implementation of this project in the schools. We assume that the success of this project (in comparison to earlier projects with Israeli and Palestinian teachers, which were less successful) was related to three important aspects:

1. The timing of the project introduced as an aspect of urgency to create a positive counterweight to the violence we experienced outside our workshops.

2. Our leadership was a role model for the possibility of a serious performance of academic, professional, financial, and managerial symmetry, which we have never experienced before in similar projects.

3. The creation of real texts, as something concrete that can be given to students and can be related to in both contexts, was very important for teachers who have difficulty with abstract forms of discussions and evaluations.

We acknowledged to each other that peace could only be a result of both sides winning; a "peace" in which only one side wins has no value. Sami said: "The disarmament of history can happen only after the disarmament of weapons. But one can prepare it now." Events of the last months have highlighted the fact that we are not yet getting close to a formal peace agreement. Still, even if that will be achieved in the future, without a bottom-up, peace-building process involving face-to-face encounters between Jewish-Israeli and Palestinian peoples, a sustainable peace will not be achieved. Furthermore, the booklet these teachers are creating and their implementation of it will provide a concrete way to spread the effects outward of this face-to-face encounter between a small group of teachers. As Margaret Mead once said, "Never doubt that a small group of thoughtful committed citizens can change the world." In this case, "Never doubt that a small group of committed teachers—Palestinian and Israeli—can change the world, or at least one part of it, when the time will be ripe."

NOTES

1. We are thankful to Dr. Dieter Hartmann and the Wye River People-to-People Exchange Program of the U.S. State Department for their 3-year grants and to the Ford Foundation for their 2-year grant that helped us implement this research project. We also wish to thank Dr. Shoshana Steinberg for her help in developing an earlier report and to Linda Livni and Bob Loeb for their administrative help.

2. While this chapter was being written, a group of Israeli Palestinians, headed by Emil Shufani, a Greek Orthodox priest from Nazareth, decided for the first time to travel to Poland and visit Auschwitz as part of their need to learn about Jewish suffering there and its impact on contemporary Jewish-Israeli society.

REFERENCES

Adwan, S., & Firer, R. (1997). *The narrative of Palestinian refugees during the War of 1948 in Israeli and Palestinian history and civic education textbooks.* Paris: UNESCO.

Adwan, S., & Firer, R. (1999). *The narrative of the 1967 war in the Israeli and Palestinian history and civics textbooks and curricula statement.* Braunschweig, Germany: Eckert Institute.

Al-Ashmawi, F. (1996). The image of the other as presented in history booklet. *International Textbooks Research, 18*(2), 221–229.

Angvik, M., & von Borries, B. (Eds) (1997). *Youth and history: A comparative European survey on historical consciousness and political attitudes among adolescents.* Hamburg, Germany: Koerber Foundation.

Apple, M. W. (1979). *Ideology and curriculum.* London: Routledge & Kegan Paul.

Bar-Tal, D. (1995). *The rocky road toward peace: Societal beliefs in times of intractable conflict, the Israeli case.* Jerusalem: Hebrew University, School of Education.

Bourdieu, P. (1973). Cultural reproduction and social reproduction. In R. Brown (Ed.), *Knowledge, education and cultural change* (pp. 71–112). London: Tavistock.

Luke, A. (1988). *Literacy, booklet, and ideology.* London: Falmer Press.

Maoz, I. (2000a). Multiple conflicts and competing agendas: A framework for conceptualizing structured encounters between groups in conflict: The case of a coexistence project between Jews and Palestinians in Israel. *Journal of Peace Psychology, 6,* 135–156.

Maoz, I. (2000b). Power relations in inter-group encounters: A case study of Jewish–Arab encounters in Israel. *International Journal of Intercultural Relations, 24,* 259–277.

Nave, E., & Yogev, E. (2002). *Histories: Towards a dialogue with yesterday.* In D. Danon (Ed.), Tel-Aviv: Bavel.

APPENDIX A: A SAMPLE OF THE TWO NARRATIVES OF THE BALFOUR DECLARATION

(In the original there are empty lines between the two narratives
for the students to write in their own reactions.)

THE ISRAELI NARRATIVE

From the Balfour Declaration to the first White Paper

Introduction

The birth of the Zionist movement.   Zionism, the Jewish national movement, was born in the 19th century when the ideology embodied in the Enlightenment was disseminated in the European Jewish community. These new ideas planted the first seeds of Jewish nationalism; the subsequent birth of Zionism was the result of several factors:

1. The rise of modern anti-Semitism—a deeply-rooted and complicated mixture of traditional religious hatred augmented by "scientific" racism, which categorized Jews as a depraved and pernicious race.
2. The disappointment of western European Jews with the emancipation, which pledged that the position of Jews in society would equal that of the Christians. The Jews were discouraged when it became clear that in many instances there was equality in name only. Discrimination continued.
3. New European nationalist movements such as those appearing in Italy and Germany inspired similar aspirations among the Jews.
4. An important element was the longing for Zion, an integral aspect of Jewish religious and national identity throughout history. This longing stemmed from the biblical promise that the Land of Israel was given to the people of Israel by the God of Israel, and on memories of those historical eras when the people of Israel lived independently in their land. This concept inspired the national anthem, written at that time:

> *Hatikvah: The Hope*
>
> As long as in our heart of hearts
> the Jewish spirit remains strong,
> And we faithfully look toward the east,
> Our eyes will turn to Zion.
> We have not yet lost our hope,
> The hope of two thousand years,
> To be a free people in our land—
> The land of Zion and Jerusalem.

The Zionist movement was born in the major centers of Jewish population in Europe, and its purpose was to return the Jewish people to its land and put an end to its abnormal situation among the nations of the world. At first there was a spontaneous emergence of local associations ("Lovers of Zion") out of which an organized political movement was established, thanks to the activities of "The Father of Zionism," Theodore Herzl [whose Hebrew name is Benjamin Ze'ev Herzl].

In 1882 there was a small wave of immigration [aliya/Aliyot] to "the land" [i.e., the Land of Israel], the first of several. The purpose of these aliyot was not just to fulfill the religious obligations connected to the land, as had been the case in the past, but rather to create a "new" kind of Jew, a productive laborer who Zionism is to create a refuge for the Jewish people in the land of Israel, guaranteed by an open and official legal arrangement.

There were two basic approaches to Zionism:

1. Practical Zionism focused on increasing immigration, purchasing land, and settling Jews on the land. By 1914, in the first two waves of immigration, nearly 100,000 people immigrated (although most of them later left the country). Dozens of agricultural settlements were established and there was a significant increase in the urban Jewish population.

2. Political Zionism focused on diplomatic efforts to get support for Zionism from the great empires in order to obtain a legal and official charter for widescale settlement in the land.

Chaim Weizmann, who became Zionism's leader after Herzl's death, integrated both aspects of the movement.

In the original there is a picture of The moshav Nahalal, a semi-cooperative agricultural settlement, established in 1921 in the Jezreel Valley.

The Balfour Declaration

The first time any country expressed support for Zionism was in a letter sent by Lord Balfour, they would work on his own land and help establish a Jewish political entity in the Land of Israel.

Minister of Foreign Affairs, to Lord Rothschild, a leader of the Jewish community in Great Britain. It came to be known as the Balfour Declaration. The letter was dated November 2, 1917, shortly before the end of World War I. It expressed the support of the British Government for establishing a national home for the Jewish people in the land of Israel:

Foreign Office

November 2nd, 1917

Dear Lord Rothschild,

I have much pleasure in conveying to you, on behalf of His Majesty's Government, the following declaration of sympathy with Jewish Zionist aspirations which has been submitted to, and approved by, the Cabinet.

"His Majesty's Government view with favor the establishment in Palestine of a national home for the Jewish people, and will use their best endeavors to facilitate the achievement of this object, it being clearly understood that nothing shall be done which may prejudice the civil and religious rights of existing non-Jewish communities in Palestine, or the rights and political status enjoyed by Jews in any other country."

I should be grateful if you would bring this declaration to the knowledge of the Zionist Federation.

Yours sincerely,

Arthur James Balfour

THE PALESTINIAN NARRATIVE

The Balfour Declaration

Historical Background

In April 1799 Napoleon Bonaparte put forth a plan for a Jewish state in Palestine. During the siege of Acre, he sought to enlist Jewish support in return for which he promised to build the Temple. The project failed after the defeat of Napoleon in the battles of Acre and Abu-Qir. It represents the first post-Renaissance expression of cooperation between a colonialist power and the Jewish people.

However, it was the events of 1831–40 that paved the way for the establishment of a Jewish state in Palestine. Lord Palmerston, the British Foreign Secretary in 1840-41, proposed establishing a British protectorate in the Ottoman Empire to be settled by as a buffer area—an obstacle to Mohammed Ali of Egypt and to political unity in the Arab regions.

Britain launched a new policy supporting Jewish settlement in Palestine after Eastern European Jews, particularly those in Czarist Russia, whose living conditions were poor in any case, suffered cruel persecution. Consequently, with the rise of nationalism, Zionism appeared as a drastic international solution to the Jewish problem, transforming the Jewish religion into a nationalist attachment to a special Jewish homeland and a special Jewish state. Other factors influencing the birth and development of the Zionist movement were the increasingly competitive interests shared by European colonialists in Africa and Asia, and the Zionist colonialist movement for control of Palestine.

British imperialism found in Zionism a perfect tool for attaining its own interests in the Arab East, which was strategically and economically important for the Empire. Likewise, Zionism used British colonialist aspirations to gain international backing and economic resources for its project of establishing a Jewish national home in Palestine.

This alliance of British imperialism and Zionism resulted in the birth of what is known in history books as the Balfour Declaration (November 2, 1917). It is a conspicuous example of the British policy of seizing another nation's land and resources and effacing its identity. It is a policy based on aggression, expansion and repression of a native people's aspirations for national liberation.

For the Palestinians, the year 1917 was the first of many—1920, 1921, 1929, 1936, 1948, 1967, 1987, 2002—marked by tragedy, war, disaster, killing, destruction, homelessness, and catastrophe.

Dividing the Arab East

Imperialist Britain called for forming a higher committee of seven European countries. The report submitted in 1907 to British Prime Minister Sir Henry Campbell-Bannerman emphasized that the Arab countries and the Muslim-Arab people living in the Ottoman Empire presented a very real threat to European countries, and it recommended the following actions:

1. To promote disintegration, division, and separation in the region.
2. To establish artificial political entities that would be under the authority of the imperialist countries.
3. To fight any kind of unity—whether intellectual, religious or historical—and taking practical measures to divide the region's inhabitants.
4. To achieve this, it was proposed that a "buffer state" be established in Palestine, populated by a strong, foreign presence that would be hostile to its neighbors and friendly to European countries and their interests.

Doubtless the recommendations of Campbell-Bannerman's higher committee paved the way for the Jews to Palestine. It gave British approval to the Zionist movement's policy of separating Palestine from the Arab lands in order to establish an imperialist core that would ensure foreign influence in the region.

Jewish imperialist projects in Palestine followed in quick succession. World War I, 1914–1918, was a critically important period for Zionist and British imperialist policies for Palestine. Included in an exchange of letters between Sharif Hussein of Mecca and Sir Henry McMahon was the Damascus Protocol (July 14, 1915). Sharif Hussein indicated to McMahon the boundaries of the Arab countries in Asia to which Britain would grant independence—the Arabian Peninsula, Iraq/Mesopotamia, Syria and southern parts of present-day Turkey. He excluded Aden because it was a British military base. McMahon's response in a Hussein–McMahon Agreement.

In May 1916 Britain and France signed a secret document—the Sykes–Picot Agreement—to divide the Arab East at a time when Britain was exchanging letters with Sharif Hussein about recognizing the independence of the region. In the agreement Britain and France pledged to divide the Ottoman Empire as follows:

(A map in the original)

1. The Lebanese and Syrian coasts were given to France.
2. South and middle Iraq were given to Britain.
3. An international administration in Palestine excluding the two ports of Haifa and Acre.
4. A French zone of influence, including eastern Syria and the Mosul province.
5. Transjordan and the northern part of Baghdad province.

CHAPTER 20

EDUCATING TOWARD A CULTURE OF PEACE

Good Governance—Peace or War

Rajayswur Bhowon

I do not want my house to be walled in on all sides and my windows to be stuffed.
I want the culture of all lands to be blown about my house as freely as possible.
But I refuse to be blown off my feet by any of them.

—Mahatma Gandhi (1959)

INTRODUCTION

The Island of Mauritius is a diminutive volcanic island in the Indian Ocean at the crossroads of Africa and Asia. This location is geopolitically significant as it has been the point of convergence of many seafaring nations, in particular the Portuguese, Dutch, French, and British. Its vulnerability to both the deleterious effects of global climatic changes and man-made political, cultural, and economic globalization forces is overwhelmingly evident. Mauritius remains, however, a unique example in its tradition of a peaceful multicultural society with a strong coexistence tradition. It is said that it is the kindness of Buddha, the nonviolence of Gandhi, and the mutual toler-

Educating Toward a Culture of Peace, pages 325–343
Copyright © 2006 by Information Age Publishing
All rights of reproduction in any form reserved.

ance among the ethnic groups that capture the essence of Mauritian tradition and facilitate its peaceful nature.

Culture is viewed in a dynamic and democratic framework. The love and affection that we show to the children are reflected in the curriculum. We are preserving and promoting our rich languages and the traditional folk-performing arts, which in no way should be disturbed by globalization. We have a pool of intellectual wealth that is honest to convert Mauritius into a cyber island and duty-free paradise. This chapter examines this important achievement by way of discussion of the effects of good governance, culture, and the reliance for inspiration on Gandhi's political philosophy in respect to peace and war within a small island state.

THE MAKING OF THE RAINBOW NATION

Mauritius, often referred to as the "Star and Key of the Indian Ocean," had no autochthonous population. Some four centuries ago, it was successively inhabited by waves of seafaring nations like the Portuguese, Dutch, French, and British, who brought with them African slaves and Indian and Chinese indentured laborers to work in the sugar cane plantations. The Dutch colonized Mauritius for almost a century and gave the island its present name after Maurice Van Nassau, the "opperhoof" of Holland, and introduced sugar cane, which became the backbone of the economy of Mauritius for three centuries. Cyclonic conditions and the infestation of the island by rats discouraged the Dutch who finally abandoned Mauritius for South Africa. The French succeeded the Dutch and continued the development of the sugar industry especially under the French Governor, Mahé de Labourdonnais, until 1810 when Mauritius was conquered by the British. The Dutch, French, and British successively brought African and Malagasy slaves to work in the sugar cane plantation until 1833 when slavery was abolished by Westminster. The British then turned to British India, which provided plenty of cheap indentured laborers to Mauritius. The laborers were brought on a contract for 5 years and Mauritius was the first British colony to receive this new form of labor (Arno et Orian, 1986; Blood, 1975; Chinapah, 1979; Toussaint, 1974).

Mauritius belongs to four diasporas. The Mauritians have their roots in India, Africa, China, and Europe. Mauritians are proud of its "Mauritianness" in which they are born with their diverse traditions and cultures. Yet they are still emotionally tied to their ancestral lands, namely India, Africa, Europe, and China. Mauritius has different parts of its heritage in which to anchor its pride. It is proud of its roots and the religious organizations working hand in hand with Government to ensure that the ancestral values are maintained and nurtured. The deep attachment of the people of Mauritius to their respective ancestral lands is reflected in the bridges that have been built and constantly strengthened through an exchange of music, arts, and culture. Music transcends all cultural barriers and serves as a strong bond between Mauritius and the ancestral lands.

In 1968, Mauritius became an independent sovereign state within the British Commonwealth. But the customs and practices established by the Colonial powers stayed for a protracted period. Mauritius continues its ties with Europe, principally with Britain and France and in Asia, with India and China. The African, Indian, Chinese, and European descents of 1 million people are all bound by a common code of conduct working toward a complementarity of cultures of African, Asian, and European traditions (Durand, 1975, 1978). English is the official language of Mauritius. English, French, and ancestral languages like Mandarin, Hindi, Urdu. Tamil, Telegu, and Marathi are taught in all primary and secondary schools. Creole, which is pidgin French, and Bhojpuri derived from Hindi are commonly spoken languages island-wide (Benedict, 1961, 1965; Carpooran, 2003; Prithipaul, 1976).

In Mauritius, February 1 is celebrated as African Slavery Day and November 2 as Indian Coolie Day. These two celebrations represent the past and the present: how the African slaves and Indian Coolie communities were landless and defenseless; how they were denied political and civil rights and even police protection. From nothing, Mauritians built an edifice of peace and tranquility. Today, Mother India has a responsibility and legitimate right to intervene wherever the interests of the Indian descents are under attack. Africa does likewise. Mauritian ancestors came as slaves and indentured laborers from different environments and in different boats. But today they are in the same boat. They have nurtured the ancestral values and tradition and in the process have learned to show respect and tolerance to the cultures of others and to find something good in them (Bhowon, 2003).

The influences from ancestral lands, namely India, China, Africa, and Europe, have been continuous for over four centuries. Although Mauritius has been blessed with the wisdom of at least four major cultures, it should never be taken for granted that Mauritians understand all of them. Even when it comes to one's own culture, there is always a lack of knowledge. The four main national cultures as represented in Mauritius point the way to respect the other one. These cultures coexist in dialogue and active learning in the same person. We have been inspired by the principles of tolerance, mutual respect, and appreciation that these cultures teach us. We have today evolved as a nation with deep faith and respect for one another through cultural unity, solidarity, and integration (Parsuramen, 1988).

ORGANIC TRADITIONS AND GOVERNMENT'S INITIATIVES
IN MAINTAINING COEXISTENCE

Government cannot create a peaceful society from scratch (Galtung, 2003). It can only supplement already existing organic traditions, habits, and tendencies, induced perhaps by the nature of local religions, experiences, and circumstances. Mauritius was blessed with such preexisting inclinations. Children from very diverse backgrounds have grown up together quite naturally in shared educational, religious, and cultural institutions. The cemetery is the place of burial for all, irrespective of color and complexion. The Catholic Church, the Hindu temple, the mosque, and the synagogue all stand side by side in many places. The Divali festival, which is the festival of lights of the Hindus, is universally celebrated. Similarly, Christmas is celebrated by all religious groups. The presence of the Virgin Mary in the Hindu house and the Hindu Trinity in the Catholic house reflects the high level of religious tolerance in Mauritius (Ramdoyal, 1994).

However, government has a role too, and can introduce policies and initiatives to promote supportive conditions for these organic traits. Since Mauritius gained independence in March 1968, each successive Government has given its support to maintain and to sustain harmonious relationships among the different cultural and ethnic groups living together on the island. Mauritius is a welfare state whereby those lying below poverty line are given special attention with respect to social aid, education, health, and housing.

Forces that have shaped the current emerging patterns of peaceful coexistence among the various groups through good governance are equal access and opportunity to education, reduction of poverty, economic growth, protecting its environment and biodiversity, and spiritual development by drawing inspiration from the great mother cultures. But above all is the right to speak the ancestral languages or any other language as a mother tongue. The acceptance of a set of ancestral values and philosophy and cooperation between different cultures altogether, and the indigenous cultural and architectural heritage, make Mauritius unique as a nation (Bhowon, 2003; Martial, 2002; Ministry of Education, Arts and Culture, 1984).

Some of the Government's top-down initiatives will be explored in the following paragraphs.

Popular Participation

"Popular participation must become a central, integral feature of people's activities at all levels of society. Problems tend to build up where people are least free to publicize them or to protest about them. Hence the features of democracy (freedom of association and assembly, free speech and a free press, free election with universal adult suffrage) are all essential to successful adaptation by all concerned" (Caring for the Future, 1966).

The Mauritian Parliament reflects the multiracial complexity of the country. It is a democratic principle that the people of Mauritius have to be well represented in governmental institutions. There has never been any cultural or ethnic clash of significance both inside and outside Parliament. The debates in Parliament cover issues like globalization, peace, security, poverty alleviation, social cohesion, and the promotion and protection of cultural heritage. Parliamentarians make the difficult choices for higher-level decisions to ensure the principles of good political governance, respect of human rights, the rule of law, and that democratic values are maintained and nurtured. Mauritius is a beacon of democracy in Africa. It is widely recognized across the nation and internationally that its vibrant economy has been due to strong policies and the involvement of the public and private partnership in the efficient implementation of its programs. The colonial powers laid the foundation of the sugar cane industry whereas the post-colonial era ushered in tourism, textiles, financial services, and information and communication technology. Mauritius is today fast becoming a cyber island and a duty-free island.

General elections are held every 5 years based on the Westminster model. The following measures further demonstrate the democratization process in Mauritius These are free and compulsory education for all up to the age of 16; free health care; decentralization and "municipalization" to enable local participation; sustained governmental participation with sociocultural groups to preserve and promote the cultural heritage; local public–private partnership and broader cooperation within the region and beyond; and positive discrimination toward the poor through the Trust Fund for the Vulnerable groups and a variety of supports and incentives to encourage entrepreneurship and the development of small and medium enterprises. Creation of opportunities for more people to become shareholders of land under sugar cane cultivation and in industrial enterprises and to become members of cooperative's societies (Bhowon, 1995).

War on Corruption

Several laws are passed that inhibit the growth of terrorism and corruption, foster the growth of civil society, and promote a more equitable distribution of resources and access to education and health. Mauritius recognizes that corruption destabilizes public institutions, impedes democratic processes, undermines economic growth, and discourages potential investors. However, good governance does not depend on governments alone, but also on the strength and independence of civil society and in its ability to monitor compliance with government-led reforms, to act as "watch-dogs" and to have its "voice" heard.

The interaction between globalization and good governance is emerging as a critical issue and the Mauritius Ministry of Industry, Financial Services and Corporate Affairs has set up a corporate sector that acts as a deterrent against money laundering. The Independent Commission Against Corruption (ICAC) set up by this Government follows closely all activities related to bribery and corruption and wherever detected appropriate action is taken. The need to create a good image in the eyes of foreign investors is a *sine qua non* for investment (ICAC, 2002).

The Best Loser System—Governance by Constitution

The core of good governance requires clearly understood rules, which are transparent, enforceable, and nondiscriminatory. It is widely recognized in Mauritius that good governance, political stability, and economic performance are closely intertwined. Mauritius continues to apply democratic principles enshrined in its Constitution. A unique feature is the Best-Loser System, that is, eight reserved seats are allocated to those who stand as candidates at the General Elections but who though not elected by first past-the-post should belong to the minority communities (The Constitution of Mauritius, 1968).

The Media—A Vibrant Vehicle of Communication

Mauritius has demonstrated a broad-based political engagement that advocates a culture of independent and impartial broadcasting of services of information, education, and entertainment in Creole, Bhojpuri, French, English, Hindustani, Tamil, Telegu, Marathi, Urdu, and Mandarin. The entertainment media with films and music in a dozen languages and regular film festivals held in Mauritius in collaboration with countries like India, China, France, and Britain fortify the Mauritian media links and exchanges with these countries. Music and films transcend all barriers. The traditional folk-performing arts that the eyes find beautiful, and the rich ancestral languages are well preserved and promoted and should in no way be disturbed by globalization. For Mauritius, interculturalism is a must against war and violence. The crucial issues in a globalized world, such as new dimensions related to mobility of the labor force, growing intercultural interaction, regional cooperation and interdependence of societies, are all on the agenda of the Mauritian Government. The Mauritius Broadcasting Corporation Television (MBCTV) provides news in five different languages on television and in 10 languages on radio (MBC Act, 1982).

Investing in Human Capital—Priority of Priorities

The main resource of Mauritius is its 1 million people. It is investing heavily in education and health to ensure that it has sufficient human capital to respond effectively to the ever-shrinking global village. Major policies are deliberately formulated and implemented to ensure political stability, security and image building, credibility, and freedom from fear. Agriculture has been a tool of social mobility and poverty reduction. Mauritius has created a class of small sugar farmers who are mainly descents from Indian indentured laborers and who have cultivated their fields to clothe their children and to send them to school (Ward, 1941). Their children are today professionals and occupy important posts in different sectors of our economy. By far the owners of the largest sugar plantations including the sugar factories are still the property of the Franco-Mauritians. In recent years, foreign land-owners have sold a part of their land to Government who in turn have sold it to local buyers who have become entrepreneurs. However, beaches and coastal resources have been sold or rented to local and foreign investors to enhance the hospitality industry. With the establishment of cybercities in Mauritius, Government has embarked on a program of training to create "an intelligent island" and a knowledge hub. A duty-free island expected to receive about 3 million tourists a year will require more services and hence the service sector is fast becoming one of the major pillars of the economy (Bhowon & Chinapah, 1992; Bunwaree, 1994; Central Statistical Office, Mauritius, 2004; CERSOI, 1984).

Besides, Mauritius is integrating in the global village. This is a natural process that makes sense for this small but overpopulated nation. Democracy, universal suffrage, and free markets are working hand in hand. The role of Government is changing from player to facilitator. It has created the right environment and incentives conducive to foreign direct investment. Mauritius recognizes the interdependent and interlocking economic structures with overseas economies and the need for global development with local and diverse vision. As it has been argued by the Nobel Prize Laureate Amartya Sen (2001), "The predicament of the poor cannot be reversed by withholding from them the great advantages of contemporary technology, the well-established efficiency of international trade and exchange, and the social as well as economic merits of living in open, rather than closed societies."

Promotion of Cultural Heritage

The current Government has taken several decisions to promote and preserve the cultural heritage of all the ethnic groups through the creation of trust funds. Thus the Marathi, Tamil, Telegu, Hindi and Chinese Speaking Union and Islamic Cultural and Mauritian Cultural Centre Trust Acts (*2001*) have been set up. Mauritius is a part of the diaspora comprising some 20 million Indians settled in over 110 countries around the world. Cultural and religious taboos are gradually changing. UNESCO has been approached to declare the Apravasi Ghat, which was the first landing place for Indian indentured laborers and Le Morne mountain, which has acted as the hideout for African slaves, as a World Heritage Memorial.

Political Commitment to Education for All and Teaching and Learning of Ancestral Languages

The most important lesson from successful countries like Mauritius is that strong political will and financial commitments are essential prerequisites to sustainable educational development and alleviation of poverty. Political will is critical to provide the finances required and for the implementation of the reforms needed to establish educational programs that are financially sustainable, technically sound, and that can be politically and socially implemented in the national context. (Clay & Schaffer, 1984). It is the firm conviction of Government that people who are poor can be educable and become intellectuals to participate as agents of change. Education enhances self-respect and self-esteem is the hearts of all (Volawsky & Friedman, 2003). Thus the building of a creative intellectual capital stands as a top priority for Government as it is an essential prerequisite for socioeconomic development.

Children between the ages of 5 and 13 have the opportunity to learn seven ancestral languages currently taught in primary schools. Mauritius seems to be unique in this respect (Chinapah, 1979, 1983, 1999). Besides English and French, which are the mother-tongue of none, are compulsory subjects at primary and secondary levels. The ancestral languages are

Hindi, Tamil, Telegu, Marathi, Urdu, Mandarin, and Arabic. The Mauritius Institute of Education set up with the help of UNESCO in 1973, is the body charged with curriculum development, teacher education, and research. It currently designs and develops new curriculum, pedagogy, professional staff training in all the ancestral languages including English and French, evaluates the teaching–learning process, and assists in the dissemination of good practice in the schools (Irvine, 1984). The Ministry of Education and Scientific Research has an inspectorial team that monitors the teaching–learning process at the school level. Education at the primary and secondary level up to 16 years is free and compulsory. Curriculum designs also include the study of history and geography of Mauritius and its relationship with the rest of the world. History-geography helps us to know how we came about to be where we are today. The curriculum also includes music, drama, the arts, and citizenship education. Yoga in the schools serves as a medication and is intended to have a therapeutic effect that reduces stress. Meditation is a component in the curriculum in management and leadership training for teachers.

The changes that are taking place in the domain of education in Mauritius are profound. Such a scope of change that is so challenging is described by Drucker (1993), who asserted: "Within a few short decades, society rearranges itself—its worldview, its basic values; its social and political structures; its arts, its key institutions. Fifty years later, there is a new world." Mauritius is currently undergoing such a change, transforming the school and its society. The latest innovation has been the establishment of the Open University of Mauritius, working in collaboration with several open learning institutions and specifically with the Indira Gandhi Open University in New Delhi, the Commonwealth of Learning in Vancouver, and the British Open University at Milton Keynes.

Toward a Learning Society

In Mauritius, conventional education has perpetuated archaic structures and approaches. Several structural reforms in the past have not induced or coerced behavioral reform. We are always wrong in education and behavioral change is not easy to attain. On the one hand, teachers who are the key decisive actors have not always been provided with the necessary incentives and lifelong training to function as professionals. On the other hand, failures and dropouts among children are common. The need for learning, unlearning, and relearning is a fact of reality (Caldwell, 1994). Learning models are becoming less academic and more polyvalent. Improving the quality of education and the efficiency and effectiveness of the system are vital challenges to Mauritian education. Policymakers in Mauritius are further confronted with the new roles and daunting challenges of global education (Bhowon, 1990). The recent evidence from KOLN Charter of the G8 Summit in Germany sees no globalization without higher standards of skills and knowledge across both the developed and developing world. That is why the heaviest investment in Mauritius in the past decade has been in education.

The printed and audio-visual media and the various communication and information networks are challenging the traditional educational practices associated with exam-driven rote learning and memorization. Twenty-first-century educators of Mauritius, as elsewhere, are confronted with increasing learner-centered developmental pedagogy rather than with the teacher-centered approach. Objectives-based curriculum is becoming outcomes-based curriculum. The curriculum has always paid attention to the universal concept of love by the inclusion of peace, love, truth, nonviolence, and the right conduct to serve others. Mauritius is a party to the report "Learning the Treasure Within" (Delors, 1996), which focuses on learning throughout life: learning what to learn, learning how to learn, and learning to live together. But little attention has been paid to the cultural dimension of information and communication technology (ICT) that has changed the nature of learning environments. How can ICT increase knowledge when information has to flow from the developed countries to developing ones? The digital divide that separates the rich from the poor can be a big challenge both locally and internationally. International cooperation between different cultures on philosophical issues and sets of values that underpin the conception of knowledge is generally slow.

MAURITIAN POLITICS ROOTED IN GANDHI'S POLITICAL THOUGHT

Gandhi's Visit to Mauritius

It should be noted that both Mauritius and India were historically governed by the British, and in a manner that was against international law and human dignity. In this context, Gandhi was the spiritual ancestor of fundamental rights. His declaration of Indian independence is likened to the famous U.S. Declaration of Independence. He said: "We believe it is an inalienable right of the Indian people as of any other people to have freedom and to enjoy the fruits of their toil and have the necessities of life so that they may have full opportunities for growth," and anything to the contrary would be "a crime against man and God" (Gandhi, 1931).

In the beginning of the 20th century, Gandhi went to South Africa where he fought against apartheid. The foundation for dismantling apartheid in South Africa was laid, amongst others, by Gandhi himself. The Truth and Reconciliation Commission in recent years in South Africa was a direct inspiration of Gandhi, intended to heal the hearts of those who suffered humiliation and discrimination. On his way back to India in 1901, Gandhi visited Mauritius. This visit was to become significant to Mauritius as it symbolized the historical, geographical, and cultural ties with Mother India. Gandhi was welcomed in Mauritius as the apostle of peace and nonviolence. He stressed the need for respect, dignity, and human rights for all workers in the sugar cane plantations in Mauritius. He was against forced labor under the supervision of the state. He was aware of the need of the majority population of Mauritius to break away from the shackles of slavery and forced labor. He was also aware that the vast majority was poor and was deprived of the basic necessities of life including basic education.

There is a strong body of evidence that suggests that Gandhi's contribution to Mauritius was made in the direction of ensuring that slaves and indentured workers would cease to work as forced labor in sugar plantations under British Colonial supervision. Gandhi left deep imprints in the minds of the majority of Mauritian citizens with respect to the spread of peace and nonviolence. The rights and liberties of individuals became a cause of concern. It was the firm conviction of Gandhi that they could be achieved only through peace.

The underlying principles concerning the means to achieve independence took roots in Mauritius after the visit of Gandhi. Manilall Doctor, a follower of Gandhi in India, was sent to Mauritius to see into the condition of work of the laborers. A Royal Commission from Britain was subsequently called in to look at the working conditions of the laborers in the sugar cane plantations. Enquiries and commissions have since then been set up with the intention to ensure that the conditions of work of laborers and the "sugar camps" in which they were living were inhuman and needed constant improvement. Furthermore, the squatter settlements that have grown extensively through time have been drastically reduced. Facilities have been provided to the poor to acquire low-cost houses built by Government. These are pragmatic steps that present the practical side of Gandhi's leadership. It is his philosophical assumptions and concepts that I believe underlined his work, and as such became influential in Mauritian political philosophy. "We who follow Gandhi Maharaj's lead have one thing in common among us: We never fill our purses with spoils from the poor nor bend our knees to the rich (Tagore, 1940).

Gandhian Nonviolence

"I have no weapon but nonviolence," says Gandhi. Simon Peres, former Prime Minister of Israel, said that Gandhi stood up alone against the British and that too without an army, without a state, within a divided nation where the vast majority was poor. Gandhi was leading a movement for "Swaraj" (independence) as the ultimate goal. He was in the midst of a struggle, how to put together the disparate forces, how to bring the vast disenfranchised poor into the mainstream of the struggle. Gandhi's statements like "I am made by Nature to side with the poor... I am not a visionary. I claim to be a practical idealist" reveal his inner feelings. Jawaharlall Nehru, the First Prime Minister of India, found Gandhi "Too weak to kill a fly... but strong enough to move the world." Albert Einstein, the Nobel Laureate, standing on the shrine of Gandhi, described him as an apostle of peace, a spiritual leader above politics and said that "Generations to come, it may be, will scarcely believe that such a one (Gandhi) as this ever in flesh and blood walked upon this earth."

Gandhi argues that peace has to do with freedom, which is the birthright of an individual; it has to do with social justice, democracy, tolerance, international understanding, the creation of safety nets for the vulnerable and marginalized societies. We are reminded by Gandhi that "The earth is capable of satisfying every human need but not every human greed." "My Experiments with Truth" by Gandhi (1959) is explicit about the need for truth and the use of proper means to reach "Swaraj."

Gandhi also shared the liberal assumption that people are by nature capable of taking care of themselves and they can demonstrate a certain level of morality. Human nature comprises both a body and a spirit. According to Gandhi, the body has passion, anger, greed, lust, envy, and hatred. Humans embody also the spirits that are a source of virtues like compassion, tolerance, and care. To use Gandhi's old terminology, both "soul force" and "brute force" are at work in human nature. However, "soul force" and "brute force" do not have equal moral status. They exist in a hierarchical relationship. Therefore, passion has to be reduced or completely removed rather than indulged in. The secret of a good life consists of the ability to manage passion and anger. Constant anger will eventually lead to loss of memory and intelligence. In order to live well as human beings, passion and anger have to be brought under the guidance of the spirit. That is why a deep spiritual life is a necessary precondition for peaceful political and social living.

It is Gandhi's treatment of nonviolence that, among other issues, turned him into one of the greatest and original political geniuses. Absolute nonviolence is impossible both in theory and practice. The political class will always use all sorts of means to protect its citizens, and realistically, this can mean violence. But though violence is a part of life, it is never the norm of life. We do not want to destroy life but to obtain freedom from the liability to kill any kind of life. This is supported by his belief in strict vegetarianism and the protection of animals against inhuman treatment.

Good life is compatible with some form of violence and is justifiable. It includes the decisions taken by the political masters with regards to military means of self-defense. This makes Gandhi fearless but also a realist with a difference. The pursuit of nonviolence is not to eliminate war but to reduce its fierceness and its horrors. The role of nonviolence is not to eliminate war but to reduce its frequency and intensity.

Gandhi (1959) experimented mentally with new ways of looking at a nonviolent army as expressed in his book *My Experiments with Truth*. Such an army would be an army in every respect with the exception that it did not possess any weapons. The army would need rigorous training like the regular army and should possess self-discipline. Such a situation might well end up with the death of innocent and unarmed soldiers. Such a scale of destruction would be massive. But these were risks worth taking. It is expected that in such a situation, the hearts of tyrants and oppressors would melt away and turn public opinion against them. The sufferings of others would tame the oppressors who will eventually receive pangs in their conscience for unjust violence. He has avoided, for example, the extremes of pacifism as proposed by Leo Tolstoy in *War and Peace* or radical realism by Thomas Hobbs. He invites us to activate our moral and institutional capacities for better economic and political well-being.

Gandhi was in favor of the right of self-defense by military means. So here, we face the myth of a pacifist, Gandhi, created by those who interpret his nonviolence in strictly pacifist terms but the reality behind Gandhi's nonviolence is more realistic than ordinarily supposed. It shows that his nonviolence is compatible with his theory of the state based on two factors: first, on his conception of human nature and the possibility of changing their hearts into human beings and second, on his adherence to Indian traditional thinking on truth and the saintliness of man, and drawing inspiration from the spiritual values as enshrined in the sacred books, namely the Bhagavad Gita and the Vedas, which are the repository of knowledge of all kinds. The means to achieve the ends have to be only through truth for he saw God in truth. Thus, he was totally against the adoption of untruthful and dishonorable means to gain Indian independence.

The Vast Majority Principle and "Civil Disobedience"

The need of governments to resort to some measure of violence is balanced by the traits of the vast majority. For Gandhi, vast dispersion of nonviolence practices and tendencies in the population is a crucial factor for lowering realistically ongoing violence. If the vast majority of people in a given state are nonviolent, then that state can be administered nonviolently. Gandhi believed in the notion that unless the vast majority of people in a given state are peaceful, the chance of reducing the horrors of war and increasing the prospect of peace remain very slim. But the vast majority principle does place the burden of war on the political classes who are the decision-makers regarding peace or war. However, he points out that the political classes can promote peace only to the extent that the masses are not violent. The Indian population whom Gandhi recognized as largely nonviolent and leading a peaceful way of life in line with the Indian tradition, however, needed to be made aware of the need for "civil disobedience" and "noncooperation," which he referred to as "Satyagrah." According to him, no one should accept whatever laws passed did not serve the interest of the vast majority.

Gandhi's main proposition was that these nonviolent habits and tendencies within the masses are powerful also during civil government's rule. The peaceful society is not easily victimized as one might expect. It has a powerful, nonviolent measure of influence, which he refers to as "civil disobedience." Any move that is not in the interest of the majority should trigger this measure. Any governmental plan should have a "human face," thereby signifying that economic consideration alone is not enough. If it goes contrary to human dignity, it will trigger off not only "civil disobedience" but complete noncooperation, leading even to the boycott of British goods.

Gandhi realized that Indian independence like Mauritian independence could not be fought with arms but with "nonviolence" and "noncooperation." Gandhi was uniting the ordinary people in his crusade against British rule in India through "civil disobedience" and "noncooperation." He called upon the vast majority of Indians and especially the Harijans, who were the low castes and downtrodden, to play their role fully and to come into the mainstream of political life. Various movements by Gandhi, like the "salt march" and fasting, unleashed the power of the Indian citizens especially in villages and thus spurred the "Quit India" movement until independence was achieved in 1947 from British rule.

Gandhi analyzed the sources of internal violence among Indians, namely between Hindus and Muslims, in the suppression of women, minorities, peasants, and scheduled castes. He came to the conclusion that if people were deprived of the basic necessities of life, then such a state would be violent. Violence and poverty are thus closely intertwined. The former President of India, Narayanan, speaking on India's Independence Celebration Day, said that the greatest problem that India was facing was not the war between India and Pakistan but between what the poor and the rich were getting.

The vast majority principle places the burden of war and peace on the ultimate shoulders of the political classes who have the responsibility to eliminate as much as possible the structures of violence in mass society and to reduce the internal violence to its maximum. Thus war and peace became a question of internal, social, and economic reforms. Furthermore, there is a close link between domestic politics and socioeconomic reforms. For instance, Communism fell because the domestic politics of the Soviet Union and Eastern Europe in general could no longer support the ideology of Communism. The fall of the Berlin Wall confirms this view.

No nation's defense should be under the control of a foreign nation or agency. This is not only against the spirit and letter of international law but it breeds tension between the rulers and the ruled. Ultimately, such a situation leads to violence and such a state cannot be administered nonviolently. Gandhi recognized that the relationship between Britain and India would not remain static for long, as the colonized population would not accept to be subservient to the British rule. In 1957, Harold Macmillan, the then Prime Minister of Britain, made a historic speech in South Africa where he said that the winds of change have started to blow over Africa and that Britain was ready to give independence to her colonies. This speech escalated the breakup of the British Empire and Mauritius would be independent in March 1968.

Gandhi was not in favor of absolute independent states warring one against another but instead a federation of friendly interdependent states. Such states would enjoy universal independence but at the same time would maintain interdependence with other states. Gandhi was firmly convinced that multinationals and richer countries could have been less greedy toward third-world countries and that economic and social exploitation of the oppressed was not only morally wrong but also a crime against humanity.

The political classes and the masses should work together by putting in place collaborative and constructive programs that will enable the moral and spiritual capacity of human beings to keep violence under control. It is only a morally and spiritually awakened population that can help the politicians to work for peace and lessen the horrors of war.

CONCLUSION

Good governance and mass peaceful behavior are both needed of a peaceful society as taught by Gandhi. This enhances inclusiveness, dialogic and interactive openness, which are most critical for living together in peace in communities of different classes, color, and complexion like Mauritius. Education, in particular, has been a critical factor in Mauritius in forging closer ties with different communities and for fostering a culture of peace. I have also argued by way of example that Gandhi, the epitome of peace, did not completely put aside the need for military action when the cause is right. The vast majority principle places the burden of peace or war on the political classes. However, Gandhi unleashed the power of the ordinary man through nonviolence and noncooperation, which were new ways of leading a crusade toward the British rule. But it was of utmost importance that passion had to be controlled and that the ferocity of war had to diminish rather than be banished totally.

In Mauritius, good governance draws from spiritualism and the wisdom of ancestral lands. Decisions with respect to peace or war rest on the shoulders of politicians. But the presence of a peaceful way of life in the majority population makes it easier for the political class to ensure peace. The fostering of peace has been enhanced by the teaching of the right action to serve others and in changing the minds and hearts of people to recognize the saintliness of humankind. Mauritius has retained its unity in diversity through a recognition of the complexity as well as the sensitivity of the major world's cultures. It has through time that the cross-fertilization of the world's major cultures was enhanced. It continues to "row its canoe" toward more tolerance, democracy, human rights, and peace, which are the essence of a "culture of peace."

APPENDIX

Country, island, and language of forefathers	Both sexes	Male	Female
All linguistic groups	1,178,848	583,756	595,092
Creole	454,763	227,449	227,314
Cantonese	348	161	187
Chinese	16,972	6,381	10,591
Hakka	4,009	1,987	2,022
Mandarin	1,209	232	977
Other Chinese	177	65	112
English	1,075	493	582
French	21,171	10,092	11,079
Other European	840	376	464
Arabic	806	417	389
Bhojpuri	361,250	179,070	182,180
Gujrati	1,975	985	990
Hindi	35,782	17,959	17,823
Marathi	16,587	8,218	8,369

Country, island, and language of forefathers	Both sexes	Male	Female
Tamil	44,731	22,265	22,466
Telegu	18,802	9,203	9,599
Urdu	34,120	16,919	17,201
Other Oriental	1,779	1,056	723
Creole & Chinese	3,473	1,767	1,706
Creole & French	18,181	8,685	9,496
Creole & Other European	4,490	2,268	2,222
Creole & Bhojpuri	65,868	32,714	33,154
Creole & Hindi	5,222	2,584	2,638
Creole & Marathi	1,809	910	899
Creole & Tamil	7,845	3,863	3,982
Creole & Telegu	2,201	1,087	1,114
Creole & Urdu	11,164	5,609	5,555
Creole & Other Oriental	2,877	1,396	1,481
Chinese & European	100	41	59
Chinese & Oriental	249	130	119
French & Other European	1,550	746	804
French & Oriental	457	226	231
Other European & Oriental	2,068	1,028	1,040
Bhojpuri & Hindi	22,977	11,472	11,505
Bhojpuri & Marathi	673	322	351
Bhojpuri & Tamil	613	293	320
Bhojpuri & Telegu	697	353	344
Bhojpuri & Urdu	3,842	1,925	1,917
Bhojpuri & Other Oriental	407	207	200
Hindi & Marathi	189	89	100
Hindi & Tamil	359	193	166
Hindi & Telegu	177	101	76
Hindi & Urdu	265	156	109
Hindi & Other Oriental	165	97	68
Marathi & Tamil	81	46	35
Marathi & Telegu	19	10	9
Marathi & Urdu	6	4	2
Marathi & Other Oriental	12	6	6
Tamil & Telegu	133	62	71
Tamil & Urdu	32	12	20
Tamil & Other Oriental	41	19	22
Other	1,040	556	484
Not stated	3,170	1,451	1,719

REFERENCES

Arno et Orian, C. (1986). *Ile Maurice: Une Ile Multiraciale.* Paris: L'Harmattan.

Benedict, B. (1961). Indians in plural societies: A report on Marituis. *Colonial Research Studies, 34.*

Benedict, B. (1965). *Mauritius: Problems of a plural society.* London: Pall Mall Press.

Bhowon, R. (1990). *Elite behaviour in educational policy-making in Mauritius.* Unpublished doctoral dissertation.

Bhowon, R. (1995). *Decentralisation in Mauritius education.* Paper presented at the World Bank Conference on Education and Training, Washington DC.

Bhowon, R. (2003). *The Indian diaspora: India without borders.* Address at the First Pravasi Bharatiya Divas (The First Gathering of Overseas Indians), New Delhi, India.

Bhowon, R. (2003). *Good governance and human rights.* Keynote address at University of Jyvaskyla, Finland.

Bhowon, R., & Chinapah, V. (1992). *Reform of Bbasic education in Mauritius: The process of information gathering, consultation and decision-making for IIEP/UNESCO, working in collaboration with Improving the Efficiency of Educational Systems (IEES) of the State University of New York at Albany.* IIEP Publication.

Blood, H. (1957). *Ethnic and cultural pluralism in Mauritius.* In *Ethnic and cultural pluralism in inter-tropical countries* (pp. 356–362). Brussels: International Institute of Differing Civilisations.

Bunwaree, S. (1994). *Mauritian education in a global economy.* Mauritius: Editions de l'Océan Indien.

Caldwell, B. J. (1994). *The global transformation of public education.* Keynote address at the annual conference of Grant Maintained Schools, Birmingham, UK.

Caring for the future: Report of the Independent Commission on Population and Quality of Life. (1966). Oxford: Oxford University Press.

Carpooran, A (2003). *Ile Maurice: Des Langues et des Lois.* Paris: L'Harmattan.

CERSOI. (1984). *L'île Maurice (Sociale, Economique et Politique) 1974–1980.* Marseille, France : Presses Universitaires d'Aix Marseille.

Chinapah, V. (1979). *Mauritius: Education and society. A baseline study* (Working paper series no. 12 Stockholm University). Stockholm: Institute of International Education, University of Stockholm.

Chinapah, V. (1983). *Participation and performance in primary schooling.* Stockholm: Institute of International Education, University of Stockholm.

Chinapah, V. (1999). *Global education: An international perspective for peace-building and sustainable human development.* Keynote address at Oulu, Finland.

Clay E. J., & Schaffer, B. (1984). *Room for Manoeuvre: An exploration in public policy in agricultural and rural development.* London: Heinemann.

Central Statistical Office, Republic of Mauritius, National Accounts Year 2004, Republic of Mauritius.

Delors, J. (1996). *Learning the treasure within.* Paris: UNESCO.

Drucker, P. (1993). *Post capitalist society.* London: Heinemann.

Durand, J. (1975). *L'île Maurice, Quelle Indépendance? La reproduction des rapports de production capitalistes dans une formation sociale dominée.* Paris: Editions Anthropos.

Education Master Plan for the Year 2000. (1991). Mauritius: Ministry of Education, Arts and Culture.

Galtung, J. (2003). *Teaching and learning intercultural understanding: Fine, but how?* Keynote address at the UNESCO conference, University of Jyvaskyla, Finland.

Gandhi, M. K. (1931). *The constitutional conference in London on the new constitution of India.* London.

Gandhi, M. K. (1959). *An autobiography or the story of my experiments with truth* (M. Desai, Trans.). Ahmedabad: Navjivan.

Gandhi, S. (2004). *Leader of Indian National Congress Party.* Keynote address at the Inauguration of Rajiv Gandhi Centre, Mauritius.

Irvine, J. (1984). *Remedial education—Primary curriculum development.* Mauritius: Mauritius Institute of Education.

Martial, D. (2002). *Identité et Politique Culturelle à l'Ile Maurice.* Paris: L'Harmattan.

Parsuramen, A. (1988). *From ancestral culture to national culture.* Mauritius: Mahatma Gandhi Institute Press.

Prithipaul, D. (1976). *A comparative analysis of French and British colonial policies in Mauritius (1735–1889).* Mauritius: Imprimerie Ideale.

Ramdoyal, R. (1976). *The development of education in Mauritius.* Mauritius: Mauritius Institute of Education.

Sen, A. (2001). If it's fair, it's good: 10 truths about globalization. *International Herald Tribune.*

Tagore, R. (1940). *Gandhi Maharaj, Udayan Shantiniketan.* Calcutta.

Toussaint, A. (1974). *Histoire de l'île Maurice.* Paris: Presse Universitaire de France.

UNDP. (2004). *Human Development Report 2004.* New York: Oxford University Press

Volawsky A., & Friedman, I. A. (Eds.). (2003). *School-based management: An international perspective.* Israel: Ministry of Education.

Ward W. E. F. (1941). *Report on education in Mauritius.* Mauritius: Port Louis Government Printing.

CONTRIBUTORS

Sami Adwan is Professor of Education at Bethlehem University and Codirector of PRIME, the Peace Research Institute in the Middle East, Palestinian National Authority.

Faisal Odeh Al-Rfou'h is Professor of International Relations and former Minister of Culture of Jordan; President of the Gandhi Center for Peace Studies (NGO); and Chairman of the Political Science Department at the University of Jordan, Amman.

Dan Bar-On is Professor and Chair of the Department of Behavioral Sciences at Ben-Gurion University of the Negev and Codirector of PRIME, the Peace Research Institute in the Middle East, Israel.

MP – Hon Rajayswur Bhowon is a member of Parliament and a Parliamentary Private Secretary and Vice President of the Forum for African Parliamentarians on Education (FAPED), The Republic of Mauritius.

Erik H. Cohen, Senior Lecturer and Chair, Board of Directors, The Lookstein Center for Jewish Education in the Diaspora, School of Education, Bar-Ilan University, Israel.

Mohammed S. Dajani Daoudi is Professor of International Political Economy and International Law; Founder/Director of the American Studies Institute at Al-Quds University; Director of the National Institute for Public Administration; and Director of the Assistance and Training Department of the Palestinian Council for Development and Reconstruction, Palestinian National Authority.

Erwin H. Epstein is Professor and Director of the Center for the Comparative Study of Education at Loyola University of Chicago. He is a former edi-

Educating Toward a Culture of Peace, pages 345–347
Copyright © 2006 by Information Age Publishing
All rights of reproduction in any form reserved.

tor of the *Comparative Education Review* and a past president of the Comparative and International Education Society and of the World Council of Comparative Education Societies.

Grace Feuerverger is Associate Professor in the Department of Curriculum, Teaching and Learning (CTL) at the Ontario Institute for Studies in Education (OISE) at the University of Toronto, Canada.

K. Peter Fritzsche, is Professor and Chairholder of UNESCO Chair in Human Rights Education at the University of Magdeburg Germany, a member of the Board of the Federal Association of Civic Education, and a speaker of the Research Group "Human Rights" of the German Association for Political Science.

Rachel Gali Cinamon is a lecturer on developmental aspects in education at the School of Education, Tel-Aviv and Bar-Ilan Universities, Israel.

Zehavit Gross is a lecturer and researcher in the School of Education, Bar Ilan University, Israel. She is involved in peace education within the framework of the UNESCO/Burg Chair in Education for Human Values, Tolerance, and Peace.

Yaacov Iram is Professor of Comparative and International Education at the School of Education of Bar Ilan University, Israel. He is the Chairholder of the UNESCO/Burg Chair in Education for Human Values, Tolerance, and Peace; recipient of the Fulbright-Yitzhak Rabin Award to advance research and promote activities of peace and tolerance; and past president of the World Association for Educational Research.

Chaim Lavie teaches social psychology and organizational behavior in the Interdisciplinary Department of Social Sciences at Bar-Ilan University, Israel.

Ben Mollov is on the faculty of the Interdisciplinary Program in Social Sciences and the Program in Conflict Management at Bar-Ilan University, Israel where he teaches Political Science and Conflict Management from an intercultural perspective.

Madhav D. Nalapat is Professor of Geopolitics and Chairholder of the UNESCO Chair for the Promotion of the Culture of Peace and Non-Violence at the Manipal Academy of Higher Education, Manipal, India.

F. Michael Perko is Professor at the Department of Educational Leadership and Policy Studies at Loyola University and Director of the Center for the Advanced Study of Christianity and Culture, in Chicago.

Shifra Sagy is Professor of Educational Psychology and Chair of the Center for Enhancement in Education at Ben-Gurion University, Israel.

Gerald Steinberg is Professor of Political Studies at Bar-Ilan University, Director of the Interdisciplinary Program on Conflict Management and Negotiation, and Editor of NGO Monitor.

Hillel Wahrman is a PhD candidate on political literacy and civic education and recipient of the doctoral "Scholarship of Excellence" at the School of Education, Bar-Ilan University, Israel. He is involved in peace education within the framework of the UNESCO/Burg Chair in Education for Human Values Tolerance and Peace.

Dietmar Waterkamp is Professor of Comparative Education at the University of Technology in Dresden, Germany and Chair of the Section for Comparative International and Intercultural Education in the German Society for Education.

Hans Werdmolder is a criminologist and anthropologist and is senior researcher at Utrecht University, The Netherlands. He is Head of the Research and Graduate Program of the School of Human Rights Research, and a member of the Advisory Committee of the Dutch Refugee Council and of the Network of UNESCO Chairs in Human Values, Tolerance and Peace.

Rivka Witenberg is a developmental and cognitive psychologist at the Australian Catholic University and is a research fellow at the University of Melbourne, Australia.

Ephraim Yaar-Yuchtman is Professor Emeritus of Sociology and Social-Psychology and Director of the Evens Program for Conflict Resolution and Mediation at Tel-Aviv University, Israel.

Yaacov B. Yablon lectures at the School of Education and a researcher at the Institute for Community Education and Research at Bar-Ilan University, Israel.

INDEX

A

Adam Institute for Democracy and Peace (Jerusalem), 298
Agha, Hussein, 43
Al-Aksa Intifada, 161
impact on young Palestinians, 157
All Children Together (ACT) movement, 235
American University, peace studies advocacy example, 19–20
Amir, Yehuda
intergroup encounter requirements, 248
application to field observations, 250–251
Anti-Defamation League (ADL)/New York, 298
Arab summit conference (Khartoum)/ "three no's," 134
Arab–Israeli conflict in peace studies programs, 17
anti-Israel and pro-Palestinian ideology, 19
Arapura, J. G., 67
Asabiyya, 122
Ashrawi, Hanan, award by peace study program, 19
Asia Pacific Free Trade Agreement (APEC), 74

B

Assefa, Hizkias, 48
Ayalon-Nusseibeh People Initiative, 47–48

B

Balfour Declaration, 132
Bar-tal, Daniel, 44
Barak, Ehud, 136
Barenboim, Daniel, 49
Baskin, Gershon, 50
Bastian, Adolf, 64
Beilen-Abd Rabbo Geneva Initiative, 47–48
Ben-Gurion, David, 132
Benigno S. Acqino, Jr. Foundation (Philippines), 298
Bertelsmann Group for Policy Research (Center for Applied Policy), 298
"Big Dream." *See* Palestinian–Israeli conflict
Bishop Doyle of Kildare and Leighlin, 234
Boulding, Kenneth, 40
Bouling, Kenneth, 13
Bowman, Mary Jean, 82
Bradford University (England), 14
and anti-Israeli propaganda, 19
Brown, Nathan, 42–43

Educating Toward a Culture of Peace, pages 349–359
Copyright © 2006 by Information Age Publishing
All rights of reproduction in any form reserved.

Printed in the United States
53711LVS00001BA/127-153